AMSCO'S
AP Calculus AB/BC

Preparing for the Advanced Placement Examinations

Maxine Lifshitz

Mathematics Department Chairperson
Friends Academy
Locust Valley, New York

with

Martha Green

Mathematics Teacher
Baldwin High School
Baldwin, New York

AMSCO

Amsco School Publications, Inc.
315 Hudson Street, New York, N.Y. 10013

Author

Maxine Lifshitz is Chair of the Math Department at Friends Academy in Locust Valley, New York. She received her A.B. degree from Barnard College with Honors in Mathematics and her Ph.D. from New York University in Mathematics Education. She has been a mathematics consultant for the College Board and a reader of Advanced Placement Calculus Examinations. Dr. Lifshitz has conducted workshops in applications of the graphing calculator both locally at Calculators Help All Teachers (CHAT) and Long Island Mathematics (Limaçon) conferences, and nationally at National Council of Teachers of Mathematics (NCTM) and Teachers Teaching with Technology (T³) conferences. Dr. Lifshitz has published articles in *Mathematics Teacher* and *The New York State Mathematics Teachers Journal*.

Collaborator

Martha Green has taught mathematics at Baldwin High School for the past 17 years and is currently a reader for the AP Calculus Examinations. She received a bachelor's degree in Engineering from Hofstra University and a master's degree in Secondary Education from Adelphi University. She instructs a graduate-level class on Teaching AP Calculus through The Effective Teachers Program of the New York State United Teachers (NYSUT). She has conducted numerous workshops on using calculators to enhance the teaching of mathematics and has presented at CHAT, Limaçon, and regional NCTM conferences. She has previously collaborated with Dr. Lifshitz to conduct workshops at T³ International Conferences. In 2001, the Nassau County Mathematics Teachers Association named Martha Green Teacher of the Year.

Reviewers

Steven J. Balasiano
Assistant Principal Supervising Mathematics
Canarsie High School
Brooklyn, NY

Brad Huff
Headmaster
University High School
Fresno, CA

Terrence Kent
Mathematics Teacher
Downers Grove High School
Downers Grove, IL

Sal Sutera
Assistant Principal (Supervision)
 for Mathematics
New Utrecht High School
Brooklyn, NY

Text design by One Dot Inc.
Composition and Line Art by Nesbitt Graphics, Inc.

Please visit our Web site at: *www.amscopub.com*

When ordering this book, please specify:
either R 781 W *or* AP CALCULUS AB/BC:
PREPARING FOR THE ADVANCED PLACEMENT EXAMINATIONS.

ISBN 978-1-56765-562-9
NYC Item 56765-562-8

Printed in the United States of America
    4 5 6 7 8 9 10   09 08 07 06

To all the AP Calculus teachers, from the ones who accept the challenge a few weeks before the course begins to those who continuously refresh and renew themselves after years of teaching. And to Seymour, Alissa, and Mariel, who provide the base and the encouragement for all my efforts.

Maxine Lifshitz

To my parents, Robert and Martha Sweeney, who raised me to believe I could accomplish anything and who helped me realize my dreams.

Martha Green

CONTENTS

AB/BC Topics

Answer Key 321

Model Examinations 371

Index 395

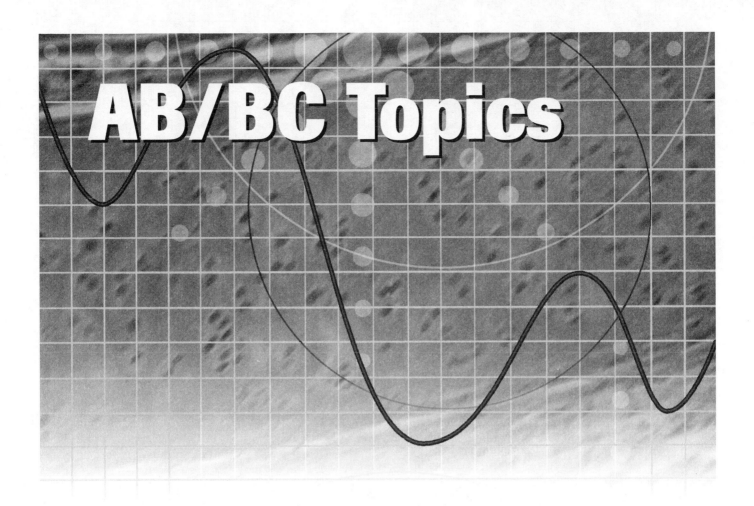

AB/BC Topics

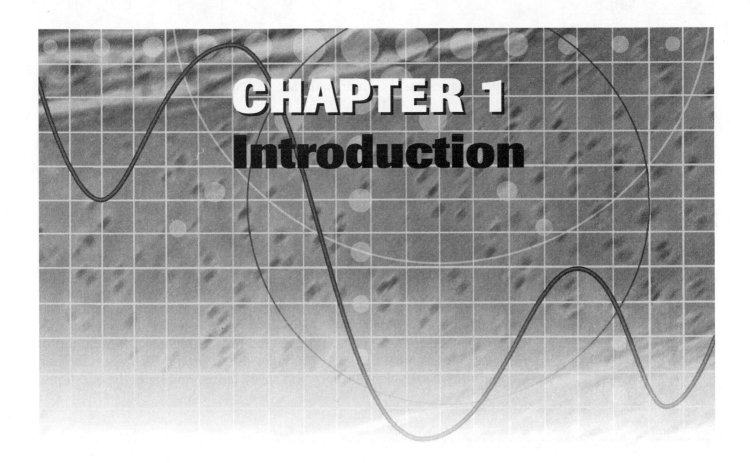

CHAPTER 1
Introduction

About the Book

This book was written to provide a thorough review for students preparing to take the AP Calculus Examinations on both the AB and BC levels. Students intending to take only the AB Examination should study Chapters 2 through 7, which cover the Calculus AB course with some extensions into BC topics. The BC topics in Chapters 2 through 7 are indicated in the text by the symbol **BC**, and may be considered optional by students concentrating on Calculus AB.

Students intending to take the Calculus BC Examination should begin their review at Chapter 3 and proceed through Chapter 10. These students may consider Chapter 2 to be optional, since it consists of a review of pre-calculus topics.

Each chapter encompasses a large topic and is divided into sections that provide focused review. The sections contain explanations of concepts, definitions of important terms (these appear in **boldface**), and rules. Examples with Solutions appear in a format similar to AP Calculus Examination questions. Every section concludes with a substantial set of Exercises containing both multiple-choice and free-response questions. These exercises allow opportunities for review and investigation of the topics in the section. The Chapter Assessment, also in the multiple-choice and free-response format, builds mastery of the topics covered in the entire chapter.

At the end of the book, there are four complete Model Examinations, two for Calculus AB and two for Calculus BC. Each test contains the same number and type of questions as the actual AP Calculus Examinations, including both multiple-choice and free-response questions. These tests can be used for practice before the actual exams. The answers to all Exercises, Chapter Assessments, and Model Examinations are in the Answer Key at the back of the book.

How to Use This Book

This book provides an excellent review for those planning to take the AP Calculus AB/BC Examinations. It is also useful to students preparing for a calculus final exam. It is not intended to be a textbook, but rather an organized review of topics already studied and a source of practice problems. Ideally, this book will be used as a companion to a textbook, supplementing each topic with additional problems. It can also be used as a review in the weeks before the AP Calculus Examinations. The Model Examinations at the end of the book can be used as part of the review and taken under simulated test conditions as indicated by the time guidelines for each part of the examination (see page 5). Taking a timed Model Examination is an opportunity to develop accuracy and speed in responding to the questions.

Prerequisites to AP Calculus

Courses in mathematics are cumulative; that is, each course depends on knowledge of the content of the previous courses. A course in calculus depends on knowledge of the content of *all* the mathematics courses that preceded it, and introduces a greater level of abstraction than is usually presented in high school math courses. Generally, students who have completed a course in precalculus before beginning calculus are better prepared and have more success in calculus. Precalculus gives an overview of functions and their properties that is essential for a successful study of calculus. Functions and their properties are basic to the foundation of calculus. A calculus student must be prepared with a strong knowledge of polynomial, trigonometric, exponential, logarithmic, and piecewise-defined functions. Additionally, calculus students should be proficient in the use of a graphing calculator.

The AP Calculus AB and BC Courses

There are two levels of AP Calculus, Calculus AB and Calculus BC. The Calculus AB course is intended to be a yearlong course that includes some time for a review of basic functions. The Calculus BC course encompasses all the topics on the Calculus AB examination and proceeds to several additional topics. The Calculus BC course is intended for students whose prior studies eliminate the need for the review of basic functions included in Calculus AB.

In general, Calculus AB is comparable to a one-semester college course. Calculus BC is comparable to a two-semester college course. Students who take the Calculus BC Examination will receive both a BC score and an AB subscore that indicates how they performed on the Calculus AB portion of the examination.

The AP Calculus Examinations

How the Examinations Are Organized

The two AP Calculus Examinations are organized in the same way. They consist of Sections I and II, which contribute equally to determining the examination grade.

Section I is made up of multiple-choice questions and has two parts, A and B. Part A consists of 28 questions to be completed in 55 minutes. No calculators are allowed in Part A of Section I.

Section I, Part B consists of 17 questions to be completed in 50 minutes. Graphing calculators are required to answer some questions in Part B of Section I.

Answers to Section I are bubbled on an answer sheet.

Section II is made up of six free-response questions and is divided into parts A and B. Students must be prepared to write clear explanations of their solutions to these questions. Part A consists of three questions to be completed in 45 minutes. Graphing calculators are required to answer some questions in Part A of Section II.

Part B also consists of three questions to be completed in 45 minutes. No calculators are allowed in Part B of Section II.

The answers to Section II are written in an answer booklet. Upon completion of Section II, Part B, students may return to the problems in Section II, Part A, but without the use of a calculator.

Organization of the AP Calculus Examinations				
Section I Multiple-Choice Questions				
	Number of Questions	**Time Allowed**	**Graphing Calculator Use**	**Answer Format**
Part A	28	55 minutes	No calculator allowed	Bubbled
Part B	17	50 minutes	Calculator required	Bubbled
Section II Free-Response Questions				
	Number of Questions	**Time Allowed**	**Graphing Calculator Use**	**Answer Format**
Part A	3	45 minutes	Calculator required	Written in booklet
Part B	3	45 minutes	No calculator allowed	Written in booklet

Using a Graphing Calculator on the Examinations

The AP Calculus Examinations are written with the assumption that the test taker has access to a graphing calculator with certain built-in capabilities. The AP Calculus Course Description lists these features as the capability to:

1. Graph a function within a window.
2. Find the roots of an equation.
3. Find the numerical value of a derivative at a point.
4. Find the numerical value of a definite integral over an interval.

While most graphing calculators have more capabilities than those listed, only these four may be utilized on the AP Calculus Examinations. A list of the graphing calculators approved for use on Advanced Placement Calculus Examinations can be found at the College Board Web site, http://apcentral.collegeboard.com.

Memories in the calculators do not have to be cleared before the examination. Students may bring any programs they have in their calculators to the examination; however, only the four capabilities listed can be used without explanation in Section II of the examinations.

When writing solutions to the free-response questions, students must use standard mathematical notation, rather than calculator syntax. For example, students must write

$$\int_1^3 2x^2\,dx = \left.\frac{2x^3}{3}\right|_1^3 = 17\frac{1}{3} \text{ or } 17.333,$$

and NOT

$$\text{fnInt}(2x^2, x, 1, 3) = 17.333.$$

Students should also note that all answers are expected to be accurate to three decimal places.

How the Examinations Are Scored The multiple-choice questions in Section I are machine scored and count equally with the free-response questions in Section II. High school and college teachers selected by the College Board grade the six questions in Section II. These teachers, called "readers," have been trained to use a grading rubric, which ensures that grading is consistent. Students' final raw scores are then converted into grades numbered from 1 to 5, with 5 being the most qualified. A score of 3 or better is generally acceptable for either advanced course placement, or a semester's or a year's credit at participating colleges. The amount of college credit given does vary from college to college; therefore, students should consult individual colleges to learn their policies on Advanced Placement.

Factors Leading to Success in AP Calculus

Course Outlines The Advanced Placement Program Course Description booklet for Calculus, published by the College Board, is updated frequently. It includes a topical outline for Calculus AB and Calculus BC, as well as statements on the philosophy, goals, and prerequisites for an AP Calculus course. If the booklet is not available to you, information on AP Calculus can also be found on the Internet at http://apcentral.collegeboard.com. Additional information on AP Calculus courses and examinations is also available for students and teachers at this site.

What to Emphasize in AP Calculus The study of calculus should include algebraic, graphical, verbal, and numerical approaches. These techniques support each other and add to a clearer understanding of calculus. In calculus, establishing connections and being able to explain relationships is as important as learning algebraic manipulations and formulas.

Test-Taking Tips

- Follow the directions given for each question on the examination. Read the question carefully and consider your answer thoughtfully. Long explanations are not necessary since a concise and clear response based on an appropriate theorem or technique is all that is required.

- Include all necessary information in your response. For example, if a problem requires units of measure in the response, be sure to include them. If a problem requires an interval in your response, write your answer in standard interval notation.

- Practice doing problems that have appeared on previous, released AP Calculus Examinations or are similar to those on the examinations. This will help you to become familiar with the format of the test and the types of questions that may appear.

- Be mindful of the list of the four capabilities required of the graphing calculator you will use on the test, since an answer to a free-response question without supporting work will receive no credit. If you employ a procedure not found on this list (see page 5) to respond to a problem, you must show your work.

- Become proficient with the graphing calculator you will use on the test *and* learn the mathematics needed to respond to the problems. Know when to use the calculator and when to use your brain. An over dependence on technology can hinder the development of the algebraic skills and content knowledge that can lead to success on the AP Calculus Examinations.

- Practice with multiple-choice and free-response questions that do not require the use of a calculator. This is one way to prepare for the non-calculator sections of the AP exam.

- Remember that the readers scoring your examination are not your calculus teacher, who is familiar with your work. They are well-trained calculus instructors who are looking for clear explanations of the questions on the examination. Learn to write clearly using standard notation.

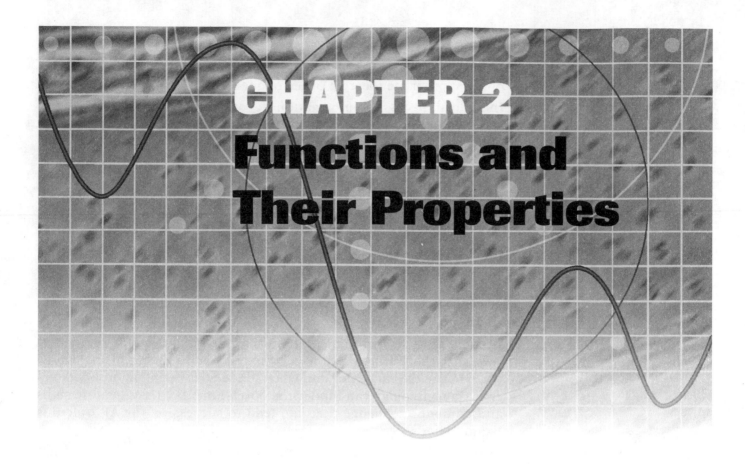

CHAPTER 2
Functions and Their Properties

2.1 A Review of Basic Functions

Calculus is the study of how things change. Functions are used to describe or model the quantities that are changing. Functions may represent areas, volumes, distances, or other quantities. Functions may also represent the *rates* at which quantities are changing. This chapter provides a review of functions and serves as a reference as you cover the topics in later chapters.

A function is a relationship between two or more variables. It is often expressed as a rule that relates the variables. AP Calculus deals with functions of a single variable, usually expressed as $y = f(x)$. By definition, a **function** is a set of ordered pairs $\{(x, y)\}$ such that for each x-value there is one and only one y-value.

On a graph, the vertical line test determines whether a graph represents a function. The **vertical line test** states that if any vertical line intersects the graph more than once, then the graph is not a function.

Analyzing the properties of a function and then applying the techniques of calculus allows us to solve many types of problems. For instance, given the perimeter of a rectangle, we can find the dimensions of the rectangle that has the maximum area. Given information on the initial height and velocity of an object, we can determine how fast the object is moving when it hits the ground. In these examples, the area of the rectangle and the velocity of the object are represented by functions.

Following is an overview of functions that are basic to the study of calculus, along with a brief summary of the important properties of each.

The Vertical Line Test

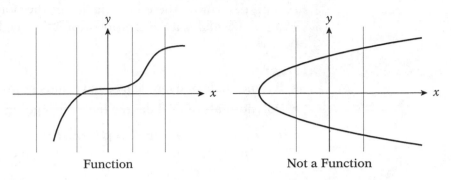

Function   Not a Function

Polynomials   A **polynomial** is a sum of terms of the form ax^n, where n is a nonnegative integer. The largest value of n is the **degree** of the polynomial, and the coefficient of the term of the highest power of x is called the **leading coefficient.** Polynomials include linear, quadratic, and cubic functions. For example, $4x^3 + 8x^2$ is a polynomial. Its degree is 3 and the leading coefficient is 4. This polynomial can also be expressed in factored form as $4x^2(x + 2)$. The zeros of the polynomial are found by solving the equation $4x^2(x + 2) = 0$. The zeros are $x = 0$ (a double root) and $x = -2$.

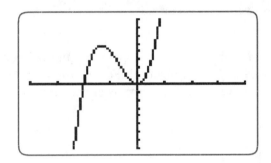

   The graph of the polynomial $f(x) = 4x^3 + 8x^2$ shows that there are two **turning points,** or places where the graph changes direction. The number of turning points can also be determined by noting the degree of the equation. The maximum number of turning points equals $n - 1$, where n is the degree of the polynomial.

Calculator Note

A graphing calculator can be used to find that the coordinates of the turning points of the polynomial $4x^3 + 8x^2$ are $(-1.333, 4.741)$ and $(0, 0)$.
Using the TI-83
Enter the function into Y= and press ZOOM 4. Then press WINDOW and change Ymax to 7. Press GRAPH.
   To find the coordinates of the turning point in the second quadrant, press 2nd CALC 4. To enter Left Bound, scroll to the immediate left of the turning point and press ENTER.
   Now scroll to the immediate right of the turning point and press ENTER. Press ENTER and round the coordinates to $x = -1.333$ and $y = 4.741$.
   The second turning point appears to be located at the origin. With the polynomial still in Y=, press 2nd CALC 3. Scroll to set the Left Bound and the Right Bound of the turning point. To enter Guess, scroll as close as possible to the turning point. Press ENTER. The calculator confirms that $(0, 0)$ is the turning point.

End Behavior Two factors, the degree of the polynomial and the sign of the leading coefficient, determine the end behavior of the polynomial. The **end behavior** of a polynomial is a description of how the right and left sides of the graph behave.

Degree
- Polynomials of even degree have ends going in the same direction.
- Polynomials of odd degree have ends going in opposite directions.

Sign of the Leading Coefficient **a**
- The end behavior of polynomials of even degree is like $f(x) = ax^2$.

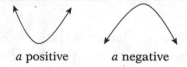

a positive   a negative

- The end behavior of polynomials of odd degree is like $f(x) = ax^3$.

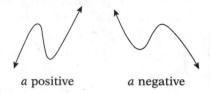

a positive   a negative

Algebraic Functions Algebraic functions that appear frequently in calculus are square roots and cube roots of a polynomial. For example, $\sqrt{(x - 3)}$ has the domain $\{x \geq 3\}$ and range $\{y \geq 0\}$. Its graph is shown below.

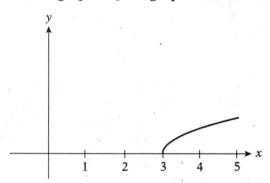

If the function is $\sqrt{(x)} - 3$, the domain will be the set $\{x \geq 0\}$ and the range will be $\{y \geq -3\}$. The graph is shown below.

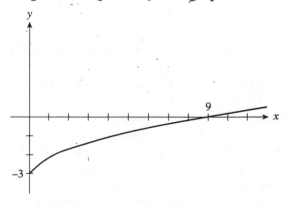

Rational Functions A **rational function** is the ratio of two polynomials. Unlike polynomials, the domain of a rational function may not be the set of all real numbers. When the polynomial in the denominator is zero for some values of x, these values are excluded from the domain. In addition, rational functions may have vertical and horizontal asymptotes. An **asymptote** is a line that the graph of a function approaches very closely, but never touches.

> **To find the vertical asymptotes of a rational function:**
> - Set the denominator equal to zero and solve for x.
> - Find the values of x that make the denominator equal to zero, but do *not* make the numerator equal to zero. The equations of the vertical asymptotes are these values of x.

If a value of x makes both the numerator and the denominator equal to zero, then there is a break or a hole in the function at that x-value. When using a graphing calculator, this hole may or may not be visible, depending on the WINDOW in which the graph of the rational function is viewed.

> **To find the horizontal asymptotes of a rational function:**
> - When the degree of the numerator is less than the degree of the denominator, the function has the line $y = 0$ as a horizontal asymptote.
> - When the degree of the numerator is equal to the degree of the denominator, then the equation of the horizontal asymptote is:
> $y = $ the ratio of the coefficients of the highest degree terms
> - When the degree of the numerator is greater than the degree of the denominator, the rational function has no horizontal asymptote.

For example, to find the vertical asymptotes of $y = \dfrac{2x + 4}{x - 1}$, set the denominator equal to zero and solve for x:

$$x - 1 = 0$$
$$x = 1.$$

When $x = 1$, the numerator *does not* equal zero; therefore, there is a vertical asymptote at $x = 1$.

To find the horizontal asymptotes, first note that the numerator and the denominator are of the same degree. Therefore, the horizontal asymptote is

$$y = \frac{2}{1} \text{ or } y = 2.$$

The rational function $y = \dfrac{2x + 4}{x - 1}$ has one vertical asymptote with equation $x = 1$, and one horizontal asymptote with equation $y = 2$. The graph of this rational function is shown on the following page.

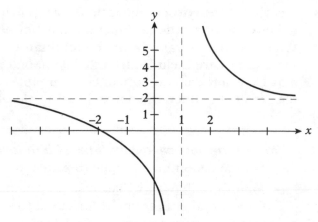

By the same procedure, the rational function $y = \dfrac{2x}{x^2 - 4}$ has two vertical asymptotes at $x = 2$ and $x = -2$, and one horizontal asymptote at $y = 0$.

Trigonometric Functions One of the basic topics in precalculus is learning the properties of and graphing the sine, cosine, and tangent functions, and finding the amplitude, frequency, and period of these graphs.

In general, a sine or cosine curve of the form $y = a \sin bx$ or $y = a \cos bx$ has amplitude $|a|$, frequency $|b|$, and period $\dfrac{2\pi}{|b|}$.

For example, for the function $y = 2 \sin x$, the amplitude is 2, the frequency is 1, and the period is 2π. Its graph is shown below.

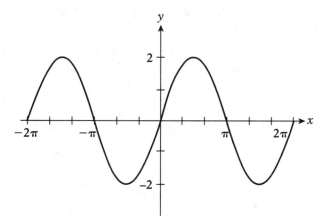

As another example, the graph of $y = -\dfrac{1}{2} \cos 4x$ has amplitude $\dfrac{1}{2}$, frequency 4, and period $\dfrac{2\pi}{4}$, which equals $\dfrac{\pi}{2}$. The negative sign makes the graph reflect in the x-axis. The graph is shown below.

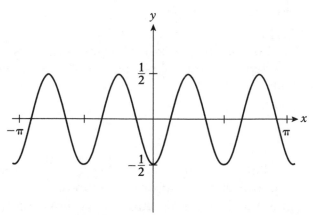

Tangent curves do not have amplitude. In general, a tangent curve of the form $y = a \tan bx$ has frequency $|b|$ and period $\frac{\pi}{|b|}$.

For example, the graph of $y = \tan 2x$ has frequency 2 and period $\frac{\pi}{2}$. Its graph is shown below.

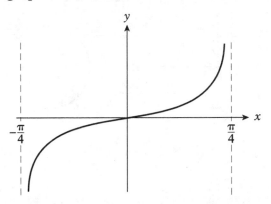

In addition to graphing trigonometric functions, it is also important to be able to solve trigonometric equations. For example, solve the equation $2 \sin x - 1 = 0$ for values of x between 0 and 2π, in the following way.

First solve for x.

$$2\sin x - 1 = 0$$
$$2\sin x = 1$$
$$\sin x = \frac{1}{2}$$

When $\sin x = \frac{1}{2}$, the equation $2 \sin x - 1 = 0$ is true. There are, however, infinitely many values of x that make $\sin x = \frac{1}{2}$ true. It is necessary to find the values of x in the domain given, between 0 and 2π. Since $\sin x$ is positive, x is an angle in quadrant I or II. The solution in the first quadrant is $x = \frac{\pi}{6}$. This value is used as a reference angle to find the solution in the second quadrant, which is $\pi - \frac{\pi}{6}$, or $\frac{5\pi}{6}$.

To solve trigonometric equations, it is necessary to know the values of sine, cosine, and tangent functions for the boundary angles 0, $\frac{\pi}{2}$, π, and $\frac{3\pi}{2}$, and the standard angles $\frac{\pi}{6}$, $\frac{\pi}{4}$, and $\frac{\pi}{3}$, as well as which functions are positive or negative in each quadrant. The values in the table below are often used in solving trigonometric equations.

Degrees	0°	30°	45°	60°	90°	180°	270°	360°
Radians	0	$\frac{\pi}{6}$	$\frac{\pi}{4}$	$\frac{\pi}{3}$	$\frac{\pi}{2}$	π	$\frac{3\pi}{2}$	2π
Sine	0	$\frac{1}{2}$	$\frac{\sqrt{2}}{2}$	$\frac{\sqrt{3}}{2}$	1	0	-1	0
Cosine	1	$\frac{\sqrt{3}}{2}$	$\frac{\sqrt{2}}{2}$	$\frac{1}{2}$	0	-1	0	1
Tangent	0	$\frac{\sqrt{3}}{3}$	1	$\sqrt{3}$	undefined	0	undefined	0

Each of the standard angles is a reference angle for another angle in quadrants II, III, and IV. The following wheels illustrate the standard angles and the angles in the remaining quadrants in radian measure.

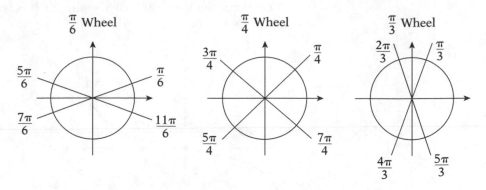

EXAMPLE

Solve for x: $2 \sin^2 x - 1 = 0$ for values of x between $-\pi$ and π.

Solution   Solving for sin x first, we have $\sin x = \pm \dfrac{\sqrt{2}}{2}$. The solution to $\sin x = \dfrac{\sqrt{2}}{2}$, $x = \dfrac{\pi}{4}$, provides the reference angle for the remaining solutions. There are four solutions, one in each quadrant. The solutions are: $x = \dfrac{\pi}{4}$, $x = \dfrac{3\pi}{4}$, $x = -\dfrac{\pi}{4}$, $x = -\dfrac{3\pi}{4}$.

BC Trigonometric Identities

The following trigonometric identities are necessary in calculus, particularly in AP Calculus BC:

Pythagorean Identities

$$\sin^2 x + \cos^2 x = 1$$
$$\tan^2 x + 1 = \sec^2 x$$
$$\cot^2 x + 1 = \csc^2 x$$

Reciprocal Identities

$$\csc x = \frac{1}{\sin x}$$

$$\sec x = \frac{1}{\cos x}$$
$$\cot x = \frac{1}{\tan x}$$

Quotient Identities

$$\tan x = \frac{\sin x}{\cos x}$$
$$\cot x = \frac{\cos x}{\sin x}$$

Double-Angle Formulas for Sine and Cosine

$$\sin 2x = 2 \sin x \cos x$$
$$\cos 2x = \cos^2 x - \sin^2 x$$
$$= 2 \cos^2 x - 1$$
$$= 1 - 2 \sin^2 x$$

Inverse Trigonometric Functions

The **inverse of a function,** f^{-1}, is itself a function only if there is a one-to-one correspondence between the domain and the range. Interchanging the x- and y-values of a trigonometric function results in a relation that is not a function. For each new x-value, there will be many values of y. To obtain inverses of the trigonometric functions that are themselves definable as functions, the domains of the trigonometric functions must be restricted as follows:

- Sin x is restricted to $-\frac{\pi}{2} \le x \le \frac{\pi}{2}$ to obtain arcsin x.

- Cos x is restricted to $0 \le x \le \pi$ to obtain arccos x.

- Tan x is restricted to $-\frac{\pi}{2} < x < \frac{\pi}{2}$ to obtain arctan x.

Arcsin x and arctan x are the inverse trigonometric functions that usually appear on the AP Calculus exams. The graphs of arcsin x and arctan x are shown below.

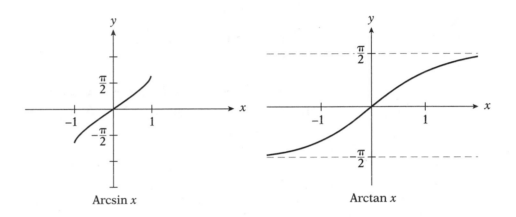

Arcsin x Arctan x

For example, arcsin $\frac{1}{2}$ is the angle (in radians) whose sine is equal to $\frac{1}{2}$, and we know this angle is $\frac{\pi}{6}$. Therefore arcsin $\frac{1}{2} = \frac{\pi}{6}$. Since it is a function, arcsin $\frac{1}{2}$ has only one answer, which must be in the range of arcsin x.

Similarly, arcsin $\left(-\frac{1}{2}\right)$ is the angle whose sine is equal to $-\frac{1}{2}$, and we know this angle is $-\frac{\pi}{6}$. Therefore arcsin $\left(-\frac{1}{2}\right) = -\frac{\pi}{6}$. Since it is a function, arcsin $\left(-\frac{1}{2}\right)$ has only one answer, which must be in the range of arcsin x.

Arccos $\frac{1}{2}$ is the angle whose cosine equals $\frac{1}{2}$, and we know this angle is $\frac{\pi}{3}$. Arccos $\left(-\frac{1}{2}\right)$ is the angle whose cosine equals $-\frac{1}{2}$. Since the range of arccos is from 0 to π, the only solution to arccos $\left(-\frac{1}{2}\right)$ is $\frac{2\pi}{3}$.

Exponential and Logarithmic Functions

Exponential functions are functions of the form $y = b^x$, where b is a positive number, $b \ne 1$. The domain of $y = b^x$ is the set of all real numbers, and the range is $\{y > 0\}$.

Properties of Exponents

$$b^0 = 1$$
$$b^1 = b$$
$$b^x \cdot b^y = b^{x+y}$$
$$\frac{b^x}{b^y} = b^{x-y}$$
$$b^{-x} = \frac{1}{b^x}$$
$$(b^x)^y = b^{xy}$$

The inverse of the exponential function $y = b^x$ is the logarithmic function $y = \log_b x$. Therefore, the domain of $y = \log_b x$ is $\{x > 0\}$ and the range is the set of all real numbers.

Properties of the Logarithmic Function

$$\log_b 1 = 0$$
$$\log_b b = 1$$
$$\log_b x + \log_b y = \log_b(xy)$$
$$\log_b x - \log_b y = \log_b\left(\frac{x}{y}\right)$$
$$\log_b x^y = y \log_b x$$

The graphs of $y = b^x$ and $y = \log_b x$ are reflections of each other across the line $y = x$. The graphs of $y = b^x$ and $y = \log_b x$ are shown in the figure below.

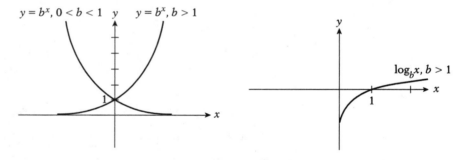

In the special case, where $b = e$, the graphs appear as follows:

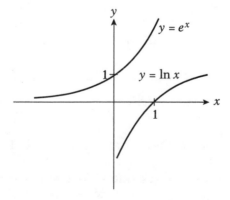

Piecewise–Defined Functions Piecewise functions (also called **split functions**) are functions defined by more than one rule in each part of their domain. The pieces of the function may be connected or not. These functions may be graphed on a graphing calculator, but students should practice graphing them by hand until they become proficient at it. Two examples follow:

$$f(x) = \begin{cases} x + 2, & \text{for } x < 1 \\ 2 - x, & \text{for } x \geq 1 \end{cases}$$

$$g(x) = \begin{cases} x^2, & \text{for } x < 0 \\ 2x, & \text{for } 0 \leq x \leq 1 \\ x + 1, & \text{for } x > 1 \end{cases}$$

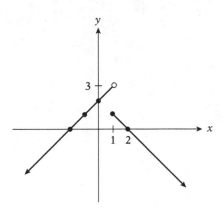

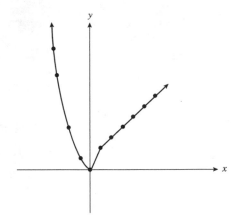

Calculator Note

The graphing calculator is a useful tool for examining functions and investigating their properties. At times, there will be exercises in this book to be done *without* a graphing calculator. Exercises done without a graphing calculator emphasize basic knowledge of details of a function. Since about half of the AP Calculus exam is now done without any calculator, it is essential that students gain experience by doing exercises without a calculator.

The graphing calculator can be used to graph functions, help determine their domains and ranges, and find points of intersection of graphs. In this book, there will be exercises in which a graphing calculator is necessary to explore a concept or practice a technique. Students should be aware that calculators might provide misleading or even incorrect information. It is vital that students of calculus understand the processes of calculus and be aware of the pitfalls of believing everything they see in the calculator window.

A student in an AP Calculus course should be skilled at using the graphing calculator to perform the four procedures allowed on the AP Calculus exam.

1. Get a complete graph of a function using the [WINDOW] key. (A complete graph is a graph that shows all the essential parts of the function.)
2. Find the zeros of a function.
3. Find a derivative numerically (covered in Chapters 4 and 5).
4. Find an integral numerically (covered in Chapters 6 and 7).

It is also useful to be able to find points of intersection of two graphs, and the maximum and minimum values of a function using the [2nd] CALC menu on the TI-82/83 series (or the [F5] Math menu on the TI-89). The examples and review exercises in this book are designed to give students practice in the types of calculations they will need to perform on the AP Calculus exam.

EXAMPLE

Use a graphing calculator to sketch the graph of each of the following functions in your notebook. Below each graph, state the window used. State the domain and range for each.

(a) $y = e^x + 1$

(b) $y = \ln |x|$

(c) $y = \sin^{-1}x$

(d) $y = \begin{cases} x^2, & x > 1 \\ 2x, & x \le 1 \end{cases}$

Solutions

(a) Domain = {all real numbers}, range = {$y > 1$}

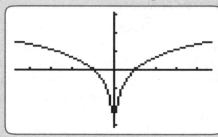

$x\,[-4, 4]\quad y\,[-3, 10]$

(b) Domain = {$x \ne 0$}, range = {all real numbers}

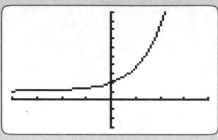

$x\,[-4.7, 4.7]\quad y\,[-3.1, 3.1]$

(c) Domain = $[-1, 1]$, range = $\left[-\dfrac{\pi}{2}, \dfrac{\pi}{2}\right]$

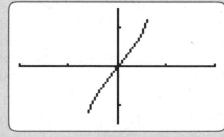

$x\,[-\pi, \pi]\quad y\,[-1.5, 1.5]$

(d) Domain = {all real numbers}, range = {all real numbers}

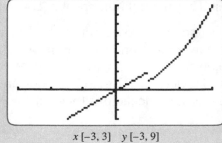

$x\,[-3, 3]\quad y\,[-3, 9]$

Exercises

Multiple-Choice Questions
No calculator is allowed for these questions.

1. The zeros of the polynomial function $f(x) = x^4 - 3x^3$ are
   (A) 0 and 3
   (B) 0 only
   (C) 3 only
   (D) 3 and 4
   (E) 4 only

2. Arctan $\sqrt{3}$ is equal to
   (A) 1
   (B) $\frac{\pi}{4}$
   (C) $\frac{\pi}{6}$
   (D) $\frac{\pi}{3}$
   (E) $\frac{\pi}{2}$

3. Find the number of solutions of the equation $\cos^2 x - 1 = 0$ for values of x in the interval $[0, 2\pi]$.
   (A) 0
   (B) 1
   (C) 2
   (D) 3
   (E) 4

4. Solve for x: $e^{2x} = 9$.
   (A) ln 9
   (B) ln 4.5
   (C) ln 3
   (D) ±4.5
   (E) no solution

5. Find the range of the piecewise function defined by $f(x) = \begin{cases} (x-1)^2, & x < 1 \\ 2x - 3, & x > 1 \end{cases}$.
   (A) {all real numbers}
   (B) {$y > -1$}
   (C) {$y \geq -1$}
   (D) {$y \neq 1$}
   (E) {$y > 0$}

6. Find the equation of the horizontal asymptote of $y = \frac{5x}{x-1}$.
   (A) $y = 1$
   (B) $y = 0$
   (C) $x = 1$
   (D) $x = 5$
   (E) $y = 5$

7. Find the equation of the vertical asymptote of $y = \frac{5x}{x-1}$.
   (A) $y = 1$
   (B) $y = 0$
   (C) $x = 1$
   (D) $x = 5$
   (E) $y = 5$

8. Given $f(x) = 2x - 3$, find $f(x + h)$.
   (A) $2x + 2h - 3$
   (B) $2x + h - 3$
   (C) $x + h$
   (D) $x + h - 3$
   (E) $2(x + h)$

9. If $f(x) = (2x - 1)(x^2 + 1)(x - 5)^2$, then $f(x)$ has how many real roots?
   (A) 0
   (B) 1
   (C) 2
   (D) 3
   (E) 4

10. Solve for x: $\log_9 x^2 = 9$.
    (A) 1
    (B) 3^3
    (C) 3^9
    (D) $\pm 3^9$
    (E) 3^{18}

11. $2 \ln e^{5x} =$
    (A) $10x$
    (B) $5x^2$
    (C) $25x^2$
    (D) e^{10x}
    (E) e^{5x^2}

12. The values of x that are solutions to the equation $\cos^2 x = \sin 2x$ in the interval $[0, \pi]$ are:
    (A) arctan $\frac{1}{2}$ only
    (B) arctan $\frac{1}{2}$ and π
    (C) arctan $\frac{1}{2}$ and 0
    (D) arctan $\frac{1}{2}$ and $\frac{\pi}{2}$
    (E) arctan $\frac{1}{2}$, 0, and $\frac{\pi}{2}$

13. The graph of $f(x) = \dfrac{x^2 - 1}{x - 1}$ has

   (A) a hole at $x = 1$
   (B) a hole at $x = -1$
   (C) a vertical asymptote at $x = 1$
   (D) a vertical asymptote at $x = -1$
   (E) $f(1) = 2$

14. If $\ln x^2 = 6$, then $x =$

   (A) $\pm 3^6$
   (B) $\pm e^6$
   (C) $9\sqrt{6}$
   (D) $e^{\sqrt{6}}$
   (E) $\pm e^3$

Free-Response Questions

A graphing calculator is required for some questions.

1. Find the domain and range and sketch the graph of $y = e^{\ln x}$.

2. The rational function $y = \dfrac{ax}{bx + c}$ has a vertical asymptote at $x = 2$ and a horizontal asymptote at $y = 3$.

   (a) Find a and c in terms of b, and express y in simplest form.
   (b) Graph the function, showing the vertical and horizontal asymptotes.

3. Write a piecewise function that has domain = {all real numbers} and range = $\{y \neq 2\}$.

4. Solve the trigonometric equation $4\sin^2 x - \cos x = 1$ for values of x in the interval $(0, \pi)$.

5. For each of the following functions, graph $f(x)$, $|f(x)|$, and $f(|x|)$. Using these graphs, write a statement about the relationship between the graphs of $f(x)$, $|f(x)|$, and $f(|x|)$.

   (a) $f(x) = \cos x$
   (b) $f(x) = \sin x$
   (c) $f(x) = x^2 - 2x$

6. (a) Write a fourth-degree polynomial that has roots 3 and $1 - i$. (There is more than one correct solution.)
   (b) Write a rational function that has a vertical asymptote at $x = 1$, a horizontal asymptote at $y = 2$, and a hole at $x = -1$.

2.2 Lines

The Formula for the Slope of a Line

$$\text{slope } m = \frac{\Delta y}{\Delta x} = \frac{y_2 - y_1}{x_2 - x_1}$$

Three Forms for the Equation of a Line

slope-intercept form	$y = mx + b$
point-slope form	$y - y_1 = m(x - x_1)$
standard form	$ax + by = c$

When the y-intercept is known, use the slope-intercept form. In most cases, however, the y-intercept is unknown, and the point-slope form should be used.

The Equations of Vertical and Horizontal Lines

horizontal line	$y = b$ (a constant)
vertical line	$x = a$ (a constant)

The Relationship Between Parallel and Perpendicular Lines

• If two lines are parallel, their slopes are equal.
• If two lines are perpendicular, their slopes are negative reciprocals.

EXAMPLE 1

Use the slope-intercept form to write the equation of a line with slope 5 that passes through the point (0, 7).

> *Solution* Since the slope is 5, and the line intercepts the y-axis at $(0, 7)$, the equation of the line is $y = 5x + 7$.

EXAMPLE 2

> Write the equation of a line that is parallel to the line with equation $4x + 3y = 9$ and that passes through the point $(0, 7)$.
>
> *Solution*
>
> METHOD 1 To find the slope of the line with equation $4x + 3y = 9$, rewrite the equation as $y = -\frac{4}{3}x + 3$. The slope is $-\frac{4}{3}$ and since the line passing through the point $(0, 7)$ means that the y-intercept is 7, the line parallel to the given line has the equation $y = -\frac{4}{3}x + 7$.
>
> METHOD 2 A line parallel to the line with equation $4x + 3y = 9$ has the same slope and has an equation of the form $4x + 3y = k$, where k is a constant. Substituting the values of x and y in $(0, 7)$ into the equation $4x + 3y = k$, we find the value of k is 21. Therefore, the equation of the line, in standard form, is $4x + 3y = 21$.

EXAMPLE 3

> Write the equation of a line perpendicular to the line with equation $2x - y = 8$ that passes through the point $(4, 5)$.
>
> *Solution*
>
> METHOD 1 The line with equation $2x - y = 8$ can be rewritten as $y = 2x - 8$. Since its slope is 2, the slope of any line perpendicular to it is $-\frac{1}{2}$. Using the point-slope form for the equation of a line, we find that the perpendicular line that passes through $(4, 5)$ has the equation $y - 5 = -\frac{1}{2}(x - 4)$
>
> *Note:* On the AP exam, the equation of a line may be left in this form and the student will receive full credit.
>
> METHOD 2 The slopes of perpendicular lines are negative reciprocals. A line perpendicular to the line with equation $2x - y = 8$ can be obtained by exchanging the coefficients of x and y, which results in the equation $x + 2y = k$, where k is a constant. Substituting the values of x and y in $(4, 5)$ into $x + 2y = k$, we find the value of k is 14. Therefore, the equation of the line perpendicular to the given line is $x + 2y = 14$.

EXAMPLE 4

> Write the equation of a line parallel to the x-axis and passing through the point $(-1, 4)$.
>
> *Solution* A line parallel to the x-axis is a horizontal line. Since it passes through $(-1, 4)$, its equation is $y = 4$.

Exercises

Multiple-Choice Questions

No calculator is allowed for these questions.

1. Write the equation of the line parallel to the graph of $4x + 3y = 8$ that passes through the point $(2, -1)$.
   - (A) $4x + 3y = 5$
   - (B) $3x - 4y = 10$
   - (C) $4x - 3y = 7$
   - (D) $3x + 4y = 2$
   - (E) $4x + 3y = 0$

2. Write the equation of the line perpendicular to the graph of $2x - 5y = 0$ that passes through the point $(-2, 3)$.
   - (A) $2x - 5y = 11$
   - (B) $2x + 5y = 11$
   - (C) $5x + 2y = -4$
   - (D) $5x + 2y = -16$
   - (E) $y = -\dfrac{2}{5}x$

3. Which is the equation of a line with slope -3 that passes through the point $(-1, -5)$?
   - (A) $y - 5 = -3(x - 1)$
   - (B) $y - 5 = -3(x + 1)$
   - (C) $y + 5 = -3(x - 1)$
   - (D) $y + 5 = -3(x + 1)$
   - (E) $y + 1 = -3(x + 5)$

4. If the point with coordinates $(3, k)$ is on the line $2x - 5y = 8$, find the value of k.
   - (A) $-\dfrac{14}{5}$
   - (B) $-\dfrac{3}{5}$
   - (C) $-\dfrac{2}{5}$
   - (D) $\dfrac{2}{5}$
   - (E) $\dfrac{14}{5}$

5. The equation of the line joining the points $(-1, 2)$ and $(5, 6)$ is
   - (A) $2x - 3y = 8$
   - (B) $2x - 3y + 8 = 0$
   - (C) $2x + 3y = 8$
   - (D) $2x + 3y + 8 = 0$
   - (E) $y = \dfrac{2}{3}x$

6. Which of the following are the equation of a line?
   - I $\quad y = 2x - 5$
   - II $\quad y = x^2 - 5$
   - III $\quad 2y - 3x = 0$
   - (A) I only
   - (B) III only
   - (C) I and III
   - (D) II and III
   - (E) I, II, and III

Free-Response Questions

No calculator is allowed for these questions.

1. Given points $A(2, 4)$, $B(0, 0)$, and $C(4, 0)$:
   - (a) Write the equation of line l, the perpendicular bisector of segment BC.
   - (b) Is point A on line l?
   - (c) Write the equation of line m, the perpendicular bisector of segment AC.
   - (d) Is B on line m?

2. Given points $A(2, 4)$, $B(0, 0)$, and $C(5, 1)$:
   - (a) Find the equation of the line through A and parallel to line BC.
   - (b) Find the coordinates of point D so that $ABCD$ is a parallelogram.

2.3 Properties of Functions

Calculus continues the study of the behavior of functions begun in pre-calculus. The basic properties of a function are its domain and its range. Functions may also have additional properties such as symmetry or asymptotes.

The **domain** of a function is the set of its x-coordinates. The x-coordinate is called the independent variable. Often the easiest way to find the domain of a function is to locate the values of x for which the function is not defined. In a rational function, for example, the function is not defined at those values of x for which the denominator is zero. The domain of a function is the set of x-values excluding those for which the function is not defined. In the case of polynomials, the domain is always the set of all real numbers. This is one of the reasons that polynomials are the functions that are studied first.

The **range** of a function is the set of its y-coordinates. The y-coordinate is called the dependent variable. The range of a function depends on the values in the domain.

Finding the range of a simple function such as a line or parabola is a straightforward process. An arbitrary function may have maximum and minimum values that are difficult to locate. In some cases, therefore, finding the range may require using the methods of calculus.

Functional Notation   The value of a function $f(x)$ at $x = 2$ is denoted $f(2)$. If the function is $f(x) = 4x + 1$, for example, then $f(2) = 4(2) + 1 = 9$.

Similarly, $f(a) = 4a + 1$, and $f(x - 1) = 4(x - 1) + 1 = 4x - 3$.

Symmetry of a Function   If a function $f(x)$ is **even,** its graph is symmetric with respect to the y-axis. An equivalent algebraic statement is that $f(-x) = f(x)$.

If a function $g(x)$ is **odd,** its graph is symmetric with respect to the origin. An equivalent algebraic statement is that $g(-x) = -g(x)$.

Note: If 0 is in the domain of an odd function $g(x)$, then $g(-0) = -g(0)$, or $g(0) = -g(0)$. Therefore, $g(0) = 0$. That is, if 0 is in the domain of an odd function, then its graph must pass through the origin.

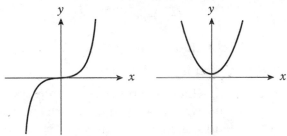

An Odd Function
Symmetric with Respect
to the Origin

An Even Function
Symmetric with Respect
to the y-Axis

Asymptotes   If there are values of x for which a function is undefined, then the function may have a **vertical asymptote** at these x-values. Many rational functions have vertical asymptotes.

If a function is not a rational function, it may still have vertical or horizontal asymptotes. Vertical asymptotes are located by finding the values of x for which the function is undefined. Finding horizontal asymptotes may involve evaluating the limit of the function. Limits will be discussed next in Chapter 3.

Multiple Representations of a Function   The AP Calculus courses emphasize the importance of being able to represent a function in multiple ways. Students should be able to represent functions graphically, numerically, algebraically, and verbally. They should also be able to convert flexibly from one representation to another. Much of the power of calculus derives from being able to approach problems from different perspectives. Students who are skilled at representing functions in multiple ways are able to approach problem-solving situations from a variety of perspectives and can choose from a number of techniques and methods when working toward a solution.

For example, looking at the graph of the $f(x) = \dfrac{x}{x^2 + 1}$ shown on page 24, we might suspect that the function is odd, since it appears to be symmetric with respect to the origin.

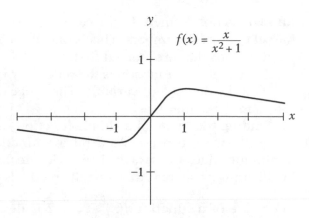

Investigating further, we can evaluate the function for several values of x. Thus,

$$f(2) = \frac{2}{5}, f(-2) = -\frac{2}{5}, f(0) = 0, f(1) = \frac{1}{2}, f(-1) = -\frac{1}{2}.$$

A pattern emerges from these values that gives us a further clue that the function is odd. This can be proved using the definition of an odd function:

$$f(-x) = \frac{-x}{(-x)^2 + 1} = -f(x).$$

We conclude that $f(x) = \frac{x}{x^2 + 1}$ is an odd function because $f(-x) = -f(x)$, which is the definition of an odd function. This is also apparent in the graph, which is symmetric with respect to the origin.

In this way, a graphical representation led to numerical analysis, which led to an algebraic proof of a property of the function and to a verbalization of this property.

EXAMPLE 1

Find the domain and range of the function $y = \sqrt{x - 8}$.

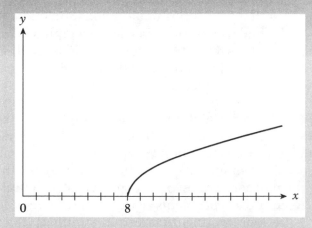

Solution   The quantity under the radical must be greater than or equal to zero; therefore, the domain is $\{x \geq 8\}$. Since the y-values are greater than or equal to zero, the range of the function is $\{y \geq 0\}$.

EXAMPLE 2

Find the domain and range of each function.
(a) $y = e^x - x$
(b) $y = |x| + x$
(c) $y = (x + 1)^2$
(d) $y = \dfrac{\sin 2x}{x}$

Solution

(a) Domain = {all reals}, range = $\{y \geq 1\}$
(b) Domain = {all reals}, range = $\{y \geq 0\}$
(c) Domain = {all reals}, range = $\{y \geq -1\}$
(d) Domain = $\{x \neq 0\}$, range = $\{-0.434 \leq y \leq 2\}$

EXAMPLE 3

Is the function $y = \dfrac{e^{x^2}}{x}$ even, odd, or neither? Explain your answer both graphically and algebraically.

Solution

GRAPHICALLY Graph the function on the calculator to see if it is symmetric to either the y-axis or the origin.

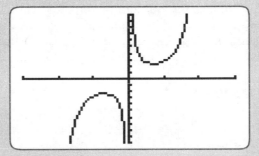

Since it is symmetric with respect to the origin, the function is odd.

ALGEBRAICALLY Choose several x-values to see if either $f(-x) = f(x)$, or $f(-x) = -f(x)$. It should appear that $f(-x) = -f(x)$. To prove this, note that

$$f(-x) = \frac{e^{(-x)^2}}{-x} = \frac{e^{x^2}}{-x} = -\frac{e^{x^2}}{x},$$

which is $-f(x)$. Therefore, $f(x)$ is odd.

Calculator Note

To see if a function is even or odd using the calculator, enter the function in Y_1. Then enter $Y_1(-x)$ into Y_2. Now graph Y_1 and Y_2.

   If the function is even, then Y_1 and Y_2 are the same function, and only one function will appear on the graph.

   If the function is odd, then Y_1 and Y_2 are opposites, and two opposite functions will appear on the graph.

EXAMPLE 4

Find the equations of the vertical asymptote(s) of $y = \frac{x+2}{x^2-1}$.

Solution   The vertical asymptotes are found by solving $x^2 - 1 = 0$.

The solutions are $x = 1$ and $x = -1$. Since neither of these values makes the numerator zero, both $x = 1$ and $x = -1$ are equations of vertical asymptotes.

Zeros   The **zeros**, or **roots**, of a function $f(x)$ are the x-values such that $f(x) = 0$. Some zeros are found by factoring. Other zeros may be approximated on a calculator. In some cases, such as complex roots, the roots do not appear on the calculator, but can sometimes be found by algebraic methods.

EXAMPLE 5

Find the asymptotes of $f(x) = \frac{x-1}{x^2-1}$.

Solution   Since $f(x)$ is a rational function and the degree of the numerator is less than the degree of the denominator, $f(x)$ has a horizontal asymptote at $y = 0$.

To find the vertical asymptotes, set the denominator equal to zero and solve for x. There are two solutions, $x = 1$ and $x = -1$. Since $x = 1$ also makes the numerator zero, $f(1)$ is not undefined (it is called indeterminate). Thus, there is a gap or hole at $x = 1$ and no vertical asymptote. Thus, $f(x)$ has only one vertical asymptote at $x = -1$.

EXAMPLE 6

For the functions that follow, find
(a) the zeros
(b) the end behavior

- $f(x) = (x - 2)^2 (x + 3)$
- $f(x) = (x - 2)^2 (x + 3)^2$

Solution   For $f(x) = (x - 2)^2 (x + 3)$

(a) The zeros are $x = 2$ and $x = -3$.
(b) Since $f(x)$ is a third-degree polynomial and the leading coefficient is positive, the graph of $f(x)$ goes up to the right and down to the left.

Solution   For $f(x) = (x - 2)^2 (x + 3)^2$

(a) The zeros are $x = 2$ and $x = -3$.
(b) Since $f(x)$ is a fourth-degree polynomial and the leading coefficient is positive, the graph of $f(x)$ rises on both the left and right sides.

EXAMPLE 7

(a) If (1, 2) is a point on the graph of an *even* function, what other point is also on the graph?
(b) If (1, 2) is a point on the graph of an *odd* function, what other point is also on the graph?

Solution

(a) By the definition of an even function $f(x) = f(-x)$. Since (1, 2) is a point on the graph of an even function, the point $(-1, 2)$ is also on the graph.
(b) By the definition of an odd function, $f(x) = -f(x)$. Since (1, 2) is on the graph of an odd function, the point $(-1, -2)$ is also on the graph.

Exercises

Multiple-Choice Questions
A graphing calculator is required for some questions.

1. If $f(x) = x^2 - x + 1$, then $f(x + 1) =$
(A) $x^2 - x + 2$
(B) $x^2 + x + 1$
(C) $x^2 + x + 3$
(D) 1
(E) 3

2. Find the domain of $f(x) = \sqrt{x^3 - x^2}$.
(A) $\{x \geq 1\}$
(B) $\{x \geq 1, x = 0\}$
(C) $\{x \geq 1\}$
(D) $\{|x| \geq 1\}$
(E) $\{|x| > 1\}$

3. Which of the following is an even function with domain = {reals}?
(A) $\ln x^2$
(B) $e^{x^2} - x$
(C) $e^{x^2} - x^2$
(D) $e^{x^3} + 1$
(E) $\dfrac{1}{x^2 - 4}$

4. Find the domain of $f(x) = \ln(\tan x)$ on the interval $[-\pi, \pi]$.
(A) all x in $(-\pi, \pi)$
(B) all x in $(0, \pi)$
(C) all x in $\left(0, \dfrac{\pi}{2}\right)$
(D) all x in $\left(-\pi, -\dfrac{\pi}{2}\right)$ and $\left(0, \dfrac{\pi}{2}\right)$
(E) all x in $\left[-\dfrac{\pi}{2}, \dfrac{\pi}{2}\right]$

5. $f(x) = \dfrac{(x - 1)^2}{x^2 - 1}$ has
(A) a hole at $x = -1$
(B) holes at $x = -1$ and $x = 1$
(C) vertical asymptotes at $x = 1$ and $x = -1$
(D) a horizontal asymptote at $y = -1$
(E) a hole at $x = 1$ and a vertical asymptote at $x = -1$

6. $f(x)$ is an odd function and the graph of f contains the point (6, 5). Which of the following points is also on the graph of f?
(A) $(-6, 5)$
(B) $(6, -5)$
(C) $(-6, -5)$
(D) $(-5, -6)$
(E) $(5, 6)$

7. If $f(x) = \sqrt{x - 2}$, then $\dfrac{f(x + h) - f(x)}{h} =$
(A) $\dfrac{\sqrt{x - 2} + \sqrt{h - 2}}{h}$
(B) $\dfrac{\sqrt{xh - 2} + \sqrt{x - 2}}{h}$
(C) $\dfrac{\sqrt{x - 2 + h} - \sqrt{x - 2}}{h}$
(D) $\dfrac{\sqrt{x + h} - \sqrt{2}}{h}$
(E) $\dfrac{\sqrt{x + h - 2} - (x - 2)}{h}$

8. If $f(x) = \dfrac{1}{x + 2}$, then $\dfrac{f(x + h) - f(x)}{h} =$
(A) $\dfrac{h + 4}{h(x + 2)(x + h + 2)}$
(B) $\dfrac{-1}{(x + 2)(x + h + 2)}$

(C) $\dfrac{-1}{(x+h)(x+h-2)}$

(D) $\dfrac{1}{h(x+2)(x+h+2)}$

(E) $\dfrac{1}{2h+2}$

9. Which of the following functions are odd?

  I $y = \ln(x^3)$
  II $y = |x^3|$
  III $y = e^{x^3}$

(A) none
(B) II only
(C) I and II
(D) II and III
(E) I, II, and III

10. Which of the following functions are even?

  I $y = \ln|x|$
  II $y = |\ln x|$
  III $y = \left|\dfrac{1}{x}\right|$

(A) none
(B) II only
(C) I and III
(D) II and III
(E) I, II, and III

Free-Response Questions

A graphing calculator is required for some questions.

1. Find all the zeros (real and complex) of $f(x) = x^3 + 2x - 3$.

2. (a) Enter into the calculator Y=: $Y_1 = x^3 - x$, $Y_2 = Y_1(-x)$. Sketch Y_1 and Y_2 on paper and describe the relationship between them. What property of the function in Y_1 is the basis for this relationship?

   (b) Enter in Y=: $Y_1 = x^2 + 1$, $Y_2 = Y_1(-x)$. Sketch Y_1 and Y_2 on paper and describe the relationship between them. What property of the function in Y_1 is the basis for this relationship?

3. Sketch $f(x) = \dfrac{x-1}{x^2 - 3x + 2}$, and state the vertical asymptote(s), horizontal asymptote(s), and holes, if any.

4. Find the zeros and describe the end behavior of $f(x) = 2x(x-1)(x+1)$. Is $f(x)$ odd, even, or neither? Explain.

2.4 Inverses

If a function is **one-to-one,** then the function has an inverse. The inverse of the function $f(x)$ is denoted $f^{-1}(x)$, and is read as "the inverse of f."

Note: Do not confuse $f^{-1}(x)$ with $\dfrac{1}{f(x)}$.

Use the **horizontal line test** to determine if a function is one-to-one from its graph.

> **Horizontal Line Test**
> If any horizontal line intersects the graph no more than once, then the function is one-to-one.

If a function is not one-to-one, it may be possible to restrict its domain in order to make it one-to-one. This is the procedure for finding inverses of functions such as $y = x^2$ and $y = \sin x$.

The *graph of the inverse of a function* is the reflection of the graph of the function (on its restricted domain) in the line $y = x$.

The *equation of the inverse of a function* can be found by exchanging x and y in the equation of the function, and then solving for y. The domain of the inverse is the range of the function, and the range of the inverse is the domain of the function.

Calculator Note

The TI-83 and TI-89 calculators have a built-in draw inverse feature.

Using the TI-83

Enter the function into Y=.

Press 2nd DRAW 8 to get DrawInv on the Home screen.

Press VARS Y-VARS 1 ENTER.

The calculator will then display the graph of the inverse of the function.

Using the TI-89

Press GRAPH WINDOW F6 3: DrawInv, then enter the function (for example, Y_1 or Y_2) and press ENTER.

EXAMPLE 1

For the functions $f(x)$ and $g(x)$ where $f(x) = x^3 - 4$ and $g(x) = \ln(x) + 2$:

(a) State the domain and range of the function.
(b) Find the equation of the inverse of the function.
(c) State the domain and range of the inverse.
(d) Graph the function and its inverse on the same set of axes.

Solution For $f(x) = x^3 - 4$:

(a) The domain is the set of all real numbers. The range is the set of all real numbers.
(b) The equation of the inverse is $y = (x + 4)^{1/3}$.
(c) The domain and range of the inverse is the set of real numbers.
(d)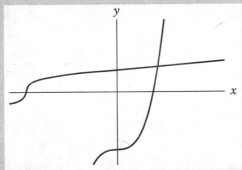

Solution For $g(x) = \ln(x) + 2$:

(a) Domain of $g(x)$ is $\{x > 0\}$. Range is the set of real numbers.
(b) Equation of the inverse of $g(x) = e^{x-2}$.
(c) Domain of the inverse of $g(x)$ is the set of real numbers. Range of the inverse of $g(x)$ is $\{y > 0\}$.
(d)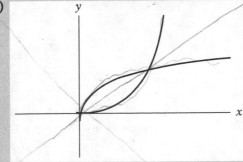

Exercises

Multiple-Choice Questions

No calculator is allowed for these questions.

1. Which of the following graphs show(s) a function that has an inverse?

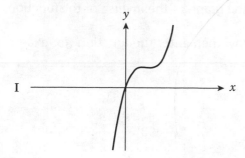

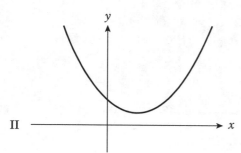

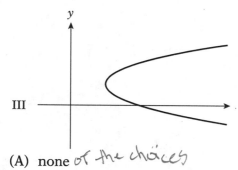

   (A) none of the choices
   (B) I only
   (C) II only
   (D) I and II
   (E) I, II, and III

2. Find the inverse of the equation $y = 2x^3 + 1$.

   (A) $y = \dfrac{2}{x^3} + 1$
   (B) $y = -2x^3 + 1$
   (C) $y = \sqrt[3]{\dfrac{x-1}{2}}$
   (D) $y = \dfrac{\sqrt[3]{x} - 1}{2}$
   (E) $y = \sqrt[3]{\dfrac{x+1}{2}}$

3. The graphs of a function and its inverse are reflections of each other across
   (A) the x-axis
   (B) the y-axis
   (C) the origin
   (D) $y = x$
   (E) $y = -x$

4. The composition of a function f and its inverse is equal to
   (A) -1
   (B) 0
   (C) 1
   (D) x
   (E) $\dfrac{1}{x}$

Free-Response Questions

A graphing calculator is required for some questions.

1. (a) Sketch the graph of $y = -e^{-x}$. State its domain and range.
   (b) On the calculator, enter [2nd] DRAW 8: DrawInv Y_1, and copy the inverse onto your graph.
   (c) Solve algebraically for the inverse of $y = -e^{-x}$.
   (d) Enter the equation of the inverse in Y_2. Graph it and examine the symmetry to check that it is in fact the equation of the inverse.

2. (a) Find the domain and range of the function $y = \sqrt{x-2} + 1$, and sketch the graph.
   (b) Find the domain and range of the inverse, and solve algebraically for the equation of the inverse.

3. Sketch the inverse of the function shown here.

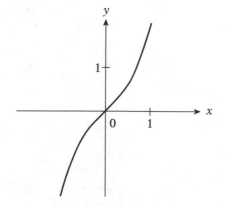

2.5 Translations and Reflections

When the graph of a function is moved to the left or right, or up or down, or is reflected in the x-axis or the y-axis, the graph maintains many of its properties. When the graph of a function is shifted or flipped, the rule for the function changes, though the graph remains essentially the same.

Rules for Translating and Reflecting Functions

- If a function $f(x)$ is translated to the right c units, its new equation is $f(x - c)$.
- If a function $f(x)$ is translated to the left c units, its new equation is $f(x + c)$.
- If a function $f(x)$ is translated down c units, its new equation is $f(x) - c$.
- If a function $f(x)$ is translated up c units, its new equation is $f(x) + c$.
- If a function $f(x)$ is reflected across the x-axis, its new equation is $-f(x)$.
- If a function $f(x)$ is reflected across the y-axis, its new equation is $f(-x)$.

For example, if the graph of $y = x^2$ is moved 5 units to the right, the new rule is $y = (x - 5)^2$.

If the graph is moved down 3 units, the new rule is $y = x^2 - 3$.

If the graph is reflected across the x-axis, the new rule is $y = -x^2$.

When the graph of a parabola is shifted or reflected, the graph remains a parabola with properties similar to those of the original graph.

If the graph of $y = \ln x$ is shifted to the left 2 units, the new rule will be $y = \ln(x + 2)$.

Practice in graphing both by hand and using a graphing calculator makes it easier to recognize that a group of functions can be understood as one function that has been shifted and/or reflected.

EXAMPLE 1

Describe the translation and/or reflection that changes:
(a) x^2 to $(x + 3)^2$
(b) $|x|$ to $-|x - k|$ $(k > 0)$
(c) 2^x to 2^{-x}
(d) $\cos x$ to $-\cos x$

Solution

(a) The graph is moved 3 units to the left.
(b) The graph is moved k units to the right and reflected in the x-axis.
(c) The graph is reflected in the y-axis.
(d) The graph is reflected in the x-axis.

Exercises

No calculator is allowed for these questions.

1. The following functions have been shifted as described. Circle the equation that matches each description, then sketch its graph.
   (a) $y = \ln x$ shifted right 2 units
   $y = \ln(x + 2)$ $y = \ln(x - 2)$
   $y = \ln x + 2$ $y = \ln x - 2$

   (b) $y = 2^x$ shifted down 1 unit
   $y = 2^x - 1$ $y = 2^{x-1}$
   $y = 2^{x+1}$ $y = 2^x + 1$

   (c) $y = |x|$ shifted left 3 units
   $y = |x + 3|$ $y = |x - 3|$
   $y = |x| + 3$ $y = |x| - 3$

   (d) $y = x^2$ shifted up 2 units and right 4 units
   $y = (x - 2)^2 - 4$ $y = (x - 2)^2 + 4$
   $y = (x^2 + 4) + 2$ $y = (x - 4)^2 + 2$

   (e) $y = \sin x$ reflected in the x-axis
   $y = \sin(-x)$ $y = \sin(x - 1)$
   $y = -\sin x$ $y = -\sin(-x)$

2. Write the domain for each of the following functions. Then sketch the graph.
   (a) $y = \ln x^2$
   (b) $y = |x + 2|$
   (c) $y = -\ln(x - 1)$

Multiple-Choice Questions

A graphing calculator is required for some questions.

1. The graph of $y = x^2$ first reflected in the x-axis and then shifted down one unit is
   (A) $y = x^2 - 1$
   (B) $y = 1 - x^2$
   (C) $y = 1 + x^2$
   (D) $y = 1 - x^{-2}$
   (E) $y = -1 - x^2$

2. The graph of $y = x^2$ first shifted down one unit and then reflected in the x-axis is
   (A) $y = x^2 - 1$
   (B) $y = 1 - x^2$
   (C) $y = 1 + x^2$
   (D) $y = 1 - x^{-2}$
   (E) $y = -1 - x^2$

3. The inverse of the function $y = x^2$ with domain = $\{x \leq 0\}$ has equation
   (A) $y = -x^2$
   (B) $y = x^2$
   (C) $y = \sqrt{x}$
   (D) $y = \pm\sqrt{x}$
   (E) $y = -\sqrt{x}$

Free-Response Questions

A graphing calculator is required for some questions.

1. Sketch the graph of $y = \frac{1}{x}$, and then use it to sketch the graphs of the following functions without a calculator. Check your results by graphing each equation in the calculator.
   (a) $y = \frac{1}{x - 1}$
   (b) $y = \frac{1}{x} - 1$
   (c) $y = \frac{1}{x + 2} + 2$
   (d) the inverse of $y = \frac{1}{x}$

2. Describe the translations and/or reflections that transform $y = x^{2/3}$ into the following:
   (a) $y = x^{2/3} + 2$
   (b) $y = -x^{2/3} - 3$
   (c) $y = (-x)^{2/3}$
   (d) $y = (x - 1)^{2/3} + 1$

BC 2.6 Parametric Equations

Functions in calculus are usually of a single variable. There are also functions defined by a set of parametric equations, where x and y are both dependent variables expressed in terms of an independent variable t, called the **parameter**. Parametric functions appear in the following form:

$$\begin{cases} x = f(t) \\ y = g(t) \end{cases}$$

Parametric equations allow us to graph a wider variety of functions and even to graph curves that are not functions, called relations. Unlike x and y, the parameter t does not appear as an axis in the coordinate plane. It is a third variable, often representing time, used only to define the values of x and y.

Calculator Note

To work with parametric equations on the graphing calculator, the MODE must be set to Par (for parametric). Expressions for both x and y may then be entered in Y=.

Press WINDOW to enter values that will define the viewing window. In addition to Tmin and Tmax, there is also a Tstep, which controls the number of points that are plotted. The bigger Tstep is, the fewer points are plotted and the less accurate the graph. The smaller Tstep is, the more points are plotted and the more accurate the graph. It also takes the calculator longer to produce a graph with a smaller Tstep.

Press GRAPH, and then TRACE, to display the values of x, y, and t.

EXAMPLE 1

On the calculator, graph the parametric function in the window given, and state the domain and range.

$$\begin{cases} x = t^2 \\ y = t + 2 \end{cases}$$

Graph the function in the WINDOW: Tmin = 0, Tmax = 3, and Tstep = 0.1, Xmin = 0, Xmax = 10, Ymin = −3, Ymax = 9.

Solution   Press Y=, and enter $X_{1T} = t^2$ and $Y_{1T} = t + 2$. Define the window and then press GRAPH.

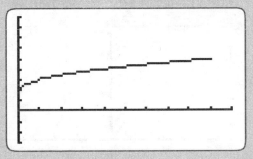

Use TRACE to find that the domain for t is [0, 3], the domain for x is [0, 9], and the range for y is [0, 5].

EXAMPLE 2

Using the parametric function from Example 1, go to WINDOW and change Tmin = −3, and press GRAPH. Find the domain and range of the graph.

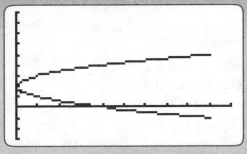

Solution   Notice that the graph is not that of a function. It is now a relation. The domain of t is [−3, 3]. The domain of x is [0, 9]. The range of y is [−1, 5].

By eliminating the parameter t, the set of parametric equations given in Example 1 on page 33, $x = t^2$ and $y = t + 2$, can be transformed into a single equation in terms of x and y as follows: solve for t in $y = t + 2$, $t = y - 2$, and substitute t into the equation for x, $x = t^2$.

Thus, $x = (y - 2)^2$. This is the equation of a parabola, but there is still a restriction on the values of x and y, depending on the values of t that are used, say t between 0 and 3 or t between -3 and 3. It is extremely important to remember that when eliminating the parameter, the values of x and y are still dependent on, that is, limited by, the values of t specified in the problem.

EXAMPLE 3

On the calculator, graph the parametric function in the window given.
$$\begin{cases} x = te^{-t^2} \\ y = t + 2 \end{cases}$$

Graph the function in the following WINDOW: Tmin $= -2$, Tmax $= 2$, Xmin $= -2$, Xmax $= 2$, Ymin $= -1$, Ymax $= 5$.
(a) Sketch the graph and indicate the direction of increasing t.
(b) Estimate the domain and range of the graph.

Solution

(a) With the calculator in parametric mode, enter the following into Y=:
$X_{1T} = te^{-t^2}$, $Y_{1T} = t + 2$. Set the WINDOW and press ENTER.

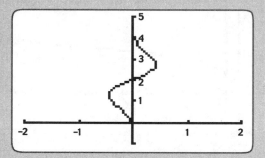

(b) The domain is approximately $[-0.429, 0.429]$, and the range is $[0, 4]$.

Exercises

Multiple-Choice Questions
No calculator is allowed for these questions.

1. For the pair of parametric equations $x(t) = 2 \cos t$ and $y(t) = \sin t$, eliminating the parameter gives which equation in the variables x and y?
   (A) $x^2 + y^2 = 4$
   (B) $x^2 - y^2 = 4$
   (C) $x^2 + 4y^2 = 4$
   (D) $4x^2 + y^2 = 4$
   (E) $4x^2 - y^2 = 4$

2. For the pair of parametric equations $x(t) = t^2 + t$ and $y(t) = t$, eliminating the parameter gives which equation in the variables x and y?
   (A) $y^2 = x + y$
   (B) $y^2 = x - y$
   (C) $x^2 + x = y$
   (D) $y^2 = x^2 + y$
   (E) $x - y = t$

3. Which of the following is a part of the graph given by the system of parametric equations $x(t) = t^2 + 2t$ and $y(t) = t$?

(A)

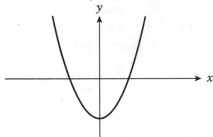

(B)

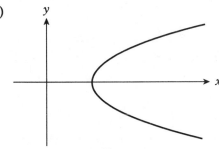

(C)

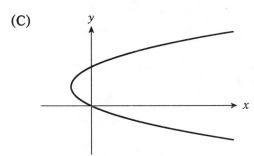

(D)

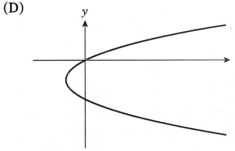

(E)

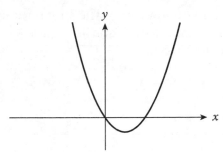

4. The parametric equations $x(t) = 2t + 1$ and $y(t) = t - 1$, for t in the interval $[0, 4]$, is the equation of
(A) a line
(B) a ray
(C) a line segment
(D) a circle
(E) a parabola

Free-Response Questions
A graphing calculator is required.

1. Given the parametric equations, sketch the curve and indicate the direction of increasing t.

$$x(t) = 2\cos t \text{ and } y(t) = \sin t,$$
for t in the interval $[0, \pi]$.

2. Sketch the graph of the parametric equations, indicating the direction of increasing t, and use the graph to identify the curve.

$$x(t) = t^2 + 1 \text{ and } y(t) = t - 1,$$
for t in the inverval $[-3, 3]$.

Chapter Assessment

Multiple-Choice Questions
No calculator is allowed for these questions.

1. Find the slope of the line with equation $2x + 3y = 5$.

(A) $-\frac{3}{2}$

(B) $-\frac{2}{3}$

(C) $\frac{2}{3}$

(D) $\frac{3}{2}$

(E) $\frac{5}{2}$

2. Find the equation of the line parallel to the line with equation $x - 2y = 6$ and passing through the point $(2, -3)$.
(A) $x - 2y = 11$
(B) $x - 2y = 8$
(C) $2x + y = 7$
(D) $2x + y = 1$
(E) $x = 6$

3. Find the equation of the line perpendicular to the line with equation $3x + 4y = 7$ and passing through $(0, -1)$.
   (A) $4x - 3y = 7$
   (B) $4x - 3y = 3$
   (C) $3x + 4y = -4$
   (D) $3x + 4y = 4$
   (E) $y = -1$

4. How many vertical and horizontal asymptotes are there to the graph of $y = \dfrac{x^2}{x^2 - 1}$?
   (A) 2 vertical and 1 horizontal
   (B) 1 vertical and 1 horizontal
   (C) 1 vertical and no horizontal
   (D) 2 vertical and no horizontal
   (E) 1 vertical and 2 horizontal

5. The graph of $y = e^{-x} + 1$ has a horizontal asymptote with equation
   (A) $x = 0$
   (B) $y = 0$
   (C) $x = 1$
   (D) $y = 1$
   (E) The graph has no horizontal asymptote.

6. The graph of $y = \ln(x + 2)$ has a vertical asymptote with equation
   (A) $x = -2$
   (B) $y = -2$
   (C) $x = 0$
   (D) $y = 0$
   (E) The graph has no vertical asymptote.

7. The domain of $y = e^{-2x} + 1$ is
   (A) $\{x \geq 0\}$
   (B) $\{x > 0\}$
   (C) $\{x \neq 0\}$
   (D) $\{x < 0\}$
   (E) {all real numbers}

8. The range of $y = \ln(x + 2)$ is
   (A) $\{x > 2\}$
   (B) $\{x > 0\}$
   (C) $\{x \neq 0\}$
   (D) $\{x > -2\}$
   (E) {all real numbers}

9. The end behavior of the graph of $f(x) = x^4 + 3x^3 - 6x$ can be described as
   (A) both ends up
   (B) left up, right down
   (C) left down, right up
   (D) both ends down
   (E) none of these

10. The end behavior of the graph of $f(x) = -3x^3 + x^2$ can be described as
    (A) both ends up
    (B) left up, right down
    (C) left down, right up
    (D) both ends down
    (E) none of these

11. Find the value(s) of arccos 1.
    (A) 0
    (B) π
    (C) 0 or π
    (D) $\dfrac{\pi}{2}$
    (E) 0 or $\dfrac{\pi}{2}$

12. Solve the equation: $\ln x^2 = 5$.
    (A) $x = \pm\, e^{\frac{5}{2}}$
    (B) $x = e^{\frac{5}{2}}$
    (C) $x = \pm\, e^{\sqrt{5}}$
    (D) $x = e^{\sqrt{5}}$
    (E) $x = \pm\, e^{\frac{2}{5}}$

13. The function $y = \log_2(x - 4)$ has an x-intercept at $x =$
    (A) 0
    (B) 1
    (C) 2
    (D) 4
    (E) 5

14. The function $y = \ln x + 2$ has a y-intercept at $y =$
    (A) 0
    (B) 1
    (C) 2
    (D) e
    (E) There is no y-intercept.

15. Solve the equation $e^{2x} - e^x = 2$.
    (A) 2 only
    (B) -1 or 2
    (C) $\ln 2$
    (D) e^{-1} or e^2
    (E) e^2 only

16. The graph of an even function has
    (A) no symmetry
    (B) symmetry with respect to the x-axis
    (C) symmetry with respect to the line $y = x$
    (D) symmetry with respect to the y-axis
    (E) symmetry with respect to the line $y = -x$

17. If the point with coordinates $(2, 1)$ is on the graph of a function, then which of the following is on the graph of its inverse?
(A) $(2, -1)$
(B) $(-2, -1)$
(C) $(-2, 1)$
(D) $(1, 2)$
(E) $(-1, -2)$

18. The inverse of $y = 2\sqrt{x}$ is

(A) $y = \frac{1}{4}x^2, x \le 0$

(B) $y = \frac{1}{4}x^2, x \ge 0$

(C) $y = \frac{1}{4}x^2$

(D) $y = -2\sqrt{x}$

(E) $y = \dfrac{1}{2\sqrt{x}}$

19. The real zero(s) of $f(x) = x^3 + 2x^2 + 9x + 18$ are
(A) -2 only
(B) $-3, -2$
(C) $\pm 3, -2$
(D) $\pm 3, \pm 2$
(E) none

20. If $f(x) = x^2 - 2x$, then $f(2 + h) =$
(A) $h^2 + 4h + 3$
(B) $h^2 + 8h + 3$
(C) $h^2 + 2h + 3$
(D) $h^2 - 2h + 3$
(E) $h^2 + 2h$

21. The domain of $f(x) = \dfrac{x - 3}{\sqrt{x - 2}}$ is

(A) $x \ge 2$
(B) $x > 2$
(C) $x > 3$
(D) $x > 2$ and $x \ne 3$
(E) $x < 2$

22. The range of $y = 2|x - 2| - 2$ in the interval $[0, 5]$ is
(A) $\{0 \le y \le 5\}$
(B) $\{2 \le y \le 5\}$
(C) $\{-2 \le y \le 5\}$
(D) $\{-2 \le y \le 4\}$
(E) $\{0 \le y \le 4\}$

23. Which of the following has an inverse?
(A) $x = y^2$
(B) $y = |x|$
(C) $y = \ln x$
(D) $y = \sqrt{4 - x^2}$
(E) $x = |y|$

24. Which of the following functions are even?
I $3y = x^4 + x$
II $y = |x - 2|$
III $y = e^{x^2} - 1$
(A) I only
(B) II only
(C) III only
(D) II and III
(E) I, II, and III

25. For which of the following functions does $f(a) + f(b) = f(a + b)$?
(A) $y = 2x + 3$
(B) $y = 2x$
(C) $y = x^2$
(D) $y = \sqrt{x}$
(E) $y = |x|$

Free-Response Questions
A graphing calculator is required for some questions.

1. (a) Sketch the graph of each function below by hand.

$$f(x) = x^4 - x^3 \quad g(x) = \ln x \quad h(x) = x - 1$$

(b) Graph the 3 functions in the calculator and use $\boxed{\text{ZOOM}}$ Box centered at $(1, 0)$.
(c) Write a sentence that describes the relationship between $f(x)$, $g(x)$, and $h(x)$ for values of x near $(1, 0)$.
(d) Find the range of $f(x)$. (*Hint:* Use the CALC menu on the calculator to find the minimum value of $f(x)$.)

2. (a) Graph $f(x) = x^3 - x$.
(b) Does $f(x)$ have an inverse? Explain your answer and find the inverse if it exists.
(c) Graph $g(x) = x^3 - 1$.
(d) Does $g(x)$ have an inverse? Explain your answer and find the inverse if it exists.

3. Copy the table below and fill in the domain, range, roots, symmetry, and asymptotes (if any) of each of the following functions. Then sketch the graph of each function *without* using a calculator

Function	Domain	Range	Roots	Symmetry	Asymptotes
(a) $y = x^2$					
(b) $y = \ln x$					
(c) $y = 2^x$					
(d) $y = \sin x$					
(e) $y = |x|$					

4. (a) Sketch the graph of $f(x) = (x - 2)^2(x - 4)^3(x - 6)$. Check your result with a calculator.
   (b) Find the degree of the function and the roots, and describe the behavior of the graph near each of the roots.

5. (a) Give an example of an odd function which has $x = 0$ in the domain and which passes through the origin.
   (b) Use the definition of an odd function to prove that the conditions in part (a) are true for all odd functions.

CHAPTER 3
Limits and Continuity

Introduction

Understanding the concept of limit is central to understanding calculus. A **limit** is a value that a function approaches as x approaches some fixed value. The definition of the derivative of a function and the concept of an integral both involve a limiting process. In this chapter, you will learn how to evaluate a limit and how to interpret a limit in relation to the graph of a function.

3.1 Functions and Asymptotes

In addition to knowing the basics about a function, its domain and range, it is important to know whether a function has vertical or horizontal asymptotes. Rational functions often have horizontal and vertical asymptotes. The process of finding the vertical and horizontal asymptotes of a rational function was explained in Section 2.1.

In general, if a function $f(x)$ has a horizontal asymptote, then $f(x)$ approaches a finite number, call it b, as x gets larger (as $x \to \infty$) or as x gets smaller (as $x \to -\infty$). The equation of the horizontal asymptote is $y = b$. Another way of expressing the fact that $f(x)$ approaches the value b as $x \to \infty$ is to use the limit symbol:

$$\lim_{x \to \infty} f(x) = b$$

The limit symbol can also be used to describe the end behavior of a function. In Section 2.1, the end behavior of polynomial functions was discussed. In general, if a function $f(x)$ is unbounded, this means that $f(x)$ approaches ∞ or $-\infty$ as x increases (as $x \to +\infty$) or as x decreases (as $x \to -\infty$). If $f(x)$ approaches ∞ as $x \to \infty$, the limit symbol expresses this as follows:

$$\lim_{x \to \infty} f(x) = \infty.$$

If a rational function has a vertical asymptote at $x = a$, then the function $f(x)$ is undefined at $x = a$, but approaches ∞ or $-\infty$ as the value of x approaches a from the right or the left.

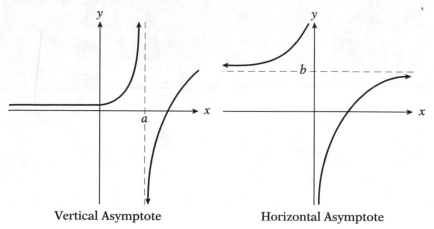

Vertical Asymptote   Horizontal Asymptote

Limits

Notation	Meaning	Asymptotes
$\lim\limits_{x \to a^-} f(x) = \infty$	$f(x)$ approaches ∞ as x approaches a from the left.	vertical asymptote at $x = a$
$\lim\limits_{x \to a^+} f(x) = -\infty$	$f(x)$ approaches $-\infty$ as x approaches a from the right.	vertical asymptote at $x = a$
$\lim\limits_{x \to \infty} f(x) = b$	$f(x)$ approaches b as x approaches ∞.	horizontal asymptote at $y = b$
$\lim\limits_{x \to -\infty} f(x) = b$	$f(x)$ approaches b as x approaches $-\infty$.	horizontal asymptote at $y = b$

Calculator Note

Another feature of the graphing calculator that is useful in studying the behavior of functions is the TABLE. For a given function, values of x are entered into the x-column and the calculator generates the corresponding values of y.

To create a table for a given function on the calculator, first enter the function in $\boxed{\text{Y=}}$.

Then go to TBLSET and set the Independent variable to Ask.

Now go to TABLE and enter the values of x that are close to the x-value in question. The table will list the corresponding values of $f(x)$ and show how large or small the values of $f(x)$ become. This process is demonstrated in Examples 1 and 2, which follow.

EXAMPLE 1

Find the horizontal asymptote of $f(x) = \dfrac{x}{x-2}$.

Solution Go to [Y=] and enter the function into Y_1. Now go to TBLSET and check to see that the independent variable is on Ask. If not, change from Auto to Ask. Go to TABLE and enter the following values of x: 10, 20, 50, 100.

The limit of $f(x)$ as x increases (as $x \to \infty$) appears to be 1. This can be written using the limit notation as

$$\lim_{x \to \infty} \frac{x}{x-2} = 1$$

Now enter these values of x: -10, -20, -50, -100.

```
  X      Y1
 10     1.25
 20     1.1111
 50     1.0417
100     1.0204
-10     .83333
-20     .90909
-50     .96154

X= -50
```

The limit of $f(x)$ as x decreases (as $x \to -\infty$) appears to be 1. This can be written using the limit notation as

$$\lim_{x \to -\infty} \frac{x}{x-2} = 1$$

Thus, $f(x)$ has a horizontal asymptote at $y = 1$.

EXAMPLE 2

Find the vertical asymptote of $f(x) = \dfrac{x}{x-2}$.

Solution Go to [Y=] and enter $Y_1 = \dfrac{x}{x-2}$ as in Example 1. Check TBLSET to see that the Independent variable is on Ask. Go to TABLE and enter the following values of x: 1.9, 1.99, and 1.999. As these values of x approach 2 from the left, the values of $f(x)$ decrease, or approach $-\infty$. This can be expressed as:

$$\lim_{x \to 2^-} \frac{x}{x-2} = -\infty.$$

Now enter the values 2.1, 2.01, and 2.001 into the TABLE. As these values of x approach 2 from the right, the values of $f(x)$ increase, or approach ∞. This can be expressed as:

$$\lim_{x \to 2^+} \frac{x}{x-2} = \infty.$$

A more concise way of finding the vertical asymptote is to note that since $x = 2$ makes the denominator equal to zero, the line $x = 2$ is the vertical asymptote of $f(x)$.

EXAMPLE 3

Describe the end behavior of $f(x) = x^4 + x + 3$.

Solution   The end behavior of $f(x)$ is unbounded and $f(x)$ approaches ∞ as $x \to +\infty$ or $-\infty$. This type of end behavior may be expressed as:

$$\lim_{x \to \infty} x^4 + x + 3 = \infty, \text{ and}$$

$$\lim_{x \to -\infty} x^4 + x + 3 = \infty.$$

Exercises

Multiple-Choice Questions

A graphing calculator is required for some questions.

1. Find the equation of the horizontal asymptote of $f(x) = \dfrac{2x - 1}{4x + 1}$.

   (A) $y = 2$
   (B) $x = 2$
   (C) $y = \dfrac{1}{2}$
   (D) $x = \dfrac{1}{2}$
   (E) $y = -1$

2. Find the equation of the vertical asymptote(s) of $f(x) = \dfrac{2x}{x^2 - 4}$.

   (A) $y = 0$
   (B) $x = 0$
   (C) $x = 2$
   (D) $x = \pm 2$
   (E) $y = 2$

3. Find the value of $\lim\limits_{x \to \infty} \dfrac{2x}{x + 2}$.

   (A) 0
   (B) $\dfrac{1}{2}$
   (C) 1
   (D) 2
   (E) ∞

4. Find the value of $\lim\limits_{x \to 2^-} \dfrac{2x}{x - 2}$.

   (A) $-\infty$
   (B) $\dfrac{1}{2}$
   (C) 1
   (D) 2
   (E) ∞

Free-Response Questions

A graphing calculator is required for some questions.

1. (a) Graph $f(x) = \dfrac{x + 3}{x - 3}$.
   (b) Use TABLE to find:
   - $\lim\limits_{x \to 3^-} f(x)$
   - $\lim\limits_{x \to 3^+} f(x)$
   - $\lim\limits_{x \to \infty} f(x)$
   - $\lim\limits_{x \to -\infty} f(x)$
   (c) State the zeros and asymptotes of $f(x)$.
   (d) Is $f(x)$ even, odd, or neither? Use your calculator to determine the answer.
   (e) Does $f(x)$ have an inverse? If yes, find the inverse and graph it. If not, explain why.

2. (a) Use the graph of $f(x)$ below to find:
   - $\lim\limits_{x \to 2^-} f(x)$
   - $\lim\limits_{x \to 2^+} f(x)$
   - $\lim\limits_{x \to \infty} f(x)$
   - $\lim\limits_{x \to -\infty} f(x)$
   (b) Does $f(x)$ have an inverse? Explain.

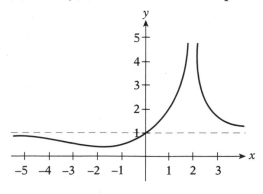

3.2 Evaluating Limits as *x* Approaches a Finite Number *c*

To evaluate a limit algebraically as x approaches a finite number c, substitute c into the expression.

1. If the answer is a finite number, that number is the value of the limit.
2. If the answer is of the form $\frac{0}{0}$, we have an indeterminate form. In this case, one of the following techniques may be useful in evaluating the limit:

   - Factor the numerator or the denominator, simplify, and then substitute the value c into the new expression.
   - Rationalize the numerator or the denominator by using the conjugate, simplify, and then substitute the value c into the new expression.
   - Simplify the complex fraction, and then substitute the value c into the new expression.

Notation	Meaning
$\lim\limits_{x \to \infty} f(x) = c$	$f(x)$ approaches c, as x approaches ∞. $f(x)$ has a horizontal asymptote at $y = c$.

EXAMPLE 1

Evaluate $\lim\limits_{x \to 3} \dfrac{x + 2}{x}$.

Solution Substitute $x = 3$ into the expression $\dfrac{x + 2}{x}$. The value of the limit is $\dfrac{5}{3}$.

EXAMPLE 2

Evaluate $\lim\limits_{x \to 0} \dfrac{x^2 - 16}{x - 4}$.

Solution Substitute $x = 0$ into the expression $\dfrac{x^2 - 16}{x - 4}$. The result is 4.

EXAMPLE 3

Evaluate $\lim\limits_{x \to 4} \dfrac{x^2 - 16}{x - 4}$.

Solution Substitute $x = 4$ into the expression $\dfrac{x^2 - 16}{x - 4}$. The result is $\dfrac{0}{0}$, which is called an indeterminate form. To evaluate the limit, factor the numerator and simplify the expression to $(x + 4)$.

$$\frac{x^2 - 16}{x - 4} = \frac{(x - 4)(x + 4)}{x - 4} = x + 4$$

Now substitute $x = 4$. The value of the limit is 8.

EXAMPLE 4

Evaluate $\lim\limits_{x \to 1} \dfrac{3x^2 - 4x + 1}{x^2 - 1}$.

Solution Substitute $x = 1$ into the expression $\dfrac{3x^2 - 4x + 1}{x^2 - 1}$. The result is $\dfrac{0}{0}$, an indeterminate form. Factor the numerator and the denominator and simplify the expression to $\dfrac{3x - 1}{x + 1}$.

$$\frac{3x^2 - 4x + 1}{x^2 - 1} = \frac{(3x - 1)(x - 1)}{(x + 1)(x - 1)} = \frac{3x - 1}{x + 1}$$

Now substitute $x = 1$ into the simplified expression. The result is 1.

EXAMPLE 5

Evaluate $\lim\limits_{x \to 25} \dfrac{\sqrt{x} - 5}{x - 25}$.

Solution Substitute $x = 25$ into the expression. The result is $\dfrac{0}{0}$, an indeterminate form. Since the numerator has a square root, rationalize the numerator by multiplying the numerator and the denominator by the conjugate $\sqrt{x} + 5$. Multiply out the conjugates in the numerator, but leave the denominator in factored form.

$$\left(\frac{\sqrt{x} + 5}{\sqrt{x} + 5}\right)\frac{\sqrt{x} - 5}{x - 25} = \frac{x - 25}{(x - 25)(\sqrt{x} + 5)} = \frac{1}{\sqrt{x} + 5}$$

Now substitute $x = 25$ into the simplified expression:

$$\lim_{x \to 25} \frac{1}{\sqrt{x} + 5} = \frac{1}{10}.$$

EXAMPLE 6

Evaluate $\lim\limits_{x \to a} \dfrac{\sqrt{x} - \sqrt{a}}{x - a}$.

Solution Substitute $x = a$ into the expression. The result is $\dfrac{0}{0}$, an indeterminate form. Rationalize the numerator by multiplying the numerator and the denominator by the conjugate $\sqrt{x} + \sqrt{a}$.

$$\left(\frac{\sqrt{x} + \sqrt{a}}{\sqrt{x} + \sqrt{a}}\right)\frac{\sqrt{x} - \sqrt{a}}{x - a} = \frac{x - a}{x - a(\sqrt{x} + \sqrt{a})} = \frac{1}{\sqrt{x} + \sqrt{a}}$$

We then have

$$\lim_{x \to a} \frac{1}{\sqrt{x} + \sqrt{a}} = \frac{1}{2\sqrt{a}}.$$

EXAMPLE 7

Evaluate $\lim\limits_{x \to 3} \dfrac{x - 3}{\dfrac{1}{x} - \dfrac{1}{3}}$.

Solution Substituting $x = 3$ into the expression gives the result $\dfrac{0}{0}$, an indeterminate form. In this case, simplify the complex fraction by multiplying the numerator and the denominator by the least common denominator of $\dfrac{1}{x} - \dfrac{1}{3}$, which is $3x$.

$$\left(\dfrac{3x}{3x}\right) \dfrac{x - 3}{\dfrac{1}{x} - \dfrac{1}{3}} = \dfrac{3x(x - 3)}{3x\left(\dfrac{1}{x}\right) - 3x\left(\dfrac{1}{3}\right)} = \dfrac{3x(x - 3)}{3 - x}$$

This produces the following result:

$$\lim\limits_{x \to 3} \dfrac{3x(x - 3)}{3 - x}.$$

Simplifying further as shown reduces the expression to $\lim\limits_{x \to 3}(-3x)$.

$$\dfrac{3x(x - 3)}{3 - x} = \dfrac{3x(x - 3)}{-x + 3} = \dfrac{-3x(\cancel{-x + 3})}{\cancel{-x + 3}} = -3x$$

Now substitute $x = 3$, and the value of the limit is -9.

Evaluating Limits Graphically as x Approaches a Finite Number c   Algebraic methods of evaluating limits provide a definitive answer. Occasionally we may wish to use an alternative method of evaluating a limit; for example, when the limit expression does not yield to the algebraic techniques described above. A graph of the function along with a table of values, as described in Section 3.1, can often yield the answer or at least provide a good approximation of the value of the limit. If additional proof is required, other methods, such as the use of L'Hôpital's Rule (see Section 10.4) can be used.
Note: Although L'Hôpital's Rule is part of the AP Calculus BC curriculum, it is often studied in AP Calculus AB courses since it is easy to understand and apply.

Exercises

Multiple-Choice Questions

No calculator is allowed for these questions

1. Evaluate $\lim\limits_{x \to -1} \dfrac{x^2 - 5x - 6}{x^2 - 1}$.
   (A) 1
   (B) 3
   (C) $\dfrac{7}{2}$
   (D) 12
   (E) indeterminate

2. Evaluate $\lim\limits_{x \to 0} \dfrac{x - 1}{x^2 - 1}$.
   (A) $-\dfrac{1}{2}$
   (B) $\dfrac{1}{4}$
   (C) $\dfrac{1}{2}$
   (D) 1
   (E) indeterminate

3. Evaluate $\lim\limits_{x \to 9} \dfrac{\sqrt{x} - 3}{x - 9}$.
   (A) 1
   (B) $\dfrac{1}{3}$
   (C) $\dfrac{1}{6}$
   (D) $-\dfrac{1}{3}$
   (E) indeterminate

4. Evaluate $\lim\limits_{x \to 2} \dfrac{x - 2}{\frac{1}{x} - \frac{1}{2}}$.

(A) -4
(B) -2
(C) 0
(D) 2
(E) 4

Free-Response Questions

A graphing calculator is required for some questions

1. Using the graph of $f(x)$ shown, find:

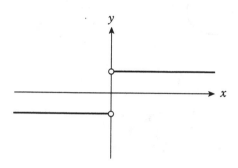

(a) $\lim\limits_{x \to -1} f(x)$
(b) $\lim\limits_{x \to 0^+} f(x)$
(c) $\lim\limits_{x \to 0^-} f(x)$
(d) $\lim\limits_{x \to 0} f(x)$

2. Sketch $f(x) = \begin{cases} x, & x < 0 \\ \sin x, & x \geq 0 \end{cases}$, and find:

(a) $\lim\limits_{x \to -3} f(x)$
(b) $\lim\limits_{x \to 0} f(x)$

3. Sketch a graph of the greatest-integer function, $f(x) = [x]$, and evaluate:

(a) $\lim\limits_{x \to \frac{1}{2}} f(x)$
(b) $\lim\limits_{x \to 1} f(x)$
(c) $\lim\limits_{x \to n} f(x)$ (where n is an integer)

4. Graph $f(x) = \dfrac{x}{e^x - 1}$ and make a table of values to find $\lim\limits_{x \to 0} f(x)$.

3.3 Evaluating Limits as *x* Approaches $\pm\infty$

The limit of a rational function as x approaches infinity is the value of the horizontal asymptote. If a function $f(x)$ is not a rational function, it may be possible to evaluate the limit as x approaches infinity. One method is to graph the function and make a table of values for increasingly large x-values and increasingly small x-values to see if the values of $f(x)$ appear to approach a finite number.

Another method is to consider the rate at which exponential, polynomial, and logarithmic functions increase as x increases without bound. In general, exponential functions increase most rapidly, polynomial functions increase less rapidly, and logarithmic functions increase least rapidly as x increases without bound.

EXAMPLE 1

Evaluate $\lim\limits_{x \to \infty} \dfrac{3x - 1}{2x + 1}$.

Solution Since this is a rational function, and the numerator and denominator have the same degree, the limit is the ratio of the leading coefficients, 3:2. This is the same as finding the horizontal asymptote.

Thus the limit is $\dfrac{3}{2}$.

EXAMPLE 2

Evaluate $\lim\limits_{x \to \infty} \dfrac{2x^2 + x + 1}{5x^2 - x + 5}$.

Solution Since this is a rational function and the degree of the numerator equals the degree of the denominator, the limit is the ratio of the leading coefficients, $\frac{2}{5}$.

EXAMPLE 3

Evaluate $\lim\limits_{x \to \infty} \dfrac{x^2 + x + 4}{5x^3 + 7x}$.

Solution Since this is a rational function and the degree of the numerator is less than the degree of the denominator, the limit is 0.

EXAMPLE 4

Evaluate $\lim\limits_{x \to \infty} \dfrac{6x^3}{7x^2 + 1000x - 9}$.

Solution Since this is a rational function and the degree of the numerator is greater than the degree of the denominator, the limit does not exist. Since $x \to +\infty$ and the coefficients of the highest degree terms are both positive, we can also say that the limit is $+\infty$.

EXAMPLE 5

Evaluate $\lim\limits_{x \to -\infty} \dfrac{x}{\sqrt{x^2 + 1}}$.

Solution $\lim\limits_{x \to -\infty} \dfrac{x}{\sqrt{x^2 + 1}} = \lim\limits_{x \to -\infty} \dfrac{1}{\sqrt{\dfrac{x^2 + 1}{x}}}$

Since $x \to -\infty$, $x < 0$ and therefore,

$$\lim_{x \to -\infty} \frac{1}{\sqrt{\dfrac{x^2 + 1}{-\sqrt{x^2}}}} = \lim_{x \to -\infty} -\sqrt{\frac{x^2}{x^2 + 1}} = \lim_{x \to -\infty} -\sqrt{\frac{1}{1 + \dfrac{1}{x^2}}} = -1$$

Exercises

Multiple-Choice Questions

No calculator is allowed for these questions.

1. Evaluate $\lim\limits_{x \to \infty} \dfrac{x^2 - 5}{2x^2 + 1}$.

   (A) -5 (D) 2

   (B) $\frac{1}{2}$ (E) ∞

   (C) 1

2. Evaluate $\lim\limits_{x \to \infty} \dfrac{x^2 - 5}{2x + 1}$.

   (A) -5 (D) 2

   (B) $\frac{1}{2}$ (E) ∞

   (C) 1

3. Evaluate $\lim\limits_{x \to \infty} \dfrac{x - 5}{2x^2 + 1}$.

   (A) -5 (D) $\frac{1}{2}$

   (B) $-\frac{1}{2}$ (E) ∞

   (C) 0

4. Evaluate $\lim\limits_{x \to \infty} \dfrac{100x}{x^2 - 1}$.

   (A) -1 (D) 100

   (B) 0   (E) does not exist

   (C) 1

A graphing calculator is required for some questions

1. (a) Graph $f(x) = \dfrac{x}{x^2 - 1}$.

    (b) Use the graph to determine:

- $\displaystyle\lim_{x \to 1^+} f(x)$
- $\displaystyle\lim_{x \to 1^-} f(x)$
- $\displaystyle\lim_{x \to -1^+} f(x)$
- $\displaystyle\lim_{x \to -1^-} f(x)$

- $\displaystyle\lim_{x \to \infty} f(x)$
- $\displaystyle\lim_{x \to -\infty} f(x)$

2. Sketch a function $f(x)$ that has all of the following properties:

- $f(0) = 1$
- $\displaystyle\lim_{x \to 1^+} f(x) = \infty$
- $\displaystyle\lim_{x \to 1^-} f(x) = \infty$
- $\displaystyle\lim_{x \to \infty} f(x) = 1$
- $\displaystyle\lim_{x \to -\infty} f(x) = 1$

3.4 Special Limits: $\displaystyle\lim_{x \to 0} \frac{\sin x}{x}$ and $\displaystyle\lim_{x \to 0} \frac{1 - \cos x}{x}$

One of the first theorems in many calculus books proves the following geometrically:

$$\lim_{x \to 0} \frac{\sin x}{x} = 1.$$

In addition to a geometric proof, evidence that the limit is 1 may also be seen by graphing the function $y = \dfrac{\sin x}{x}$ in a graphing calculator, and using the TABLE method shown in Section 3.1. Enter values in the TABLE that approach 0 from the positive side and from the negative side. The corresponding values of the function will be closer and closer to 1.

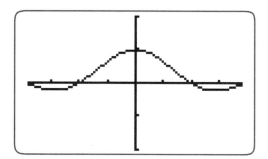

An abbreviated version of the TABLE method is simply to TRACE values of the function in the graph to the right and left of 0. The corresponding values of the function will be close to 1.

Using the fact that $\displaystyle\lim_{x \to 0} \frac{\sin x}{x} = 1$, similar limits can be evaluated.

The symbol x can be replaced by another expression as long as that expression also approaches 0. For example, suppose we replace x by $2x$. We want to evaluate:

$$\lim_{2x \to 0} \frac{\sin 2x}{2x}.$$

This limit is the same as $\displaystyle\lim_{x \to 0} \frac{\sin x}{x}$, since as $2x \to 0$, so does $x \to 0$.

Since $\displaystyle\lim_{x \to 0} \frac{\sin 2x}{2x} = 1$, $\dfrac{1}{2} \displaystyle\lim_{x \to 0} \frac{\sin 2x}{x} = 1$. Therefore,

$$\lim_{x \to 0} \frac{\sin 2x}{x} = 2.$$

If x in $\displaystyle\lim_{x \to 0} \frac{\sin x}{x}$ is replaced by $\frac{1}{y}$, then

$$\lim_{\frac{1}{y} \to 0} \frac{\sin\left(\frac{1}{y}\right)}{\frac{1}{y}} = \lim_{y \to \infty} y \sin\left(\frac{1}{y}\right),$$

since as $\frac{1}{y} \to 0$, $y \to \infty$. Therefore,

$$\lim_{y \to \infty} y \sin\left(\frac{1}{y}\right) = 1.$$

Look carefully at the limits. For example, to evaluate $\displaystyle\lim_{x \to \frac{\pi}{2}} \frac{\sin x}{x}$, the

limit is $\dfrac{\sin \frac{\pi}{2}}{\frac{\pi}{2}} = \dfrac{1}{\frac{\pi}{2}} = \dfrac{2}{\pi}$.

EXAMPLE 1

Evaluate $\displaystyle\lim_{x \to 0} \frac{\sin 4x}{x}$.

Solution $\displaystyle\lim_{x \to 0} \frac{\sin 4x}{4x} = 1$. By multiplying both sides of the equation by

4, we find that $\displaystyle\lim_{x \to 0} \frac{\sin 4x}{x} = 4$.

EXAMPLE 2

Evaluate $\displaystyle\lim_{x \to 0} \frac{\sin ax}{bx}$.

Solution $\displaystyle\lim_{x \to 0} \frac{\sin ax}{ax} = 1$. By multiplying both sides of the equation by

$\frac{a}{b}$, we find that $\displaystyle\lim_{x \to 0} \frac{\sin ax}{bx} = \frac{a}{b}$.

EXAMPLE 3

Evaluate $\displaystyle\lim_{x \to 0} \frac{1 - \cos^2 x}{x}$.

Solution Use the Pythagorean Identity that $\sin^2 x = 1 - \cos^2 x$. Thus,

$\displaystyle\lim_{x \to 0} \frac{\sin^2 x}{x} = \lim_{x \to 0} \frac{\sin x}{x} \cdot \sin x = 1 \cdot \sin 0 = 0$.

Exercises

Multiple-Choice Questions
No calculator is allowed for these questions.

1. Evaluate $\displaystyle\lim_{x \to 0} \frac{\sin 7x}{7x}$.

(A) 0

(B) $\frac{1}{7}$

(C) 1

(D) 7

(E) indeterminate

2. Evaluate $\displaystyle\lim_{x \to 0} \frac{\sin 7x}{x}$.

(A) 0

(B) $\frac{1}{7}$

(C) 1

(D) 7

(E) indeterminate

3. Evaluate $\lim\limits_{x \to 0} \dfrac{\sin x}{7x}$.

(A) 0

(B) $\dfrac{1}{7}$

(C) 1

(D) 7

(E) indeterminate

4. Find the value of $\lim\limits_{x \to \pi} \dfrac{\sin x}{x}$.

(A) $-\pi$

(B) -1

(C) 0

(D) 1

(E) π

Free-Response Questions
No calculator is allowed for these questions.

1. Use the special trigonometric limits to find the value of each of the following:

(a) $\lim\limits_{x \to 0} \dfrac{\tan x}{x}$

(b) $\lim\limits_{x \to 0} \dfrac{\sin^2 x}{x}$

(c) $\lim\limits_{x \to 0} \dfrac{\cos^2 x}{x}$

(d) $\lim\limits_{x \to 0} \dfrac{x^2}{\sin x}$

2. Prove $\lim\limits_{x \to 0} \dfrac{1 - \cos x}{x} = 0$ using $\lim\limits_{x \to 0} \dfrac{\sin x}{x}$ and a Pythagorean Identity.

3.5 Evaluating Limits of a Piecewise-Defined Function

A **piecewise-defined function,** or **split function,** has two or more pieces, each of which is defined on a specific domain. When evaluating the limit of a piecewise-defined function, first consider whether x is approaching a value where the function splits.

> ***To find the limit of the function as x approaches a value where the function does not split:***
> * Evaluate the limit of the function as before, using the piece of the function that has that value of x in its domain.

> ***To find the limit of the function as x approaches a value where the function does split:***
> * Since there are two distinct pieces on either side of this value, evaluate a left-hand limit using the piece of the function defined on the left of this value. Evaluate a right-hand limit using the piece of the function defined on the right of this value.
> * If the left-hand limit and the right-hand limit are the same, then this is the limit of the function. If the left-hand limit and the right-hand limit are not the same, then the limit of the function does not exist at this value in the domain.

EXAMPLE

For the function $f(x) = \begin{cases} x - 1, & x \geq 0 \\ x^2, & x < 0 \end{cases}$, find:

(a) $\lim\limits_{x \to -1} f(x)$

(b) $\lim\limits_{x \to 0} f(x)$

Solution Consider the graph of $f(x)$.

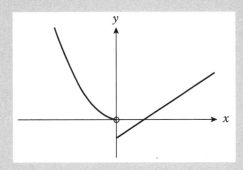

The split occurs at $x = 0$. To find the limit as $x \to -1$, find the value of

$$\lim_{x \to -1} f(x) = \lim_{x \to -1} x^2 = 1.$$

Since the split occurs at $x = 0$, to find the limit as $x \to 0$, find

$$\lim_{x \to 0^+} f(x) = \lim_{x \to 0^+} (x - 1) = -1, \text{ and}$$

$$\lim_{x \to 0^-} f(x) = \lim_{x \to 0^-} x^2 = 0.$$

Since $\lim\limits_{x \to 0^+} f(x) \neq \lim\limits_{x \to 0^-} f(x)$, $\lim\limits_{x \to 0} f(x)$ does not exist.

Exercises

Multiple-Choice Questions

A graphing calculator is required for some questions.

In Exercises 1–5, use $f(x) = \begin{cases} x + 3, & x < 0 \\ x - 3, & x \geq 0 \end{cases}$.

1. $\lim\limits_{x \to 0^-} f(x) =$
- (A) -3
- (B) 0
- (C) 1
- (D) 3
- (E) does not exist

2. $\lim\limits_{x \to 0^+} f(x) =$
- (A) -3
- (B) 0
- (C) 1
- (D) 3
- (E) does not exist

3. $\lim\limits_{x \to 0} f(x) =$
- (A) -3
- (B) 0
- (C) 1
- (D) 3
- (E) does not exist

4. $\lim\limits_{x \to 1} f(x) =$
- (A) -2
- (B) -1
- (C) 0
- (D) 1
- (E) does not exist

5. $\lim\limits_{x \to -2} f(x) =$
- (A) -3
- (B) 0
- (C) 1
- (D) 3
- (E) does not exist

A graphing calculator is required for some questions

1. (a) Graph $f(x) = \begin{cases} x + 2, & x < 0 \\ \sqrt{x} + 2, & 0 \le x < 4. \\ \ln x, & x \ge 4 \end{cases}$

   (b) Use the graph to determine
   - $f(0)$
   - $\lim\limits_{x \to 0} f(x)$
   - $f(4)$
   - $\lim\limits_{x \to 4} f(x)$

2. Sketch the graph of a function $f(x)$ that has all of the following properties:
   - continuous for all $x \ne 3$
   - has a hole at $x = -1$
   - $\lim\limits_{x \to 3} f(x) = -\infty$
   - $\lim\limits_{x \to \infty} f(x) = 0$
   - $\lim\limits_{x \to -\infty} f(x) = -\infty$

3.6 Continuity of a Function

Continuity is a property of a function. An intuitive definition of a continuous function is a function whose graph can be drawn without lifting the pencil from the paper. A continuous function has no breaks or holes in its graph.

> **By definition, a function f(x) is *continuous* at x = c if all of the following conditions exist:**
>
> 1. The function has a value at $x = c$; that is, $f(c)$ exists.
> 2. $\lim\limits_{x \to c} f(x)$ exists.
> 3. $\lim\limits_{x \to c} f(x) = f(c)$.

By this definition, a function is continuous at c if the function is defined at c, and has a limit as x approaches c, and if that limit as x approaches c is equal to c.

A function is *everywhere continuous* if it is continuous at each point of its domain. A function is *continuous on an interval* if it is continuous at every point on that interval.

EXAMPLE 1

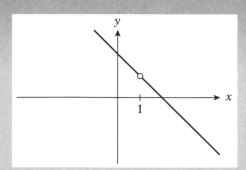

Is $f(x)$ continuous at $x = 1$?

Solution Using the definition of continuity, this function is not defined at $x = 1$. Therefore, $f(x)$ is not continuous there.

EXAMPLE 2

Is f(x) continuous at x = 1?

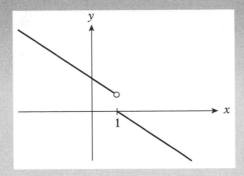

Solution Using the definition of continuity, the function is defined at x = 1: f(1) = 0. Thus, the first condition of continuity is satisfied.

To satisfy the second part of the definition, find the limit as $x \to 1$. Since x = 1 is where the function splits, we find that the right-hand limit and the left-hand limit are different.

The right-hand limit is $\lim_{x \to 1^+} f(x) = \lim_{x \to 1^+} (-x + 1) = 0$.

The left-hand limit is $\lim_{x \to 1^-} f(x) = \lim_{x \to 1^-} (-x + 2) = 1$.

Since the right-hand limit is not equal to the left-hand limit, the limit of the function as $x \to 1$ does not exist, and the function is not continuous at x = 1.

EXAMPLE 3

Is f(x) continuous at x = 1?

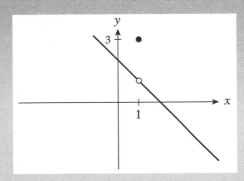

Solution Using the definition of continuity, f(x) is defined at x = 1: f(1) = 3. $\lim_{x \to 1} f(x) = 1$, thus the limit exists. However, the value of the function is not equal to the value of the limit, and f(x) is not continuous at x = 1.

Notice that in Example 3, the function was almost continuous. If the point (1, 3) is removed and replaced by (1, 1) to fill the gap, then f(x) would be continuous. This type of discontinuity is called **removable discontinuity.** That is, we can make the function continuous by redefining it at a finite number of points.

In Example 1 on page 52, f(x) has a removable discontinuity at x = 1. Since there is no value of f(x) at x = 1, redefine f(1) = 1, and f(x) is continuous.

Exercises

Multiple-Choice Questions

A graphing calculator is required for some questions

For Exercises 1–4, use $f(x) = \begin{cases} x^2, & x \neq 2 \\ 2, & x = 2 \end{cases}$.

1. $f(2) =$
- (A) 0
- (B) 1
- (C) 2
- (D) 4
- (E) does not exist

2. $\lim\limits_{x \to 2^-} f(x) =$
- (A) 0
- (B) 1
- (C) 2
- (D) 4
- (E) does not exist

3. $\lim\limits_{x \to 2^+} f(x) =$
- (A) 0
- (B) 1
- (C) 2
- (D) 4
- (E) does not exist

4. $\lim\limits_{x \to 2} f(x) =$
- (A) 0
- (B) 1
- (C) 2
- (D) 4
- (E) does not exist

For Exercises 5–8, use $f(x) = \begin{cases} e^x, & x < 1 \\ \ln x, & x \geq 1 \end{cases}$.

5. $f(1) =$
- (A) 0
- (B) 1
- (C) 2
- (D) e
- (E) does not exist

6. $\lim\limits_{x \to 1^-} f(x) =$
- (A) 0
- (B) 1

- (C) 2
- (D) e
- (E) does not exist

7. $\lim\limits_{x \to 1^+} f(x) =$
- (A) 0
- (B) 1
- (C) 2
- (D) e
- (E) does not exist

8. $\lim\limits_{x \to 1} f(x) =$
- (A) 0
- (B) 1
- (C) 2
- (D) e
- (E) does not exist

Free-Response Questions

No calculator is allowed for these questions

1. $f(x) = \begin{cases} kx + 1, & x < 1 \\ x^2, & x \geq 1 \end{cases}$

   (a) Find the value of k so that $f(x)$ is continuous at $x = 1$.

   (b) Using the value of k found in part (a), sketch the graph of $f(x)$.

2. $g(x) = \begin{cases} x^2 + 2, & x < -1 \\ x - p, & x \geq -1 \end{cases}$

   (a) Find the value of p so that $f(x)$ is continuous at $x = -1$.

   (b) Using the value of p found in part (a), sketch the graph of $f(x)$.

3. $f(x) = \begin{cases} 2x - 3, & x \neq 2 \\ 0, & x = 2 \end{cases}$ has a removable discontinuity. Redefine $f(x)$ so that it is continuous at $x = 2$.

4. (a) Write a function $f(x)$ that has a removable discontinuity.

   (b) Write a function $g(x)$ that has a non-removable discontinuity.

Chapter Assessment

Multiple-Choice Questions

No calculator is allowed for these questions

1. $\lim\limits_{x \to 2} \dfrac{x}{x - 2} =$
- (A) -1

- (B) 0
- (C) 1
- (D) 2
- (E) does not exist

2. $\lim\limits_{x \to 5} \dfrac{x - 5}{x^2 - 25} =$
   (A) -1
   (B) 0
   (C) $\dfrac{1}{10}$
   (D) 1
   (E) does not exist

3. $\lim\limits_{x \to \frac{\pi}{2}} \dfrac{\sin x}{x} =$
   (A) 0
   (B) 1
   (C) $\dfrac{2}{\pi}$
   (D) $\dfrac{\pi}{2}$
   (E) does not exist

4. $\lim\limits_{x \to 0} \dfrac{\sin 2x}{x \cos x} =$
   (A) -1
   (B) 0
   (C) 1
   (D) 2
   (E) does not exist

5. $f(x) = \begin{cases} x^2 + 1, & x < 2 \\ 4, & x > 2 \end{cases}$
   $\lim\limits_{x \to 2^-} f(x) =$
   (A) 0
   (B) 2
   (C) 4
   (D) 5
   (E) does not exist

6. The vertical asymptote of $f(x) = \dfrac{x}{x - 1}$ has equation
   (A) $x = 0$
   (B) $x = 1$
   (C) $y = 0$
   (D) $y = 1$
   (E) There is no vertical asymptote.

7. The horizontal asymptote of $f(x) = \dfrac{x}{x - 1}$ is
   (A) $x = 0$
   (B) $x = 1$
   (C) $y = 0$
   (D) $y = 1$
   (E) There is no horizontal asymptote.

8. The vertical asymptote of $f(x) = \dfrac{4}{x + 1}$ is
   (A) $x = -1$
   (B) $x = 0$
   (C) $y = -1$
   (D) $y = 0$
   (E) There is no vertical asymptote.

9. The horizontal asymptote of $f(x) = \dfrac{4}{x + 1}$ is
   (A) $x = -1$
   (B) $x = 0$
   (C) $y = -1$
   (D) $y = 0$
   (E) There is no horizontal asymptote.

10. The domain of $y = \ln x - 1$ is
    (A) $\{x > 0\}$
    (B) $\{x < 0\}$
    (C) $\{x \neq 0\}$
    (D) $\{x > 1\}$
    (E) {all real numbers}

11. The inverse of $y = \ln x - 1$ is
    (A) $y = e^{x-1}$
    (B) $y = e^x - 1$
    (C) $y = e^x + 1$
    (D) $y = e^{x+1} - 1$
    (E) $y = e^{x+1}$

12. Find the slope of a line parallel to the line with equation $y - 2x = 7$.
    (A) -2
    (B) 0
    (C) 1
    (D) 2
    (E) 7

13. For what value(s) of x is $f(x) = \dfrac{x - 1}{x^2 - 1}$ discontinuous?
    (A) $x = 0$
    (B) $x = 1$
    (C) $x = -1$
    (D) $x = 1$ and $x = -1$
    (E) all real numbers

14. $f(x) = \dfrac{1}{x^2}$ is continuous for all real numbers EXCEPT
    (A) $x = 0$
    (B) $x = 1$ only
    (C) $x = 1$ and $x = -1$
    (D) $x = -1$ only
    (E) $x = 2$

15. $\lim\limits_{x \to \frac{\pi}{3}} \dfrac{1 - \cos x}{x} =$
    (A) $\dfrac{\pi}{3}$
    (B) $\dfrac{3}{\pi}$
    (C) $\dfrac{3}{2\pi}$
    (D) $\dfrac{3(1 - \sqrt{3})}{2\pi}$
    (E) 0

16. $\lim\limits_{x \to 0} \dfrac{\sin 3x}{7x} =$

   (A) $\dfrac{3}{7}$

   (B) $\dfrac{7}{3}$

   (C) 3

   (D) 7

   (E) does not exist

17. $\lim\limits_{x \to 2} \dfrac{2-x}{x^2-4} =$

   (A) $-\dfrac{1}{2}$

   (B) $-\dfrac{1}{4}$

   (C) $\dfrac{1}{4}$

   (D) $\dfrac{1}{2}$

   (E) does not exist

18. The slope of $3x + 4y = 7$ is

   (A) $-\dfrac{4}{3}$

   (B) $-\dfrac{3}{4}$

   (C) $\dfrac{4}{7}$

   (D) $\dfrac{3}{4}$

   (E) $\dfrac{4}{3}$

19. $\lim\limits_{x \to \infty} \dfrac{x^2 - 4x + 4}{4x^2 - 1} =$

   (A) $\dfrac{1}{4}$

   (B) 1

   (C) 4

   (D) 8

   (E) does not exist

20. Find the equation of the vertical asymptote of $f(x) = \dfrac{x}{4x + 8}$.

   (A) $y = \dfrac{1}{4}$

   (B) $y = -2$

   (C) $x = -2$

   (D) $y = 2$

   (E) $x = 2$

21. Find the equation of the horizontal asymptote of $y = \dfrac{x^2}{2x^2 - 2}$.

   (A) $y = 0$

   (B) $x = \dfrac{1}{2}$

   (C) $y = \dfrac{1}{2}$

   (D) $x = 1$

   (E) $x = \pm 1$

22. Find $f(2)$ for $f(x) = \begin{cases} x^2 + 4, & x < 0 \\ 3 - x, & x \geq 0 \end{cases}$.

   (A) 1

   (B) 3

   (C) 4

   (D) 8

   (E) does not exist

23. Which of the following graphs shows a function that is continuous for all real numbers?

   (A)

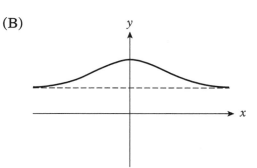

   (B)

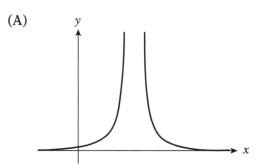

   (C)

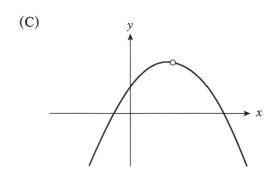

(D)

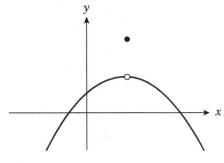

(E)

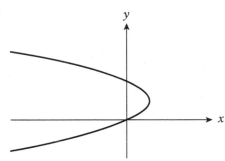

24. $\lim\limits_{x \to \infty} \dfrac{\sqrt{x-2}}{x-2} =$

  (A) -2

  (B) 0

  (C) 1

  (D) 2

  (E) does not exist

25. $\lim\limits_{x \to 3} \dfrac{\dfrac{1}{x} - \dfrac{1}{3}}{x-3} =$

  (A) $-\infty$

  (B) $-\dfrac{1}{3}$

  (C) $-\dfrac{1}{9}$

  (D) 0

  (E) $\dfrac{1}{3}$

Free-Response Questions

No calculator is allowed for Questions 1–3.

1. Find the value of a so that $f(x) = \begin{cases} 2x + a, & x < 1 \\ x^2 - a, & x \geq 1 \end{cases}$ is continuous for all real numbers.

2. Find the zeros, holes, and vertical and horizontal asymptotes of $f(x) = \dfrac{3x-6}{x+5}$.

3. On the graph of $f(x)$, sketch the graph of $f^{-1}(x)$ and find $f(f^{-1}(-1))$.

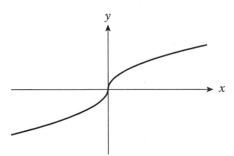

For Questions 4–6, a graphing calculator is required.

4. Set the $\boxed{\text{WINDOW}}$ in the graphing calculator to Xmin $= -1$, Xmax $= 5$, Ymin $= -2$, Ymax $= 10$, and sketch $Y_1 = x^2$, $Y_2 = 4x - 4$.

  (a) Find the slope of Y_2.

  (b) Graph the inverse of Y_1 and estimate the slope of the graph at $x = 4$.

5. Use the graph of $f(x)$ shown below to find the following limits:

- $\lim\limits_{x \to -1} f(x)$
- $\lim\limits_{x \to 1} f(x)$
- $\lim\limits_{x \to 2} f(x)$

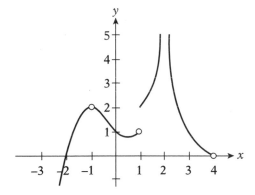

6. Sketch a function $f(x)$ with all of the following properties:

- $f(x)$ is odd.
- $f(1) = 2$
- The x-axis is a horizontal asymptote.

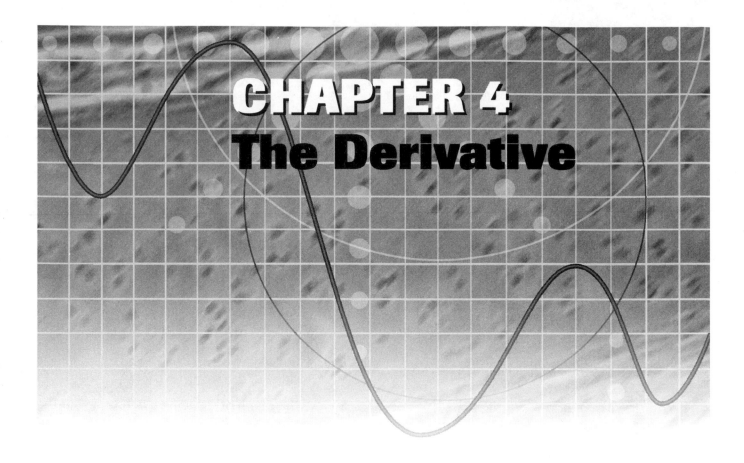

CHAPTER 4
The Derivative

4.1 The Derivative of a Function

The derivative of a function describes the behavior of the function. On the graph of $y = f(x)$, the **derivative** of the function at x is the slope of the line tangent to the graph at the point $(x, f(x))$. (*Note:* A tangent line is a line that touches a curve at a point.)

Recall that a line with a positive slope rises or increases (from left to right), and that a line with a negative slope falls or decreases (from left to right).

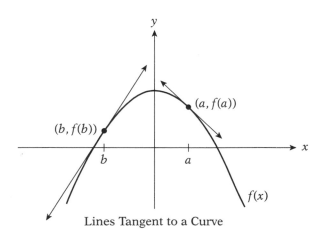

Lines Tangent to a Curve

Since the derivative of a function is the slope of the line tangent to the graph of the function, we can ascertain the following:

- If the derivative is positive at a value, the function is increasing.
- If the derivative is negative at a value, the function is decreasing.
- If the derivative is zero or undefined at a value, this value is called a **critical value** of the function.
- If the derivative equals zero, the tangent line at that value of the function is horizontal.
- If the derivative is undefined, there may be a vertical tangent or no tangent to the graph of the function at that value.

Critical Points **Critical points** (or **critical values**) are points on the graph of a function where the derivative is zero or is undefined. These points may locate the **turning points** of the function, where the function stops increasing and starts decreasing, or stops decreasing and starts increasing. The vertex of a parabola is an example of a critical point on the graph of a function. At the vertex of a parabola, the tangent line is horizontal and therefore has a slope of zero. It is possible, using the critical values of a function and several values near them, to sketch the graph of the derivative of the function. We can do this even before we have a formal definition of the derivative. (Section 5.2 shows how to identify a critical value as a relative or absolute extrema.)

EXAMPLE 1

(a) Sketch the graph of the function $f(x) = x^2 - 2x$.
(b) State whether the following are positive, negative, or zero: the slope of the line tangent to the graph of $f(x)$
    i.   at $x = 1$
    ii. for $x < 1$
    iii. for $x > 1$
(c) Sketch the graph of the derivative.

Solution

(a)

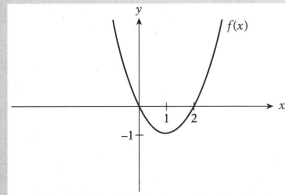

(b) i. The graph is a parabola with vertex at the point $(1, -1)$. Thus the slope of the line tangent to $f(x)$ at $x = 1$ is zero.
   ii. The slope of the line tangent to $f(x)$ for $x < 1$ is negative, because the function is decreasing for $x < 1$.
  iii. The slope of the line tangent to $f(x)$ for $x > 1$ is positive, because the function is increasing for $x > 1$.

Therefore, we know that the graph of the *derivative* of $f(x)$ is below the *x*-axis for $x < 1$, that it crosses the *x*-axis at $x = 1$, and that it is above the *x*-axis for $x > 1$.

(c)

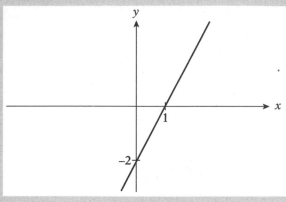

EXAMPLE 2

(a) Sketch the graph of $f(x) = \sin(x)$ on the interval $[0, 2\pi]$.
(b) At what value(s) of *x* is the slope of the line tangent to the graph of $f(x)$ positive? At what value(s) is it negative? At what value(s) is it zero?
(c) Write a brief description of the graph of the derivative of $f(x)$ and sketch it.

Solution

(a)

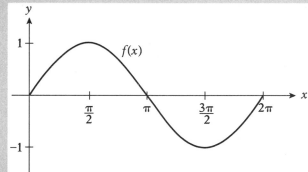

(b) The sine curve has two turning points on $[0, 2\pi]$, a high point at $x = \dfrac{\pi}{2}$ and a low point at $x = \dfrac{3\pi}{2}$. Thus, the slope of the tangent of $f(x)$ is zero at $x = \dfrac{\pi}{2}$ and at $x = \dfrac{3\pi}{2}$.

The slope of the tangent is positive at any point in the interval $\left[0, \dfrac{\pi}{2}\right)$ and at any point in the interval $\left(\dfrac{3\pi}{2}, 2\pi\right]$, where the function is increasing.

The slope of the tangent is negative at any point in the interval $\left(\dfrac{\pi}{2}, \dfrac{3\pi}{2}\right)$, where the function is decreasing.

(c) The graph of the derivative of $\sin(x)$ crosses the x-axis at $x = \frac{\pi}{2}$ and at $x = \frac{3\pi}{2}$; it is above the x-axis on the intervals $\left[0, \frac{\pi}{2}\right)$ and $\left(\frac{3\pi}{2}, 2\pi\right]$, and is below the x-axis on the interval $\left(\frac{\pi}{2}, \frac{3\pi}{2}\right)$.

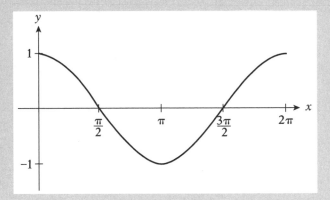

EXAMPLE 3

(a) Sketch the graph of $f(x) = x^3$.
(b) At what value(s) of x is the slope of the line tangent to the graph of $f(x)$ positive? At what value(s) is it negative? At what value(s) is it zero?
(c) Write a brief description and sketch the graph of the derivative.

Solution

(a)

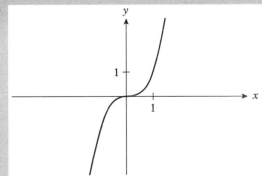

(b) The slope of the tangent is positive for $x < 0$ and for $x > 0$. The slope of the tangent at $x = 0$ is zero.
(c) The graph of the derivative of $f(x) = x^3$ is above the x-axis for $x < 0$ and for $x > 0$, and touches the x-axis at $x = 0$.

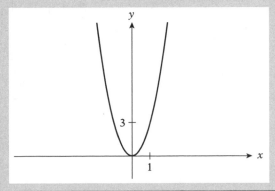

Exercises

Match the graphs of the functions I, II, and III to the graphs of their derivatives A, B, and C.

I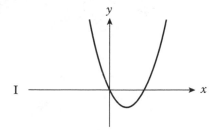

(A)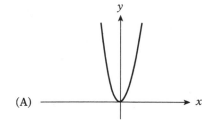

II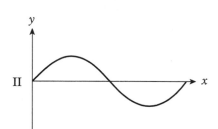

(B)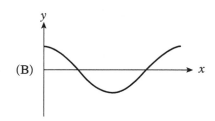

III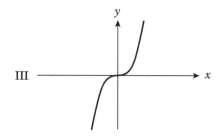

(C)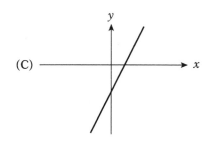

Multiple-Choice Questions

No calculator is allowed for these questions. Refer to the figure for Questions 1−4.

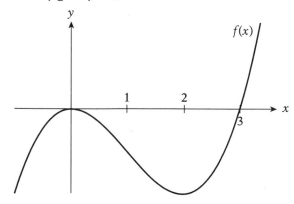

1. On what interval is $f(x)$ positive?
   (A) $(0, \infty)$
   (B) $[1, \infty)$
   (C) $[2, \infty)$
   (D) $(3, \infty)$
   (E) $(0, 3)$

2. On what interval(s) is the slope of the tangent to the graph of $f(x)$ positive?
   (A) $(-\infty, 0)$ and $(2, \infty)$
   (B) $(-\infty, 0)$
   (C) $(0, 2)$
   (D) $(2, \infty)$
   (E) $(-\infty, 2)$

3. The critical value(s) of $f(x)$ is (are) $x =$
- (A) 2
- (B) 0 and 2
- (C) 0
- (D) 0 and 3
- (E) 3

4. On what interval(s) is the derivative of $f(x)$ increasing?
- (A) $(0, \infty)$
- (B) $(1, \infty)$
- (C) $[3, \infty)$
- (D) $(-\infty, 1]$ and $[3, \infty)$
- (E) $[2, \infty)$

5. The graph of the derivative of $f(x) = 2x + 3$ is
- (A) a horizontal line
- (B) a vertical line
- (C) a line with a positive slope
- (D) a line with a negative slope
- (E) a parabola

6. The derivative of $f(x) = -\frac{1}{2}x + 5$ has the equation
- (A) $x = 0$
- (B) $y = 0$
- (C) $x = -\frac{1}{2}$
- (D) $y = -\frac{1}{2}$
- (E) $y = 5$

7. The graph of the derivative of $f(x) = x^2$ is
- (A) a horizontal line
- (B) a vertical line
- (C) a line with positive slope
- (D) a line with negative slope
- (E) a line with y-intercept 2

Free-Response Questions
No calculator is allowed for these questions.

1. Sketch the graph of the derivative of each function.
- (a) $y = x$
- (b) $y = 2$

2. Sketch the graph of the derivative of $y = |x - 1|$.

3. Sketch the graph of the derivative of
$$f(x) = \begin{cases} x + 2, x \le 1 \\ x - 2, x > 1 \end{cases}.$$

4. Discuss the continuity of the functions in Questions 2 and 3, and the existence of the derivative of each function at $x = 1$.

4.2 The Average Rate of Change of a Function on an Interval

The average rate of change of a function $f(x)$ on an interval $[a, b]$ is found by computing the slope of the line joining the endpoints of the function on that interval.

The average rate of change of $f(x)$ on $[a, b] = \dfrac{f(b) - f(a)}{b - a}$.

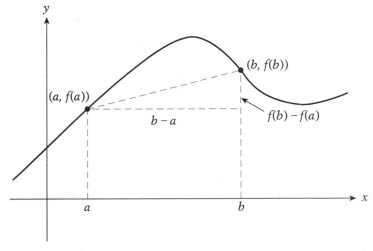

EXAMPLE 1

Find the average rate of change of $f(x) = x^2$ on the interval $[-1, 2]$.

Solution   The average rate of change of $f(x) = x^2$ on the interval $[-1, 2]$ is equal to

$$\frac{f(2) - f(-1)}{2 - (-1)} = \frac{4 - 1}{2 + 1} = \frac{3}{3} = 1$$

Notice that the average rate of change is positive on the interval $[-1, 2]$. This means that the function must be increasing at some values in the interval.

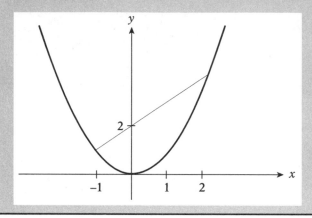

Calculator Note

The graphing calculator can be used to graph a function and its derivative. Use the following procedures to graph the function $f(x) = 4x - x^2$ and its derivative.

Using the TI-83

Press Y= and enter the function into Y_1. Then enter the derivative into Y_2 as MATH 8 VARS Y-VARS Function Y_1 , X,T,Θ,n , X,T,Θ,n) .

Press ZOOM 6.

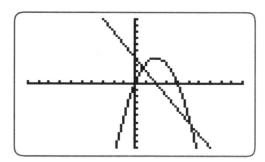

Using the TI-89
Enter the function into Y_1. Enter the derivative into Y_2 as $d(Y_1(x), x)$.

After entering Y_2, you can distinguish between the graphs of the function and the derivative in the following way. Go to F6 (Style) and scroll down to 4: Thick. The graph of Y_2, in this case the derivative, will be displayed as a thicker line.

Use ZOOM 6 to graph Y_1 and Y_2.

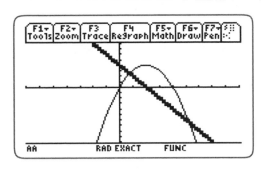

Exercises

No calculator is allowed for these exercises.

Multiple-Choice Questions

1. The average rate of change of $f(x) = 4x - x^2$ on the interval $[1, 3]$ is
   (A) 2
   (B) 1
   (C) 0
   (D) −1
   (E) −2

2. If $f(x) = 3x + 2$, then the graph of the derivative of $f(x)$ is
   (A) a horizontal line
   (B) a line with a positive slope
   (C) a line with a negative slope
   (D) not a line
   (E) a vertical line

3. If the average rate of change of a function on $[a, b]$ equals zero, then the graph of the function
   (A) can be a line with a positive slope
   (B) can be quadratic
   (C) cannot be a horizontal line
   (D) can be a line with a negative slope
   (E) is a vertical line

4. The average rate of change of $f(x) = mx + b$ on the interval $[a, c]$ is
   (A) 0
   (B) 1
   (C) m
   (D) $\dfrac{mc - ma + 2b}{c - a}$
   (E) $m(c - a)$

Free-Response Questions

1. (a) Sketch the graph of $f(x) = 4x - x^2$ on $[0, 4]$.
   (b) Complete the following table by estimating the slope of the tangent to $f(x)$ at each of the values of x.

x	0	1	2	3	4
Slope					

   (c) Plot the points in the table on a new set of axes and sketch a curve that connects the points.

2. (a) Find the average rate of change of $f(x) = 4x - x^2$ on each of the following intervals.

    i.   [0, 2]
    ii. [1, 3]
    iii. [2, 4]

(b) Find an approximate value of x so that the slope of the tangent to $f(x)$ at $(x, f(x))$ has the same value as your answers to i, ii, and iii.

4.3 The Definition of the Derivative

There are two definitions of the derivative, the standard definition and the alternate form of the derivative. It is useful to know both forms of the definition.

The standard definition of the derivative is:

$$f'(x) = \lim_{h \to 0} \frac{f(x + h) - f(x)}{h}$$

In this definition, Δx may be used instead of h. In this case, the definition of the derivative is:

$$f'(x) = \lim_{\Delta x \to 0} \frac{f(x + \Delta x) - f(x)}{\Delta x}$$

This definition is the limit of the average rate of change of $f(x)$ on the interval $[x, x + h]$ as $h \to 0$. It is also called the **instantaneous rate of change** of $f(x)$.

Note: There are two ways of writing a derivative, the $f'(x)$ notation, which is read "f prime of x"; or the $\dfrac{dy}{dx}$ notation (or Leibniz notation), which is read "the derivative of y with respect to x." In most cases, these two notations can be used interchangeably.

EXAMPLE

Use the definition of the derivative to find a formula for the derivative of $f(x) = x^2$.

Solution   Using the standard form for the definition of the derivative:

$$f'(x) = \lim_{h \to 0} \frac{f(x + h) - f(x)}{h}$$

$$= \lim_{h \to 0} \frac{(x + h)^2 - x^2}{h}$$

$$= \lim_{h \to 0} \frac{x^2 + 2xh + h^2 - x^2}{h}$$

$$= \lim_{h \to 0} \frac{2xh + h^2}{h} = \lim_{h \to 0} (2x + h) = 2x$$

Therefore, the derivative of $f(x) = x^2$ is $f'(x) = 2x$.

Alternative Form of the Derivative At the beginning of this chapter, the derivative was described as the slope of the line tangent to the graph of the function. If the average rate of change of a function is over a small interval $[a, b]$, then this is close to the value of the derivative. In fact, the alternate form of the derivative, stated below, looks very much like the definition of the average rate of change of $f(x)$, where the interval $[a, b]$ is replaced by the interval $[a, x]$.

$$f'(a) = \lim_{x \to a} \frac{f(x) - f(a)}{x - a}$$

The Rule of Four While it is important for AP Calculus students to learn and practice the rules for finding the derivatives, the focus should be on understanding the *relationships* between a function and its derivatives rather than on extensive computation. For example, examine the relationship between a function f and its derivative f' in several ways: graphically, numerically, algebraically, and verbally. This rule of four is the basis for studying calculus with the graphing calculator as a tool.

Exercises

No calculator is allowed for these exercises.

Multiple-Choice Questions

1. If $f(x) = 5$, $f'(x) =$
   (A) 0
   (B) 1
   (C) 5
   (D) $5x$
   (E) undefined

2. If $f(x) = 5x$, $f'(x) =$

   (A) $-\frac{1}{5}$
   (B) 0
   (C) $\frac{1}{5}$
   (D) 1
   (E) 5

3. If $f(x) = 5x + 5$, then $f'(x) =$
   (A) -1
   (B) 0
   (C) 1
   (D) 5
   (E) undefined

4. If $f(x) = 5x - 5$, $f'(x) =$
   (A) -5
   (B) 0
   (C) 1
   (D) 5
   (E) 10

Free-Response Questions

1. Use the definition of the derivative to find $f'(x)$ if $f(x) = 5x^2$.   10x

2. Use the definition of the derivative to find $f'(x)$ if $f(x) = 5x^2 + 5x + 5$.

   10x + 5

4.4 Rules for Derivatives

The rules for derivatives of functions commonly seen in AP Calculus courses are given below. These rules for finding derivatives should be memorized.

Constant Rule

If $f(x) = c$, a constant, then $f'(x) = 0$

Constant-Multiple Rule

If c is a constant, $(cf(x))' = c \cdot f'(x)$

Power Rule

$(x^n)' = nx^{n-1}$

Chain Rule Extension

$((f(x))^n)' = n(f(x))^{n-1} \cdot f'(x)$

The Chain Rule Extension can be used to find the derivative of a composite function. The rule involves taking the derivative of the exterior function, with the interior function inside it, and then multiplying by the derivative of the interior function. Example 1 involves a function whose derivative can be found with or without the Chain Rule Extension.

Note: The lists of derivative rules that follow in this chapter include the specific Chain Rule Extensions.

EXAMPLE 1

Find the derivative of $f(x) = (2x^2)^3$.

Solution

METHOD **1** Simplifying and applying the Power Rule:

$f(x) = (2x^2)^3$
$f(x) = 8x^6$
$f'(x) = 48x^5$

METHOD **2** Applying the Chain Rule Extension:

$f(x) = (2x^2)^3$
$f'(x) = 3(2x^2)^2 \cdot f'(2x^2)$
$f'(x) = 12x^4 \cdot 4x$
$f'(x) = 48x^5$

Observe that Method 1 and Method 2 yield the same value for the derivative.

EXAMPLE 2

Find the derivative of $f(x) = (x^5 + 3x)^8$.

Solution Using the Chain Rule Extension to the Power Rule, the derivative of $(x^5 + 3x)^8$ is

$8(x^5 + 3x)^7 \cdot (x^5 + 3x)'$
$= 8(x^5 + 3x)^7 \cdot (5x^4 + 3)$.

Exponential Rules

$$(e^x)' = e^x$$
$$(e^{f(x)})' = e^{f(x)} \cdot f'(x)$$
$$(a^x)' = a^x \ln a$$
$$(a^{f(x)})' = a^{f(x)} \cdot f'(x) \ln a$$

EXAMPLE 3

Find the derivative of $f(x) = 6^{3x+2}$.

Solution   Using the Chain Rule Extension of the Exponential Rule, the derivative of 6^{3x+2} is

$$6^{3x+2}(3x + 2)' \cdot \ln 6$$
$$= 6^{3x+2}(3) \cdot \ln 6$$
$$= 3(\ln 6)6^{3x+2}$$

EXAMPLE 4

Find the derivative of $f(x) = e^{x^2}$.

Solution   Using the Chain Rule Extension of the Exponential Rule, the derivative of e^{x^2} is $e^{x^2} \cdot (x^2)' = e^{x^2} \cdot (2x) = 2xe^{x^2}$.

Logarithmic Rules

$$(\ln x)' = \frac{1}{x}$$

$$(\ln f(x))' = \frac{1}{f(x)} \cdot f'(x)$$

$$(\log_a x)' = \frac{1}{x \ln a}$$

$$(\log_a f(x))' = \frac{1}{f(x) \ln a} \cdot f'(x)$$

EXAMPLE 5

Find the derivative of $f(x) = \log_2(4x - 9)$.

Solution   Using the Chain Rule Extension of the Log Rules, the derivative of $\log_2(4x - 9)$ is

$$\frac{1}{(4x - 9) \ln 2} \cdot (4x - 9)'$$

$$= \frac{1}{(4x - 9) \ln 2} \cdot 4$$

$$= \frac{4}{(4x - 9) \ln 2}$$

EXAMPLE 6

Find the derivative of $f(x) = \ln(x^2 + x)$.

Solution Using the Chain Rule Extension of the Log Rule, the derivative of $\ln(x^2 + x)$ is

$$\frac{1}{x^2 + x} \cdot f'(x^2 + x)$$

$$= \frac{1}{x^2 + x} \cdot (2x + 1)$$

$$= \frac{2x + 1}{x^2 + x}$$

Trigonometric Rules

$(\sin x)' = \cos x$

$(\sin f(x))' = \cos f(x) \cdot f'(x)$

$(\cos x)' = -\sin x$

$(\cos f(x))' = -\sin f(x) \cdot f'(x)$

$(\tan x)' = \sec^2 x$

$(\tan f(x))' = \sec^2 f(x) \cdot f'(x)$

$(\cot x)' = -\csc^2 x$

$(\cot f(x))' = -\csc^2 f(x) \cdot f'(x)$

$(\sec x)' = \sec x \tan x$

$(\sec f(x))' = \sec f(x) \tan f(x) \cdot f'(x)$

$(\csc x)' = -\csc x \cot x$

$(\csc f(x))' = -\csc f(x) \cot f(x) \cdot f'(x)$

Inverse Trigonometric Rules

$$(\arcsin x)' = \frac{1}{\sqrt{1 - x^2}}$$

$$(\arctan x)' = \frac{1}{1 + x^2}$$

Note: All trigonometric functions have an **argument.** In $\sin(3x)$, $3x$ is the argument. In $\tan(x^2)$, x^2 is the argument. When taking trigonometric derivatives, it helps to remember that the argument always stays the same.

EXAMPLE 7

Find the derivative of $f(x) = \sin(3x)$.

Solution Using the Chain Rule Extension of the trigonometric rule:

$f(x) = \sin(3x)$

$f'(x) = \cos(3x) \cdot (3x)'$

$f'(x) = \cos(3x) \cdot 3$

$f'(x) = 3 \cos(3x)$

EXAMPLE 8

Find the derivative of $f(x) = \tan(x^2)$.

Solution   Using the Chain Rule Extension of the trigonometric rule:

$$f(x) = \tan(x^2)$$
$$f'(x) = \sec^2(x^2) \cdot (x^2)'$$
$$f'(x) = \sec^2(x^2) \cdot 2x$$
$$f'(x) = 2x \sec^2(x^2)$$

EXAMPLE 9

Find the derivative of $f(x) = \sec(e^x)$.

Solution   Using the Chain Rule Extension of the trigonometric rule and the Exponential Rule:

$$f(x) = \sec(e^x)$$
$$f'(x) = \sec(e^x)\tan(e^x) \cdot (e^x)'$$
$$f'(x) = \sec(e^x)\tan(e^x) \cdot e^x = (e^x)\sec(e^x)\tan(e^x)$$

Sum and Difference Rule

$$(f(x) \pm g(x))' = f'(x) \pm g'(x)$$

Product Rule

$$(f(x) \cdot g(x))' = f(x)g'(x) + g(x)f'(x)$$

Quotient Rule

$$\left(\frac{f(x)}{g(x)}\right)' = \frac{g(x)f'(x) - f(x)g'(x)}{(g(x))^2}$$

EXAMPLE 10

Find the derivative of $f(x) = x + \ln x$.

Solution   Using the Sum Rule and the Log Rule:

$$f(x) = x + \ln x$$
$$f'(x) = (x)' + (\ln x)'$$
$$f'(x) = 1 + \frac{1}{x}$$

EXAMPLE 11

Find the derivative of $f(x) = x \ln x$.

Solution   Using the Product Rule and the Log Rule:

$$f(x) = x \ln x$$
$$f'(x) = x(\ln x)' + \ln x \cdot (x)'$$
$$f'(x) = x \cdot \frac{1}{x} + \ln x \cdot 1$$
$$f'(x) = 1 + \ln x$$

EXAMPLE 12

Find the derivative of $f(x) = \dfrac{\sin(x)}{x}$.

Solution   Using the Quotient Rule and the trigonometric rule:

$$f(x) = \frac{\sin(x)}{x}$$

$$f'(x) = \frac{x(\sin x)' - \sin x \cdot (x)'}{x^2}$$

$$f'(x) = \frac{x\cos(x) - \sin(x) \cdot 1}{x^2}$$

$$f'(x) = \frac{x\cos(x) - \sin(x)}{x^2}.$$

Exercises

Multiple-Choice Questions

No calculator is allowed for these questions.

1. Find the derivative of $y = (x^3 + x)^5$.
   (A) $3x^2 + 1$
   (B) $5(x^3 + x)^4$
   (C) $(15x^2 + 5)(x^3 + x)^4$
   (D) $5(3x^2 + 1)$
   (E) $\frac{1}{6}(x^3 + x)^6$

2. Find the derivative of $y = 6\ln\left(\dfrac{1}{x^2}\right)$.
   (A) -6
   (B) $-\dfrac{12}{x^3}$
   (C) $\dfrac{6}{x}$
   (D) $-\dfrac{12}{x}$
   (E) $-\dfrac{12}{x^2}$

3. The derivative of $f(x) = \ln(x^2 + 2x + 1)$ is
   (A) $\dfrac{2x}{x^2 + 2x + 1}$
   (B) $\dfrac{2}{x + 1}$
   (C) $\dfrac{1}{x^2 + 2x + 1}$
   (D) $\dfrac{1}{x + 1}$
   (E) $\dfrac{2x + 3}{x^2 + 2x + 1}$

4. Find the derivative of $y = \sin(x^2)$.
   (A) $\cos(x^2)$
   (B) $2\sin x \cos x$
   (C) $2x\sin(x^2)$

   (D) $2x \sin x$
   (E) $2x \cos(x^2)$

5. If $y = \ln(\tan x)$, then $y' =$
   (A) $\dfrac{2}{\sin 2x}$
   (B) $\sec^2 x$
   (C) $\dfrac{1}{x \tan x}$
   (D) $\cot x$
   (E) $\sec^2 x \tan x$

6. If $y = e^{5x+5}$, then $y'(0) =$
   (A) e^5
   (B) 1
   (C) $5e^5$
   (D) 5
   (E) $\frac{1}{5}e^5$

7. Find the derivative of $y = e^x \sin x$.
   (A) $e^x \cos x$
   (B) $e^x + \cos x$
   (C) $e^x(\sin x + \cos x)$
   (D) $\ln(\sin x)$
   (E) $e \cos x$

8. If $y = \sqrt{x^2 - 2x}$, then $y' =$
   (A) $\frac{1}{2}(x^2 - 2x)$
   (B) $\frac{1}{2}(x^2 - 2x)^{-\frac{1}{2}}$
   (C) $(x^2 - 2x)^{-\frac{1}{2}}(x - 1)$
   (D) $x - 1$
   (E) $(x^2 - 2x)(x - 1)$

9. If $f(x) = \cos x$ and $g(x) = \sqrt{x}$, the derivative of $f \circ g(x)$ is equal to

(A) $\cos\left(\dfrac{1}{2\sqrt{x}}\right)$

(B) $-\sin \sqrt{x}$

(C) $\sin \sqrt{x}$

(D) $-\dfrac{\sin x}{2\sqrt{x}}$

(E) $-\dfrac{\sin \sqrt{x}}{2\sqrt{x}}$

10. The derivative of $y = \tan (x^2)$ is

(A) $\sec^2(x^2)$

(B) $2x \sec^2(x^2)$

(C) $2x \sec(x^2)$

(D) $\sec(x^2)$

(E) $2x \sec^2(x^2) \tan(x^2)$

11. If $y = \ln e^{\tan^2 x}$, find $y'\left(\dfrac{\pi}{4}\right)$.

(A) -2

(B) 1

(C) 2

(D) $2\sqrt{2}$

(E) 4

12. Given $f(x) = x \cos x$, find the second derivative of $f(x)$.

(A) $-x \sin x$

(B) $-\cos x$

(C) $-x \cos x$

(D) $-x \cos x - 2 \sin x$

(E) $x \sin x$

13. $(\arctan 3x)' =$

(A) $\dfrac{3}{1 + 3x^2}$

(B) $\dfrac{3}{1 + x^2}$

(C) $\dfrac{3}{1 + 9x^2}$

(D) $\dfrac{1}{1 + 9x^2}$

(E) $\dfrac{3x}{1 + 3x^2}$

14. $\dfrac{d}{dx}(\arcsin(x^2)) =$

(A) $\dfrac{x^2}{\sqrt{1 - x^4}}$

(B) $\dfrac{2x}{\sqrt{1 - x^4}}$

(C) $\dfrac{2x}{\sqrt{1 - x^2}}$

(D) $\dfrac{1}{\sqrt{1 - x^4}}$

(E) $\dfrac{4x}{\sqrt{1 - x^2}}$

Free-Response Questions

A graphing calculator is required for some questions.

1. (a) Enter $Y_1 = \sqrt{x^2 + 2x + 1}$ in [Y=] on a graphing calculator, and sketch the graph.
   (b) Write another name for this function.
   (c) Enter the derivative of Y_1 into Y_2 and graph as follows:
   TI-83: $Y_2 =$ [MATH] 8 nDeriv(Y_1, x, x).
   Change [MODE] from Connected to Dot and graph in [ZOOM] 4.
   TI-89: $Y_2 = d(Y_1(x), x)$. In [Y=], change F6: Style to Dot.
   (d) Explain the relationship between the graph of Y_1 and the graph of Y_2.

2. Sketch the derivative of $f(x) = \begin{cases} x^2 + 2x, & x < 1 \\ 4x, & x \geq 1 \end{cases}$
   (a) by hand
   (b) on the graphing calculator
   (c) Is $f'(x)$ continuous at $x = 1$? Explain why or why not.

3. Find the derivative of $y = (x^2 + 1)(x^3 + 1)$
   (a) by using the Product Rule
   (b) by multiplying first
   (c) Compare the results of parts (a) and (b).

4.5 Recognizing the Form of the Derivative

Recognizing the form of the derivative may be helpful in answering AP Calculus questions. Recall that the standard definition of the derivative is $f'(x) = \lim\limits_{h \to 0} \dfrac{f(x + h) - f(x)}{h}$. On the AP Calculus Examinations, it may be useful to work backward from the definition of the derivative to the function. For example, to evaluate the expression $\lim_{h \to 0} \dfrac{(2 + h)^4 - 2^4}{h}$, note that it is in the form of the definition of the derivative where $f(x) = x^4$ and $x = 2$. Thus, the value of the limit is the value of the derivative of $f(x) = x^4$ at $x = 2$; that is, the value of $f'(x) = 4x^3$ at $x = 2$ or $4(2^3) = 32$.

EXAMPLE 1

Evaluate $\lim_{h \to 0} \dfrac{(1 + h)^3 - 1}{h}$.

Solution Since this limit is in the form of the definition of the derivative, we see that it is the derivative of the function $f(x) = x^3$ at $x = 1$.

Since we have a rule for the derivative of powers, the derivative of the function $f(x) = x^3$ is $f'(x) = 3x^2$. At $x = 1$, $f'(x) = 3$. This is the value of the limit.

EXAMPLE 2

Evaluate $\lim_{h \to 0} \dfrac{\ln(e + h) - 1}{h}$

Solution Recognizing that the limit may be in the form of the definition of the derivative, we substitute ln e for 1 in the numerator. We now have

$$\lim_{h \to 0} \frac{\ln(e + h) - \ln(e)}{h}.$$

This is the derivative of $f(x) = \ln x$ at $x = e$. Using the Log Rule for the derivative $f(x) = \ln x$, we have $f'(x) = \frac{1}{x}$. At $x = e$, $f'(e) = \frac{1}{e}$. This is the value of the limit.

Inverse Functions and Their Derivatives If $f(x)$ and $g(x)$ are inverse functions, then $f(g(x)) = x$. Taking the derivative of each side of this equation,

$$\frac{d}{dx}(f(g(x))) = \frac{d}{dx}(x),$$

and $f'(g(x)) \cdot g'(x) = 1$.

Therefore, $g'(x) = \dfrac{1}{f'(g(x))}$.

EXAMPLE 3

$f(x) = \sqrt{x} - 4$ and $g(x)$ is the inverse of $f(x)$. Find $g'(1)$.

Solution There are several methods of finding $g'(1)$. One way is to use the formula above: $g'(1) = \dfrac{1}{f'(g(1))}$.

Since $f(x)$ and $g(x)$ are inverses, $g(1)$ is the value in the domain of $f(x)$ that makes $f(x) = 1$. Thus, $g(1) = 5$, and $g'(1) = \dfrac{1}{f'(5)}$.

$$f'(x) = \frac{1}{2\sqrt{x-4}} \text{ and } f'(5) = \frac{1}{2}$$

Therefore, $g'(1) = \dfrac{1}{\frac{1}{2}} = 2$.

Another method is to find $g(x)$. Solving for the inverse of $f(x)$, $g(x) = x^2 + 4$, $x \geq 0$. Then $g'(x) = 2x$ and $g'(1) = 2$.

EXAMPLE 4

$f(x)$ and $g(x)$ are inverses, and $f(x) = \sqrt{x^3 + 1}$. Find $g'(3)$.

Solution Using the formula on page 74, $g'(3) = \dfrac{1}{f'(g(3))}$. $g(3)$ is the value in the domain of $f(x)$ such that $f(x) = 3$. Thus, $g(3) = 2$, and $g'(3) = \dfrac{1}{f'(2)}$.

$$f'(x) = \frac{3x^2}{2\sqrt{x^3+1}} \text{ and } f'(2) = 2$$

Therefore, $g'(3) = \dfrac{1}{2}$.

EXAMPLE 5

$f(x) = \tan x$. If $g(x)$ is the inverse of $f(x)$, find $g'(1)$.

Solution Using the formula from page 74, $g'(1) = \dfrac{1}{f'(g(1))}$. $g(1)$ is the

value in the domain of $f(x) = \tan x$ such that $\tan x = 1$. In order to define the inverse of $\tan x$, the domain must be restricted to an interval where the graph of $\tan x$ is one-to-one. By convention, the domain of $\tan x$ is restricted to the interval $\left(-\dfrac{\pi}{2}, \dfrac{\pi}{2} \right)$. Therefore, there is only one

solution of the equation $\tan x = 1$, namely, $x = \dfrac{\pi}{4}$, and $g(1) = \dfrac{\pi}{4}$.

Thus, $g'(1) = \dfrac{1}{f'\left(\dfrac{\pi}{4} \right)} = \dfrac{1}{\sec^2\left(\dfrac{\pi}{4} \right)} = \dfrac{1}{2}$.

The Second Derivative The derivative of a function may itself be a function that can be differentiated. The **second derivative** is the derivative of the derivative of a a function. The second derivative of $f(x)$ is denoted by $f''(x)$ or $\dfrac{d^2y}{dx^2}$. Finding the second derivative of a function is a two-step process: first find the derivative of the function, and then find the derivative of that function. Second derivatives and concavity are covered in Section 5.2.

EXAMPLE 6

For each function, find $f''(x)$.

(a) $f(x) = (x - 3)^3$

(b) $f(x) = \dfrac{x + 1}{x + 2}$

(c) $f(x) = \sin^2(3x)$

Solution

(a) The first derivative is $3(x - 3)^2$. The second derivative is $6(x - 3)$.

(b) The first derivative is $\dfrac{1}{(x + 2)^2}$. The second derivative is $\dfrac{-2}{(x + 2)^3}$.

(c) Use the Chain Rule to find the first derivative:

$$f'(x) = 2(\sin(3x))(\cos(3x)(3)) = 6 \sin 3x \cos 3x.$$

Then use the Product Rule to find the second derivative:

$$f''(x) = 6 \sin 3x(-3 \sin 3x) + \cos 3x(18 \cos 3x)$$
$$= -18 \sin^2 3x + 18 \cos^2 3x,$$
$$= 18 \cos(6x), \text{ by the double angle identity}$$

Exercises

Multiple-Choice Questions

A graphing calculator is required for some questions.

1. The derivative of $2x - x^{-2}$ is

(A) $2 + 2x$

(B) $2 - x^{-1}$

(C) $x^2 + 2x^{-3}$

(D) $2 + 2x^{-3}$

(E) $2 + 2x^{-1}$

2. The second derivative of $f(x) = \ln(x)$ at $x = 3$ is

(A) $-\dfrac{1}{3}$

(B) $-\dfrac{1}{9}$

(C) $\dfrac{1}{9}$

(D) $\dfrac{1}{3}$

(E) $\dfrac{2}{3}$

3. Evaluate $\lim\limits_{h \to 0} \dfrac{e^{1+h} - e}{h}$.

(A) 0

(B) 1

(C) 2

(D) e

(E) e^2

4. The slope of the line tangent to $f(x) = \tan(x^2)$ at $x = 1$ is

(A) 1.557

(B) 1.851

(C) 3.115

(D) 3.426

(E) 6.851

5. Find the slope of the line tangent to $f(x) = \dfrac{\sin(x)}{x}$ at $x = \dfrac{\pi}{2}$.

(A) $\dfrac{2}{\pi}$

(B) 1

(C) -1

(D) $\dfrac{4}{\pi^2}$

(E) $-\dfrac{4}{\pi^2}$

6. Evaluate the derivative of $f(x) = x + e^{2x}$ at $x = 0$.

(A) 0

(B) 1

(C) 2

(D) 3

(E) 4

7. Find $\dfrac{dy}{dx}$ if $y = 3x(x-2)^3$.

(A) $9(x-2)^2$
(B) $9x(x-2)^2$
(C) $(12x-6)(x-2)^2$
(D) $3(x-2)^3$
(E) $(2x-1)(x-2)^2$

8. Find y' if $y = -\dfrac{\cos(x)}{x}$.

(A) $\dfrac{x\sin(x) - \cos(x)}{x^2}$

(B) $\dfrac{x\sin(x) + \cos(x)}{x^2}$

(C) $\dfrac{\sin(x)}{x}$

(D) $\dfrac{\sin(x) - x}{x^2}$

(E) $\dfrac{x\sin(x) - 1}{x^2}$

9. Find the derivative of $\cos^2 x$.

(A) $\sin^2 x$
(B) $1 - \sin^2 x$
(C) $2\cos(x)$
(D) $-2\sin(x)\cos(x)$
(E) $-2\sin(2x)$

10. Find the value of the derivative of $e^x \sin(x)$ at $x = \pi$.

(A) 0
(B) 1
(C) e
(D) e^π
(E) $-e^\pi$

11. If $f(x) = \ln x$ and $g(x)$ is the inverse of $f(x)$, find $g'(1)$.

(A) 0
(B) 1
(C) e
(D) $\dfrac{1}{e}$
(E) does not exist

12. $f(x) = \arcsin x$ and $g(x) = f^{-1}(x)$. Find $g'(0)$.

(A) 0
(B) 1
(C) $\dfrac{\pi}{2}$
(D) $\dfrac{2}{\pi}$
(E) does not exist

13. $g(x) = -\sqrt{x}$ and $f(x) = g^{-1}(x)$. Find $f'(-1)$.

(A) -2
(B) $-\dfrac{1}{2}$

(C) $\dfrac{1}{2}$
(D) 2
(E) does not exist

Free-Response Questions
A graphing calculator is required for some questions.

1. Use the definition of the derivative to find $f'(x)$ if $f(x) = x^2 + x$. Check your answer with the Power Rule.

2. Find the derivative of $f(x) = \dfrac{2x}{\sqrt{(x^2 + x)}}$.

3. For $y = \dfrac{x^2 + 4}{x}$:

(a) Find y' using the Quotient Rule.
(b) Rewrite y as a product and use the Product Rule to find y'.
(c) Write y as a sum and use the Sum Rule to find y'.
(d) Find y''.

4. For each of the following graphs (a)–(e), sketch the graph of its derivative:

(a) y

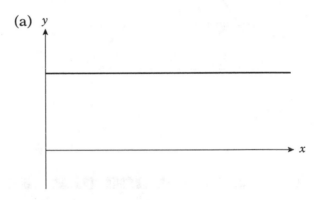

(b) y

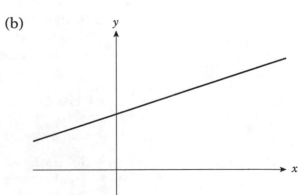

(c)

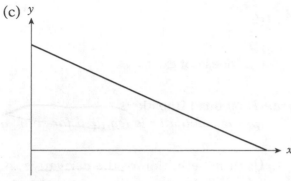

(d)

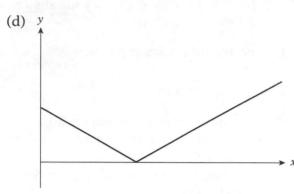

(e)

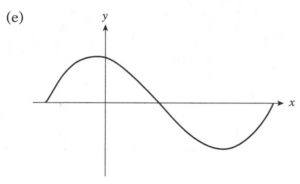

5. $f(x) = \sin x$.

   (a) State the domain of $f(x)$ so that $f(x)$ has an inverse.

   (b) Write an expression for $g(x) = f^{-1}(x)$, and state the domain and range of $g(x)$.

   (c) Write an expression for $g'(x)$, and use it to show that $g'(x) = \dfrac{1}{f'(g(x))}$ for $x = \dfrac{1}{2}$.

6. $f(x) = 2x^2 - 3$ for $x \geq 0$.

   (a) Is $f(x)$ one-to-one?

   (b) If $g(x)$ is the inverse of $f(x)$, use the formula $g'(x) = \dfrac{1}{f'(g(x))}$ to find $g'(0)$.

   (c) Find an algebraic expression for $g(x)$ and use it to confirm the answer in part (b).

   (d) Sketch the graphs of $f(x)$ and $g(x)$. Then use the calculator to confirm the value of $g'(0)$ found in part (b).

7. For the function $f(x) = x^3 + 2x^2 + 4x - 5$:

   (a) Find the first, second, and third derivatives of $f(x)$.

   (b) Determine which derivative is a constant.

   (c) Generalize the result and determine what order derivative is a constant for an nth-degree polynomial.

4.6 The Equation of a Tangent Line

Using the formula for the derivative of a function, find the value of the derivative at the given point to find the slope of the tangent line. To find the equation of the tangent line to the graph of the function, use one of the forms of the equation of a line. The point-slope form is usually the easiest to use.

EXAMPLE 1

Find the equation of the line tangent to $f(x) = 2x^2 + 5x$ at the point $(1, 7)$.

Solution   Since a point is given, we must find the slope of the tangent line. First find the derivative: $f'(x) = 4x + 5$. Substituting the value of x, the slope of the tangent is $f'(1) = 9$. Using the point-slope form for the equation of a line, the equation of the tangent is

$$y - 7 = 9(x - 1).$$

The equation may be left in this form in a free-response question on the AP exams.

EXAMPLE 2

Find the equation of the line tangent to $f(x) = 6 - x^3$ at $x = 1$.

Solution   To write the equation, we must find the slope of the tangent line and the coordinates of a point on the line.

METHOD 1   First find the derivative: $f'(x) = -3x^2$. Substituting the value of x, the slope of the tangent is $f'(1) = -3$. By substituting $x = 1$ into $f(x)$, the y-coordinate is $f(1) = 5$.

Using the point-slope form for the equation of a line, the equation of the tangent is

$$y - 5 = -3(x - 1).$$

The equation may be left in this form in a free-response question on the AP exams.

METHOD 2   Using the graphing calculator: Enter $f(x)$ into Y_1.

By the definition of the derivative, the slope of the line tangent to $f(x)$ at $x = 1$ will be equal to the $f'(1)$. This value can be found by graphing the derivative and using the CALC function.

Enter $Y_2 = $ MATH 8 VARS Y-VARS ENTER ENTER , X,T,Θ,n , X,T,Θ,n).

Press GRAPH to see a graph of the function $f(x)$ and its derivative $f'(x)$.
Press 2nd CALC ENTER and enter $x = 1$. Use the ▲ ▼ keys to move the cursor to the graph of the derivative. Press ENTER to calculate the y-coordinate -3, which is also the slope of the tangent to $f(x)$ at $x = 1$.

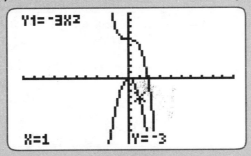

By moving the cursor to the graph of $f(x)$, we can determine also that $f(1) = 5$. We can then use the point-slope form with the point $(1, 5)$ and slope -3 to get the equation $y - 5 = -3(x - 1)$.

EXAMPLE 3

Find the y-intercept of the line tangent to $f(x) = \tan x - x$ at $x = \frac{\pi}{4}$.

Solution   First find the derivative: $f'(x) = \sec^2 x - 1$. Substituting the value of x, the slope of the tangent is $f'\left(\frac{\pi}{4}\right) = 1$. By substituting $x = \frac{\pi}{4}$ into $f(x)$, the y-coordinate is $1 - \frac{\pi}{4}$.

Using the point-slope form for the equation of a line, the equation of the tangent is

$$y - \left(1 - \frac{\pi}{4}\right) = x - \frac{\pi}{4}, \text{ or } y = x + 1 - \frac{\pi}{2}.$$

Thus, the y-intercept of the tangent line is $1 - \frac{\pi}{2}$.

EXAMPLE 4

Find the coordinates of the point on the curve $f(x) = xe^{2x} + 1$ where the tangent line is horizontal.

Solution The slope of the tangent line is the derivative of the function.

$$f'(x) = x(2e^{2x}) + e^{2x} = e^{2x}(2x + 1).$$

A horizontal line has a slope of zero.

Solving $f'(x) = 0$, $x = -\dfrac{1}{2}$.

$$f\left(-\frac{1}{2}\right) = -\frac{1}{2}e^{-1} + 1 = 1 - \frac{1}{2e}.$$

Thus, the coordinates of the point where the tangent line is horizontal are $\left(-\dfrac{1}{2}, 1 - \dfrac{1}{2e}\right)$.

Exercises

Multiple-Choice Questions
No calculator is allowed for these questions.

1. Find the equation of the line tangent to $f(x) = 2x + 2e^x$ at $x = 0$.
   (A) $y = 4x + 2$
   (B) $y = 2x + 2$
   (C) $y = 4x$
   (D) $y = 4x - 2$
   (E) $y = -\dfrac{1}{4}x + 2$

2. Find the equation of the line perpendicular to the line tangent to $f(x) = \ln(3 - 2x)$ at $x = 1$.
   (A) $y = -2x + 1$
   (B) $y = \dfrac{1}{2}x + 1$
   (C) $y = \dfrac{1}{2}(x - 1)$
   (D) $y = \dfrac{1}{2}(x + 1)$
   (E) $y = -2x + 2$

3. Find the slope of the line tangent to $f(x) = \dfrac{1}{x^2 + 1}$ at $x = -1$.
   (A) -2
   (B) $\dfrac{1}{2}$
   (C) 1
   (D) 2
   (E) undefined

4. The y-intercept of the line tangent to $y = x \sin x$ at $x = \pi$ is
   (A) $-\pi$
   (B) π

   (C) $-\pi^2$
   (D) π^2
   (E) 1

Free-Response Questions
A graphing calculator is required for some questions.

1. (a) Find the equations of the tangent lines at the zeros of $f(x) = x^2 - 2x - 3$, and find their point of intersection.
   (b) Repeat part (a) for $f(x) = \sin x$ on the interval $[0, 2\pi]$.

2. (a) Sketch the graph of $f(x) = x^3 - 13x + 12$ on the calculator by setting x-range from -8 to 8 and y-range from -15 to 35.
   (b) Use the calculator to find the equations of the tangent lines at the following values of x, and complete the table below. Sketch each tangent line on the graph from part (a).

x	Equation of tangent line	Is tangent line above or below graph?
-3		
-1		
2		
3		

   (c) At what value of x does the tangent line appear to change from being above the curve to below the curve?

4.7 Differentiability vs. Continuity

If a function is differentiable at a value of x, then the function is continuous at that value of x.

Be careful to use the statement above correctly, since the *converse* is NOT true. A function that is continuous at a value of x may or may not be differentiable at x.

There are many examples of functions that are continuous but NOT differentiable. A standard example is $f(x) = |x|$. The absolute value of x is continuous for all values of x, but its derivative does not exist at $x = 0$.

Another example is $f(x) = x^{2/3}$. This function is continuous for all values of x, but it does not have a derivative at $x = 0$.

Note: All polynomial functions, $\sin(x)$, $\cos(x)$, e^x, and $\ln x$ are differentiable at every value in their domains, so it follows that they are continuous at every value in their domains.

If a question asks to verify the continuity of a function, check each of the three conditions in the definition of continuity. (See Section 3.6 for the definition of continuity.)

If a question asks to verify whether or not a function has a derivative (that is, if the function is differentiable), first check to see if the function is continuous. If it is continuous, then check to see if the derivative exists.

EXAMPLE

For $f(x) = \begin{cases} x^2, & x < 1 \\ 2x, & x \geq 1 \end{cases}$, is $f(x)$ differentiable at $x = 1$?

Solution   First use the definition of continuity to see if $f(x)$ is continuous at $x = 1$.

1. Is $f(x)$ is defined at $x = 1$? Yes.

2. Does $\lim\limits_{x \to 1} f(x)$ exist? This means does $\lim\limits_{x \to 1^-} f(x) = \lim\limits_{x \to 1^+} f(x)$?

$$\lim\limits_{x \to 1^-} f(x) = \lim\limits_{x \to 1^-} x^2 = 1 \text{ and}$$

$$\lim\limits_{x \to 1^+} f(x) = \lim\limits_{x \to 1^+} 2x = 2.$$

Since $\lim\limits_{x \to 1^-} f(x) \neq \lim\limits_{x \to 1^+} f(x)$, $\lim\limits_{x \to 1} f(x)$ does not exist and $f(x)$ is not continuous at $x = 1$.

Since $f(x)$ is not continuous at $x = 1$, it is not differentiable at $x = 1$.

Exercises

Multiple-Choice Questions

A graphing calculator is required for some questions.

1. $f(x) = \dfrac{1}{\ln x}$ is continuous and differentiable on which interval(s)?

   (A) $(0, 1)$ or $(1, \infty)$
   (B) $(0, \infty)$
   (C) $(-\infty, \infty)$
   (D) $[0, \infty)$
   (E) $[1, \infty)$

2. Every polynomial is continuous and differentiable

   (A) for all $x \geq 0$
   (B) for all real x
   (C) for all $x > 0$
   (D) for $0 < x < 1$
   (E) for no values of x

3. For what values of x is $f(x) = |x + 1|$ differentiable?

(A) for all $x \neq 0$
(B) for all $x \geq 0$
(C) for all real numbers
(D) for all $x \neq 1$
(E) for all $x \neq -1$

4. $f(x) = \begin{cases} 4, & x < 2 \\ x^2, & x \geq 2 \end{cases}$ is differentiable for

(A) all real numbers
(B) $x \neq 2$
(C) $x > 2$
(D) $x \geq 2$
(E) $x < 2$

Free-Response Questions

A graphing calculator is required for some questions.

1. Write a function that is continuous for all real numbers and differentiable except at $x = 1$.

2. The graph of $f(x)$ is shown in the figure.

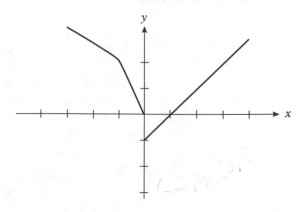

(a) For what values of x is $f(x)$ continuous?
(b) Sketch the graph of the derivative of $f(x)$.

Note: Graphing split functions on the calculator may be misleading. Pieces that appear connected may not be. Be sure to check the values at the break points to determine the actual values.

4.8 Particle Motion

In questions about particle motion, the particle may be moving in one dimension along a line, usually the x-axis (though it could also be moving along the y-axis). The particle may also be moving in two dimensions, in which case it may be referred to as a freely falling object.

The **position** of the particle at time t, usually denoted $x(t)$ or $s(t)$, is its location on the number line if it moves in one dimension, or its height if it moves in two dimensions. Position is expressed in linear units such as meters or feet.

The **velocity** $v(t)$ of the particle is the rate of change of position with respect to time, or the derivative of position. Velocity is calculated using $v(t) = x'(t)$ or $s'(t)$. Velocity has magnitude and direction: it tells how fast *and in what direction* the particle is moving. Velocity can be positive, negative, or zero. When the velocity is zero, the particle is at rest. When the velocity is positive, the particle is moving to the right (or moving up). When the velocity is negative, the particle is moving to the left (or moving down). Velocity is expressed as a ratio of linear units and time units, such as m/sec or ft/sec.

The **speed** of the particle tells us only *how fast* the particle is moving. Speed can be positive or zero. Speed is the absolute value of velocity.

Particle Velocity	
$v(t) = 0$	Particle at rest
$v(t) > 0$	Particle moves to right (or up)
$v(t) < 0$	Particle moves to left (or down)
Sign of $v(t)$ changes	Particle changes direction

The **acceleration** $a(t)$ of the particle is the rate of change of velocity with respect to time, or the derivative of velocity. Since velocity is the *first* derivative of position, acceleration is the *second* derivative of position. Acceleration is calculated using $a(t) = v'(t) = x''(t)$ or $s''(t)$. Acceleration can be positive, negative, or zero and is expressed as a ratio of linear units and time units squared, such as m/sec² or ft/sec².

EXAMPLE 1

Suppose a particle is moving along a line with its position at time t given by $s(t) = t^3 - 3t + 2$, for $t \geq 0$. (t is in seconds and s is in feet.)
(a) Find the velocity function.
(b) Find $v(0)$ and $v(2)$.
(c) When is the velocity zero? Where is the particle at that time?
(d) Draw a number line indicating the position and the velocity of the particle at $t = 0$, $t = 1$, and $t = 2$.
(e) Refer to the number line to write a description of the motion of the particle from $t = 0$ to $t = 2$.

Solution

(a) The velocity function $v(t) = s'(t) = 3t^2 - 3$.
(b) $v(0) = -3$ ft/sec and $v(2) = 9$ ft/sec.
(c) To find when the velocity is zero, solve the equation $3t^2 - 3 = 0$.
   $t = 1$ is the only solution for $t \geq 0$.
   At $t = 1$, $s(1) = 0$.

(d)

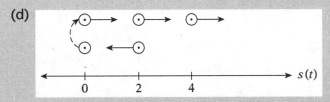

Particle Motion				
Time	t	0	1	2
Position	$s(t) = t^3 - 3t + 2$	2	0	4
Velocity	$v(t) = s'(t) = 3t^2 - 3$	−3 ft/sec	0 ft/sec	9 ft/sec

(e) As seen in the number line and the table, at $t = 0$, the particle is at $s = 2$ and is moving to the left at 3 ft/sec. One second later at $t = 1$, the particle is at $s = 0$ and is at rest. The particle then turns and at $t = 2$, the particle is at $s = 4$ and is moving to the right at 9 ft/sec.

EXAMPLE 2

A particle moves along a number line with position function $s(t) = t - \ln t$, for $t \geq 1$.
(a) Find the velocity and the acceleration functions.
(b) Find $s(1)$, $s(5)$, $v(2)$, and $v(4)$.
(c) Is there a value of t that makes the velocity zero? If yes, find the value of t. If no, explain why not.
(d) As t increases, does the velocity increase or decrease? Explain your answer in a complete sentence. (*Hint:* What does the velocity approach as t gets larger; that is, find $\lim\limits_{t \to \infty} v(t)$.)

(e) Is the acceleration positive or negative for $t \geq 1$? Explain your answer in a complete sentence.

(f) Draw a number line indicating the position and velocity for $t = 1$, $t = 3$, and $t = 5$.

(g) Refer to the number line and your answers to parts (c), (d), and (e) to write a description of the motion of the particle.

Solution

(a) The velocity function $v(t) = 1 - \frac{1}{t}$. The acceleration function $a(t) = \frac{1}{t^2}$.

(b) $s(1) = 1$, $s(5) = 5 - \ln 5 \approx 3.391$, $v(2) = 0.5$, and $v(4) = 0.75$.

(c) Since $1 - \frac{1}{t} > 0$ for $t > 1$, the velocity is positive for $t > 1$. The velocity is zero only at $t = 1$.

(d) As t increases, the value of $\frac{1}{t}$ decreases. Therefore, $v(t) = 1 - \frac{1}{t}$ always increases.

Note: As t gets larger, the velocity approaches 1; that is, $\lim\limits_{t \to \infty} v(t) = 1$.

(e) Since t^2 is always positive, $\frac{1}{t^2}$ is always positive. Thus, the acceleration is always positive.

(f)

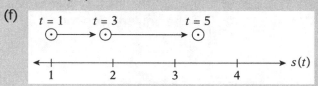

Particle Motion						
Time	t	1	2	3	4	5
Position	$s(t) = t - \ln t$	1	1.31	1.901	2.61	3.391
Velocity	$v(t) = 1 - \frac{1}{t}$	0	0.5	$0.6\overline{6}$	0.75	0.8
Acceleration	$a(t) = \frac{1}{t^2}$	1	0.25	0.111	0.0625	0.04

(g) As seen in the number line and the table, the particle starts from rest at $s = 1$ when $t = 1$. As t increases, the particle accelerates and the velocity increases. Since the velocity is positive for $t > 1$, the particle is always moving to the right. The velocity increases and approaches 1 as a limiting value.

Exercises

Multiple-Choice Questions

For Questions 1–6, consider a particle whose motion is represented by the position equation $s(t) = t^2 - t$, $t \geq 0$, where s is feet and t is seconds. No calculator is allowed for these questions.

1. The velocity of the particle after two seconds is
   (A) 0 ft/sec
   (B) 1 ft/sec
   (C) 2 ft/sec
   (D) 3 ft/sec
   (E) 4 ft/sec

2. The acceleration of the particle after two seconds is
- (A) 0 ft/sec^2
- (B) 1 ft/sec^2
- (C) 2 ft/sec^2
- (D) 3 ft/sec^2
- (E) 4 ft/sec^2

3. What is the position of the particle at $t = 2$?
- (A) 0 ft
- (B) 1 ft
- (C) 2 ft
- (D) 3 ft
- (E) 4 ft

4. At what value(s) of t does the particle change direction?
- (A) $t = \frac{1}{2}$
- (B) $t = 1$
- (C) $t = 1$ and $t = 2$
- (D) $t = 2$
- (E) The particle never changes direction.

5. Find the distance traveled by the particle in the first two seconds.
- (A) 1.75 ft
- (B) 2 ft
- (C) 2.25 ft
- (D) 2.5 ft
- (E) 3 ft

6. The particle moves to the right when
- (A) $t > 0$
- (B) $t > \frac{1}{2}$
- (C) $t > 1$
- (D) $t > 2$
- (E) It does not move right.

For Questions 7 and 8, a graphing calculator is required. Consider a particle moving along a line, with its position given by $s(t) = t^3 - 3t$, $t \geq 0$.

7. The particle moves to the left for
- (A) $0 < t < 1$
- (B) $0 < t < 2$
- (C) $1 < t < 2$
- (D) $0 < t < 3$
- (E) It does not move left.

8. Find the distance traveled by the particle in the first two seconds.
- (A) 0
- (B) 2
- (C) 4

- (D) 6
- (E) 8

Free-Response Questions

A graphing calculator is required for some questions.

1. A particle travels on a number line with position given by $s(t) = t \sin t$ for t in the interval $[0, 2\pi]$.

- (a) Find the velocity and acceleration functions.
- (b) For what value(s) of t is the particle at rest?
- (c) Draw the path of the particle on a number line and show the direction of increasing t.
- (d) Is the distance traveled by the particle greater than 10? Explain your answer.

Exercises 2 and 3 provide practice with two techniques of using the graphing calculator in parametric mode to illustrate the motion of a particle on a number line.
- Set the MODE to Par.
- In Y=, enter: $X_{1T} = t^2 - 4t$ and $Y_{1T} = 2$.
- In WINDOW, set Tmin = 0, Tmax = 5, and Tstep = 0.03. Set Xmin = −6, Xmax = 8, Ymin = −2, and Ymax = 5.

The bigger the value of Tstep, the faster the particle moves. When you press GRAPH, you will see the particle moving along a number line two units above the x-axis. Press TRACE and hold down ▶ to see the particle moving again. As it moves, you can see the values of t, x, and y at the bottom of the screen.

2. Use the calculator to answer the following:
- (a) When is the particle at rest?
- (b) Describe the behavior of the particle as its position moves left toward −4.
- (c) Describe the behavior of the particle as it moves to the right away from $x = -4$.
- (d) Make a number line and draw the path of the particle showing the direction of increasing t.

3. In Y=, deselect X_{1T} and Y_{1T}, and enter $X_{2T} = 2t - 4$ and $Y_{2T} = 4$. Change Tstep to 0.01 and press GRAPH. Describe the motion of the particle and explain how this second function relates to the motion in Exercise 2.

4.9 Motion of a Freely Falling Object

The motion of an object in two dimensions, such as a ball being dropped from a height or thrown up into the air, can be modeled by an equation that gives the position of the object as a function of time. The general equation that describes this kind of motion is

$$s(t) = \frac{1}{2}at^2 + v_0 t + s_0,$$

where t is time, a is the acceleration due to gravity, v_0 is the initial velocity, and s_0 is the initial height.

> If the height is in feet and time is in seconds, then $a = -32$ ft/sec^2.
> If the height is in meters and time is in seconds, then $a = -9.8$ m/sec^2.

EXAMPLE 1

Suppose a ball is dropped from a window 20 feet above the ground.
(a) Find the height of the ball after 1 second.
(b) Find the velocity of the ball after 1 second.
(c) When will the ball hit the ground? What is its speed at that moment?

Solution   The equation of motion is

$$s(t) = \frac{1}{2}(-32t^2) + v_0 t + s_0$$
$$s(t) = -16t^2 + v_0 t + s_0$$

Since the ball was dropped from a height of 20 feet, $v_0 = 0$ and $s_0 = 20$. Thus the equation of motion is $s(t) = -16t^2 + 20$.
(a) The height of the ball after one second is $s(1) = 4$ feet.
(b) The velocity is calculated using $v(t) = s'(t) = -32t$. Therefore, the velocity of the ball after 1 second is $v(1) = -32$ ft/sec.
(c) The ball hits the ground when $s(t) = 0$. Solving $-16t^2 + 20 = 0$, we have

$$t = \frac{\sqrt{5}}{2} \text{ or } 1.118 \text{ seconds.}$$

Since speed $= |v(t)|$, the speed at that time is $\left| -32\left(\frac{\sqrt{5}}{2}\right) \right|$ ft/sec or 35.776 ft/sec.

EXAMPLE 2

A ball is thrown upward from the hand of a player. When the ball leaves the player's hand, it is at a height of 2 meters and traveling at a speed of 5 meters per second.
(a) What is the speed of the ball one second later?
(b) When is the ball 3 meters above the ground? 1.5 meters above the ground?
(c) When does the ball hit the ground?
(d) When is the ball at its highest point?

Solution   The equation of motion for a freely falling object in meters and seconds is $s(t) = -4.9t^2 + v_0t + s_0$. Since the ball is thrown from a height of 2 meters at 5 m/sec, $v_0 = 5$ and $s_0 = 2$. Thus, the equation of motion is $s(t) = -4.9t^2 + 5t + 2$.

(a) The speed of the ball one second later is $|v(1)|$.

$$v(t) = -9.8t + 5.$$

Thus, $v(1) = -4.8$, and the speed is 4.8 m/sec.

(b) The ball is 3 meters above the ground when $s(t) = 3$. Solving

$$-4.9t^2 + 5t + 2 = 3,$$

the values of t are 0.273 and 0.747 seconds.

The ball is 1.5 meters above the ground when $s(t) = 1.5$. Solving

$$-4.9t^2 + 5t + 2 = 1.5,$$

we find that there are two solutions, but only one value of t that is positive. That solution is $t = 1.112$ seconds.

(c) The ball hits the ground when $s(t) = 0$. Solving

$$-4.9t^2 + 5t + 2 = 0,$$

we find that there are two solutions, but only one value of t that is positive. That solution is $t = 1.328$ seconds.

The solutions for parts (b) and (c) are shown on the graph.

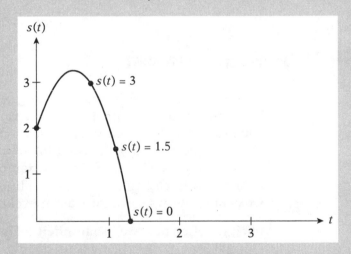

(d) The ball is at its highest point when $v(t) = 0$. Solving

$$-9.8t + 5 = 0,$$

the solution is $t = 0.510$ seconds.

Exercises

Multiple-Choice Questions

For Questions 1–4, the position of a freely falling object is given by, s(t) = −16t² + v₀t + s₀, *where s is feet and* t *is seconds. The initial position is s and the initial velocity is* v₀. *A graphing calculator is required.*

1. A ball is thrown upward from the top of a building 100 feet high at initial velocity of 20 ft/sec. How long will it take until the ball hits the ground?
   (A) 1.952 sec
   (B) 2.5 sec

(C) 3.202 sec

(D) 10 sec

(E) 50 sec

2. A ball is thrown ~~upward~~ *down* from the top of a building 100 feet high with initial speed 20 ft/sec. The ball hits the ground after

(A) 1.952 sec

(B) 2.5 sec

(C) 3.202 sec

(D) 5 sec

(E) 10 sec

3. A ball is dropped from the top of a building 100 feet high. After how many seconds does the ball hit the ground?

(A) 1.952 sec

(B) 2.5 sec

(C) 3.202 sec

(D) 5 sec

(E) 10 sec

4. A ball is dropped from the top of a building 200 feet high. It hits the ground after

(A) 2 sec

(B) 2.5 sec

(C) 3 sec

(D) 3.536 sec

(E) 5 sec

Free-Response Questions

No calculator is allowed for these questions.

1. Multiple-Choice Questions 1–4 investigate a freely falling object given different initial velocities and initial heights. Compare your answers to the four questions, and explain how initial velocity and initial height affect the time that the ball hits the ground.

2. A ball is thrown downward from the top of a building 80 feet high toward a 6-foot-tall friend who reaches up to catch it. With what initial velocity must the ball be thrown downward to reach the friend's hand in 3 seconds?

4.10 Implicit Differentiation

Most of the functions in calculus are given in the form $f(x) =$ or $y =$. These functions are *explicit* functions of the variable. In addition, we often study equations that do not have an explicit form and may not even be functions. For example, we study the equation of a circle centered at the origin with standard form $x^2 + y^2 = r^2$. In this example, y is related to x *implicitly*. This means that given a value of x, we can find the corresponding y-value(s), but we cannot always solve for y as an explicit function of x. When y is an implicit function of x, we use **implicit differentiation** to find y' or $\dfrac{dy}{dx}$.

EXAMPLE 1

Find $\dfrac{dy}{dx}$ for the equation $x^2 + y^2 = r^2$.

Solution   Use the $\dfrac{d}{dx}$ notation instead of the y' notation to make it clear that we are taking the derivative of y with respect to the variable x.

Take the derivative on each side of the equation:

$$\frac{d}{dx}(x^2 + y^2) = \frac{d}{dx}(r^2).$$

Expanding on the left, since r^2 is a constant, we have

$$\frac{d}{dx}(x^2) + \frac{d}{dx}(y^2) = 0.$$

We know that $\frac{d}{dx}(x^2) = 2x$, but what is $\frac{d}{dx}(y^2)$?

Solve: $\frac{d}{dx}(y^2) = \frac{d}{dy}(y^2) \cdot \frac{dy}{dx} = 2y\frac{dy}{dx}$.

Therefore, from $\frac{d}{dx}(x^2) + \frac{d}{dx}(y^2) = 0$, we have $2x + 2y\frac{dy}{dx} = 0$.

Now solve for $\frac{dy}{dx}$: $\frac{dy}{dx} = -\frac{x}{y}$, which is in terms of both x and y.

EXAMPLE 2

Find $\frac{dy}{dx}$ for $y^2 + xy = 2$.

Solution   Since y is implicitly related to x, we use the method of implicit differentiation to find $\frac{dy}{dx}$.

Take the derivative on each side with respect to x:

$$\frac{d}{dx}(y^2) + \frac{d}{dx}(xy) = \frac{d}{dx}(2).$$

Thus, we have $2y\frac{dy}{dx} + x\frac{d}{dx}(y) + y\frac{d}{dx}(x) = 0$, or

$$2y\frac{dy}{dx} + x\frac{dy}{dx} + y = 0.$$

Now solve for $\frac{dy}{dx}$ as follows:

$$(2y + x)\frac{dy}{dx} = -y, \text{ and } \frac{dy}{dx} = \frac{-y}{x + 2y}.$$

EXAMPLE 3

Find the slope of the line tangent to $\ln(xy) + y = x$ at the point $(1, 1)$.

Solution   Using the logarithmic properties, first rewrite the equation:

$$\ln x + \ln y + y = x.$$

Next find the derivative using implicit differentiation:

$$\frac{1}{x} + \frac{1}{y}\frac{dy}{dx} + \frac{dy}{dx} = 1$$

$$\frac{dy}{dx}\left(1 + \frac{1}{y}\right) = 1 - \frac{1}{x}.$$

At $x = 1$, $\frac{dy}{dx} = 0$. Therefore the slope of the line tangent at $(1, 1)$ is zero.

EXAMPLE 4

Find the equation of the line tangent to $y \sin x + e^x = y^2$ at $(0, 1)$.

Solution   By implicit differentiation:

$$y \cos x + \frac{dy}{dx}\sin x + e^x = 2y\frac{dy}{dx}$$

$$\frac{dy}{dx}(2y - \sin x) = y \cos x + e^x$$

At $(0, 1)$, $2\frac{dy}{dx} = 2$, and $\frac{dy}{dx} = 1$.
The equation of the tangent line is $y - 1 = x - 0$, or $y = x + 1$.

Exercises

No calculator is allowed for these exercises.

1. Use the formula derived in Example 1 to find $\frac{dy}{dx}$ for $x^2 + y^2 = 25$ at the point $(3, 4)$.

2. Use the formula derived in Example 2 for the derivative of $y^2 + xy = 2$ to find the slope of the tangent to the curve at $(1, 1)$.

3. Use the process of implicit differentiation to find $\frac{dy}{dx}$ for the equation $x^2 + y^2 + xy = 5$.

Multiple-Choice Questions

1. Find $\frac{dy}{dx}$ if $x^2 + y^2 = -2xy$.
   (A) 1
   (B) -1
   (C) $\frac{x - y}{x + y}$
   (D) $\frac{x + y}{x - y}$
   (E) $-\frac{x + 2y}{x}$

2. Find the slope of the line tangent to the graph of $2xy^2 + xy = y$ when $y = 1$.
   (A) $-\frac{9}{2}$
   (B) $-\frac{2}{9}$
   (C) $\frac{2}{9}$
   (D) $\frac{1}{3}$
   (E) $\frac{9}{2}$

3. The equation of the tangent line to the graph of $x \cos y + y = x^2$ at the point $(1, 0)$ is
   (A) $y = 2x$
   (B) $y = x$
   (C) $y = x - 1$
   (D) $y = -x + 1$
   (E) $y = -x$

Free-Response Questions

1. (a) Find $\frac{dy}{dx}$ if $x^2 y + y^2 = 2x$.
   (b) Find the point(s) on the graph where there is a horizontal tangent.
   (c) Find the point(s) on the graph where there is a vertical tangent.

2. (a) Find the derivative $\frac{dy}{dx}$ for the graph of $1 + x \ln(y + 1) = x + y$.
   (b) Show that there is a vertical tangent to the graph at the point $(1, 0)$.

4.11 Related Rates

Suppose a particle starts from the origin and moves along the curve $y = x^2$ in the first quadrant. As it moves, both the x-coordinate and the y-coordinate of its position change. If the rate of change of the x-coordinate is $\frac{1}{2}$ unit/sec, that is, $\frac{dx}{dt} = \frac{1}{2}$ unit/sec, then the rate of change of the y-coordinate can be calculated as follows:

$$\frac{dy}{dt} = \frac{dy}{dx} \cdot \frac{dx}{dt}.$$

Since $y = x^2$, $\frac{dy}{dt} = 2x \cdot \frac{dx}{dt} = 2x\left(\frac{1}{2}\right) = x.$

That is, the rate of change of the y-coordinate at a point on the curve is equal to the value of the x-coordinate at that point. For example, at the point $(1, 1)$, $\frac{dy}{dt} = 1$ unit/sec, and at the point $(3, 9)$, $\frac{dy}{dt} = 3$ units/sec.

Thus, for a function $y = f(x)$, the rates of change of the x-coordinate and the y-coordinate are related by the equation

$$\frac{dy}{dt} = \frac{dy}{dx} \cdot \frac{dx}{dt}.$$

EXAMPLE 1

A particle moves along the curve $y = 3x^2 - 6x$ so that the rate of change of the x-coordinate $\frac{dx}{dt}$ is 2 units/sec. Find the rate of change of the y-coordinate, $\frac{dy}{dt}$, when the particle is at the origin.

Solution   The relationship between $\frac{dx}{dt}$ and $\frac{dy}{dt}$ is given by the equation

$$\frac{dy}{dt} = \frac{dy}{dx} \cdot \frac{dx}{dt}.$$

Substituting $\frac{dy}{dx} = 6x - 6$ and $\frac{dx}{dt} = 2$ into the equation, we have

$$\frac{dy}{dt} = (6x - 6) \cdot 2.$$

Therefore, at the origin, where $x = 0$, $\frac{dy}{dt} = -12$ units/sec.

In Example 2, a particle moves along a curve where y is an implicit function of x. To find the relationship between the rates of change of the x-coordinate $\frac{dx}{dt}$ and the y-coordinate $\frac{dy}{dt}$, take the derivative of each side of the equation with respect to t.

EXAMPLE 2

Suppose a particle moves along a circle with equation $x^2 + y^2 = 25$. If the particle is at the point $(-4, 3)$ and the y-coordinate is increasing so that $\frac{dy}{dt} = 2$ units/sec, find the rate of change of x-coordinate $\frac{dx}{dt}$.

Solution To find the rates of change of the x-coordinate $\frac{dx}{dt}$ and the y-coordinate $\frac{dy}{dt}$, find the derivative of the equation with respect to t as follows:

$$\frac{d}{dt}(x^2 + y^2) = \frac{d}{dt}(25).$$

This gives us the result:

$$\frac{d}{dt}(x^2) + \frac{d}{dt}(y^2) = \frac{d}{dt}(25) \text{ or,}$$

$$\frac{d}{dt}(x^2) \cdot \frac{dx}{dt} + \frac{d(y^2)}{dy} \cdot \frac{dy}{dt} = 0$$

Thus, we have $2x\frac{dx}{dt} + 2y\frac{dy}{dt} = 0$, or $x\frac{dx}{dt} + y\frac{dy}{dt} = 0$.

Substituting the values of x, y, and $\frac{dy}{dt}$, we find that:

$$-4\frac{dx}{dt} + 3(2) = 0, \text{ and } \frac{dx}{dt} = \frac{3}{2} \text{ units/sec.}$$

Exercises

Multiple-Choice Questions
No calculator is allowed for these questions.

1. A pebble is thrown into a pond forming ripples whose radius increases at the rate of 4 in./second. How fast is the area of the ripple changing when the radius is one foot?
   (A) 2π in.²/sec
   (B) 24π in.²/sec
   (C) $\frac{2\pi}{3}$ ft²/sec
   (D) 2π ft²/sec
   (E) 8π ft²/sec

2. A piece of ice cut in the shape of a cube melts uniformly so that its volume decreases at 3 cm³/sec. How fast is its surface area decreasing when the edge of the cube is 5 cm?
   (A) $\frac{12}{25}$ cm²/sec
   (B) 2.4 cm²/sec
   (C) 3 cm²/sec
   (D) 6 cm²/sec
   (E) 150 cm²/sec

3. A 20-foot ladder leans against the wall of a building. The ladder starts sliding down the wall so that the top of the ladder moves down at the rate of 0.5 ft/sec. How fast is the foot of the ladder moving away from the wall when the foot of the ladder is 12 feet from the wall?

(A) 0.5 ft/sec

(B) $\frac{5}{8}$ ft/sec

(C) $\frac{2}{3}$ ft/sec

(D) $\frac{4}{3}$ ft/sec

(E) $\frac{8}{3}$ ft/sec

4. A spherical balloon is filled with air at 8 in.³/sec. How fast is the diameter of the balloon increasing when the volume of the balloon is 36π in.³?

(A) $\frac{4}{9\pi}$ in./sec

(B) $\frac{2}{3\pi}$ in./sec

(C) $\frac{2}{9\pi}$ in./sec

(D) $\frac{8}{27\pi}$ in./sec

(E) $\frac{2}{27\pi}$ in./sec

Free-Response Questions
A graphing calculator is required for some questions.

1. A conical paper cup (vertex down) is being filled with water at the rate of 3 cm³/sec. If the depth of the water is always twice the radius at the surface, find the following:

(a) How fast is the radius increasing when the water is 2 cm deep?

(b) How fast is the area of the surface of the water increasing when the water is 2 cm deep?

2. A coffee maker has a filter holder and filter in the shape of a cone with radius 5 cm. 500 cm³ of water are poured into the filter holder. Brewed coffee drips out of the cone at the rate of 20 cm³/min into a cylindrical coffee pot that has the same radius as the filter holder.

(a) Find a formula for the rate of change of the depth of the coffee in the coffee pot.

(b) What is the final depth of the coffee in the coffee pot?

BC 4.12 Derivatives of Parametric Equations

In systems of parametric equations, the *x*- and *y*-coordinates of a point are given in terms of another variable called the parameter, often denoted by the letter *t*. To find the derivative $\frac{dy}{dx}$, use the formula $\frac{dy}{dx} = \frac{\frac{dy}{dt}}{\frac{dx}{dt}}$. The derivative $\frac{dy}{dx}$ is defined for values of *t* where $\frac{dy}{dt}$ exists. The components of the velocity are $(x'(t), y'(t))$.

EXAMPLE

$x(t) = 3t^2 - 2t$, $y(t) = 6t + 2$.

Find $\frac{dy}{dx}$ at $t = 1$ and the velocity vector at $t = 1$.

Solution $\frac{dy}{dx} = \frac{\frac{dy}{dt}}{\frac{dx}{dt}} = \frac{6}{6t - 2}$.

At $t = 1$, $\frac{dy}{dx} = \frac{6}{4} = \frac{3}{2}$.

The velocity vector is $(6t - 2, 6)$. At $t = 1$, the velocity vector is $(4, 6)$.

Exercises

A graphing calculator is required for these exercises.

Multiple-Choice Questions

For Questions 1 and 2, the motion of a particle is given parametrically by $x(t) = 3t^2 - 3$, $y(t) = 2t + 1$, *for* $t \geq 0$.

1. Find the slope of the tangent at $t = 1$.
   (A) $\dfrac{1}{3}$
   (B) 1
   (C) 2
   (D) 3
   (E) 6

2. Find the speed of the particle at $t = 1$.
   (A) 0.333
   (B) 2.828
   (C) 6.164
   (D) 6.325
   (E) 12

Free-Response Question

Sketch the graph of the system of parametric equations:

$$x(t) = 3 \sin t - 3, \, y(t) = t - 1 \text{ for } 0 \leq t \leq 2\pi.$$

   (a) Sketch the path of the particle, indicating the direction of increasing t.
   (b) Find the position of the particle at $t = 3$.
   (c) Find the velocity of the particle at $t = 3$.
   (d) Find the speed of the particle at $t = 3$.
   (e) Find the slope of the line tangent to the graph at $t = 3$.

Chapter Assessment

Multiple-Choice Questions

A graphing calculator is required for some questions.

1. Find the value(s) of x for which $f(x) = e^x$ is increasing.
   (A) $x > 0$
   (B) all real numbers
   (C) $x < 0$
   (D) $x = 0$
   (E) no values

2. For what part of the interval $[-\pi, \pi]$ is $y = -2 \sin x$ decreasing?
   (A) $\left[-\dfrac{\pi}{2}, \dfrac{\pi}{2} \right]$
   (B) $\left[-\dfrac{\pi}{3}, \dfrac{\pi}{3} \right]$
   (C) $\left[-\dfrac{\pi}{4}, \dfrac{\pi}{4} \right]$
   (D) $[-\pi, 0]$
   (E) $[-\pi, \pi]$

3. For what values of x is $f(x) = -x^2 + 2x$ increasing?
   (A) $x > 0$
   (B) $x < 1$
   (C) $x > 2$
   (D) $x < 2$
   (E) $0 < x < 2$

4. Find the number of horizontal asymptotes of $y = 2 - \ln x$.
   (A) 0
   (B) 1
   (C) 2
   (D) 3
   (E) 4

5. Find the average rate of change of $y = \ln (x^2)$ on the interval $[1, 2]$.
   (A) -1.386
   (B) 0
   (C) 1.386
   (D) 2
   (E) 4

6. Find the value of $\displaystyle\lim_{h \to 0} \dfrac{\tan\left(\dfrac{\pi}{4} + h \right) - \tan\left(\dfrac{\pi}{4} \right)}{h}$.
   (A) -1
   (B) 0
   (C) 1
   (D) 2
   (E) does not exist

7. If $f(x) = x^4 - 4x$, evaluate $\lim_{x \to -1} \dfrac{f(x) - f(-1)}{x + 1}$.

(A) -8
(B) 0
(C) 1
(D) 2
(E) 4

8. $f(x) = \frac{1}{2}(x - 1)^3$. Find $f'(0)$.

(A) -6
(B) -3
(C) $-\dfrac{3}{2}$
(D) $-\dfrac{1}{2}$
(E) $\dfrac{3}{2}$

9. $f(x) = \ln(\sin x)$. Find $f'\left(\dfrac{\pi}{4}\right)$.

(A) $-\dfrac{1}{2}\ln 2$
(B) $\dfrac{\sqrt{2}}{2}$
(C) 0
(D) 1
(E) undefined

10. $y = \sin 2x - x$. Find $y'\left(\dfrac{\pi}{2}\right)$.

(A) -3
(B) -1
(C) 0
(D) 1
(E) undefined

11. $y = 3\tan^2\left(\dfrac{x}{3}\right)$. Find $y'(\pi)$.

(A) 1
(B) $8\dfrac{\sqrt{3}}{3}$
(C) 9
(D) $8\sqrt{3}$
(E) 27

12. $y = \ln(e^{x^2-1})$. Find $y'(1)$.

(A) 0
(B) $\dfrac{1}{2}$
(C) 1
(D) 2
(E) undefined

13. $y = e^{x^3}$. Find $y'(1)$.

(A) $3e^2$
(B) $3e$
(C) e

(D) $\dfrac{1}{e}$
(E) e^3

14. For what values of x is $f(x) = \dfrac{\sin x}{x}$ continuous?

(A) $x \neq 0$
(B) $x > 0$
(C) $x > 1$
(D) $x \geq 1$
(E) all real x

15. For what values of x is $f(x) = \sqrt{(\ln x)^2}$ differentiable?

(A) $x > 0$
(B) $x \geq 1$
(C) $x \neq 0$
(D) $x > 0$ and $x \neq 1$
(E) all real x

16. Find $\dfrac{dy}{dx}$ for $xy + x - y = 2$ when $x = 0$.

(A) -2
(B) -1
(C) 0
(D) 1
(E) 2

17. A particle moves along the y-axis with a motion defined by the equation $s(t) = \dfrac{\ln t}{t}$ for $t > 0$. Find the velocity at $t = 2$.

(A) 0
(B) 0.0767
(C) 0.693
(D) 1
(E) 2

18. Find the derivative of $f(x) = x^2 - \ln x$.

(A) $2x - 1$
(B) $2x - \ln x$
(C) $2x - \dfrac{1}{x}$
(D) $x - \dfrac{1}{x}$
(E) $\dfrac{2x - 1}{x}$

19. Find the second derivative of $\sqrt{(x^2 + 1)}$.

(A) $(x^2 + 1)^{-\frac{3}{2}}$
(B) $(x^2 + 1)^{-\frac{1}{2}}$
(C) $x(x^2 + 1)^{-\frac{1}{2}}$
(D) $2x(x^2 + 1)^{-\frac{3}{2}}$
(E) $2(x^2 + 1)^{-\frac{3}{2}}$

20. Find y'' for $y = x \ln x - 3x$.
   (A) $\frac{1}{x} - 3$
   (B) $1 + \ln x$
   (C) $\ln x - 2$
   (D) $\frac{1}{x}$
   (E) $\frac{1}{x} - 2$

21. Find the slope of the tangent to the graph of $y = \sqrt{(x + 2)}$ at $x = -1$.
   (A) $-\frac{\sqrt{2}}{2}$
   (B) $-\frac{1}{2}$
   (C) $\frac{1}{2}$
   (D) $\frac{\sqrt{2}}{2}$
   (E) undefined

22. Write the equation of the line tangent to the graph of $x = y^2 + 4$ at the point $(5, 1)$.
   (A) $2y = x - 2$
   (B) $2y = x - 3$
   (C) $2y = x + 9$
   (D) $2y = x - 7$
   (E) $x = 5$

23. Write the equation of the line tangent to the graph of $f(x) = \dfrac{1}{(x^2 + 2)}$ at $x = 0$.
   (A) $y = \frac{1}{2}$
   (B) $x = \frac{1}{2}$
   (C) $y = -\frac{16}{81}x + \frac{1}{2}$
   (D) $y = -\frac{1}{2}$
   (E) $y = -\frac{1}{4}x + \frac{1}{2}$

24. Find the equation of the line tangent to $y = \arctan x$ at $x = 1$.
   (A) $x - 2y = 1 - \pi$
   (B) $2x - 4y = 2 - \pi$
   (C) $2x - 4y = \pi - 2$
   (D) $4x - 4y = 4 - \pi$
   (E) $x - 2y = 2 - \pi$

25. $f(x) = \dfrac{1}{x^2}$, $x > 0$. If $g(x)$ is the inverse of $f(x)$, find $g'(2)$.
   (A) $-4\sqrt{2}$
   (B) $-\dfrac{1}{\sqrt{2}}$
   (C) $-\sqrt{2}$
   (D) $-\dfrac{\sqrt{2}}{8}$
   (E) -8

BC *For questions 26 and 27, use* $x(t) = 2t^2$ *and* $y(t) = 4t - 1$.

26. Find the slope of the line tangent to the curve at $t = 1$.
   (A) -4
   (B) $\frac{1}{4}$
   (C) 1
   (D) 4
   (E) undefined

27. Find the equation of the line tangent to the curve at $t = 1$.
   (A) $y = x + 1$
   (B) $y = 4x - 5$
   (C) $y = \frac{1}{4}x + \frac{5}{2}$
   (D) $y = -4x + 11$
   (E) $x = 2$

Free-Response Questions
A graphing calculator is required for some questions.

1. (a) Sketch the graph of $y = \ln x$ on the interval $\left[\frac{1}{e}, e\right]$.

   (b) Write the range of the function on this interval.

   (c) Find the average rate of change of $y = \ln x$ on the interval $\left[\frac{1}{e}, e\right]$.

   (d) Estimate the slope of the graph of $y = \ln x$ at $x = \frac{1}{e}$, $x = 1$, and $x = e$.

   (e) Plot the slopes at the corresponding x-values on a separate graph.

2. Use the standard definition of the derivative to find $f'(x)$ for:

   (a) $f(x) = \dfrac{2}{x+1}$

   (b) $f(x) = x^2 - 2x$

3. Use the fact that $\dfrac{d(\sin x)}{dx} = \cos x$ and $\dfrac{d(\cos x)}{dx} = -\sin x$ to find the derivative of:

   (a) $\tan x$

   (b) $\cot x$

   (c) $\sec x$

   (d) $\csc x$

4. Given $f(x) = \begin{cases} -x, & \text{for } x \geq 1 \\ x + k, & \text{for } x < 1 \end{cases}$:

   (a) Find the value of k so that $f(x)$ will be continuous at $x = 1$.

   (b) Using the value of k found in part (a), is $f(x)$ also differentiable at $x = 1$?

5. What is the minimum initial velocity needed so that a ball thrown upwards from the ground reaches the top of a building 40 feet high?

6. A cylindrical terrarium hanging from the ceiling leaks sand at the rate of 5 cm³/minute. The sand falls to the floor, forming a conical pile. The radius and the height of the cone are in the ratio 3:2. How fast is the height of the pile increasing when the radius is 9 cm?

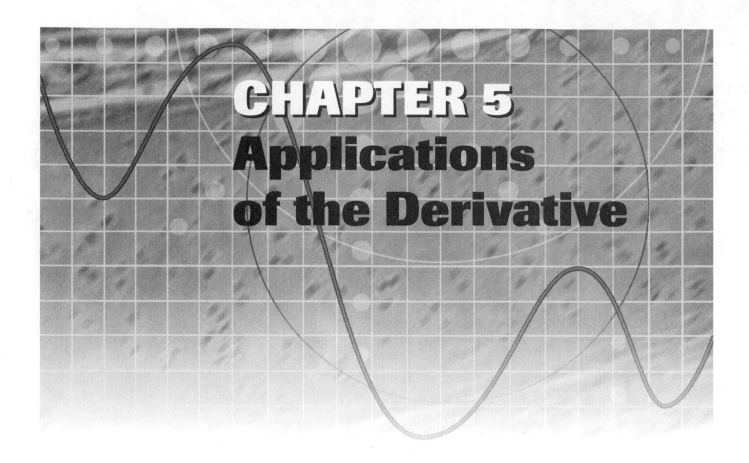

CHAPTER 5
Applications of the Derivative

5.1 Three Theorems: The Extreme Value Theorem, Rolle's Theorem, and the Mean Value Theorem

In this chapter, the rules for finding derivatives outlined in Section 4.4 are applied to analyze the properties of functions. The first derivative of a function helps us find the minimum and maximum values of the function, which may be located at the turning points. These **turning points** allow us to locate the intervals where the function is increasing or decreasing. The second derivative of a function enables us to find the points of inflection of the function and where the function is concave up or concave down. Later in the chapter, we investigate optimization problems and create functions in order to find the largest or the smallest values of the function as required by the problem.

Three theorems are the foundation for these processes: the Extreme Value Theorem, Rolle's Theorem, and the Mean Value Theorem.

The Extreme Value Theorem   A continuous function on a closed interval $[a, b]$ has a maximum value and a minimum value on $[a, b]$.

The Extreme Value Theorem says that any continuous function on a closed interval has a largest and a smallest value on that interval. The largest and smallest values can be located inside the interval or at the endpoints.

Rolle's Theorem   The proof of the Mean Value Theorem uses another theorem called Rolle's Theorem. The idea behind Rolle's Theorem is a simple one:

If

- a function is continuous on a closed interval $[a, b]$, and
- has a derivative on the open interval (a, b), and
- has the same y-value at the endpoints, a and b

Then

There must be at least one value of x, call it c, between a and b where the function has a horizontal tangent.

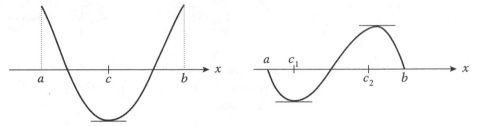

The hypotheses of Rolle's Theorem are that the function $f(x)$ must be continuous on the closed interval $[a, b]$, must have a derivative on the open interval (a, b), and must have $f(a) = f(b)$. The conclusion of Rolle's Theorem is that there is at least one number, call it c, in the open interval (a, b) where $f'(c) = 0$.

EXAMPLE 1

Find the value of c guaranteed by Rolle's Theorem for $f(x) = 1 - x^2$ in the interval $[-1, 1]$.

Solution   First check to see if $f(x)$ satisfies the three conditions.

- Is $f(x)$ is continuous on $[-1, 1]$? Yes.
- Does $f(x)$ have a derivative on $(-1, 1)$? Yes.
- Is $f(-1) = f(1)$? Yes.

Since all three conditions are satisfied, there must be a value c in the open interval $(-1, 1)$ where $f'(c) = 0$.

$$f'(c) = -2c$$

Solving $-2c = 0$, we have $c = 0$. Since 0 lies in the interval $(-1, 1)$, this is the value guaranteed by Rolle's Theorem.

EXAMPLE 2

Does $f(x) = x - x^3$ satisfy the conditions of Rolle's Theorem on the interval $[-1, 1]$?

Solution   Check to see if $f(x)$ satisfies the three conditions of Rolle's Theorem.

- Is $f(x)$ is continuous on $[-1, 1]$? Yes.
- Does $f(x)$ have a derivative on $(-1,1)$? Yes.
- Is $f(-1) = f(1)$? Yes.

Thus, all three conditions are satisfied for $f(x)$.

EXAMPLE 3

Does $f(x) = \sin x$ satisfy the three conditions of Rolle's Theorem on the interval $\left[-\dfrac{\pi}{2}, \dfrac{3\pi}{2} \right]$?

Solution   Check to see if $f(x)$ satisfies the three conditions.

- Is $f(x)$ is continuous on the interval? Yes.
- Does $f(x)$ have a derivative on the interval? Yes.
- Is $f\left(-\dfrac{\pi}{2}\right) = f\left(\dfrac{3\pi}{2}\right)$? Yes.

Thus, all three conditions of Rolle's Theorem are satisfied.

EXAMPLE 4

Find the value of c guaranteed by Rolle's Theorem for $f(x) = x^3 - 3x^2 + 2$ in the interval $[0, 3]$.

Solution   First check to see if $f(x)$ satisfies the three conditions.

- Is $f(x)$ is continuous on $[0, 3]$? Yes.
- Does $f(x)$ have a derivative on $(0, 3)$? Yes.
- Is $f(0) = f(3)$? Yes.

   Since all three conditions are satisfied, there must be a value c where $f'(c) = 0$.

$$f'(c) = 3c^2 - 6c$$

Solving $3c^2 - 6c = 0$, the solutions are $c = 0$ and $c = 2$.
   Since c must be in the *open* interval $(0, 3)$, $c = 2$ is the only value that satisfies the conclusion of Rolle's Theorem.

The Mean Value Theorem

If
- a function $f(x)$ is continuous on the closed interval $[a, b]$, and
- has a derivative on the open interval (a, b)

Then
If a line AB is drawn joining endpoints $(a, f(a))$ and $(b, f(b))$, there must be at least one value of x in the open interval (a, b), call it c, where the tangent line at $(c, f(c))$ is parallel to line AB. That is, the slope of the tangent to the graph of $f(x)$ at $x = c$ is equal to the slope of line AB.

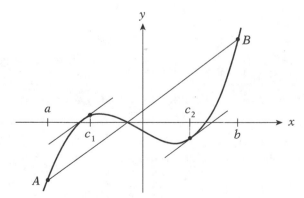

Therefore, if $f(x)$ satisfies the two hypotheses of the Mean Value Theorem, then there is a value of x, call it c, in (a, b) such that $f'(c) = \dfrac{f(b) - f(a)}{b - a}$.

EXAMPLE 5

Show that $f(x) = x^2 - 2x$ satisfies the conditions of the Mean Value Theorem on the closed interval $[-1, 2]$.

Solution   Check to see if $f(x)$ satisfies the two conditions.

- Is $f(x)$ continuous on the closed interval $[-1, 2]$? Yes.
- Does $f(x)$ have a derivative on the open interval $(-1, 2)$? Yes.

Thus, both conditions of the Mean Value Theorem are satisfied.

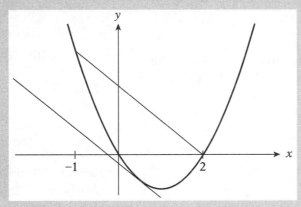

EXAMPLE 6

Find the value of c guaranteed by the Mean Value Theorem for $f(x) = \ln x$ on the closed interval $[1, e^2]$.

Solution   First check to see if $f(x)$ satisfies the two conditions.

- Is $f(x)$ continuous on the closed interval $[1, e^2]$? Yes.
- Does $f(x)$ have a derivative on the open interval $(1, e^2)$? Yes.

Since both conditions are satisfied, there must be a value c where

$$f'(c) = \frac{f(b) - f(a)}{b - a}.$$

That is, $f'(c) = \dfrac{\ln(e^2) - \ln 1}{e^2 - 1}$.

Solving for c, $\dfrac{1}{c} = \dfrac{2}{e^2 - 1}$.

Thus, $c = \dfrac{e^2 - 1}{2} \approx 3.195$, and c is in the open interval $(1, e^2)$.

Exercises

A graphing calculator is required for these exercises. For each function in Exercises 1–4:

(a) Determine if the function satisfies the two hypotheses of the Mean Value Theorem on the indicated interval.

(b) If the function satisfies the hypotheses of the Mean Value Theorem, find the value of $f'(c)$ guaranteed by the theorem on the indicated interval.

1. $f(x) = \dfrac{1}{x}$ on $[1, 3]$

2. $f(x) = \dfrac{x}{x - 2}$ on $[1, 3]$

3. $f(x) = |x - 2|$ on $[1, 3]$

4. $f(x) = x^{2/3}$ on $[0, 1]$

Multiple-Choice Questions

A graphing calculator is required for some questions.

1. Which of the following functions satisfy the hypotheses of Rolle's Theorem on the interval [0, 2]?

   I $f(x) = \dfrac{1}{|x - 1|}$

   II $f(x) = |x - 1|$

   III $f(x) = x^2 - 2x$

   (A) I only
   (B) II only
   (C) III only
   (D) II and III
   (E) I, II, and III

2. Which of the following functions satisfy the hypotheses of the Mean Value Theorem on the interval [0, 2]?

   I $f(x) = \sin \pi x + \cos 2x$

   II $f(x) = \sqrt[3]{x - 8}$

   III $f(x) = |x^2 - 2x|$

   (A) I only
   (B) II only
   (C) III only
   (D) I and II
   (E) I, II, and III

3. At what value(s) of x in the interval [0, 2] is the slope of the line tangent to $f(x) = x^3 - 3x^2$ equal to the slope of the line joining $(0, f(0))$ and $(2, f(2))$?

   (A) 0
   (B) 0.423
   (C) 1.577
   (D) 2
   (E) 0.423 and 1.577

4. Find the absolute minimum value of $f(x) = x^2 - 3x^4$ on the interval [−1, 1].

   (A) −2
   (B) 0

(C) 0.408
(D) 1
(E) There is no absolute minimum on the interval.

5. How many values of c satisfy the conclusion of the Mean Value Theorem for $f(x) = x^3 + 1$ on the interval [−1, 1]?

   (A) 0
   (B) 1
   (C) 2
   (D) 3
   (E) 4

6. How many values of c are guaranteed by Rolle's Theorem for the function $f(x) = \dfrac{\sin x}{x}$ on the interval [−10, 10]?

   (A) 4
   (B) 5
   (C) 6
   (D) 7
   (E) The theorem does not apply.

Free-Response Questions

A graphing calculator is required for some questions.

1. Find the value(s) of c guaranteed by Rolle's Theorem for $f(x) = x \sin x$ on the interval [−3, 3].

2. (a) Find the value of c guaranteed by the Mean Value Theorem for $f(x) = e^x - x$ on the interval [−2, 2].

   (b) Using the DRAW menu on the calculator (2nd DRAW 5: Tangent), draw a line tangent to the graph of $f(x) = e^x - x$ at the value of c found in part (a). Then go to 2nd DRAW 2: Line, and draw a line joining $(-2, f(-2))$ and $(2, f(2))$.

   (c) Write a sentence describing the tangent line and the line joining the endpoints of the curve.

5.2 Critical Values

When Is a Function Increasing or Decreasing?

The Mean Value Theorem leads to the following conclusions:

- When the first derivative of a function is positive, the function is increasing.

- When the first derivative of a function is negative, the function is decreasing.

Note: The converses of the two statements above are not true.

If a function is increasing, its first derivative may be positive or it may be zero. For example, by the definition of an increasing function, $f(x) = x^3$ is strictly increasing. Yet its first derivative is zero at $x = 0$.

What Are Critical Values and How Do We Find Them?

Critical values, first introduced in Section 4.1, are values in the domain of a function where its derivative is zero or is undefined. Critical values are candidates for the x-coordinates of the high and low points on the function. The corresponding y-coordinates of these points may be **relative maxima** (the high points) or **relative minima** (the low points) of the function. Together these y-values are called **relative extrema** of the function.

The First Derivative Test

Once the critical values have been found, use the following procedure to determine whether each critical number is a relative maximum, a relative minimum, or neither. Draw a number line, mark the number line f', and put the critical numbers on it. Next to the number line, make a table of values of x and f'. The x-values in the table are values to the left of, in between, and to the right of the critical numbers on the number line. The corresponding values in the f' column can be found by hand or by using TABLE in the calculator.

Using the numbers in the f' column, find the sign changes for each critical number. These sign changes determine the nature of each critical number. This is called the **First Derivative Test.**

The First Derivative Test

- If the sign of f' changes from positive to negative at a critical value, then f has a relative maximum at that value of x.

- If the sign of f' changes from negative to positive at a critical value, then f has a relative minimum at that value of x.

- If f' does not change sign at a critical value, then there is neither a relative minimum nor a relative maximum at that value of x.

After drawing the number line and completing the table of values of x and f', use the First Derivative Test to write a statement that identifies each critical value as a relative maximum, a relative minimum, or neither. This written statement is an important step in the justification of an answer.

EXAMPLE 1

(No Calculator)
(a) Find the critical values of $f(x) = x^3 + 3x^2 + 4$, and identify each as a relative maximum, a relative minimum, or neither. Justify your answer.
(b) State the intervals where f is increasing.

Solution

(a) The derivative of $f(x) = 3x^2 + 6x$. To solve for the critical values, set the derivative equal to zero and solve for x:

$$3x^2 + 6x = 0$$
$$3x(x + 2) = 0$$
$$x = 0 \text{ or } x = -2$$

Thus, 0 and -2 are the critical values of $f(x)$.

The next step is to put the critical values on a number line labeled f', and choose values of x and f' for the table that are to the left of, in between, and to the right of the critical values.

x	$f'(x) = 3x^2 + 6x$
-3	$3(-3)^2 + 6(-3) = 9$
-1	$3(-1)^2 + 6(-1) = -3$
1	$3(1)^2 + 6(1) = 9$

Now mark the intervals on the number line with a $+$ sign or a $-$ sign as shown:

Using the First Derivative Test, we conclude the following:

- Since f' changes from $+$ to $-$ at $x = -2$, $f(-2)$ is a relative maximum.
- Since f' changes from $-$ to $+$ at $x = 0$, $f(0)$ is a relative minimum.

(b) Since f' is positive on the intervals to the left of -2 and to the right of 0, f is increasing on the intervals $(-\infty, -2)$ and $(0, \infty)$.

EXAMPLE 2

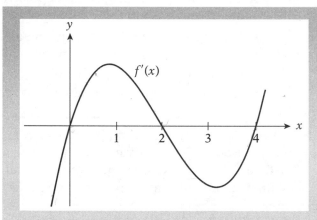

(a) The graph shown is the graph of f', the derivative of f. Using the graph, find the critical values of f, and identify each as a relative maximum, a relative minimum, or neither. Justify your answer.
(b) Use the graph of f' to state the intervals where f is increasing.

Solution

(a) Since $f'(x) = 0$ at $x = 0$, $x = 2$, and $x = 4$, these are the critical values of $f(x)$. Put these values on a number line and label it f'.

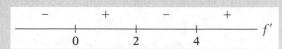

While we cannot make a table of values of x and f' as in the previous example, we can see the following from the graph of f':

- For values of x to the left of 0, f' is negative.

- For values of x between 0 and 2, f' is positive.
- For values of x between 2 and 4, f' is negative.
- For values of x to the right of 4, f' is positive.

Thus, by the First Derivative Test we arrive at the following conclusions:

- Since f' changes from $-$ to $+$ at $x = 0$, $f(0)$ is a relative minimum.
- Since f' changes from $+$ to $-$ at $x = 2$, $f(2)$ is a relative maximum.
- Since f' changes from $-$ to $+$ at $x = 4$, $f(4)$ is a relative minimum.

(b) Since f' is positive on the intervals between 0 and 2, and to the right of 4, f is increasing on the intervals $(0, 2)$ and $(4, \infty)$.

EXAMPLE 3

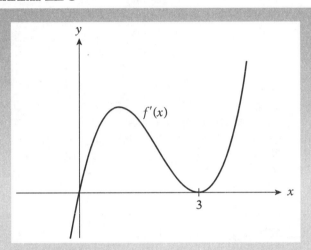

(a) Given the graph of f' above, find the critical values of f and identify each as a relative maximum, a relative minimum, or neither. Justify your answer.
(b) Use the graph of f' to find the intervals where the graph of f is increasing.

Solution

(a) Since $f' = 0$ at $x = 0$ and $x = 3$, these are the critical values of f.
(b) Put the critical values on a number line and label it f'.

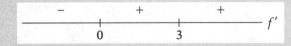

While we cannot make a table of values of x and f' as in the previous example, we can look at the graph of f' and arrive at the following conclusions.

- For values of x to the left of 0, f' is negative.
- For values of x between 0 and 3, f' is positive.
- For values of x to the right of 3, f' is positive.

Thus, by the First Derivative Test,

- Since f' changes from $-$ to $+$ at $x = 0$, $f(0)$ is a relative minimum.
- Since f' does not change sign at $x = 3$, $f(3)$ is neither a relative maximum nor a relative minimum.

EXAMPLE 4

(No Calculator)
(a) Find the critical values of $f(x) = \sin(x) + \cos(x)$ on the interval $[0, 2\pi]$.
(b) Identify each critical value as a relative maximum, a relative minimum, or neither. Justify your answer.
(c) State the intervals where f is increasing on the interval $[0, 2\pi]$.
(d) Find the absolute maximum and the absolute minimum of $f(x)$ on $[0, 2\pi]$.

Solution

(a) To find the critical values, set the derivative equal to zero and solve for x. The derivative of $f(x)$ is $f'(x) = \cos(x) - \sin(x)$. Setting this equation equal to zero and solving for x on $[0, 2\pi]$:

$$\cos(x) = \sin(x)$$

$$x = \frac{\pi}{4} \text{ or } \frac{5\pi}{4}.$$

Therefore, $\frac{\pi}{4}$ and $\frac{5\pi}{4}$ are the critical values for $f(x)$.

(b) Put the critical values on a number line labeled f', and choose values for the table of x and f' that are to the left, in between, and to the right of the critical values. Notice that the endpoints of the interval are also marked on the number line.

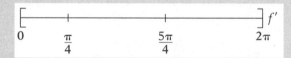

x	$f'(x) = \cos x - \sin x$
$\frac{\pi}{6}$	0.366
π	-1
$\frac{3\pi}{2}$	1

Marking the intervals on the number line with $+$ or $-$, according to the value of f' in the table, the number line should now look like this:

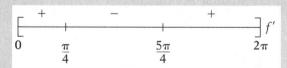

Thus, by the First Derivative Test:

• Since f' changes from $+$ to $-$ at $x = \frac{\pi}{4}$, $f\left(\frac{\pi}{4}\right)$ is a relative maximum.

• Since f' changes from $-$ to $+$ at $x = \frac{5\pi}{4}$, $f\left(\frac{5\pi}{4}\right)$ is a relative minimum.

(c) Since f' is positive on the intervals between 0 and $\frac{\pi}{4}$ and between $\frac{5\pi}{4}$ and 2π, f is increasing on the intervals $\left(0, \frac{\pi}{4}\right)$ and $\left(\frac{5\pi}{4}, 2\pi\right)$.

(d) Evaluating the critical values and the endpoints, we see that the absolute maximum of f is $\sqrt{2}$ at $x = \frac{\pi}{4}$, and the absolute minimum of f is $-\sqrt{2}$ at $x = \frac{5\pi}{4}$.

	x	$f(x) = \sin x + \cos x$
Critical Points	$\frac{\pi}{4}$	$\sqrt{2}$
	$\frac{5\pi}{4}$	$-\sqrt{2}$
Endpoints	0	1
	2π	1

EXAMPLE 5

(No Calculator)
(a) Find the critical values of $f(x) = e^x - x$.
(b) Identify each critical value as a relative maximum, a relative minimum, or neither. Justify your answer.
(c) State the intervals where f is increasing.

Solution

(a) To find the critical values, set the derivative equal to zero and solve for x. The derivative of $f(x)$ is $f'(x) = e^x - 1$. Setting this equation equal to zero and solving for x:

$$e^x - 1 = 0$$
$$e^x = 1$$
$$x = 0.$$

(b) Put the critical value on a number line labeled f', and choose values for the table of x and f' that are to the left of and to the right of the critical value.

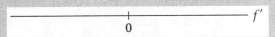

x	$f'(x) = e^x - 1$
-1	-0.632
1	1.718

Marking the intervals on the number line with $+$ or $-$, according to the value of f' in the table, the number line should now look like this:

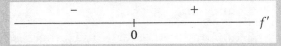

Thus, by the First Derivative Test we conclude that since f' changes from $-$ to $+$ at $x = 0$, $f(0)$ is a relative minimum.
(c) Since f' is positive to the right of 0, f is increasing on the interval $(0, \infty)$.

EXAMPLE 6

Find the absolute maximum and absolute minimum values of $f(x) = x^3 + 2x^2 + x$ on the interval $[-2, 1]$.

Solution   The critical values of f are -1 and $-\frac{1}{3}$. On the graphing calculator, use [2nd] TABLE to find y-values at the critical values and the endpoints of the interval.

	x	$f(x) = x^3 + 2x^2 + x$
Critical Points	-1	0
	$-\frac{1}{3}$	-0.1481
Endpoints	-2	-2
	1	4

Examining the values of the function, we see that the greatest y-value, and therefore the absolute maximum, is 4. The least y-value, and therefore the absolute minimum, is -2.

EXAMPLE 7

Find the absolute maximum and the absolute minimum of $f(x) = x^4 - 3x^2 + 5$ on the interval $[-2, 2]$.

Solution   The critical values of f are 0 and ± 1.225. Next, we must examine the y-values at the critical values and the endpoints.

	x	$f(x) = x^4 + 3x^2 + 5$
Critical Points	0	5
	-1.225	2.75
	1.225	2.75
Endpoints	-2	-9
	2	9

Thus, on the interval $[-2, 2]$, the absolute maximum of f is 0 and the absolute minimum of f is 2.75.

EXAMPLE 8

Repeat Example 7 for the following intervals:
(a) $[-1, 1]$
(b) $[0, 2]$

Solution

(a) On the interval $[-1, 1]$, there is only one critical value, $x = 0$. The absolute maximum of f is 5 and the absolute minimum is 3.
(b) On the interval $[0, 2]$, the absolute maximum of f is 9 and the absolute minimum of f is 2.75.
Note: Examples 7 and 8 demonstrate that the absolute extrema depend on the interval given.

EXAMPLE 9

Find the absolute extrema of $f(x) = \ln x - 2x - 5$ on $[0.3, 1]$.

Solution The critical number is $x = 0.5$.

	x	$f(x) = \ln x - 2x - 5$
Critical Points	0.5	-6.693
Endpoints	0.3	-6.804
	1	-7

Thus, the absolute maximum of f is -6.693 and the absolute minimum is -7.

Exercises

Multiple-Choice Questions

No calculator is allowed for Questions 1–4.

1. The critical values of $f(x) = 9x^4 + 16x^3 + 6x^2 + 7$ are at $x =$
   (A) 0 only
   (B) -1 and 0
   (C) -1 and $-\frac{1}{3}$
   (D) -1, $-\frac{1}{3}$, and 0
   (E) $-\frac{1}{3}$ only

2. The function $f(x) = e^x - x + 2$ has
   (A) a relative minimum at $(0, 3)$
   (B) a relative minimum at $(0, 0)$
   (C) a relative maximum at $(0, 3)$
   (D) two critical values
   (E) a relative minimum at $(0, 0)$ and a relative maximum at $(0, 3)$

3. The absolute minimum of $f(x) = x^2 - 2x + 3$ on the interval $[0, 5]$ is
   (A) -1
   (B) 0
   (C) 1
   (D) 2
   (E) 15

4. The relative minimum of the function $f(x) = 2x^3 - \frac{5}{2}x^2 - 4x + 2$ on the interval $[-1, 2]$ is at $x =$
   (A) -1
   (B) $-\frac{1}{2}$
   (C) $\frac{4}{3}$
   (D) $\frac{5}{3}$
   (E) 2

For Questions 5–8, a graphing calculator is required.

5. The absolute maximum of $y = \dfrac{x}{x^2 - 1}$ on the interval $[2, 4]$ is
   (A) 0
   (B) $\frac{4}{15}$
   (C) $\frac{2}{3}$
   (D) 2
   (E) 4

6. Find the relative minimum value of $f(x) = 3x^4 - 5x^2$ on the interval $[-3, 0]$.
   (A) -2.083
   (B) -2
   (C) -1
   (D) 0
   (E) 0.913

7. On the interval $[-\pi, \pi]$, the function $f(x) = 2\cos x - \sin 2x$ has
   (A) one relative maximum and one relative minimum
   (B) one relative maximum and two relative minima
   (C) two relative maxima and one relative minimum
   (D) only a relative maximum
   (E) only a relative minimum

8. The number of critical points of the function $f(x) = -x \sin x$ on $[-6, 6]$ is
(A) 2
(B) 3
(C) 4
(D) 5
(E) an infinite number

Free-Response Questions

A graphing calculator is required for some questions.

1. A function $f(x)$ with domain all real numbers has critical values at $x = 1, 2,$ and 3. The number line shows the sign of $f'(x)$ on intervals between and outside these critical values. Use the number line to answer the following questions. Justify your conclusions.

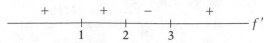

(a) At what value(s) of x does $f(x)$ have a relative maximum? a relative minimum?
(b) On what intervals is $f(x)$ increasing? decreasing?

2. (a) Find the critical values of $f(x) = x^3 - x$ on the interval $[-1, 1]$.
(b) At which critical values in $[-1, 1]$ does $f(x)$ have a relative maximum? a relative minimum?
(c) Find the absolute maximum and absolute minimum values of $f(x)$ on $[-1, 8]$.

3. Repeat Question 2 for $f(x) = x^{2/3} - 1$ on the interval $[-1, 8]$.

5.3 Concavity and the Second Derivative

The first derivative of a function helps determine the absolute extrema and tells where the function is increasing or decreasing. The second derivative of a function tells us about the shape of the curve, about its **concavity.**

Consider the two curves below. In the figure on the left, the slopes of the tangent lines change from negative to zero to positive (looking from left to right). Thus, the slope of the tangent, which is the derivative of $f(x), f'(x)$, is increasing. When a function is increasing, *its* derivative is positive. That is, when $f'(x)$ is increasing, the derivative of $f'(x), f''(x)$, is positive. This type of shape is called **concave up.** Even if we see only a small part of this graph, the shape is still called concave up.

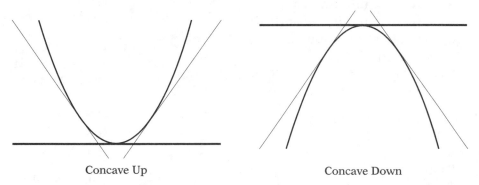

Concave Up   Concave Down

In the figure on the right, the slopes of the tangent lines change from positive to zero to negative (looking from left to right). Thus, the slope of the tangent, which is $f'(x)$, is decreasing. When a function is decreasing, *its* derivative is negative. That is, when $f'(x)$ is decreasing, the derivative of $f'(x)$, or $f''(x)$, is negative. This type of shape is called **concave down.** Even if we see only a small part of this graph, the shape is still called concave down.

Note: For graphs that are *concave up*, tangent lines lie *below* the graph. For graphs that are *concave down*, tangent lines lie *above* the graph.

In the graph on the left that is concave up, this would be the shape of a curve at a point where there is a relative minimum. In the graph on the right that is concave down, it appears that this would be the shape of a curve at a point where there is a relative maximum. This is the essence of the Second Derivative Test.

The Second Derivative Test

If c is a critical number of $f(x)$, and

$f''(c) > 0$, then there is a relative minimum at c.
$f''(c) < 0$, then there is a relative maximum at c.
$f''(c) = 0$, then there is no conclusion possible.

Note: The Second Derivative Test is easy to use, but it is also limiting since there is no conclusion when the second derivative is zero. In that case, use the First Derivative Test, which can be applied in every case.

Points of Inflection Points where the concavity of a function changes are called **points of inflection.** Points of inflection are at values in the domain of the function where the second derivative changes sign from + to − or from − to +.

To find points of inflection, find the second derivative and solve for the values of x where the second derivative is either zero or undefined. Call these x-values PPI's (possible points of inflection). Next draw a number line and put these values of x on it. Then make a table of values of x and $f''(x)$. Choose values of x on the number line that are to the left of, between, and to the right of the PPI's, and list them in the table. The corresponding values of $f''(x)$ can be found by hand or by using TABLE in the calculator.

If the sign of f'' changes around the x-values on the number line, then that value of x is a point of inflection.

The justification for determining which of these x-values is a point of inflection is to use the number line and the table to show whether or not the sign of f'' changes.

EXAMPLE 1

(No Calculator)
Find the points of inflection of $f(x) = x^3 + 3x^2 + 4$.

Solution $f'(x) = 3x^2 + 6x$ and $f''(x) = 6x + 6$. Since $f''(x)$ is never undefined, find the points of inflection by solving $f''(x) = 0$:

$$6x + 6 = 0, \text{ and } x = -1.$$

Thus the point of inflection for $f(x)$ is $(-1, 6)$.

Note: In a previous example, we found that the critical numbers for this function were $x = 0$ and $x = -2$. It is not difficult to prove that if a cubic polynomial has a relative maximum and a relative minimum, the point of inflection is the midpoint of the line segment joining the relative maximum and the relative minimum. This is a convenient shortcut when working with cubic polynomials.

EXAMPLE 2

Find the x-coordinates of the points of inflection of $f(x)$ given the graph of $f'(x)$ shown below.

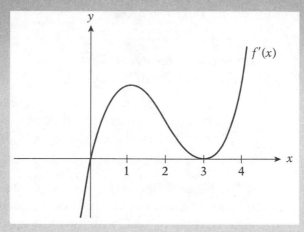

Solution   The x-coordinates of the possible points of inflection of $f(x)$ are the values of x where $f''(x) = 0$ or where $f''(x)$ is undefined. On the graph of $f'(x)$, these are the values of x where the derivative of $f'(x)$ is zero or undefined. Looking for points where there is a tangent line whose slope is zero or undefined, we find the values $x = 1$ and $x = 3$. These are x-coordinates of the points of inflection of $f(x)$.

EXAMPLE 3

(No Calculator)
Find the coordinates of the points of inflection of $f(x) = \sin(x) + \cos(x)$ for values of x in the interval $[0, 2\pi]$.

Solution   To find the x-coordinates of the PPI's of $f(x)$ since f'' is never undefined, find solutions to $f''(x) = 0$. $f'(x) = \cos(x) - \sin(x)$, and $f''(x) = -\sin(x) - \cos(x)$.

Solving $f''(x) = 0$ on $[0, 2\pi]$, we have

$$-\sin(x) - \cos(x) = 0$$

$$\sin(x) = -\cos(x)$$

$$x = \frac{3\pi}{4} \text{ and } \frac{7\pi}{4}.$$

Thus, the points of inflection of $f(x)$ are $\left(\frac{3\pi}{4}, 0\right)$ and $\left(\frac{7\pi}{4}, 0\right)$.

EXAMPLE 4

(No Calculator)
Find the coordinates of the points of inflection of $f(x) = e^x - x$.

Solution

To find the x-coordinates of the PPI's of $f(x)$ since f'' is never undefined, find solutions to $f''(x) = 0$.

$$f'(x) = e^x - 1 \quad \text{and} \quad f''(x) = e^x$$

Setting $f''(x) = 0$, we have $e^x = 0$. Since there are no solutions to this equation, $f(x)$ has no points of inflection. Since $f(x)$ has no points of inflection, its graph is either always concave up or always concave down. The second derivative $f''(x) = e^x$ is always positive; therefore, $f(x)$ is always concave up.

Exercises

Multiple-Choice Questions

A graphing calculator is required for some questions.

1. On what interval is $f(x) = x^3 + x$ concave down?
   (A) $(-\infty, \infty)$
   (B) $(0, \infty)$
   (C) $(-\infty, 0)$
   (D) $(0, 1)$
   (E) $(-1, 0)$

2. The x-coordinate(s) of the point(s) of inflection of $f(x) = \dfrac{x}{x^2 + 1}$ is (are)
   (A) 0
   (B) ± 1
   (C) $\pm\sqrt{3}$
   (D) 0 and $\pm\sqrt{3}$
   (E) no points of inflection

3. On what parts of the interval $[-2, 2]$ is the graph of $f(x) = x \sin x^2$ concave up?
   (A) $(0, 1)$
   (B) $(0, 0.994)$
   (C) $(-1, 1)$
   (D) $(-0.994, 0.994)$
   (E) $(0, 0.994)$ and $(-2, -0.994)$

4. On what interval is the graph of $f(x) = \ln(x^2 + 1)$ concave up?
   (A) $(0, 1)$
   (B) $(-1, 1)$
   (C) $(-0.5, 0.5)$
   (D) $\left(-\dfrac{\sqrt{3}}{3}, \dfrac{\sqrt{3}}{3}\right)$
   (E) The graph is never concave up.

Free-Response Questions

A graphing calculator is required for some questions.

1. Sketch $f(x) = |x^2 - 2x|$ and
   (a) Identify critical values of the function.
   (b) Find the relative extrema and justify your conclusion.
   (c) Find the intervals where the function is concave up and concave down.

2. Sketch $f(x) = e^{-x^2}$ and state
   (a) the domain and range
   (b) asymptotes
   (c) whether the function is even, odd, or neither
   (d) the critical values
   (e) relative extrema
   (f) absolute extrema
   (g) points of inflection
   (h) intervals where the graph is concave up

3. Draw the graph of a function that has the following properties:
   - the function is continuous for all real numbers
   - the function is odd
   - there are two points of inflection
   - $y = 0$ is a horizontal asymptote
   - the relative maximum = the absolute maximum
   - the relative minimum = the absolute minimum

5.4 Curve Sketching and the Graphing Calculator

With the introduction of the graphing calculator, the focus of curve sketching has changed. In the past, a function was given, and students found its first and second derivatives, its critical values, its relative extrema, and its points of inflection, and then used this information to sketch the graph of the function. More often now the function is first graphed in a graphing calculator, and then students find its derivatives, its critical values, its relative extrema, and its points of inflection algebraically to support the graph they see in the window. In addition, the basics of a function, domain, range, asymptotes, and intercepts (if any), are included in stating the properties of a function. This is a good time to review some of these topics and incorporate them in a unified approach to graphing.

It may seem that graphing a function first leaves little else to be done, but a graph is only one representation of a function. The graphing calculator is a tool, and being able to use it effectively requires an understanding of the theorems and procedures that are fundamental to the study of calculus. Furthermore, the calculator does not always show the true function, and may even mislead or give erroneous information about a function. These calculator discrepancies emphasize the fact that the graph does not stand alone: the mathematical processes that truly describe a function, ones that use the first and second derivatives, must support it. The developers of AP Calculus Examination questions are aware of this. While the calculator is required on about half of the exam, students earn credit by demonstrating an understanding of mathematics, not for their ability to press buttons.

EXAMPLE 1

Graph $y = x\sqrt{4 - x}$ in different windows, and use the graph to find its x-intercepts.

Solution   In the TI-83, graph y in [ZOOM] 4 and [ZOOM] 6 windows.

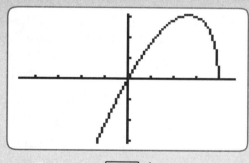

[ZOOM] 4

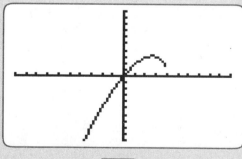

[ZOOM] 6

In [ZOOM] 4, the graph appears to touch the x-axis at $x = 4$, while in [ZOOM] 6, the graph does not appear to touch the x-axis at $x = 4$. This disparity is easily resolved by looking at the function and solving for the x-intercepts. Solving $y = 0$, the x-intercepts are $x = 0$ and $x = 4$. Thus, $x = 4$ is one of the x-intercepts though the calculator may not show this.

In the TI-89, the graph does not appear to touch the x-axis at $x = 4$ using either [ZOOM] 4 or [ZOOM] 6.

Calculator Note

The different appearances of the graphs in Example 1 are due to the number of pixels in the screen of the calculator. In ZOOM 4, or ZOOM Decimal, the pixels are located at decimal values of x. Since 4 is equal to 4.0, this value appears on the graph in ZOOM 4. In ZOOM 6, the pixels are not located at decimal values of x. Thus $x = 4$ does not appear on the graph.

EXAMPLE 2

Find the derivative of $y = |x|$ at $x = 0$.

Solution   Using the definition of the derivative, find the limit

$$\lim_{h \to 0} \frac{|0 + h| - |0|}{h} = \lim_{h \to 0} \frac{|h|}{h}.$$

If h approaches 0 from the right, then h is positive, $|h| = h$, and the limit from the right equals

$$\lim_{h \to 0^+} \frac{h}{h} = 1.$$

If h approaches 0 from the left, then h is negative, $|h| = -h$, and the limit from the left equals

$$\lim_{h \to 0^-} \frac{-h}{h} = -1.$$

Since the limits from the right and left are not the same, the limit as h approaches 0 does not exist, and therefore, the derivative of $|x|$ does not exist at $x = 0$.

In the TI-83, use the numerical derivative nDeriv (press MATH 8) to find the derivative of $|x|$ at $x = 0$. The syntax for nDeriv is nDeriv(function, variable, value). Thus, the numerical derivative of $|x|$ at $x = 0$ should be nDeriv($|x|$, x, 0). The TI-83 gives the value 0, which is incorrect.

In the TI-89, calculate the derivative using the derivative d(2nd 8) key. The syntax to find the derivative at $x = 0$ is d(function, variable)$|x = 0$. Entering d(abs(x), x)$|x = 0$ gives the answer ± 1, indicating that the values of the limit from the left and right are unequal. Therefore, there is no limit and hence no value for the derivative of $y = |x|$ at $x = 0$.

EXAMPLE 3

Sketch the graph of a function with the following properties:

- a vertical asymptote at $x = 1$
- a horizontal asymptote at $y = 2$
- $f'(x) < 0$ for $x < 1$
- $f'(x) < 0$ for $x > 1$

Solution

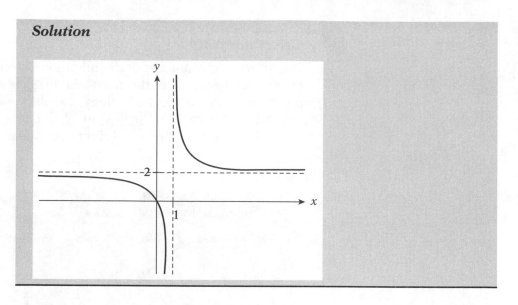

EXAMPLE 4

Enter the function $f(x) = \dfrac{9 - x^2}{3 - x}$ into Y= and sketch the graph. State the domain and range of the function, and give equations of asymptotes (if any).

Solution   In the TI-83, the graph of the function appears to be a straight line. If the graph is in the ZOOM 4 window, press ZOOM Fit and use TRACE to confirm that there is a gap at $x = 3$.

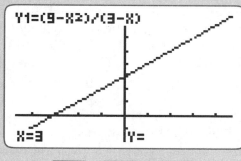

Looking closely, we see a gap at $x = 3$.

ZOOM 4 ZOOM Fit TRACE

If the graph is in the ZOOM 6 window, no gap will appear.

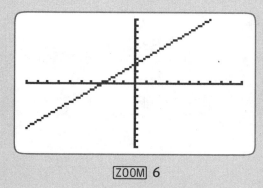

ZOOM 6

In the TI-89, the graph of the function appears to be a straight line.

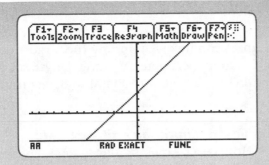

The graph of $f(x)$ is different in each of these windows due to the differences between the calculators and between the two ZOOM windows.

The value of the function at $x = 3$ is $f(3)$, but $f(3) = \frac{0}{0}$, which is an indeterminate quantity. Thus, there is no value of the function at $x = 3$. The domain is $\{x \neq 3\}$ and the range is $\{y \neq 6\}$. Though $x = 3$ makes the denominator zero, it also makes the numerator zero. Therefore, there are no asymptotes to the graph.

Exercises

Multiple-Choice Questions
A graphing calculator is required for some questions.

1. The graph of $y = \ln(x + 2)$ has an asymptote with equation
   (A) $x = -2$
   (B) $y = -2$
   (C) $x = 0$
   (D) $x = 2$
   (E) $y = 2$

2. $y = e^{x-2} - 2$ has which of the following as an asymptote?
   (A) $x = -2$
   (B) $y = -2$
   (C) $x = 0$
   (D) $x = 2$
   (E) $y = 2$

Questions 3 and 4 refer to the graph of the function $f(x) = x^2\sqrt{4 - x^2}$.

3. The critical values of $f(x)$ are
   (A) 0 only
   (B) 0, ±2
   (C) 2 only
   (D) $0, \pm\dfrac{2\sqrt{6}}{3}$
   (E) $\pm\dfrac{8}{3}$

4. The range of $f(x)$ is
   (A) $(0, 3)$
   (B) $[0, 3]$
   (C) $(0, 3.072)$
   (D) $[0, 3.072]$
   (E) $[0, 3.079]$

Free-Response Questions
A graphing calculator is required for some questions.

1. (a) Sketch a function $f(x)$ that is always increasing, is always concave up, and has $f(0) = 1$.
   (b) Sketch a function $f(x)$ that is decreasing and concave down on the interval $[0, 1]$, is decreasing and concave up on the interval $[1, 2]$, and has $f(0) = 1$.
   (c) Sketch a function $f(x)$ that is always increasing, is concave up on the interval $(0, 1)$, is concave down on the interval $(0, 2)$, and has $f(0) = 1$.

2. A function $f(x)$ and its first and second derivatives have values described in the table below. Sketch the graph of $f(x)$.

x	0	(0, 1)	1	(1, 2)	2	(2, 3)	3	(3, 4)	4
f	0		1		0		−1		0
f'		+	undef.	−	0	−	undef.	+	0
f''		+			+	0	−		−

5.5 Optimization

Optimization involves finding the largest or smallest values of a function, such as area, perimeter, volume, length, or time. As with all functions, the domain of the function is vital to determining the solution.

Typical optimization problems ask:

- How large a rectangular area can be enclosed with a fixed amount of fencing?

  In this case, the dimensions of the region are non-negative quantities.

- What is the largest volume that can be enclosed by making a box from a rectangular piece of material?

  In this case, the dimensions of the box are non-negative quantities.

- What is the minimum distance from a given point to a curve?

  In this case, the domain of the distance function is restricted to the domain of the curve given.

  The examples that follow illustrate these problems.

EXAMPLE 1

A rectangular vegetable garden is to be enclosed by 60 feet of fencing. Find the length and width that will give the maximum area.

Solution If the length $= x$ and the width $= y$, then the amount of fencing is represented by the equation $2x + 2y = 60$. Solving this equation for y, we have $y = \dfrac{60 - 2x}{2} = 30 - x$.

Then $A(x) = x(30 - x) = 30x - x^2$.

The dimensions of the rectangle are non-negative quantities. Since $y = 30 - x$ and $y \geq 0$, this means that $x \leq 30$. Thus, the domain of $A(x)$ is $\{0 \leq x \leq 30\}$.

There are two methods of solving for the value of x that will maximize the area function.

METHOD 1 This method uses the fact that the area function is quadratic. Therefore the value of x that will give the maximum value of the function is found by using the formula $x = -\dfrac{b}{2a}$. (This is also the x-coordinate of the vertex of the graph of the area function.)

Thus $x = \dfrac{-30}{-2} = 15$, and $y = 30 - x = 15$.

The rectangle that will give the maximum area is a square. This method requires no justification. Since the area function is a parabola that opens down, the vertex must be a maximum.

METHOD 2 Find the critical points of the derivative of the area function $A(x)$ by finding $A'(x) = 30 - 2x$ and solving $A'(x) = 0$. Thus, $x = 15$ and $y = 30 - x = 15$.

This answer must be justified as the absolute maximum by the First Derivative Test and by checking values at the endpoints.

JUSTIFICATION First, make a number line, mark it A', and put the value $x = 15$ on it along with the endpoints of the domain, $x = 0$ and $x = 30$.

A' ⊢————————+————————————⊣
0   15   30

Now make a table for values of x and A', choosing values of x from the intervals (0, 15) and (15, 30).

x	5	20
A'	+	−

Since A' changes from + to − at $x = 15$, by the First Derivative Test, $x = 15$ is the x-coordinate of a relative maximum. Since $A(0) = 0$, $A(30) = 0$, and $A(15) > 0$, $A(15) = 225$ is the absolute maximum on [0, 30]. Thus, the length and width that give the maximum area are $l = 15$ ft and $w = 15$ ft.

EXAMPLE 2

(Variation of Example 1) A rectangular vegetable garden is to be enclosed using the wall of a building as one side and 60 feet of fencing on the other three sides. Find the length and width that will give the maximum area.

Solution   If the length = x and the width = y, then the amount of fencing is represented by the equation $2x + y = 60$.

The area of the garden is length × width or $A = xy$.

Solving the first equation for y, we have $y = 60 - 2x$.

The area equation can then be rewritten as

$A = x(60 - 2x)$ or $60x - 2x^2$.

Since x and y are the dimensions of the rectangle, $x \geq 0$ and $y \geq 0$. Since $y = 60 - 2x$ and $y \geq 0$, this means that $x \leq 30$. Thus, the domain of $A(x)$ is $\{0 \leq x \leq 30\}$.

METHOD **1**   Use the fact that the area function is quadratic. As described in Method 1, Example 1, $x = \dfrac{-60}{-4} = 15$ and $y = 60 - 2x = 30$.

METHOD **2**   Find the critical points of the derivative of the area function $A(x)$ by finding $A'(x) = 30 - 4x$ and solving $A'(x) = 0$. Thus $x = 15$ and $y = 60 - 2x = 30$.

This answer must be justified as the maximum by the First Derivative Test.

JUSTIFICATION   First, make a number line, mark it A', and put the value $x = 15$ on it along with the endpoints of the domain, $x = 0$ and $x = 30$.

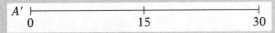
A' ⊢————————+————————————⊣
0   15   30

Now make a table for values of x and A', choosing values of x from the intervals (0, 15) and (15, 30).

x	5	20
A'	+	−

Since A' changes from + to − at $x = 15$, by the First Derivative Test, $x = 15$ is the x-coordinate of a relative maximum. Since $A(0) = 0$, $A(30) = 0$, and $A(15) > 0$, $A(15) = 450$ is the absolute maximum of $A(x)$ on [0, 30]. Thus, the length and width that give the maximum area are: length = 15 ft, width = 30 ft.

EXAMPLE 3

A box is constructed from a square sheet of cardboard 20 inches on a side by cutting out squares of the same size from each of the four corners and turning up the sides. How long should the side of the square be so that the box has the maximum volume?

Solution If the sides of the squares that are cut out have length x, then the length and width of the box are $20 - 2x$, and the volume of the box is $V(x) = x(20 - 2x)(20 - 2x)$.

Since the dimensions of the box are all nonnegative, $x \geq 0$ and $20 - 2x \geq 0$. Thus $x \leq 10$, and the domain of $V(x)$ is $\{0 \leq x \leq 10\}$.

$$V = x(20 - 2x)^2$$
$$V' = (20 - 2x)(20 - 6x)$$

Solving $V' = 0$, $x = 10$ or $x = \frac{10}{3}$.

JUSTIFICATION

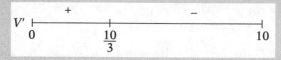

x	V'
1	$+$
4	$-$

The value of V' changes from $+$ to $-$ at $x = \frac{10}{3}$. Thus, $V\left(\frac{10}{3}\right)$ is a relative maximum.

Since $V\left(\frac{10}{3}\right) > 0$, and $V(0) = 0$, and $V(10) = 0$; therefore, $V\left(\frac{10}{3}\right)$ is the absolute maximum of V on $[0, 10]$. The length of the sides of the squares to be cut is $\frac{10}{3}$ inches.

Exercises

Multiple-Choice Questions

A graphing calculator is required for some questions.

1. Two positive numbers have a sum of 10. Find their largest possible product.
   (A) 5
   (B) 10
   (C) 25
   (D) 50
   (E) 100

2. Find the x-coordinate of the point on the graph of $4x + 3y = 7$ that is closest to the origin.
   (A) 0
   (B) 1
   (C) 1.120
   (D) 1.960
   (E) 2.333

3. A rectangle is inscribed in the semicircle $y = \sqrt{4 - x^2}$. Find its largest possible area.
   (A) 1.4
   (B) $\sqrt{3}$
   (C) $2\sqrt{3}$
   (D) 4
   (E) undefined

4. Squares of equal size are cut off the corners of an 8×10 piece of cardboard. The sides are then turned up to form an open box. What is the largest possible volume of the box?
(A) 1.472
(B) 1.5
(C) 23.986
(D) 52.50
(E) 52.514

Free-Response Questions

A graphing calculator is required for some questions.

1. A rectangle is inscribed above the x-axis in the parabola $y = a^2 - x^2$. Find the area of the largest possible rectangle.

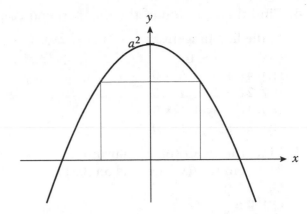

2. A rectangular plot is to be fenced in using the side of an existing barn that is 50 feet long as one side of the plot. Two hundred feet of fencing are available for the other three sides of the plot. Find the largest possible area that can be enclosed.

3. Twenty feet of wire are to be used to create a wire sculpture that consists of a square and a circle. Find the largest number of square feet of area that can be enclosed by the square and the circle.

Chapter Assessment

Multiple-Choice Questions

A graphing calculator is required for some questions.

1. Find the value of c guaranteed by the Mean Value Theorem for $f(x) = \dfrac{2}{x-1}$ on the interval $[3, 5]$.
(A) $1 + 2\sqrt{2}$
(B) $2\sqrt{2}$
(C) $1 + \sqrt{2}$
(D) 2
(E) $1 - 2\sqrt{2}$

2. Which of the following is a hypotheses of Rolle's Theorem *not* satisfied by $f(x) = \dfrac{2}{x-1}$ on the interval $[3, 5]$?
(A) f is continuous on $[3, 5]$.
(B) f is differentiable on $(3, 5)$.
(C) $f(3) = f(5)$
(D) $f'(c) = 0$
(E) $f'(x)$ is defined on $[3, 5]$.

3. Write the equation of the line tangent to $f(x) = \dfrac{2}{x-1}$ at $x = 3$.

(A) $x + 2y = 5$
(B) $x - 2y = 1$
(C) $2x - y = 5$
(D) $2x + y = 7$
(E) $y = 1$

4. Which of the following are true about the function $f(x) = \dfrac{2x}{x^2 + 1}$?
  I $f(x)$ is an odd function.
  II $f(x)$ has a horizontal asymptote.
  III $f(x)$ has a relative maximum at $x = 1$.
(A) I only
(B) II only
(C) I and II only
(D) II and III only
(E) I, II, and III

5. Find the value of c guaranteed by the Mean Value Theorem for $f(x) = \dfrac{2x}{x^2 + 1}$ on the interval $[0, 1]$.
(A) 0.475
(B) 0.486
(C) 0.488
(D) 0.577
(E) 1.000

6. Find the equation of the line perpendicular to the line tangent to $y = 2x - x^2$ at $x = \frac{1}{2}$.
   (A) $4y - 3 = 0$
   (B) $4x + 4y - 5 = 0$
   (C) $2x - 2y - 1 = 0$
   (D) $4x - 4y + 1 = 0$
   (E) $2x + 2y - 1 = 0$

7. Find the value of c guaranteed by Rolle's Theorem for $f(x) = x - x^3$ on $[0, 1]$.
   (A) 0.638
   (B) 0.6
   (C) 0.577
   (D) 0.5
   (E) Rolle's Theorem does not apply.

8. Find the absolute maximum of $f(x) = x - x^3$ on the interval $[-1, 1]$.
   (A) 0.375
   (B) 0.384
   (C) 0.385
   (D) 0.577
   (E) 0.6

9. Find the absolute maximum of $f(x) = x^3$ on the interval $[-1, 3]$.
   (A) -1
   (B) 0
   (C) 3
   (D) 27
   (E) none

10. How many critical values are there for $f(x) = x^3 - e^x$?
   (A) 0
   (B) 1
   (C) 2
   (D) 3
   (E) 4

11. How many points of inflection are there for $f(x) = x^3 - e^x$?
   (A) 0
   (B) 1
   (C) 2
   (D) 3
   (E) 4

12. How many critical values are there for $f(x) = x^3 - 3x^5$?
   (A) 0
   (B) 1
   (C) 2
   (D) 3
   (E) 4

13. How many points of inflection are there for $f(x) = x^3 - 3x^5$?
   (A) 0
   (B) 1
   (C) 2
   (D) 3
   (E) 4

14. If $f(x) = |x - 3| + x^2$, which of the following is true about $f(x)$?
   (A) The function is not continuous and not differentiable at $x = 3$.
   (B) The function is not continuous but differentiable at $x = 3$.
   (C) The function is continuous but not differentiable at $x = 3$.
   (D) The function is continuous and differentiable at $x = 3$.
   (E) $f'(3) = 6$

15. Which of the following is true about the function $f(x) = 9x^3 - \ln x$?
   (A) Its domain is all real numbers.
   (B) It is always concave up.
   (C) It has no relative minima.
   (D) It has one relative maximum.
   (E) It has one point of inflection.

16. Find the interval(s) where $f(x) = -x^4 + 3x^2 - 2$ is greater than zero.
   (A) $(-\infty, -1.225)$ and $(0, 1.225)$
   (B) $\left(-\infty, -\dfrac{\sqrt{6}}{2}\right)$ and $\left(0, \dfrac{\sqrt{6}}{2}\right)$
   (C) $(\sqrt{2}, -1)$ and $(1, \sqrt{2})$
   (D) $(-0.707, 0.707)$
   (E) $(-1.414, -1)$ and $(1, 1.414)$

17. If $f(x) = -x^4 + 3x^2 - 2$, find the interval(s) where $f'(x)$ is greater than zero.
   (A) $(-\infty, -1.225)$ and $(0, 1.225)$
   (B) $\left(-\infty, -\dfrac{\sqrt{6}}{2}\right)$ and $\left(0, \dfrac{\sqrt{6}}{2}\right)$
   (C) $(-\sqrt{2}, -1)$ and $(1, \sqrt{2})$
   (D) $(-0.707, 0.707)$
   (E) $(-1.414, -1)$ and $(1, 1.414)$

18. If $f(x) = -x^4 + 3x^2 - 2$, find the interval(s) where $f''(x)$ is greater than zero.
   (A) $(-\infty, -1.225)$ and $(0, 1.225)$
   (B) $\left(-\infty, -\dfrac{\sqrt{6}}{2}\right)$ and $\left(0, \dfrac{\sqrt{6}}{2}\right)$
   (C) $(-\sqrt{2}, -1)$ and $(1, \sqrt{2})$
   (D) $(-0.707, 0.707)$
   (E) $(-1.414, -1)$ and $(1, 1.414)$

19. If $f(x) = x \sin(x^2)$, which of the following is true?
    (A) There is a relative maximum at $x = 0$.
    (B) There is a relative minimum at $x = 0$.
    (C) There is no point of inflection at $x = 0$.
    (D) $f(2\pi) = 0$
    (E) $f''(0) = 0$

20. Find the coordinates of the point on the curve $y = \frac{1}{x}$ that is closest to the point with coordinates $(0, 3)$.
    (A) $(1, 1)$
    (B) $(0.329, 3.036)$
    (C) $(0.25, 4)$
    (D) $\left(\frac{1}{3}, 3\right)$
    (E) There is no closest point.

21. Which of the following are true for the function $f(x) = 3x^3 - x$?
    I $f(x)$ is an odd function.
    II $f(x)$ has one relative maximum and one relative minimum.
    III Its point of inflection is at $x = 0$.
    (A) I only
    (B) II only
    (C) I and II
    (D) I and III
    (E) I, II, and III

22. Which of the following are true for the function $f(x) = \frac{3x^2}{x - 1}$?
    I   Its domain is all real numbers.
    II Its range is $\{y \le 0\}$.
    III It has two relative extrema.
    (A) I only
    (B) II only
    (C) III only
    (D) I and III
    (E) I, II, and III

23. What is the relative minimum value of $f(x) = x - \ln(\sin(x))$ on the interval $(0, \pi)$?
    (A) 1.132
    (B) 1.136
    (C) 1.768
    (D) 4.798
    (E) 7.415

24. $f(x) = x^2 - 3x^3$ has a point of inflection at
    (A) $x = 0$
    (B) $x = \frac{1}{9}$
    (C) $x = \frac{2}{9}$
    (D) $x = \frac{1}{3}$
    (E) There is no point of inflection.

25. The graph of $f(x) = \ln|x|$ has
    (A) domain $= \{x > 0\}$
    (B) range $= \{y > 0\}$
    (C) range $= \{$all real numbers$\}$
    (D) symmetry with the respect to the origin
    (E) a vertical and a horizontal asymptote

Free-Response Questions
A graphing calculator is required for some questions.

1. (a) Find the value of c guaranteed by the Mean Value Theorem for $y = \cos x$ on the interval $\left[0, \frac{\pi}{2}\right]$.

    (b) Draw a sketch of the graph of $y = \cos x$ on the interval $\left[0, \frac{\pi}{2}\right]$. Draw the line joining the endpoints of the graph and a tangent line at the value of x found in part (a).

2. Given the graph of $f'(x)$ on $[-2, 3]$ as shown:

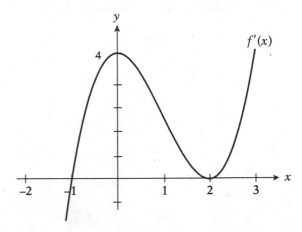

    (a) Find the critical values of $f(x)$ and identify each critical value as a relative maximum, a relative minimum, or neither.
    (b) Find the intervals where $f(x)$ is increasing.
    (c) Find the points of inflection of $f(x)$.
    (d) If $f(0) = 1$, sketch a graph of $f(x)$ on $[-1, 3]$.

3. (a) Sketch the function $f(x) = x - \sin(e^x)$ on the interval $[0, \pi]$.
   (b) Find its critical values and identify each as a relative maximum or a relative minimum.
   (c) State the interval(s) where the function is increasing.
   (d) Find its points of inflection and state the interval(s) where the function is concave up.
   (e) Find the range of the function.

4. (a) Sketch $f(x) = |x| + x \sin(x)$ in the following window:

   Xmin $= -2\pi$ Xmax $= 2\pi$
   Ymin $= -5$ Ymax $= 10$

   (b) Prove that $f(x)$ is an even function.
   (c) Is $f(x)$ continuous at $x = 0$? Explain.
   (d) Does $f'(0)$ exist? Explain.
   (e) Use your calculator to find $f'(0)$. Describe the procedure you use.

5. An archaeologist wishes to enclose a rectangular plot of land in front of a 100-foot long ancient wall and divide the plot into six smaller rectangles as shown. She has 200 feet of fencing with which to enclose the area, and she plans to use the ancient wall as one side, where no fencing will be needed. Find the dimensions of the rectangle that will produce the maximum area.

Ancient Wall

6. A box with a square base is needed to package 100 cm³ of powdered milk. Find the dimensions of the box that will use the minimum amount of material.

7. For the function $f(x) = x^3 - 4x^2 - 4x + 16$:
   (a) Find the critical values of the function.
   (b) Find the points of inflection of the function.
   (c) Find the value of c guaranteed by the Mean Value Theorem on the interval $[0, 2]$.
   (d) Find the absolute extrema on the interval $[0, 4]$.

8. (a) Find the value of a so that
   $$f(x) = \begin{cases} x^2 + ax, & x \leq 2 \\ \ln(x - 1), & x > 2 \end{cases}$$
   is continuous for all real numbers.
   (b) Find $f'(x)$.
   (c) Using the value of a found in part (a) above, is $f(x)$ continuous and differentiable for all real numbers? Is there another value of a for which $f(x)$ is continuous and differentiable for all real numbers? Explain your thinking.

CHAPTER 6
Techniques and Applications of Antidifferentiation

6.1 Antiderivatives

The **antiderivative** of a function $f(x)$ is any function $F(x)$ whose derivative is $f(x)$. The function $F(x)$ is also referred to as the **indefinite integral** of $f(x)$.

In general, finding antiderivatives is a more complex task than finding derivatives. There are formulas for finding antiderivatives of certain types of functions, which correspond to the formulas for derivatives. (Refer to Section 4.4 for lists of formulas for the derivatives of the basic functions.) These antiderivative formulas are part of the Calculus AB curriculum. There are several additional methods of finding antiderivatives of other types of functions, which are part of the Calculus BC curriculum. Finally, there are some functions whose antiderivatives either are difficult to find or do not exist in a standard form. In these cases, methods of approximating the solution to the antiderivative are used.

> **Vocabulary Notes**
> - The process of finding an antiderivative is called **antidifferentiation** or **integration**.
> - The **antiderivative** is also called the **indefinite integral**.

Formulas for Antiderivatives   Formulas for antiderivatives involve a function called the integrand, and a symbol indicating the variable with respect to which we are taking the derivative.

In the expression $\int f(x)\, dx$, the symbol $\int$ is an integral sign; $f(x)$ is the **integrand,** the function that is to be integrated; and dx indicates that x is the variable of integration.

Power Rule

In the Power Rule for antiderivatives, x^n is the integrand and dx indicates that the antiderivative is with respect to x. The Power Rule has two parts:

1. For $n \neq -1$,

$$\int x^n \, dx = \frac{x^{n+1}}{n+1} + c.$$

Note: Since the denominator, $n + 1$, cannot be equal to zero, this formula is restricted to values of n other than -1.

2. For $n = -1$,

$$\int \frac{1}{x} \, dx = \ln|x| + c.$$

The Constant c

The derivative of x^2 is $2x$; thus, the antiderivative of $2x$ should be x^2. This is almost correct, but observe that the derivative of $x^2 + 2$ is also $2x$, and the derivative of $x^2 - 20$ is again $2x$. Therefore, $2x$ is really the derivative of $x^2 + c$, where c is a constant. Therefore, the *antiderivative* of $2x$ is $x^2 + c$, where c is a constant. The antiderivative of $2x$ is described as a family of curves of the form $F(x) = x^2 + c$, where c is a constant. The value of the constant c can be determined with additional information.

EXAMPLE 1

Find $\int x^3 \, dx$.

Solution   Using the Power Rule with $n = 3$, $\int x^3 \, dx = \frac{x^4}{4} + c$.

EXAMPLE 2

Find $\int 6 \, dx$.

Solution   Using the Power Rule with $n = 0$, $\int 6 \, dx = 6x + c$.

EXAMPLE 3

Find $\int \frac{1}{x^2} \, dx$.

Solution First rewrite the integrand as x^{-2}. Then use the Power Rule with $n = -2$.

$$\int \frac{1}{x^2}\, dx = \int x^{-2}\, dx$$

$$\int x^{-2}\, dx = \frac{x^{-1}}{-1} + c$$

$$= -\frac{1}{x} + c$$

EXAMPLE 4

Find $\int \sqrt{x}\, dx$.

Solution Rewrite $\sqrt{x}$ as $x^{1/2}$, and use the Power Rule with $n = \frac{1}{2}$. Thus,

$$\int \sqrt{x}\, dx = \int x^{1/2}\, dx = \frac{x^{3/2}}{\frac{3}{2}} = \frac{2}{3}\, x^{3/2} + c.$$

The Addition-Subtraction Rule and the Constant Rule

Addition-Subtraction Rule

$$\int (f(x) \pm g(x))\, dx = \int f(x)\, dx \pm \int g(x)\, dx$$

Constant Rule

$$\int cf(x)\, dx = c \int f(x)\, dx$$

EXAMPLE 5

Find $\int \frac{2 + 7x^2}{2x^2}\, dx$.

Solution First simplify the fraction $\frac{2 + 7x^2}{2x^2}$:

$$\frac{2 + 7x^2}{2x^2} = \frac{2}{2x^2} + \frac{7x^2}{2x^2} = \frac{1}{x^2} + \frac{7}{2} = x^{-2} + \frac{7}{2}.$$

Then use the Power Rule on each part of the integrand to find

$$\int \left(x^{-2} + \frac{7}{2} \right) dx = \frac{x^{-1}}{-1} + \frac{7}{2}x + c = -\frac{1}{x} + \frac{7}{2}x + c.$$

EXAMPLE 6

Find $\int (2x + 5)^2 \, dx$.

Solution Expand $(2x + 5)^2$ as $4x^2 + 20x + 25$; then find the antiderivative of each term.

$$\int (2x + 5)^2 \, dx = \int (4x^2 + 20x + 25) \, dx = \frac{4}{3}x^3 + 10x^2 + 25x + c.$$

More Antiderivative Rules

Exponential Rules

$$\int e^x \, dx = e^x + c$$

$$\int a^x \, dx = \frac{a^x}{\ln a} + c, \text{ where } a \text{ is a positive constant, } a \neq 1$$

Trigonometric Rules

$$\int \sin x \, dx = -\cos x + c$$

$$\int \cos x \, dx = \sin x + c$$

$$\int \sec^2 x \, dx = \tan x + c$$

$$\int \csc^2 x \, dx = -\cot x + c$$

$$\int \sec x \tan x \, dx = \sec x + c$$

$$\int \csc x \cot x \, dx = -\csc x + c$$

$$\int \tan x \, dx = -\ln|\cos x| + c = \ln|\sec x| + c$$

$$\int \cot x \, dx = \ln|\sin x| + c$$

$$\int \sec x \, dx = \ln|\sec x + \tan x| + c$$

$$\int \csc x \, dx = \ln|\csc x - \cot x| + c$$

Properties of Integrals

1. For any real number a, $\int_a^a f(x) \, dx = 0$.

2. For any real numbers a and b, $\int_a^b f(x) \, dx = -\int_b^a f(x) \, dx$.

3. For real numbers a, b, and c, where $a < b < c$, $\int_a^c f(x) \, dx + \int_c^b f(x) \, dx = \int_a^b f(x) \, dx$.

4. If $f(x)$ is an even function, $\int_{-a}^a f(x) \, dx = 2\int_0^a f(x) \, dx$.

5. If $f(x)$ is an odd function, $\int_{-a}^a f(x) \, dx = 0$.

EXAMPLE 7

Evaluate $\int_{-\frac{\pi}{3}}^{\frac{\pi}{3}} \cos x \, dx$

Solution Since $\cos x$ is an even function,

$$\int_{-\frac{\pi}{3}}^{\frac{\pi}{3}} \cos x \, dx = 2\int_0^{\frac{\pi}{3}} \cos x \, dx = 2 \sin x \Big|_0^{\frac{\pi}{3}} = 2\left(\sin \frac{\pi}{3} - \sin 0 \right)$$

$$= 2\left(\frac{\sqrt{3}}{2} - 0 \right) = \sqrt{3}.$$

EXAMPLE 8

Evaluate $\int_{-\frac{\pi}{3}}^{\frac{\pi}{3}} \sin x \, dx$.

Solution Since $\sin x$ is an odd function, $\int_{-\frac{\pi}{3}}^{\frac{\pi}{3}} \sin x \, dx = 0$.

Exercises

No calculator is allowed for these questions.

1. Evaluate the integrals.

   (a) $\int (e^x + x) \, dx =$

   (b) $\int \frac{\sin x - 1}{\cos x} \, dx =$

2. Evaluate the integrals.

   (a) $\int \frac{\sqrt{x} + \sqrt[3]{x}}{x} \, dx =$

   (b) $\int \frac{x^4 - 3x^2 + 2}{x^2 - 2} \, dx =$

Multiple-Choice Questions
No calculator is allowed for these questions.

1. $\int \dfrac{x+1}{3x^2}\,dx =$

   (A) $-\dfrac{1}{3x^2} - \dfrac{2}{3x^3} + c$

   (B) $\dfrac{1}{x} + \dfrac{1}{x^2} + c$

   (C) $\dfrac{1}{3}\ln|x| - \dfrac{1}{3x} + c$

   (D) $\dfrac{1}{6x} + c$

   (E) $\dfrac{1}{6}\ln 3x^2 + c$

2. $\int 2x^{-3}\,dx =$

   (A) $-\dfrac{1}{x^2} + c$

   (B) $-\dfrac{1}{2x^4} + c$

   (C) $2\ln x^3 + c$

   (D) $-\dfrac{1}{8x^2} + c$

   (E) $-\dfrac{1}{4x^2} + c$

3. $\int \left(\sqrt{x} + 5\right)^2 dx =$

   (A) $\dfrac{x^2}{2} + 25x + \dfrac{20}{3}x^{3/2} + c$

   (B) $\dfrac{\left(\sqrt{x} + 5\right)^3}{3} + c$

   (C) $\left(\sqrt{x} + 5\right) + c$

   (D) $1 + \dfrac{5}{\sqrt{x}} + c$

   (E) $\dfrac{\left(\sqrt{x} + 5\right)^3}{6\sqrt{x}} + c$

4. $\int_{-2}^{2}(4x^3 + 6x)\,dx =$

   (A) -56
   (B) -28
   (C) 0
   (D) 28
   (E) 56

5. $\int_{-1}^{1}(3x^2 + 5x^4)\,dx =$

   (A) -4
   (B) 0
   (C) 4
   (D) 26
   (E) 52

6. $\int \dfrac{e^{2x} - e^{3x}}{e^x}\,dx =$

   (A) -1

   (B) $\dfrac{1}{2}e^{-x} + c$

   (C) $e^{-2x} + c$

   (D) $e^x - 2e^{2x} + c$

   (E) $e^x - \dfrac{1}{2}e^{2x} + c$

7. If $\int_{1}^{5} f(x)\,dx = 3$ and $\int_{1}^{10} f(x)\,dx = -7$, then

   $\int_{5}^{10} f(x)\,dx =$

   (A) -10
   (B) -4
   (C) -2
   (D) 4
   (E) 10

8. $\int \dfrac{10^x}{\ln 10}\,dx =$

   (A) $10^x + c$

   (B) $\dfrac{10^x}{(\ln 10)^2} + c$

   (C) $\dfrac{x}{\ln 10} + c$

   (D) $\dfrac{x(10^{x-1})}{\ln 10} + c$

   (E) $\dfrac{x^2}{2} + c$

9. $\int_{-\frac{\pi}{6}}^{\frac{\pi}{6}} \sin(2x)\,dx =$

   (A) $-\dfrac{1}{2}$

   (B) 0

   (C) $\dfrac{1}{2}$

   (D) 1

   (E) $\sqrt{3}$

10. $\int_{-1}^{1} \tan x\,dx =$

    (A) 0
    (B) 1
    (C) $\sqrt{3}$
    (D) 3
    (E) undefined

6.2 Area Under a Curve: Approximation by Riemann Sums

Ancient Greek mathematicians such as Eudoxus and Archimedes studied the problem of finding the area inside a closed curve. One method of finding a formula for the area of a circle was found by inscribing a regular polygon with n sides.

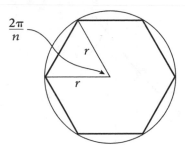

Each triangle has two sides of length r and an included angle with measure $\frac{2\pi}{n}$.

The area of each triangle is $\frac{1}{2}r^2 \sin\left(\frac{2\pi}{n}\right)$.

Thus, the area of the polygon is $n \cdot \frac{1}{2}r^2 \sin\left(\frac{2\pi}{n}\right)$.

The area of the circle is the limit of the area of the polygon as n increases without bound. Thus, area of the circle is $\lim\limits_{n \to \infty}\left(n \cdot \frac{1}{2}r^2 \sin\left(\frac{2\pi}{n}\right)\right)$. Using the special trigonometric limit presented in Section 3.4, we can evaluate this limit as

$$\lim_{n \to \infty} \frac{1}{2}r^2 \frac{\sin\left(\frac{2\pi}{n}\right)}{\frac{1}{n}} = \frac{1}{2}r^2(2\pi) = \pi r^2.$$

Using a similar method to that described above, we can evaluate the area between a curve and the x-axis. The region enclosed by the curve $y = x^2$, the x-axis, and the line $x = 2$ is called R.

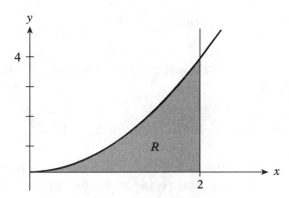

If the interval $[0, 2]$ is divided into n equal subintervals, the length of each subinterval is $\frac{2}{n}$. The x-coordinates of the partitions are $\frac{0}{n}, \frac{2}{n}, \frac{4}{n}, \frac{6}{n}$, ..., $\frac{2n}{n}$. To approximate the area, draw rectangles with bases of length $\frac{2}{n}$ and heights equal to the value of the function $y = x^2$ at the *right* endpoint of each subinterval.

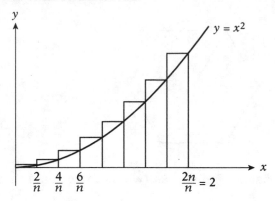

The sum of the areas of these rectangles is

$$\frac{2}{n}\left(\left(\frac{2}{n}\right)^2 + \left(\frac{4}{n}\right)^2 + \left(\frac{6}{n}\right)^2 + \cdots + \left(\frac{2n}{n}\right)^2\right).$$

This expression can be rewritten as

$$\frac{2}{n}\left(\frac{2^2}{n^2} + \frac{4^2}{n^2} + \frac{6^2}{n^2} + \cdots + \frac{(2n)^2}{n^2}\right)$$

$$= \frac{2}{n^3}(2^2 + 4^2 + 6^2 + \cdots + (2n)^2)$$

$$= \frac{2}{n^3} \cdot 2^2(1^2 + 2^2 + 3^2 + \cdots + n^2).$$

Now using a formula for the sum of the first n squares

$$1^2 + 2^2 + 3^2 + \cdots + n^2 = \frac{n(n + 1)(2n + 1)}{6},$$

the sum of the rectangles is

$$\frac{2}{n^3} \cdot 2^2 \cdot \frac{n(n + 1)(2n + 1)}{6} = \frac{4}{3n^2}(2n^2 + 3n + 1).$$

Taking the limit of this expression as n approaches ∞, the area of region R is

$$\text{Area} = \lim_{n \to \infty} \frac{4}{3n^2}(2n^2 + 3n + 1) = \frac{8}{3}.$$

If the same subintervals were used to partition the interval $[0, 2]$, but the height of each rectangle is the value of the function $y = x^2$ at the *left* endpoint of each subinterval, the process described above would give the same answer. The rectangles would then be inscribed in the region R as shown.

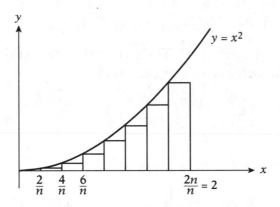

The sum of the areas of the rectangles is

$$\frac{2}{n}\left(\left(\frac{0}{n}\right)^2 + \left(\frac{2}{n}\right)^2 + \left(\frac{4}{n}\right)^2 + \left(\frac{6}{n}\right)^2 + \cdots + \left(\frac{2(n-1)}{n}\right)^2\right),$$

which can be rewritten as

$$\frac{2}{n}\left(\frac{0^2}{n^2} + \frac{2^2}{n^2} + \frac{4^2}{n^2} + \frac{6^2}{n^2} + \cdots + \frac{2^2(n-1)^2}{n^2}\right),$$

or $\frac{2}{n^3} \cdot 2^2(1^2 + 2^2 + 3^2 + \cdots + (n-1)^2)$.

Using the formula for the sum of the first $(n-1)$ squares

$$1^2 + 2^2 + 3^2 + \cdots + (n-1)^2 = \frac{(n-1)n(2n-1)}{6},$$

the sum of the rectangles inscribed in region R is

$$\frac{2}{n^3} \cdot 2^2 \cdot \frac{(n-1)n(2n-1)}{6} \text{ or } \frac{4}{3n^2}(2n^2 - 3n + 1).$$

Taking the limit of this expression as n approaches ∞, the area of region R is

$$\text{Area} = \lim_{n \to \infty} \frac{4}{3n^2}(2n^2 - 3n + 1) = \frac{8}{3}.$$

If the same partition of $[0, 2]$ is used but the height of each rectangle is the value of the function $y = x^2$ at the *midpoint* of each subinterval, the process described above would give the same answer for the area of region R. In this case, however, the rectangles are neither above the curve nor inscribed in the region, but partly above and partly under the curve.

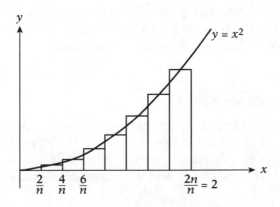

The base of each rectangle is still $\frac{2}{n}$, but the midpoints have x-coordinates $\frac{1}{n}, \frac{3}{n}, \frac{5}{n}, \dots, \frac{2n-1}{n}$. The sum of the areas of the rectangles, using the midpoints of each subinterval, is then

$$\frac{2}{n}\left(\left(\frac{1}{n}\right)^2 + \left(\frac{3}{n}\right)^2 + \left(\frac{5}{n}\right)^2 + \dots + \left(\frac{2n-1}{n}\right)^2\right).$$

This sum can be rewritten as

$$\frac{2}{n^3}\left(1^2 + 3^2 + 5^2 + \dots + (2n-1)^2\right).$$

Using the formula for the sum of odd integers from 1 to $(2n-1)$, the sum is equal to

$$\frac{2}{n^3} \cdot \frac{(2n-1)(2n)(2n+1)}{6} \text{ or } \frac{2}{3n^2}(4n^2 - 1).$$

Taking the limit of this expression as n approaches ∞, the area of region R is

$$\text{Area} = \lim_{n \to \infty} \frac{2}{3n^2}(4n^2 - 1) = \frac{8}{3}.$$

> ### Vocabulary Notes
> The first sum above using the right-hand endpoints of each subinterval is called a **right-hand sum.** The second sum using the left-hand endpoints of each subinterval is called a **left-hand sum.** The third sum using the midpoints of each subinterval is called a **midpoint sum.** Since the function $y = x^2$ is increasing on the interval [0, 2], the left-hand sum is also a **lower sum,** and the right-hand sum is also an **upper sum.**

The graphing calculator can be useful in finding a lower or an upper sum for any function. Instructions are given below for entering the data into a list on either the TI-89 or the TI-83. There are also programs that calculate upper and lower sums.

On the AP exam, whether you are using a program or entering the data into a calculator yourself, be sure to follow the instructions given in the problem. In many cases, work must be shown to receive full credit. The answer alone is generally not acceptable.

 ### Calculator Notes

The graphing calculator can be used to find left-hand, right-hand, and midpoint sums. For the previous example, first enter the function $y = x^2$ into $\boxed{\text{Y=}}$. Using five subdivisions on the interval [0, 2], the partition points are 0, 0.4, 0.8, 1.2, 1.6, and 2, and the length of the subinterval is 0.4.

Using the TI-89

To find the left-hand sum, go to [APPS] 6: Data/Matrix Editor 3: New. For Type: Data [▶] List [ENTER]. Variable x [ENTER] [ENTER]. The word LIST should appear in the upper left corner.

Use arrows to highlight c_1, and type in the entry line:

$c_1 = 0.4$ [×] y_1 (seq(x, x, 0, 1.6, 0.4)).

Now press [HOME] and type into the entry line: sum (x). The answer should be 1.92.

To find the right-hand sum, enter [APPS] 6: Data/Matrix Editor 1: Current.

Use arrows to highlight c_1, and type into the entry line:

$c_1 = 0.4$ [×] y_1(seq(x, x, 0.4, 2, 0.4)).

Now press [HOME] and type into the entry line: sum (x). The answer should be 3.52.

To find the midpoint sum, enter [APPS] 6: Data/Matrix Editor 1: Current.

Use arrows to highlight c_1, and type into the entry line:

$c_1 = 0.4$ [×] y_1 (seq(x, x, 0.2, 1.8, 0.4)).

Now press [HOME] and type into the entry line: sum(x). The answer should be 2.64.

Using the TI-83

To find the left-hand sum, enter the function $y = x^2$ into [Y=]. Go to [STAT] EDIT. Highlight L1. Use the following keystrokes to type L1 = $0.4Y_1$(seq(x, x, 0, 1.6, 0.4)) into the entry line:

0.4 [VARS] Y-VARS [ENTER] [ENTER] [(] [2nd] LIST OPS 5 [X,T,Θ,n] [,] [X,T,Θ,n] [,] 0 [,] 1.6 [,] 0.4 [)] [)].

Press [ENTER].

Press [2nd] QUIT, and then type into the home screen: [2nd] [STAT] MATH 5.

The screen prompt sum(will appear. Enter sum(L1) by pressing [2nd] L1 [)] [ENTER]. The answer should be 1.92.

To find the right-hand sum, go to [STAT] EDIT. Highlight L1. Use the following keystrokes to type L1 = $0.4Y_1$(seq(x, x, 0.4, 2, 0.4)) into the entry line:

0.4 [VARS] Y-VARS [ENTER] [ENTER] [(] [2nd] LIST OPS 5 [X,T,Θ,n] [,] [X,T,Θ,n] [,] 0.4 [,] 2 [,] 0.4 [)] [)].

Press [ENTER].

Press [2nd] QUIT, and then type into the home screen: [2nd] [STAT] MATH 5.

The screen prompt sum(will appear. Enter sum(L1) by pressing [2nd] L1 [)] [ENTER]. The answer should be 3.52.

To find the midpoint sum, go to [STAT] EDIT. Highlight L1. Use the following keystrokes to type L1 = $0.4Y_1$(seq(x, x, 0.2, 1.8, 0.4)) into the entry line:

0.4 [VARS] Y-VARS [ENTER] [ENTER] [(] [2nd] LIST OPS 5 [X,T,Θ,n] [,] [X,T,Θ,n] [,] 0.2 [,] 1.8 [,] 0.4 [)] [)].

Press [ENTER].

Press [2nd] QUIT, and then type into the home screen: [2nd] [STAT] MATH 5.

The screen prompt sum(will appear. Enter sum(L1) by pressing [2nd] L1 [)] [ENTER]. The answer should be 2.64.

Riemann Sums   The left-hand, right-hand, and midpoint sums are all examples of a more general approach to finding areas called Riemann sums. In a **Riemann sum,** a function and an interval are given, the interval is partitioned, and the height of each rectangle can be the value of the function at *any* point in the subinterval. In fact, even the subintervals do not necessarily need to be the same length. All you need to remember is that a Riemann sum uses rectangles to find the area between a curve and the *x*-axis; the left-hand, right-hand, and midpoint sums are all examples of a Riemann sum.

In the case of the left-hand sum, the height of each rectangle is the value of the function at the left point in each subinterval. In the case of the right-hand sum, the height of the rectangle is the value of the function at the right point in each subinterval. In the case of the midpoint sum, the height of the rectangle is the value of the function at the midpoint of each subinterval. In the example above, since the function $y = x^2$ is increasing on the interval [0, 2], the left-hand sum is the lowest estimate of the area of region R, the right-hand sum is the highest estimate of the area of region R, and the midpoint sum is between the two.

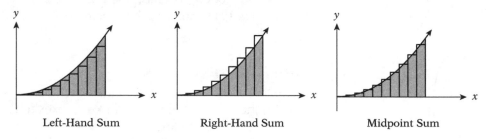

Left-Hand Sum   Right-Hand Sum   Midpoint Sum

The actual area of region R lies between the lower sum and the upper sum. As the number of subintervals n increases, the lower sum increases, while the upper sum decreases. For any value of n,

Lower Sum ≤ Area of the Region ≤ Upper Sum

In the example above for the function $y = x^2$ on the interval [0, 2], the limit of the lower sum $= \dfrac{8}{3} =$ the limit of the upper sum. Since the actual area of region R is sandwiched between the lower and upper sums for every value of n, and since the limits of both the lower and upper sums are the same, the area of region R is also $\dfrac{8}{3}$.

The essential part of the process of finding the area between a curve and the *x*-axis is to start with a function $f(x)$ on a closed interval $[a, b]$, and create rectangles on the subintervals. In a general Riemann sum, a rectangle may be drawn using any value x_i in each of the n subintervals, and the subintervals are not necessarily of equal length. The height of the rectangle is then $f(x_i)$, and the length of the rectangle is Δx_i. The sum of the areas of the rectangles may be written as $\sum\limits_{i=1}^{n} f(x_i)\Delta x_i$, and the area under the curve is the limit of this sum. Thus, the area between the curve and the *x*-axis is

$$\lim_{n \to \infty} \sum_{i=1}^{n} f(x_i)\Delta x_i.$$

Exercises

Multiple-Choice Questions

A graphing calculator is required for some questions.

1. The lower sum of $f(x) = \sqrt{x}$ on the interval $[0, 1]$ with four equal subintervals is
   (A) 0.25
   (B) 0.518
   (C) 0.667
   (D) 0.768
   (E) 3.073

2. The limit of the right-hand sum $\lim\limits_{n \to \infty} \frac{1}{n}$

$$\left[\left(\frac{n+1}{n} \right)^3 + \left(\frac{n+2}{n} \right)^3 + \left(\frac{n+3}{n} \right)^3 + \cdots + \left(\frac{n+n}{n} \right)^3 \right]$$ represents the area of which function on which interval?

   (A) $f(x) = x^3$ on $[0, 1]$

   (B) $f(x) = \frac{1}{x^3}$ on $[0, 1]$

   (C) $f(x) = x^3$ on $[1, 2]$

   (D) $f(x) = x^3$ on $[0, 2]$

   (E) $f(x) = x^3$ on $[0, n]$

3. The lower sum of $f(x) = -(x - 1)^2 + 1$ on the interval $[0, 2]$ with four equal subintervals is

   (A) $\frac{1}{2}$

   (B) $\frac{3}{4}$

   (C) $\frac{4}{3}$

   (D) $\frac{3}{2}$

   (E) 2

4. Which of the following is true for $f(x) = 4 - x^2$ on the interval $[0, 2]$ with n equal subintervals?
   (A) the left-hand sum = the right-hand sum
   (B) the left-hand sum > the right-hand sum
   (C) the left-hand sum < the right-hand sum
   (D) the area under the curve > the left-hand sum
   (E) the area under the curve < the right-hand sum

5. The left-hand sum for $f(x) = x^5$ on the interval $[-1, 1]$ using four equal subintervals is
   (A) -1

   (B) $-\frac{1}{2}$

   (C) 0

   (D) $\frac{1}{2}$

   (E) 1

6. Which of the following is true for $f(x) = \cos x$ on the interval $\left[-\frac{\pi}{2}, \frac{\pi}{2} \right]$ using four equal subintervals?
   (A) left-hand sum < right-hand sum
   (B) right-hand sum < left-hand sum
   (C) midpoint sum < left-hand sum
   (D) midpoint sum = left-hand sum
   (E) left-hand sum = right-hand sum

7. Which value of n gives the largest upper sum for $f(x) = 2x^2$ on the interval $[-1, 1]$?
   (A) $n = 4$

   (B) $n = 10$

   (C) $n = 20$

   (D) $n = 30$

   (E) $n = 50$

8. Which of the following is true for the lower sum of $f(x) = \frac{1}{x}$ on the interval $[1, 2]$ for any number of subintervals?
   (A) lower sum > ln 2

   (B) lower sum $\geq \frac{1}{2}$

   (C) lower sum = ln 2

   (D) lower sum $= \frac{1}{2}$

   (E) lower sum < 0.5

Free-Response Questions

A graphing calculator is required for some questions.

1. During a recent snowfall, several students monitored the accumulation of snow on the flat roof of their school. The table records the data they collected for the 12-hour period of the snowfall.

Number of Hours	Rate of Snowfall (in./hour)
0	0
2	1.5
3	2.1
4.5	2.4
6.5	2.8
8	2.2
10.5	1.8
12	1.6

(a) Use a right-hand sum to approximate the total depth of snow in the 12-hour period.

(b) Using the right-hand sum approximation, estimate the average rate of snowfall in the 12-hour period.

2. A car slows down as it approaches a red light at an intersection. When the light turns green, the velocity of the car increases as shown in the table.

Time t (sec)	Velocity v (ft/sec)
0	8
2	14
4	22
6	30
8	40
10	45

(a) Find the average rate of change of the velocity v on the interval [0, 10].

(b) Approximate the distance traveled in the first ten seconds using five equal subintervals.

(c) Approximate the acceleration of the car at $t = 6$.

6.3 The Fundamental Theorem of Calculus

The Fundamental Theorem of Calculus: Part One

In the previous section, we used Riemann sums to approximate the area of a region. This is an important step in understanding how calculus is used to find the area under a curve. (*Note:* The area under a curve usually refers to the area between the curve and the x-axis.)

Now that we know how to find the antiderivative and how to use Riemann sums to find areas, we are in a position to define the relationship between the antiderivative of a function and the area under the graph of that function. We have seen that they are the same! This relationship is the basis for the Fundamental Theorem of Calculus. The Fundamental Theorem of Calculus has two parts.

> **The Fundamental Theorem of Calculus: Part One**
> If $f(x)$ has an antiderivative called $F(x)$, then
>
> $$\int_a^b f(x)\,dx = F(b) - F(a).$$

Part One of the theorem is used to compute the area under a curve. Since area is a nonnegative quantity, if $f(x)$ is positive on the interval $[a, b]$, then the definite integral $\int_a^b f(x)\, dx$ represents the area between the graph of $f(x)$ and the x-axis on the interval $[a, b]$. If $f(x)$ is negative on the interval $[a, b]$, then the absolute value of $\int_a^b f(x)\, dx$ represents the area between the curve and the x-axis. If $f(x)$ crosses the x-axis on the interval $[a, b]$, then the area between the curve and the x-axis is calculated by breaking the interval $[a, b]$ into where $f(x)$ is positive and where $f(x)$ is negative. The area is then the sum of the absolute values of the integrals.

Another method of computing the area between the graph of $f(x)$ and the x-axis is to find $\int_a^b |f(x)|\, dx$. Using this method, it is not necessary to find the points where $f(x)$ crosses the x-axis.

This part of the Fundamental Theorem is also used to find the area between two curves. If $f(x) \geq g(x)$ on an interval $[a, b]$, then the area between the two curves is found using the formula

$$\int_a^b (f(x) - g(x))\, dx.$$

This formula always works for $f(x)$ and $g(x)$ whether they are above or below the x-axis.

Thus, to find the area of the region under the curve $y = x^2$ on the interval $[0, 2]$, simply take the antiderivative of x^2, and evaluate it as follows:

$$\text{area of the region} = \int_0^2 x^2\, dx = \frac{x^3}{3}.$$

The limits on the top and bottom of the integral symbol, $\int$, indicate that this is a **definite integral.** Now evaluate the antiderivative $\frac{x^3}{3}$ at the limits: substitute the upper limit 2 for x; then substitute the lower limit 0 for x. Subtract the value at the lower limit from the value at the upper limit to find the area. Thus, the area of the region $= \frac{8}{3} - \frac{0}{3} = \frac{8}{3}$. This is exactly the same value calculated using Riemann sums!

EXAMPLE 1

Find the area under the curve $y = x^2$ on the interval $[0, 3]$.

Solution   Use the Power Rule to find the antiderivative, and then substitute in the upper and lower limits.

$$\int_0^3 x^2\, dx = \frac{x^3}{3}\Big|_0^3 = \frac{3^3}{3} - \frac{0^3}{3} = \frac{27}{3} - 0 = 9.$$

EXAMPLE 2

Find the area under the curve $y = 4 - x^2$ on the interval $[-1, 1]$.

Solution Use the Power Rule and the Addition-Subtraction Rule to find the antiderivative, and then substitute in the upper and lower limits.

$$\int_{-1}^{1} (4 - x^2)\,dx = \left(4x - \frac{x^3}{3}\right)\Big|_{-1}^{1}$$

$$= \left(4 - \frac{1}{3}\right) - \left(-4 - \left(-\frac{1}{3}\right)\right) = \frac{22}{3}$$

EXAMPLE 3

Find the area under the curve $y = e^x$ on the interval $[0, \ln 2]$.

Solution Use the Exponential Function Rule to find the antiderivative, and then substitute in the upper and lower limits.

$$\int_{0}^{\ln 2} e^x\,dx = e^x\Big|_{0}^{\ln 2} = e^{\ln 2} - e^0 = 2 - 1 = 1$$

EXAMPLE 4

Find the area under the curve $y = \frac{1}{x}$ on the interval $[1, 4]$.

Solution Use the Log Function Rule to find the antiderivative, and then substitute in the upper and lower limits.

$$\int_{1}^{4} \frac{1}{x}\,dx = \ln x\Big|_{1}^{4} = \ln 4 - \ln 1 = \ln 4.$$

EXAMPLE 5

Find the area between the graphs of $f(x) = 4 - x^2$ and $g(x) = x^2 + 1$ on the interval $[-1, 1]$.

Solution Since over the entire interval $f(x) = 4 - x^2 \geq g(x) = x^2 + 1$, the area between $f(x)$ and $g(x)$ on the interval $[-1, 1]$ is calculated using the integral

$$\int_{-1}^{1} (f(x) - g(x))\,dx = \int_{-1}^{1} ((4 - x^2) - (x^2 + 1))\,dx.$$

Thus the area between $f(x)$ and $g(x)$ on $[-1, 1]$ is

$$\int_{-1}^{1} (3 - 2x^2)\,dx = (3 - 2) + (3 - 2) = 2$$

EXAMPLE 6

Find the area under the curve $f(x) = 2x^2 + 1$ on the interval $[0, 1]$.

Solution   Area $= \int_0^1 (x^2 + 1)\, dx = \left[\frac{2}{3}x^3 + x\right]_0^1 = \frac{2}{3} + 1 = \frac{5}{3}.$

EXAMPLE 7

Find the area between the curve $f(x) = x^2 - 1$ and the x-axis.

Solution   Since $f(x)$ is below the x-axis and intersects the x-axis at $x = -1$ and $x = 1$, the area between the curve and the x-axis is calculated using the absolute value of the integral $\int_{-1}^{1}(x^2 - 1)\, dx$.

$$\int_{-1}^{1}(x^2 - 1)\, dx = \left[\frac{x^3}{3} - x\right]_{-1}^{1} = \left(\frac{1}{3} - 1\right) - \left(\frac{-1}{3} - (-1)\right) = -\frac{4}{3}.$$

The area is the absolute value of $-\frac{4}{3}$, or $\frac{4}{3}$.

Note: $\int_a^b f(x)\, dx$ may be positive or negative. It is only when you are asked to find the *area* that your answer must be positive.

The Fundamental Theorem of Calculus: Part Two

The second part of the Fundamental Theorem says that the derivative of the antiderivative is the original function.

> **The Fundamental Theorem of Calculus: Part Two**
>
> $$\frac{d}{dx}\left(\int_a^x f(t)\, dt\right) = f(x)$$

Part Two may seem obvious, but it reveals an important fact. It says that the rate at which the area between the graph of a function and the horizontal axis is changing will be equal to the height of the function at that value of x. To make this clear, two variables, t and x, are used, but f is the same function. The following examples will clarify the second part of the Fundamental Theorem by going through the process for several functions $f(t)$.

EXAMPLE 8

Find $\dfrac{d}{dx}\displaystyle\int_3^x (t^2 + t)\, dt$.

Solution In this example, $f(t) = t^2 + t$, and $a = 3$. According to the first part of the Fundamental Theorem, $\dfrac{d}{dx}\displaystyle\int_3^x (t^2 + t)\, dt = x^2 + x$. We can check this ourselves. Use the first part of the Fundamental Theorem to find the antiderivative on the interval $[3, x]$:

$$\int_3^x (t^2 + t)\, dt = \left[\frac{t^3}{3} + \frac{t^2}{2}\right]_3^x = \frac{x^3}{3} + \frac{x^2}{2} - \left(\frac{3^3}{3} - \frac{3^2}{2}\right) = \frac{x^3}{3} + \frac{x^2}{2} - \frac{9}{2}.$$

The antiderivative here is the area between the graph of f and the t-axis from $t = a$ to $t = x$. The area depends on the upper limit, x.

Now find the derivative of the result with respect to x:

$$\frac{d}{dx}\left(\frac{x^3}{3} + \frac{x^2}{2} - \frac{9}{2}\right) = x^2 + x = f(x), \text{ the height of the curve at } x.$$

The derivative here is the rate at which the area found above is changing with respect to x.

EXAMPLE 9

Find $\dfrac{d}{dx}\left(\displaystyle\int_1^{5x} e^t\, dt\right)$.

Solution Calculating the antiderivative directly, the antiderivative of e^t is e^t. Use the first part of the Fundamental Theorem to evaluate e^t on the interval $[1, 5x]$. The result is $e^{5x} - e$. Now take the derivative of $e^{5x} - e$ with respect to x, and the result is $5e^{5x}$.

This example illustrates a further complexity of the second part of the Fundamental Theorem. When one of the limits of the integral is not just x, but a function of x, in this case $5x$, not only is the variable t in the integrand replaced by $5x$, but since the Chain Rule is applied, the result is also multiplied by the derivative, 5. Therefore, the final answer is $5e^{5x}$.

EXAMPLE 10

Find $\dfrac{d}{dx}\displaystyle\int_x^4 \sin t\, dt$.

Solution The antiderivative of $\sin t$ is $-\cos t$. Using the first part of the Fundamental Theorem, evaluate $-\cos t$ on the interval $[x, 4]$. The result is $-\cos 4 + \cos x$. The derivative of $-\cos 4 + \cos x$ is $-\sin x$.

This result illustrates that when the variable is at the lower limit of the integral, the answer is the opposite of the expression after replacing the variable t in the integrand with the variable x.

Examples 8–10 use integrands for which the antiderivative can be found. Examples 11 and 12, which follow, apply the second part of the Fundamental Theorem to integrands for which the antiderivatives are difficult or impossible to find.

EXAMPLE 11

Find $\dfrac{d}{dx}\left(\displaystyle\int_2^x \sqrt{t^3 + 1}\ dt\right)$.

Solution   The antiderivative of $\sqrt{t^3 + 1}$ can be found by a long and complex computation. Instead, apply the second part of the Fundamental Theorem. The derivative with respect to x of the antiderivative of $\sqrt{t^3 + 1}$ replaces the variable t with x, with the result $\sqrt{x^3 + 1}$.

EXAMPLE 12

Find $\dfrac{d}{dx}\left(\displaystyle\int_1^{2x} \sin(t^2)\ dt\right)$.

Solution   By the second part of the Fundamental Theorem, replace the variable t in $\sin(t^2)$ with $2x$. Since the derivative of $2x$ is 2, apply the Chain Rule and multiply the result by 2. The final answer is $2 \sin(4x^2)$.

Exercises

A graphing calculator is required for some questions.

1. For each of the following, sketch the region whose area is defined by the integral and calculate the area:

   (a) $\displaystyle\int_0^1 (x^2 + 2x)\,dx$

   (b) $\displaystyle\int_0^1 e^x\,dx$

   (c) $\displaystyle\int_1^e \ln x\,dx$

   (d) $\displaystyle\int_0^{\frac{\pi}{2}} \sin x\,dx$

   (e) $\displaystyle\int_{-2}^2 (4 - x^2)\,dx$

   (f) $\displaystyle\int_0^{\frac{\pi}{4}} \tan x\,dx$

   (g) $\displaystyle\int_{-1}^1 -x^2\,dx$

   (h) $\displaystyle\int_{-\frac{\pi}{4}}^{\frac{\pi}{4}} \cos 2x\,dx$

2. For each of the following regions (a)–(e), write one or more integral expressions that represent the area of the region. Then compute the area of the region.

   (a) $y = \cos x$ on the interval $\left[-\dfrac{\pi}{2}, \dfrac{\pi}{2}\right]$

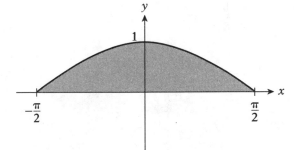

   (b) $y = e^x - 1$ on the interval $[0, 1]$

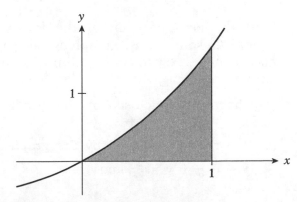

(c) The region in the first quadrant enclosed by the graphs of $y = 4 - x^2$, $y = 4x - x^2$, and $x = 0$

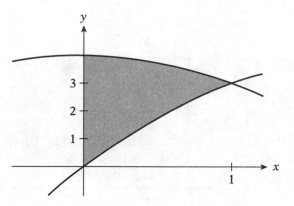

(d) The region enclosed by $y = x^4 - 1$ and $y = -x + 1$

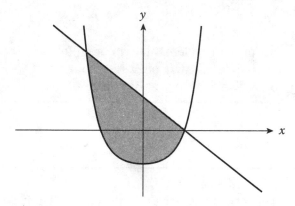

(e) The region above the x-axis enclosed by $y = x^3 + 1$ and $y = -x + 3$

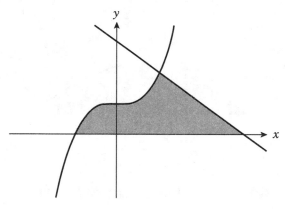

3. Find the area of each of the following regions. In some cases, a graphing calculator may be necessary to find the limits of integration.

(a) the region enclosed by the graphs of $x = y^2$ and $x = y + 2$

(b) the region enclosed by the graphs of $y = x^2 - 1$, $y = \dfrac{2}{x^2}$, and $x = 1$

(c) the region in the first quadrant enclosed by the graphs of $y = e^{-2x}$ and $x = \ln 3$

(d) the region under the curve $y = \sin x + 1$ on the interval $[0, 2\pi]$

(e) the region enclosed by the graphs of $y = e^x$ and $y = \cos x$

Multiple-Choice Questions
No calculator is allowed for these questions.

1. Find the area under the graph of $y = x + 2$ on the interval $[1, 3]$.
(A) 2
(B) 3
(C) 5
(D) 8
(E) 15

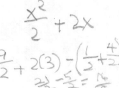

2. Find the area between the x-axis and the graph of $y = |x|$ on the interval $[-10, 10]$.
(A) 0
(B) 10
(C) 20
(D) 50
(E) 100

3. Find the area between the x-axis and the graph of $y = 3 - |x|$ on the interval $[0, 6]$.
(A) 0
(B) $\dfrac{9}{2}$
(C) 9
(D) 18
(E) 36

4. Find the area bounded by the graph of $f(x) = \sqrt{16 - x^2}$ and the x-axis.
(A) π
(B) 2π
(C) 4π
(D) 8π
(E) 16π

5. Which of the following graphs shows a shaded region whose area is represented by
$$\int_{-1}^{2} 2 \, dx?$$

(A)
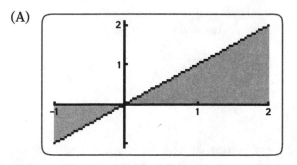

(B)

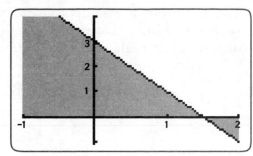

(C)

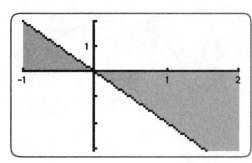

(D)

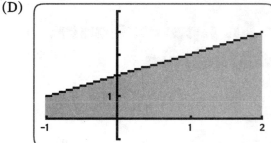

(E

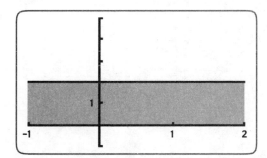

6. $\int_{-1}^{1} (e^x - 1)\, dx =$

(A) -2

(B) 0

(C) $\dfrac{e^2 - 2e - 1}{e}$

(D) $\dfrac{e^2 - 2e + 1}{e}$

(E) $\dfrac{e^2 - 1}{e}$

7. Find the area bounded by the graphs of $y = x^2 - 4x$ and $y = x$.

(A) $\dfrac{25}{3}$

(B) 10

(C) 12.5

(D) $\dfrac{125}{6}$

(E) 21

8. The area enclosed by the graphs of $y = e^x$, $y = x$, the y-axis, and the line $x = 2$ is equal to

(A) e^2

(B) $e^2 - 1$

(C) $e^2 + 1$

(D) $e^2 - 3$

(E) $e^2 - 2$

9. Find the area bounded by the curve $y = \cos x$ and the x-axis from $x = -\pi$ to $x = \pi$.

(A) -4

(B) -2

(C) 0

(D) 2

(E) 4

10. Find the area bounded by the graphs of $y = x + 2$, $y = -x + 4$, and the x-axis.

(A) 4.5

(B) 6

(C) 7

(D) 9

(E) 18

11. Find the area enclosed by the graphs of $y = \sqrt{x}$ and $y = x^3$.

(A) $\dfrac{1}{4}$

(B) $\dfrac{1}{3}$

(C) $\dfrac{5}{12}$

(D) $\dfrac{2}{3}$

(E) $\dfrac{5}{4}$

Free-Response Questions
A graphing calculator is required for Questions 1–3.

1. Find the value of k so that the line $x = k$ divides into two equal areas the region enclosed by the graph of $y = x^2$, the line $x = 2$, and the x-axis.

2. Region R is enclosed by the graph of $f(x) = \dfrac{1}{x^2}$, the lines $x = 1$ and $x = 2$, and the x-axis. The lines $x = p$ and $x = q$ divide region R into three regions of equal area. Find the values of p and q.

3. For what value of k does the line $x = k$ divide the region bounded by the graphs of $y = e^x$ and $y = -x$, the y-axis, and the line $x = 2$ so that the area of the region on the interval $[0, k]$ is 50% of the area of the region on the interval $[k, 2]$?

No calculator is allowed for Questions 4 and 5.

4. Sketch the graph of a function $f(x)$ so that $f(x) > 0$ on the closed interval $[-2, 2]$ and $\displaystyle\int_{-2}^{2} f(x)\, dx = 5$.

5. The graph of f is a semicircle and two line segments. Find the area between the graph of f on the interval $[-8, 8]$ and the x-axis.

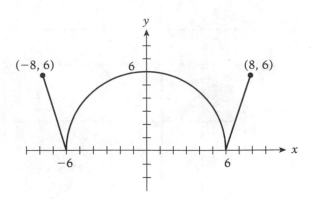

6.4 The Accumulation Function: An Application of Part Two of the Fundamental Theorem

The graph of function f is shown below.

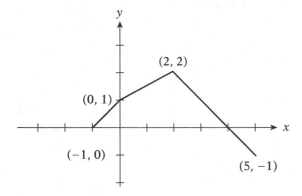

The graph of f consists of three line segments.

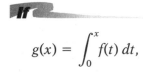

$$g(x) = \int_{0}^{x} f(t)\, dt,$$

Then

Part Two of the Fundamental Theorem can be used to determine:
- where $g(x)$ is increasing or decreasing
- the values of x where $g(x)$ has a relative maximum or a relative minimum
- where $g(x)$ is concave up or concave down
- the values of x that are points of inflection of g

The function $g(x)$ is called the **accumulation function** because it accumulates the area under the graph of f as x increases. By the second part of the Fundamental Theorem, $g'(x) = f(x)$.

Since $g'(x) = f(x)$, $g' > 0$ means g is increasing and $g' < 0$ means g is decreasing. Thus when $f > 0$, g is increasing and when $f < 0$, g is decreasing. Looking at the graph of f, $f > 0$ on the interval $(-1, 4)$ and $f < 0$ on the interval $(4, 5)$. Therefore, g is increasing on the interval $(-1, 4)$ and g is decreasing on the interval $(4, 5)$.

Critical values can be found by analyzing the values of x for which $g'(x) = 0$ or $g'(x)$ is undefined. Additionally, each critical value can be identified as a relative maximum or a relative minimum.

$g'(x) = 0$ means that $f(x) = 0$ and $g'(x)$ is undefined means that $f(x)$ is undefined.

Since $f(x)$ is always defined on $[-1, 5]$, $f(x) = 0$ at $x = -1$ and $x = 4$.

Since $x = -1$ is an endpoint of the interval, only $x = 4$ can be a relative maximum or minimum. This can be illustrated on a number line:

$$\underset{-1}{\vdash}\ \overset{+}{\rule{8cm}{0pt}}\ \underset{4}{\dashv}\ \overset{-}{\rule{1cm}{0pt}}\ \underset{5}{\dashv} \quad g'(x) = f(x)$$

By the First Derivative Test, since g' changes sign from $+$ to $-$ at $x = 4$, $g(4)$ is a relative maximum. To find the absolute maximum and the absolute minimum values of $g(x)$ on the interval $[-1, 5]$, find the value of g at the endpoints and the value of $g(4)$ by using basic geometry to evaluate the definite integral $\int_0^x f(t)\, dt$ for several values of x as follows:

$$g(-1) = \int_0^{-1} f(t)\, dt = -\int_{-1}^0 f(t)\, dt = -\frac{1}{2}$$

$$g(4) = \int_0^4 f(t)\, dt = \int_0^2 f(t)\, dt + \int_2^4 f(t)\, dt = 3 + 2 = 5 \quad \text{(using the formula for the area of a triangle and the area of a trapezoid)}$$

$$g(5) = \int_0^5 f(t)\, dt = \int_0^4 f(t)\, dt + \int_4^5 f(t)\, dt = 5 + \left(-\frac{1}{2}\right) = 4.5$$

Since $g(4) = 5$, $g(-1) = -\frac{1}{2}$, and $g(5) = 4.5$, the absolute maximum of g is 5 and the absolute minimum of g is $-\frac{1}{2}$.

The second derivative of g, $g''(x)$, can be found by taking the derivative of $g'(x) = f(x)$. Thus $g''(x) = f'(x)$. To find the points of inflection of g, find the values of x where $g''(x) = 0$ or $g''(x)$ is undefined. Since $g''(x) = f'(x)$, find the values of x where $f'(x) = 0$ or $f'(x)$ is undefined. There are no values of x where $f'(x) = 0$, but $f'(x)$ is undefined at $x = 0$ and $x = 2$. Putting these values on a number line, indicate where $g''(x)$ is positive or negative.

$$\underset{-1}{\vdash}\ \overset{+}{\rule{1cm}{0pt}}\ \underset{0}{\dashv}\ \overset{+}{\rule{1cm}{0pt}}\ \underset{2}{\dashv}\ \overset{-}{\rule{3cm}{0pt}}\ \underset{5}{\dashv} \quad g''(x) = f'(x)$$

Since $g''(x)$ changes sign at $x = 2$, there is a point of inflection on the graph of g at $x = 2$. Additionally, g is concave up on the intervals $(-1, 0)$ and $(0, 2)$, and concave down on the interval $(2, 5)$.

Using the information about the graph of $g(x)$, it is possible to sketch the graph.

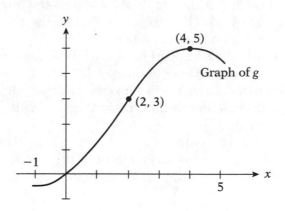

Exercises

Multiple-Choice Questions
No calculator is allowed for these questions.

1. If $F(x) = \displaystyle\int_0^x \sin^2(2t)\, dt$, then $F'(x) =$
(A) $-\cos^2(2x)$
(B) $\cos^2(2x)$
(C) $\sin^2(2x)$
(D) $\dfrac{1}{2}\sin^2(2x)$
(E) $4\sin(2x)\cos(2x)$

2. $\dfrac{d}{dx}\left(\displaystyle\int_2^5 (1 + t^{2/3})\, dt\right) =$
(A) 0
(B) $1 + 5^{2/3}$
(C) $t + \dfrac{3}{5}t^{5/3}$
(D) $5^{2/3} - 2^{2/3}$
(E) $\dfrac{(1 + t^{2/3})^2}{2}$

3. $\dfrac{d}{dt}\left(\displaystyle\int_{6t}^1 \left(1 + \sqrt{x}\right)^2 dx\right) =$
(A) $\sqrt{1 + 6t}$
(B) $-\left(1 + \sqrt{6t}\right)^2$
(C) $\left(1 + \sqrt{6t}\right)^2$
(D) $-6\left(1 + \sqrt{6t}\right)^2$
(E) $-\dfrac{1}{6}\left(1 + \sqrt{6t}\right)^2$

For Questions 4 and 5, if $F(x) = \displaystyle\int_{-x}^x e^{-t^2}\, dt$, *then*

4. $F'(1) =$
(A) 0
(B) $2e^{-1}$
(C) 2
(D) $2e$
(E) $-2e^{-1}$

5. $F''(x) =$
(A) 0
(B) $-4xe^{-x^2}$
(C) $-2xe^{-x^2}$
(D) $4xe^{-x^2}$
(E) $2e^{x^2}$

For Questions 6–9, $f(x) = \displaystyle\int_0^x f'(t)\, dt$ *and the graph of* f' *is shown.*

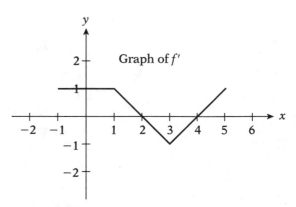

6. Which of the following are true?

6. Which of the following are true?
- I $f(-1) = -1$
- II $f(1) < f(3)$
- III $f'(1) < f'(3)$
- (A) I only
- (B) II only
- (C) III only
- (D) I and II
- (E) I, II, and III

7. Which of the following are true about the graph of f?
- I f is increasing on $(-1, 2)$ only
- II f is increasing on $(-1, 2)$ or $(4, 5)$
- III f is decreasing on $(1, 3)$
- (A) I only
- (B) II only
- (C) III only
- (D) I and III
- (E) none

8. Which of the following are true about the graph of f?
- I f is concave up on $(-1, 1)$
- II f is concave up on $(1, 3)$
- III f is concave down on $(3, 5)$
- (A) I only
- (B) II only
- (C) III only
- (D) II and III
- (E) none

9. Which of the following are true about the graph of f?
- I f has a relative minimum at $x = 2$
- II f has a relative minimum at $x = 4$
- III f has a relative maximum at $x = 2$
- (A) I only
- (B) II only
- (C) III only
- (D) I and II
- (E) II and III

A graphing calculator is required for Question 10.

10. $F(x) = \int \cos(x^2)\, dx$ and $F(2) = 10$. Find $F(3)$.
- (A) 0.140
- (B) 0.241
- (C) 0.703
- (D) 10.241
- (E) 2.414

Free-Response Questions
No calculator is allowed for these questions.

1. The graph of f shown consists of a semicircle and two line segments on the interval $[-2, 6]$.

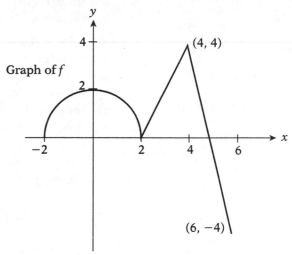

Graph of f

If $g(x) = \int_2^x f(t)\, dt$, use the graph of f to do the following:
- (a) Find $g(-2)$, $g(0)$, $g(2)$, $g(4)$ and $g(6)$.
- (b) Find the intervals where g is decreasing.
- (c) Find the intervals where g is concave up.
- (d) Find the absolute extrema of g on the interval $[-2, 6]$.
- (e) Find the point(s) of inflection of g.
- (f) Sketch g on the interval $[-2, 6]$.

2. The graph of $g(t)$ is shown on the interval $[0, 6]$ and $f(x) = \int_0^x g(t)\, dt$.

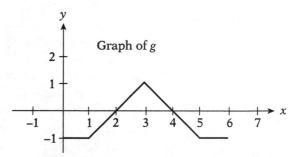

Graph of g

- (a) Find the critical points of $f(x)$, and identify each as a relative maximum, a relative minimum, or neither. Justify your conclusion.
- (b) Find the absolute extrema of $f(x)$. Justify your conclusion.
- (c) If $f(0) = k$, is there a number c in the interval $[0, 6]$ such that $f(c) = k$? Justify your conclusion.
- (d) On what interval(s) is $f(x)$ concave up? On what interval(s) is $f(x)$ concave down?
- (e) Sketch a graph of $f(x)$.

6.5 Integration by the Change of Variable or *u*-Substitution Method

There are rules for finding antiderivatives of many functions, but additional methods are required to find the antiderivatives of many other integrands. Suppose we needed to evaluate $\int x\sqrt{x+2}\,dx$. Since a function whose derivative is $x\sqrt{x+2}$ does not easily come to mind, we need another method of integration.

The only method of integration required in the AP Calculus AB curriculum is the change of variable method, often called the *u*-substitution method. The ***u*-substitution method** involves using the variable *u* to replace part of a complicated function. For example, if $u = x + 2$, then $x = u - 2$. We can then proceed by making these substitutions in the original integral:

$$\int x\sqrt{x+2}\,dx \text{ becomes } \int (u-2)\,\sqrt{u}\,du = \int (u^{3/2} - 2u^{1/2})\,du.$$

While there are other methods of integration required in the BC curriculum, the *u*-substitution method is one of the most powerful tools for finding antiderivatives since it applies to so many different situations where the antiderivative is not obvious.

> **The most important things to remember in using the u-*substitution method are:**
> * Choose an appropriate quantity for the variable *u*.
> * Find *du*.
> * Express all parts of the integrand in terms of *u*.

Hint: In choosing a quantity to substitute for *u*, look for the expression inside parentheses or under a radical sign. Then mentally take the derivative and check to see if the derivative is part of the integrand. Don't worry if the coefficients are not the same; you can always adjust for a constant.

After making the *u*-substitution, there are two possibilities. If the integral has no limits (indefinite integral), then substitute the expression for *u* in the final answer. If the integral has limits (definite integral), you have two choices. Either you can substitute the expression for *u* back into the antiderivative and use the limits of the original variable, or you can use the expression for *u* to replace the limits with the corresponding values of *u*, and then evaluate the integral. Remember, a definite integral is a number; an indefinite integral is a family of functions.

EXAMPLE 1

Find $\int 2x(x^2 - 5)^4\,dx$.

Solution It would be a tedious task to expand $(x^2 - 5)^4$, multiply each term by $2x$, and find the antiderivative of each term of this polynomial function. Instead let $u = x^2 - 5$. Then $\frac{du}{dx} = 2x$, or $du = 2x\,dx$. The integrand $\int 2x(x^2 - 5)^4\,dx$ can be rewritten as

$$\int (x^2 - 5)^4(2x\,dx) = \int u^4\,du.$$

The antiderivative is easily found using the Power Rule as $\frac{u^5}{5} + c$.

The final step for evaluating this indefinite integral is to replace u with $x^2 - 5$, giving the final answer $\frac{(x^2 - 5)^5}{5} + c$.

EXAMPLE 2

Find $\int x\sqrt{4x^2 + 9}\,dx$.

Solution By the method of u-substitution, choose $u = 4x^2 + 9$. Then $\frac{du}{dx} = 8x$, or $du = 8x\,dx$. The integrand can be rewritten as $\sqrt{4x^2 + 9}\,(x\,dx)$.

To find an expression to substitute for $x\,dx$, multiply both sides of the equation $du = 8x\,dx$ by $\frac{1}{8}$ to get $\frac{1}{8}\,du = x\,dx$.

The integrand is then replaced in terms of u by $\sqrt{u}\left(\frac{1}{8}\,du\right)$ or $\frac{1}{8}\sqrt{u}\,du$.

To find $\int \frac{1}{8}\sqrt{u}\,du$, rewrite the integral as

$$\frac{1}{8}\int \sqrt{u}\,du = \frac{1}{8}\int u^{1/2}\,du,$$

and use the Power Rule. The result is

$$\frac{1}{8}\,u^{3/2}\left(\frac{2}{3}\right) + c = \frac{1}{12}\,u^{3/2} + c.$$

Replacing u with $4x^2 + 9$, the final answer is $\frac{1}{12}(4x^2 + 9)^{3/2} + c$.

EXAMPLE 3

Find $\int \cos 4x \, dx$.

Solution   Let $u = 4x$. Then $\frac{du}{dx} = 4$ or $du = 4 \, dx$.

Multiply both sides of the equation $du = 4 \, dx$ by $\frac{1}{4}$, and the result is $\frac{1}{4} \, du = dx$.

Substituting $u = 4x$ and $dx = \frac{1}{4} \, du$ into the integrand, $\int \cos 4x \, dx$ becomes $\frac{1}{4} \int \cos u \, du$.

Using the trigonometric rules for antiderivatives, the antiderivative in terms of u becomes $\frac{1}{4} \sin u + c$.

Replacing u by $4x$, the final antiderivative is $\frac{1}{4} \sin 4x + c$.

EXAMPLE 4

Find $\int 2xe^{3x^2} \, dx$.

Solution   Let $u = 3x^2$. Then $\frac{du}{dx} = 6x$ or $du = 6x \, dx$.

Multiply both sides of the equation $du = 6x \, dx$ by $\frac{1}{3}$ to get $\frac{1}{3} \, du = 2x \, dx$.

Thus $\int 2xe^{3x^2} \, dx = \frac{1}{3} \int e^u \, du$. Use the exponential rule for antiderivatives to get $\frac{1}{3} e^u + c$.

Finally, replace u with $3x^2$ and the final antiderivative is $\frac{1}{3} e^{3x^2} + c$.

EXAMPLE 5

Find $\int \frac{x}{x^2 + 2} \, dx$.

Solution   Using the method of u-substitution, let $u = x^2 + 2$.

Then $\frac{du}{dx} = 2x$ or $du = 2x \, dx$.

Multiplying both sides of the equation $du = 2x \, dx$ by $\frac{1}{2}$, the equation becomes $\frac{1}{2} \, du = x \, dx$.

Replacing $x^2 + 2$ by u and $x \, dx$ by $\frac{1}{2} \, du$, the integral becomes $\frac{1}{2} \int \frac{du}{u} = \frac{1}{2} \int \frac{1}{u} \, du$.

Using the Power Rule for $n = -1$, the integral is $\frac{1}{2} \ln|u| + c$.

Replacing u by $x^2 + 2$, the final answer is $\frac{1}{2} \ln|x^2 + 2| + c$. Since $x^2 + 2$ is always positive, the answer could also be written $\frac{1}{2} \ln(x^2 + 2) + c$.

EXAMPLE 6

Find $\int_1^e \frac{\ln x}{x}\,dx$.

Solution Think of the quantity $\frac{\ln x}{x}$ as $\frac{1}{x}\ln x$. The integral $\int_1^e \frac{\ln x}{x}\,dx$ can be rewritten as $\int_1^e \ln x\left(\frac{1}{x}dx\right)$. Then choose $u = \ln x$, since $du = \frac{1}{x}\,dx$.

After substituting for u and du, the integral becomes $\int u\,du$. Notice that the limits of 1 and e are not written on this integral, since the variable is now u, and the original limits were expressed in terms of x. The antiderivative is found using the Power Rule: $\frac{u^2}{2}$.

There are now two methods of evaluating the integral:

METHOD 1   Return to x as the variable. Replace u by $\ln x$, and use the original limits. The antiderivative is then

$$\int u\,du = \frac{u^2}{2} = \left[\frac{(\ln x)^2}{2}\right]_1^e = \frac{(\ln e)^2}{2} - \frac{(\ln 1)^2}{2} = \frac{1}{2}.$$

METHOD 2   An alternative method is to leave the antiderivative in terms of u, $\frac{u^2}{2}$. Use the change of variable formula, $u = \ln x$, to convert the original limits from the x-values 1 and e to values of u. Therefore, the lower limit 1 becomes $\ln 1 = 0$, and the upper limit e becomes $\ln e = 1$, and the new limits are 0 and 1. Evaluating the antiderivative, we get the same answer:

$$\left.\frac{u^2}{2}\right|_0^1 = \frac{1^2}{2} - \frac{0^2}{2} = \frac{1}{2}.$$

Exercises

Multiple-Choice Questions
No calculator is allowed for these questions.

1. Find $\int \dfrac{2x}{\sqrt{x^2 + 6}}\,dx$.

   (A) $(x^2 + 6)^{1/2} + c$

   (B) $2(x^2 + 6)^{1/2} + c$

   (C) $\ln(x^2 + 6) + c$

   (D) $\frac{2}{3}(x^2 + 6)^{3/2} + c$

   (E) $2x(x^2 + 6)^{-1/2} + c$

2. Find $\int x^2(x^3 - 1)^5\,dx$.

   (A) $\dfrac{(x^3 - 1)^6}{18} + c$

   (B) $\dfrac{(x^3 - 1)^6}{6} + c$

   (C) $\dfrac{(x^3 - 1)^6}{2} + c$

   (D) $6(x^3 - 1)^6 + c$

   (E) $2x(x^3 - 1)^5 + c$

3. Find $\displaystyle\int \frac{2x + 2}{(x^2 + 2x)^5}\, dx$.

(A) $\displaystyle\frac{1}{4(x^2 + 2x)^4}\, dx$

(B) $\displaystyle -\frac{1}{4(x^2 + 2x)^4} + c$

(C) $\displaystyle -\frac{1}{2(x^2 + 2x)^4} + c$

(D) $\displaystyle -\frac{1}{8(x^2 + 2x)^4} + c$

(E) $\displaystyle\frac{(x^2 + 2x)^{-6}}{-6} + c$

4. Find $\displaystyle\int \frac{x^3}{x^4 + 1}\, dx$.

(A) $\displaystyle\frac{3(x^4 + 1)^2}{2} + c$

(B) $\displaystyle\frac{(x^4 + 1)^2}{2} + c$

(C) $\ln(x^4 + 1) + c$

(D) $\displaystyle\frac{\ln(x^4 + 1)}{4} + c$

(E) $\displaystyle\frac{(x^4 + 1)^2}{6} + c$

5. Find $\displaystyle\int \frac{e^x}{e^x + 4}\, dx$.

(A) $\displaystyle\frac{1}{e^x(e^x + 4)} + c$

(B) $e^x \ln(e^x + 4) + c$

(C) $\displaystyle x + \frac{1}{4} e^x + c$

(D) $\displaystyle\frac{(e^x + 4)^{-2}}{-2} + c$

(E) $\ln(e^x + 4) + c$

6. Find $\displaystyle\int \frac{e^x + 4}{e^x}\, dx$.

(A) $\displaystyle\frac{e^{-x}(e^x + 4)^2}{2} + c$

(B) $\displaystyle\frac{(e^x + 4)^2}{2} + c$

(C) $4e^{-x} + c$

(D) $\ln(e^x + 4) + c$

(E) $x - 4e^{-x} + c$

7. Find $\displaystyle\int \frac{e^{-x} + 4}{e^x}\, dx$.

(A) $\displaystyle -\frac{1}{2}(e^{-2x} + 4e^{-x}) + c$

(B) $\displaystyle -\frac{1}{2}(e^{-2x} + 8e^{-x}) + c$

(C) $-2e^{-2x} + 4e^{-x} + c$

(D) $\displaystyle\frac{(e^{-x} + 4)^2}{2} + c$

(E) $\ln(e^{-x} + 4) + c$

8. Find the area under the curve $y = \sec^2 x$ on the interval $\left[0, \dfrac{\pi}{3}\right]$.

(A) $\displaystyle\frac{1}{2}$

(B) $\sqrt{3}$

(C) $\displaystyle\frac{\sqrt{3}}{3}$

(D) $\sqrt{3} - 1$

(E) $\displaystyle\frac{\pi^2}{9}$

9. Find the area of the region enclosed by $y = \sin x$ and $y = \cos x$ on the interval $[0, 2\pi]$.

(A) $\sqrt{2}$
(B) $2\sqrt{2}$
(C) $\displaystyle\frac{\sqrt{2}}{2}$
(D) 1
(E) 0

10. Find the area under the curve $y = \dfrac{1}{x - 2}$ on the interval $[3, 7]$.

(A) $\ln 4$
(B) $\ln\left(\dfrac{7}{3}\right)$
(C) $\ln 5$
(D) 2
(E) $\dfrac{4}{5}$

Free-Response Questions

A graphing calculator is required for Questions 1 and 2.

1. Use your calculator to find the area enclosed by $y = 3 - x^2$ and $y = \dfrac{1}{x + 1}$.

2. Find $\displaystyle\int \frac{x^3 + 5x^2 + 8x + 5}{x^2 + 5x + 6}\, dx$. (*Hint:* Use long division first.)

3. Without the use of a calculator, find all values of b such that $\displaystyle\int_{-1.5}^{b} x\sqrt{2x + 3}\, dx = 0$. Show the work that leads to your answer.

6.6 Applications of the Integral: Average Value of a Function

If $f(x)$ is continuous on the interval $[a, b]$, then the **average value** of the function on the interval is

$$\frac{1}{b-a}\int_a^b f(x)\, dx.$$

This can also be expressed as

$$\text{(the average value of } f(x)\text{)}\,(b-a) = \int_a^b f(x)\, dx.$$

If $f(x) \geq 0$ for the entire interval, the above expression can be represented as two areas that are equal. The right side of the equation represents the area under the curve, enclosed by the lines $x = a$, $x = b$, and the x-axis. The left side of the equation represents the area of a rectangle with $(b - a)$ as its base and the average value of the function as its height.

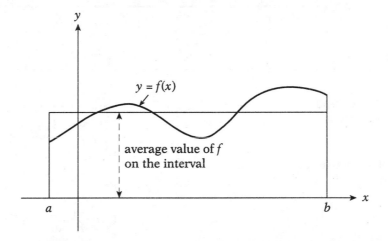

EXAMPLE 1

Find the average value of $f(x) = x^2$ on the interval $[0, 2]$.

Solution   The average value of the function $f(x) = x^2$ on the interval $[0, 2] = \frac{1}{2}\int_0^2 x^2\, dx.$

Evaluating this integral, the average value is

$$\frac{1}{2}\left(\frac{x^3}{3}\right)_0^2 = \frac{1}{2}\left(\frac{8}{3}\right) = \frac{4}{3}.$$

Notice that the average value of the function is NOT the average of the values at the endpoints.

EXAMPLE 2

Find the average value of $f(x) = \sin x$ on the interval $\left[0, \frac{\pi}{2}\right]$.

Solution   The average value of $f(x) = \sin x$ on the interval $\left[0, \frac{\pi}{2}\right] =$

$$\left(\frac{1}{\frac{\pi}{2} - 0}\right)\int_0^{\frac{\pi}{2}} \sin x \, dx = \frac{2}{\pi}(-\cos x)\Big|_0^{\frac{\pi}{2}} = \frac{2}{\pi}(0 + 1) = \frac{2}{\pi}.$$

EXAMPLE 3

Find the average value of $f(x) = e^{-x}$ on the interval $[0, 2]$.

Solution   The average value of $f(x) = e^{-x}$ on the interval $[0, 2] =$

$$\frac{1}{2}\int_0^2 e^{-x} \, dx = \frac{1}{2}(-e^{-x})\Big|_0^2 = \frac{1}{2}(-e^{-2} + 1) = \frac{1}{2}\left(1 - \frac{1}{e^2}\right) = \frac{e^2 - 1}{2e^2}.$$

Exercises

Multiple-Choice Questions
A graphing calculator is required for some questions.

1. Find the average value of $f(x) = 2x - x^2$ on the interval $[0, 2]$.
   (A) 0
   (B) $\frac{1}{2}$
   (C) 1
   (D) $\frac{2}{3}$
   (E) $\frac{4}{3}$

2. Find the average value of $f(x) = x^2 - 2$ on the interval $[0, 2]$.
   (A) $-\frac{4}{3}$
   (B) $-\frac{2}{3}$
   (C) 0
   (D) $\frac{2}{3}$
   (E) $\frac{4}{3}$

3. Find the average value of $f(x) = \sqrt{x}$ on the interval $[1, 4]$.
   (A) $\frac{1}{3}$
   (B) $\frac{7}{9}$
   (C) $\frac{14}{9}$
   (D) $\frac{7}{2}$
   (E) $\frac{14}{3}$

4. Find the average value of $y = \sqrt[3]{x + 3}$ on the interval $[-3, -2]$.
   (A) 0.681
   (B) 0.75
   (C) 0.909
   (D) 1.282
   (E) 2.280

Free-Response Questions
A graphing calculator is required for some questions.

1. The average daily temperature (°F) in Atlanta, t months after July 1, is approximated by the

function $T = 61 + 18 \cos \frac{\pi t}{6}$. Find the average temperature between September 1 ($t = 2$) and December 1 ($t = 5$).

2. (a) Find the average value of $f(x) = \sqrt{x}$ on the interval $[0, 1]$.
   (b) Find the average value of $f(x) = \sqrt[3]{x}$ on the interval $[0, 1]$.

(c) Find the average value of $f(x) = \sqrt[n]{x}$ on the interval $[0, 1]$.
(d) Find $\lim_{n \to \infty}$ (average value of $f(x) = \sqrt[n]{x}$ on the interval $[0, 1]$).

3. Find the average value of $f(x) = \sqrt[3]{x}$ on the interval $[-a, a]$.

6.7 Volumes

Both AP Calculus courses include the application of integrals to finding the volumes of solids of revolution and solids with a known cross section.

Solids of Revolution

A **solid of revolution** is formed by revolving an enclosed area around an **axis of revolution.** The axis of revolution may be vertical or horizontal. The first step in finding the volume of a solid of revolution is to sketch the area and to attempt to draw the solid. Though the drawing may not be perfect, it will assist you in visualizing the solid and identifying its radius or radii, which is necessary for finding the volume.

The figures on page 159 are representative of solids of revolution that students will encounter on the AP Calculus examinations. The solids are formed by revolving the region A (enclosed by $y = x^2$, the x-axis, and $x = 2$) around the given axes of revolution.

The two main methods for finding the area of solids of revolution are the disc method and the washer method.

The Disc Method

To use the disc method, begin with the area of a disc (or circle), which is $A = \pi r^2$, where r is the radius of the circle. Write an expression for r, and write the formula for the area of the disc. The volume of the solid of revolution is the antiderivative of the area of the disc followed by dx if the axis of revolution is the x-axis or a line parallel to the x-axis, or followed by dy if the axis of revolution is the y-axis or a line parallel to the y-axis.

If the region enclosed by the graph of $f(x)$ and the x-axis on an interval $[a, b]$ is rotated around the x-axis, then slices in the region perpendicular to the x-axis are circles with radius $f(x)$. The area of each circle or disc is

$$\text{Area} = \pi(f(x))^2.$$

The thickness of the disc is a small dx, and the volume of the solid is given by the formula

$$\text{Volume} = \pi \int_a^b (f(x))^2 \, dx.$$

The Washer Method

To use the washer method, begin with the area of a washer, $A = \pi(R^2 - r^2)$, where R is the radius of the outer circle and r is the radius of the inner circle. Write expressions for R and r, and write the formula for the area of the washer. The volume of the solid of revolution is the antiderivative of the area of the washer.

If the region enclosed by the graphs of $f(x)$ and $g(x)$ on an interval $[a, b]$ where $f(x) \geq g(x)$ is rotated about the x-axis, then slices in the region perpendicular to the x-axis are washers with outer radius $R = f(x)$ and inner radius $r = g(x)$. The area of the washer is

$$A = \pi(R^2 - r^2) = \pi((f(x))^2 - (g(x))^2).$$

The thickness of the washer is a small dx, and the volume of the solid is given by the formula

$$V = \pi \int_a^b ((f(x))^2 - g((x))^2)\, dx.$$

If the region is rotated about a line other than the x-axis, draw a slice in the region perpendicular to the line of rotation. Extend the line segment drawn to the line of rotation. The length from the point on the line of rotation to the first point in the region is r and the length from the point on the line of rotation to the last point in the region is R.

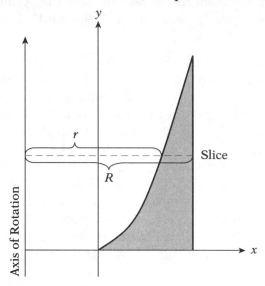

If $r = 0$, then the slice will become a disc when rotated; otherwise, the slice will become a washer when rotated.

The endpoints of the slice are the coordinates of the point or points on the graphs of $f(x)$ and $g(x)$. Use these coordinates to find expressions for r and R, the radius or radii of the disc or washer.

The designation dx or dy takes on greater importance here than in area problems. The thickness of the disc or washer is dx if it is measured in the x-direction (horizontally) or dy if it is measured in the y-direction (vertically). If an antiderivative is to be found dx, that is, with respect to x, then the integrand must be an expression in terms of x and the limits of the integral must be x-values. If the antiderivative is found dy, then the integrand must be in terms of y and the limits of the integral must be y-values.

	Horizontal Axis of Revolution	Vertical Axis of Revolution
Disc Method	$\pi \int_a^b r^2\, dx$	$\pi \int_a^b r^2\, dy$
Washer Method	$\pi \int_a^b (R^2 - r^2)\, dx$	$\pi \int_a^b (R^2 - r^2)\, dy$

Solids of Revolution

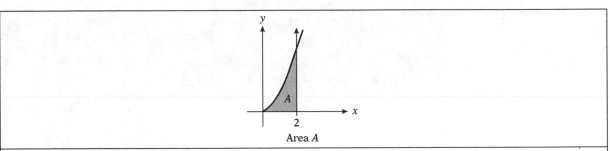

Area A

Vertical Axes of Revolution

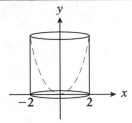

Axis: $x = 0$

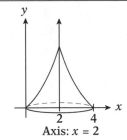

Axis: $x = 2$

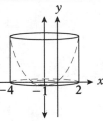

Axis: $x = -1$

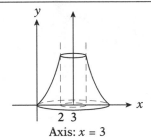

Axis: $x = 3$

Horizontal Axes of Revolution

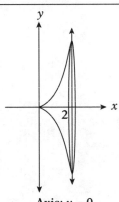

Axis: $y = 0$

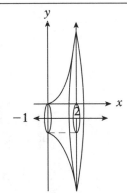

Axis: $y = -1$

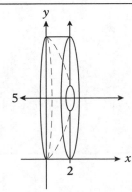

Axis: $y = 5$

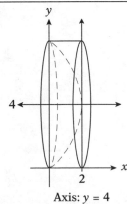

Axis: $y = 4$

EXAMPLE 1

Find the volume of the solid generated when the region enclosed by the graph of $f(x) = x^2$ and the x-axis in the interval $[0, 2]$ is rotated about the x-axis.

Solution   Begin by sketching the solid.

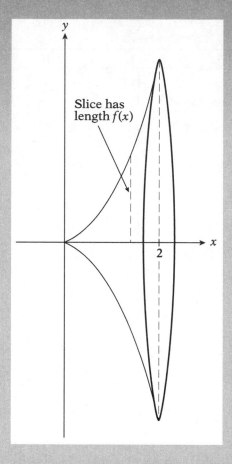

Slice has length $f(x)$

A slice in the region perpendicular to the x-axis has length $f(x)$ or x^2. When this slice is rotated about the x-axis, it will generate a disc with radius x^2. The area of the disc is

$$A = \pi r^2 = \pi(x^2)^2.$$

Since the thickness is measured with respect to x, the volume is

$$V = \pi \int_0^2 \left(f(x)\right)^2 dx = \pi \int_0^2 x^4\, dx.$$

The integral can be evaluated either by hand or by using a calculator. The volume is $\dfrac{32\pi}{5}$ or 20.106.

EXAMPLE 2

Using the region described in Example 1, find the volume when the region is rotated about the y-axis.

Solution   Begin by sketching the solid.

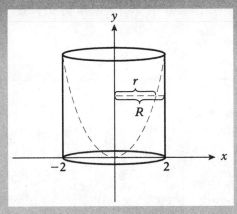

A slice drawn in the region perpendicular to the line of rotation will produce a washer with inner radius $r = x = \sqrt{y}$ and outer radius $R = 2$.

The area of the washer is $A = \pi\left(2^2 - \left(\sqrt{y}\right)^2\right) = \pi(4 - y)$.

Since the thickness is with respect to y, the area must be expressed in terms of y, and the limits of the integral must be y-values. Thus, the volume of the solid generated is given by the formula

$$V = \pi \int_0^4 (4 - x^2)\, dy$$

$$= \pi \int_0^4 (4 - y)\, dy = 8\pi \text{ or } 25.133$$

EXAMPLE 3

Rotate the region described in Example 1 about the line $x = 2$. Find the volume of the solid generated.

Solution   Begin by sketching the solid.

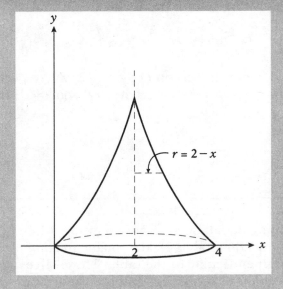

A slice drawn perpendicular to the line $x = 2$ produces a line segment that becomes a disc when rotated about the line $x = 2$.

The radius of the disc is $r = 2 - x$, and the area of the disc is

$$A = \pi r^2 = \pi(2 - x)^2.$$

The thickness is dy and $x = \sqrt{y}$, so the volume of the solid is

$$V = \pi \int (2 - x)^2 \, dy = \pi \int_0^4 \left(2 - \sqrt{y}\right)^2 dy = \frac{8\pi}{3} = 8.378.$$

EXAMPLE 4

Find the volume of the solid generated when the region enclosed by the graphs of $y = x^2$ and $y = \sqrt{x}$ is rotated about the x-axis.

Solution   Sketch the region and the solid.

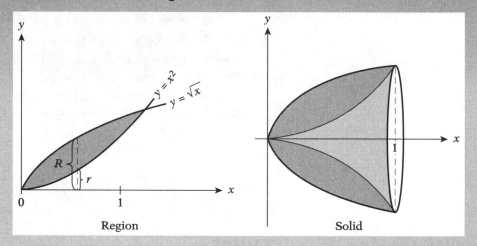

| Region | Solid |

A slice in the region perpendicular to the x-axis is a line segment that forms a washer when rotated about the x-axis. The inner radius r is the y-coordinate of the graph of $y = x^2$ and the outer radius R is the y-coordinate of the graph of $y = \sqrt{x}$.

The area of the washer is

$$A = \pi(R^2 - r^2) = \pi\left(\left(\sqrt{x}\right)^2 - (x^2)^2\right) = \pi\,(x - x^4).$$

Since the thickness of the slice is with respect to x, and the graphs of $y = x^2$ and $y = \sqrt{x}$ intersect at $x = 0$ and $x = 1$, the formula for the volume is

$$V = \pi \int_0^1 (x - x^4) \, dx.$$

The solution is $V = \frac{3\pi}{10} = 0.942.$

Solids with Known Cross Sections

Imagine taking an orange, cutting it in half, and placing one half cut-side down on a table. Next, imagine making paper-thin slices in one direction, perpendicular to the table. These slices are **cross sections.** Each cross section of the orange half is a semicircle, with each one having a different radius. The sum of the volumes of all these paper-thin semicircles forms the volume of the orange.

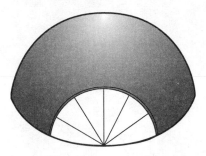

Now imagine another solid, with cross-sectioned slices that are squares of different sizes. The sum of the volumes of the paper-thin squares is the volume of the solid. In finding the volume of a solid with known cross sections, the base of the solid is given, as is the shape of the cross section. While this type of solid may be more difficult to visualize than the orange, finding its volume involves the same two-step process.

1. Find an expression for the area of the geometric shape of the cross section.
2. Take the antiderivative of the area expression.

Thus, the volume V of a solid with known cross sections is given by the formula

$$V = \int \text{Area } (dx \text{ or } dy).$$

Note: If the cross sections are perpendicular to the x-axis, the integral is with respect to dx. If the cross sections are perpendicular to the y-axis, the integral is with respect to dy.

EXAMPLE 5

A solid has a base that is a circle with equation $x^2 + y^2 = 1$. Cross sections perpendicular to the x-axis are semicircles with their diameters in the plane of the base. Find the volume of the solid.

Solution   First sketch the base of the solid and the solid itself.

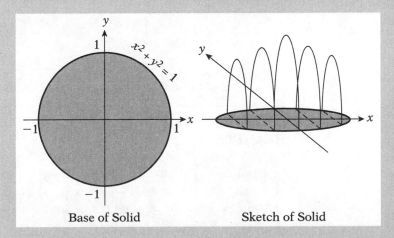

Base of Solid   Sketch of Solid

Since the cross sections are perpendicular to the x-axis, the integral will be with respect to dx. The bounds of integration are -1 and 1. Each cross section is a semicircle with radius $y = \sqrt{1 - x^2}$. The area of the semicircle is

$$A = \frac{1}{2}\pi r^2$$

$$A = \frac{1}{2}\pi y^2$$

$$A = \frac{1}{2}\pi\left(\sqrt{1 - x^2}\right)^2$$

$$A = \frac{1}{2}\pi(1 - x^2).$$

Therefore, the volume is given by

$$V = \frac{1}{2}\pi \int_{-1}^{1} (1 - x^2)\, dx.$$

Since the graph of the base is symmetrical, this can be expressed as

$$V = 2\left(\frac{1}{2}\right)\pi \int_{0}^{1} (1 - x^2)\, dx$$

$$V = \pi \int_{0}^{1} (1 - x^2)\, dx.$$

Integrating, we get

$$V = \pi \left[x - \frac{x^3}{3} \right]_{0}^{1},$$

and by substitution of the limits,

$$V = \pi\left(1 - \frac{1}{3} \right).$$

The volume is $\frac{2\pi}{3}$, or 2.094 cubic units.

EXAMPLE 6

The base of a solid is the region enclosed by the graph of $x = y^2$, the x-axis, and the line $x = 4$. Cross sections perpendicular to the x-axis are squares. Find the volume of the solid.

Solution   First sketch the base of the solid and the solid itself.

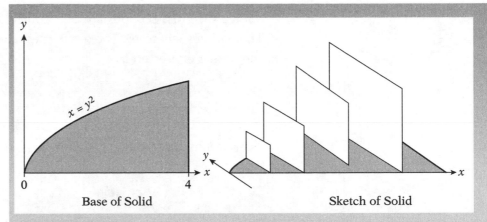

Base of Solid   Sketch of Solid

Since the cross sections are perpendicular to the x-axis, the integral will be with respect to dx. The bounds of integration are 0 and 4. The length of the side of each square is $y = \sqrt{x}$. The area of each square is

$$A = (\text{side})^2 = y^2 = \left(\sqrt{x}\right)^2 = x.$$

Therefore, the volume is given by

$$V = \int_0^4 x \, dx$$

$$V = \left[\frac{x^2}{2}\right]_0^4$$

The volume is 8 cubic units.

EXAMPLE 7

The base of a solid is the region enclosed by the graphs of $y = \frac{1}{2}x^2$ and $y = 8$. Cross sections perpendicular to the y-axis are semicircles with diameter in the plane of the region. Find the volume of the solid.

Solution   First sketch the base of the solid and the solid itself.

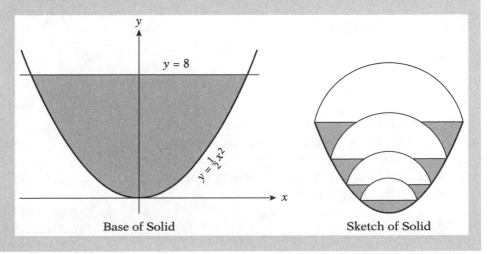

Base of Solid   Sketch of Solid

Since the cross sections are perpendicular to the y-axis, the integral will be with respect to dy. The semicircles have radius $x = \sqrt{2y}$. The area of the base is expressed as

$$A = \frac{1}{2}\pi\left(\sqrt{2y}\right)^2.$$

The volume of the solid is then expressed by

$$V = \int_0^8 \frac{1}{2}\pi\left(\sqrt{2y}\right)^2 dy$$

$$V = \int_0^8 \frac{1}{2}\pi(2y)\, dy$$

$$V = \pi \int_0^8 y\, dy$$

$$V = \pi\left(\frac{y^2}{2}\right)\Bigg|_0^8.$$

The volume is 32π cubic units.

Exercises

Multiple-Choice Questions

A graphing calculator is required for some questions.

1. The base of a solid is the region enclosed by $y = \sin x$ and the x-axis on the interval $[0, \pi]$. Cross sections perpendicular to the x-axis are semicircles with diameter in the plane of the base. Write an integral that represents the volume of the solid.

   (A) $\dfrac{\pi}{8}\displaystyle\int_0^\pi (\sin x)^2\, dx$

   (B) $\dfrac{\pi}{8}\displaystyle\int_0^1 (\sin x)^2\, dx$

   (C) $\dfrac{\pi}{4}\displaystyle\int_0^\pi (\sin x)^2\, dx$

   (D) $\dfrac{\pi}{8}\displaystyle\int_0^\pi \sin x\, dx$

   (E) $\dfrac{\pi}{2}\displaystyle\int_0^\pi (\sin x)^2\, dx$

2. The base of a solid is the region enclosed by $y = e^x$, the x-axis, the y-axis, and the line $x = \ln 3$. Cross sections perpendicular to the x-axis are squares. Write an integral that represents the volume of the solid.

   (A) $\displaystyle\int_0^{\ln 3} e^x\, dx$

   (B) $\displaystyle\int_0^{(\ln 3)^2} e^{2x}\, dx$

   (C) $\displaystyle\int_0^{\ln 3} e^{2x}\, dx$

   (D) $\pi\displaystyle\int_0^{\ln 3} e^{2x}\, dx$

   (E) $\pi\displaystyle\int_0^3 e^{2x}\, dx$

3. The base of a solid is the region enclosed by the x-axis, $y = \tan x$, and the line $x = \frac{\pi}{4}$. Cross sections perpendicular to the x-axis are isosceles right triangles with one leg in the plane of the base. Write an integral that represents the volume of the solid.

   (A) $\dfrac{1}{2}\displaystyle\int_0^{\frac{\pi}{4}} \tan^2 x\, dx$

   (B) $\displaystyle\int_0^{\frac{\pi}{4}} \tan^2 x\, dx$

   (C) $\dfrac{\pi}{2}\displaystyle\int_0^{\frac{\pi}{4}} \tan^2 x\, dx$

   (D) $\dfrac{1}{2}\displaystyle\int_0^1 \tan^2 x\, dx$

   (E) $\dfrac{\pi}{2}\displaystyle\int_0^1 \tan^2 x\, dx$

4. The base of a solid is the region enclosed by $y = e^x$ and the lines $y = 1$ and $x = \ln 3$. Cross sections perpendicular to the y-axis are squares. Write an integral that represents the volume of the solid.

(A) $\pi \int_1^3 (\ln 3 - \ln y)^2 \, dy$

(B) $\int_1^3 (\ln 3 - \ln y)^2 \, dy$

(C) $\int_0^{\ln 3} (\ln 3 - \ln y)^2 \, dy$

(D) $\int_1^3 ((\ln 3)^2 - (\ln y)^2) \, dy$

(E) $\int_0^1 (e^{2x} - 1) \, dx$

5. Find the volume of the solid formed by rotating about the x-axis the region enclosed by the graph of $y = \sqrt{x} + 1$, the x-axis, the y-axis, and the line $x = 4$.
   (A) 7.667
   (B) 9.333
   (C) 22.667
   (D) 37.699
   (E) 71.209

6. Find the volume of the solid formed by rotating the region bounded by the graph of $y = \sqrt{x} + 1$, the y-axis, and the line $y = 3$ about the y-axis.
   (A) 6.40
   (B) 8.378
   (C) 20.106
   (D) 100.531
   (E) 145.77

7. Find the volume of the solid formed by rotating the region bounded by the graph of $y = \sqrt{x} + 1$, the y-axis, and the line $y = 3$ about the line $y = 5$.
   (A) 13.333
   (B) 17.657
   (C) 41.888
   (D) 92.153
   (E) 242.95

8. The base of a solid is the region enclosed by the graph of $x^2 + 4y^2 = 4$. Cross sections of the solid perpendicular to the x-axis are squares. Find the volume of the solid.
   (A) $\frac{8}{3}$
   (B) $\frac{8}{3} \pi$
   (C) $\frac{16}{3}$
   (D) $\frac{32}{3}$
   (E) $\frac{32}{3} \pi$

9. Find the volume of the solid formed by rotating the graph of $x^2 + 4y^2 = 4$ about the x-axis.
   (A) $\frac{8}{3}$
   (B) $\frac{8}{3} \pi$
   (C) $\frac{16}{3}$
   (D) $\frac{32}{3}$
   (E) $\frac{32}{3} \pi$

10. Which of the following integrals represents the volume of the solid obtained by rotating the region bounded by the graph of $y = -\sqrt{x}$, the x-axis, and the line $x = 4$ about the x-axis?
    (A) $\pi \int_0^4 y^2 \, dy$
    (B) $\pi \int_0^2 y^2 \, dy$
    (C) $\pi \int_0^4 \left(\sqrt{x}\right)^2 \, dx$
    (D) $\pi \int_0^2 \left(-\sqrt{x}\right)^2 \, dx$
    (E) $\pi \int_0^4 (-x) \, dx$

Free-Response Questions
A graphing calculator is required for some questions.

1. The area enclosed by the graph of $x^2 + 4y^2 = 4$ is the base of a solid.
   (a) Find the ratio of the volume of the solid whose cross sections perpendicular to the x-axis are squares to the volume of the solid whose cross sections perpendicular to the x-axis are equilateral triangles.
   (b) Find the ratio of the volume of the solid whose cross sections perpendicular to the x-axis are squares to the volume of the solid whose cross sections perpendicular to the y-axis are squares.

2. Given the function $x^2 + 4y^2 = 4$:
   (a) Find the ratio of the volumes of the solids generated by rotating the graph of the function about the x-axis and about the y-axis.
   (b) Find the ratio of the volumes of the solids generated by rotating the graph of the function about the line $y = 2$ and about the line $x = 3$.

3. A cake is formed by rotating the region bounded by the graph of $y = \sqrt{25 - x^2}$, the y-axis, and the line $y = 3$ about the x-axis.

   (a) Find the volume of the cake.
   (b) If the cake weighs about 0.25 ounce/unit^3, about how much does the entire cake weigh?

4. A giant soda glass is formed by rotating the graph of

$$f(x) = \begin{cases} 0.03x^2 + 1.125, & 0 \le x < 5 \\ -0.2(x - 5)^2 + 1.875, & 5 \le x < 6 \\ 0.1(x - 6)^2 + 1.675, & 6 \le x \le 7 \end{cases}$$

   about the x-axis.

   (a) If the measurements are in inches, find the capacity of the glass in cubic inches.
   (b) If 16.387 cm^3 = 1 in.^{3}, and 1000 cm^3 = 1 liter, will the glass hold more than 0.5 liter of soda? Justify your conclusion.

5. R_1 is the region in the first quadrant bounded by the graph of $y = \frac{1}{2}x^2$, the y-axis, and the line $y = 2$. R_2 is the region in the first quadrant bounded by the graph of $y = \frac{1}{2}x^2$, the x-axis, and the line $x = 2$.

   (a) Find the ratio of the volumes of the solids generated when R_1 and R_2 are rotated about the x-axis.
   (b) Find the ratio of the volumes of the solids generated when R_1 and R_2 are rotated about the line $y = 2$.

6.8 The Trapezoidal Rule

The **Trapezoidal Rule** is used to approximate the value of a definite integral, particularly a definite integral whose antiderivative is difficult or impossible to evaluate. A trapezoidal approximation gives a more accurate estimate than a lower or upper sum, and may be found using subintervals of equal or unequal length. If an interval [a, b] is partitioned into equal subintervals, then the process of finding an approximation to the definite integral is called the trapezoidal rule. This is the same process as was used in Section 6.2 to find lower and upper sums. The difference here is that instead of rectangles, connect the points on the graph of $f(x)$ to form trapezoids.

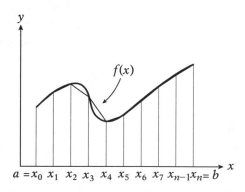

Trapezoidal Rule

Each subinterval has length $\frac{b - a}{n}$. If the partition points are $a = x_0, x_1, x_2,$ ..., $x_{n-1}, x_n = b$, the values of the function are $f(a) = f(x_0), f(x_1), f(x_2),...,$ $f(x_{n-1}), f(x_n) = f(b)$.

The Trapezoidal Rule approximates the definite integral as

$$\frac{b-a}{2n}\left[f(x_0) + 2f(x_1) + 2f(x_2) + \cdots + 2f(x_{n-1}) + f(x_n)\right].$$

 ### Error in the Trapezoidal Rule

If $f(x)$ has a continuous second derivative, the error E in approximating the definite integral of $f(x)$ on the interval $[a, b]$ is

$$E \leq \frac{(b-a)^3}{12n^2}\max|f''(x)|.$$

EXAMPLE 1

Use the Trapezoidal Rule with five subintervals to approximate the area under the curve $y = x^2$ on the interval $[0, 1]$. Then find the actual value of the area and find the error.

Solution The partition points are 0, 0.2, 0.4, 0.6, 0.8, and 1. By the Trapezoidal Rule, the area is approximately equal to

$$\frac{1}{10}[0 + 2(0.2)^2 + 2(0.4)^2 + 2(0.6)^2 + 2(0.8)^2 + 1] = 0.34.$$

The actual value of the definite integral $\int_0^1 x^2\, dx = \frac{1}{3}$, which is a difference of about 0.0067.

 ### Calculator Note

For a large number of terms, the trapezoidal approximation can be performed on a graphing calculator as follows. In Example 1 above, the approximation can be rewritten as

$$\frac{1}{10}[0 + 1 + 2((0.2)^2 + (0.4)^2 + (0.6)^2 + (0.8)^2)].$$

First enter x^2 into Y= Y_1.

Then find the sum of the sequence by entering the following in the home screen: 1 ÷ 10 (0 + 1 + 2 (.

To get the sum term, enter 2nd STAT MATH 5.

To get the sequence term, enter 2nd STAT OPS 5.

Then enter VARS Y-VARS 1 1 (X,T,Θ,n)) , X,T,Θ,n , 0.2 , 0.8 , 0.2))).

Pressing ENTER will give the following result:

```
1/10(0+1+2(sum(s
eq(Y1(X),X,.2,.8
,.2)))
                .34
■
```

In the calculator screen, the last three numbers in the parentheses indicate where the sequence starts, where the sequence ends, and the increment from one term in the sequence to the next. This is one way to add the terms in the formula for the Trapezoidal Rule and is especially useful as the number of subintervals increases.

EXAMPLE 2

(a) Use the Trapezoidal Rule with ten subintervals to approximate the area under the curve $y = \frac{1}{x}$ on the interval [1, 2].

(b) Compute the error bound E.

Solution

(a) The partition points are 1, 1.1, 1.2, 1.3, ... ,1.9, 2. By the Trapezoidal Rule, the area is approximately equal to

$$\frac{1}{20}\left[1 + 2\left(\frac{1}{1.1}\right) + 2\left(\frac{1}{1.2}\right) + \cdots + 2\left(\frac{1}{1.9}\right) + \frac{1}{2}\right] = 0.69377.$$

(b) Using the graphing calculator, enter $Y_1 = \frac{1}{x}$, and the trapezoidal approximation can be rewritten as

$$\frac{1}{20}\left[1 + \frac{1}{2} + 2(\text{sum}(\text{seq}(Y_1(x), x, 1.1, 1.9, 0.1)))\right].$$

The error bound $E \le \frac{1}{1,200} \max \left|\frac{2}{x^3}\right|$ on [1, 2].

$$E \le \frac{1}{1,200}(2) = \frac{1}{600} = 0.00167$$

EXAMPLE 3

Use the Trapezoidal Rule with five subintervals to approximate the area under the curve $y = \sin x$ on the interval $\left[0, \frac{\pi}{2}\right]$.

Solution   The partition points for the interval $\left[0, \frac{\pi}{2}\right]$ are $0, \frac{\pi}{10}$, $\frac{\pi}{5}, \frac{3\pi}{10}, \frac{2\pi}{5}, \frac{\pi}{2}$. The Trapezoidal Rule approximation to the area is:

$$\frac{\frac{\pi}{2}}{10}\left[\sin 0 + 2\sin\left(\frac{\pi}{10}\right) + 2\sin\left(\frac{\pi}{5}\right)\right.$$

$$\left. + 2\sin\left(\frac{3\pi}{10}\right) + 2\sin\left(\frac{2\pi}{5}\right) + \sin\left(\frac{\pi}{2}\right)\right],$$

which is approximately 0.9918.

The trapezoidal approximation can be performed on the calculator by rewriting it as follows and entering $Y_1 = \sin x$:

$$\frac{\frac{\pi}{2}}{10}\left[\sin 0 + \sin\frac{\pi}{2} + 2\left(\text{sum}\left(\text{seq}\left(Y_1(x), \frac{\pi}{10}, \frac{2\pi}{5}, \frac{\pi}{10}\right)\right)\right)\right].$$

Exercises

Multiple-Choice Questions
A graphing calculator is required for some questions.

1. Which of the following expressions is the Trapezoidal Rule approximation for $y = x^2$ on the interval $[0, 2]$ with 10 equal subintervals?

   (A) $\frac{1}{20}\left[(0.2)^2 + 2(0.4)^2 + \cdots + 2(1.8)^2 + 2^2\right]$

   (B) $\frac{1}{10}\left[2(0.2)^2 + 2(0.4)^2 + \cdots + 2(1.8)^2 + 2^2\right]$

   (C) $\frac{1}{5}\left[2(0.2)^2 + 2(0.4)^2 + \cdots + 2(1.8)^2 + 2^2\right]$

   (D) $\frac{1}{20}\left[2(0.2)^2 + 2(0.4)^2 + \cdots + 2(1.8)^2 + 2^2\right]$

   (E) $\frac{1}{10}\left[(0.2)^2 + 2(0.4)^2 + \cdots + 2(1.8)^2 + 2^2\right]$

2. Which of the following statements is true about the graph of $y = \ln x$ on the interval $[1, e]$ with 10 equal subintervals?
   (A) the trapezoidal approximation < the area under the curve
   (B) the trapezoidal approximation = the left-hand sum
   (C) the trapezoidal approximation = the right-hand sum
   (D) the trapezoidal approximation > the area under the curve
   (E) the left-hand sum > the right-hand sum

3. Which of the following is the trapezoidal approximation for $f(x) = \frac{1}{x}$ on the interval $[1, 3]$ with n equal subintervals?

   (A) $\frac{1}{n}\left[1 + \frac{2}{1+\frac{2}{n}} + \frac{2}{1+\frac{4}{n}} + \frac{2}{1+\frac{6}{n}} + \cdots \right.$
   $\left. + \frac{2}{1+\frac{2(n-1)}{n}} + \frac{1}{3}\right]$

   (B) $\frac{2}{n}\left[1 + \frac{2}{1+\frac{2}{n}} + \frac{2}{1+\frac{4}{n}} + \frac{2}{1+\frac{6}{n}} + \cdots \right.$
   $\left. + \frac{2}{1+\frac{2(n-1)}{n}} + \frac{1}{3}\right]$

   (C) $\frac{2}{n}\left[1 + \frac{2}{1+\frac{1}{n}} + \frac{2}{1+\frac{2}{n}} + \frac{2}{1+\frac{3}{n}} + \cdots \right.$
   $\left. + \frac{2}{1+\frac{n-1}{n}} + \frac{1}{3}\right]$

   (D) $\frac{2}{n}\left[1 + \frac{1}{1+\frac{2}{n}} + \frac{1}{1+\frac{4}{n}} + \frac{1}{1+\frac{6}{n}} + \cdots \right.$
   $\left. + \frac{1}{1+\frac{2(n-1)}{n}} + \frac{1}{3}\right]$

   (E) none of these

4. Which of the following is true about the trapezoidal approximation for the graph of $f(x) = e^{-x}$ on the interval $[-1, 1]$ with n equal subintervals?
   (A) Using $n = 5$ gives a closer approximation to the area under the curve than $n = 10$.
   (B) The trapezoidal approximation on the interval $[-1, 0]$ is equal to the trapezoidal approximation on the interval $[0, 1]$.
   (C) The trapezoidal approximation is greater than the area under the curve.
   (D) The trapezoidal approximation is greater than the upper sum.
   (E) The trapezoidal approximation for $f(x) = e^{-x}$ on the interval $[-1, 1]$ is less than the trapezoidal approximation for $f(x) = e^x$ on the interval $[-1, 1]$.

A graphing calculator is required for some questions.

1. (a) Use the Trapezoidal Rule with ten subintervals to approximate $\int_0^2 (x^2 + 1)\, dx$.

   (b) Compare the approximation with the actual value of the antiderivative.

2. (a) Use the Trapezoidal Rule with ten subintervals to approximate $\int_0^2 (x^2 - 2)\, dx$.

   (b) Compare the approximation with the actual value of the antiderivative.

3. (a) Use the Trapezoidal Rule with ten subintervals to approximate $\int_{-1}^1 \cos x\, dx$.

   (b) Compare the approximation with the actual value of the antiderivative.

4. Based on the comparisons between the actual and approximated values in Questions 1–3, write an explanation of why some approximations are greater than the actual value and why some are less.

BC 6.9 Arc Length and Area of a Surface of Revolution

Arc Length The process of finding the length of the arc of a curve is similar to the process described in Section 6.2 for finding the area under a curve. A function $y = f(x)$ is given on an interval $[a, b]$. The interval is partitioned into equal subintervals, each of length Δx. Each tiny piece of arc on the curve is approximated by the hypotenuse Δs of a right triangle with legs Δx and Δy.

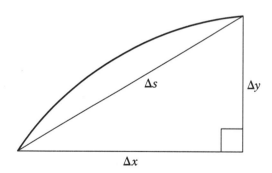

As the number of subintervals increases, the length of Δx approaches zero, and the length of the arc is closer to the hypotenuse of the triangle. The hypotenuse is expressed as

$$\Delta s = \sqrt{(\Delta x)^2 + (\Delta y)^2},$$

and the arc length is

$$\lim_{\Delta x \to 0} \sum \Delta s = \lim_{\Delta x \to 0} \sum \sqrt{(\Delta x)^2 + (\Delta y)^2}.$$

Thus, the formula for the arc length of a curve is

$$s = \int_a^b \sqrt{(dx)^2 + (dy)^2}.$$

Note: The formula in this form may be easier to remember, since the integrand is a form of the Pythagorean Theorem. In addition, by manipulating the integrand of this formula, formulas for arc length can be adjusted in the following ways.

If y is a function of x, that is, $y = f(x)$,

Then

$$\sqrt{(dx)^2 + (dy)^2} = \sqrt{1 + \left(\frac{dy}{dx}\right)^2}\, dx,$$

and the length of the arc of the curve on $[a, b]$ is

$$s = \int_a^b \sqrt{1 + \left(\frac{dy}{dx}\right)^2}\, dx.$$

If x is a function of y, that is, $x = f(y)$,

Then

$$\sqrt{(dx)^2 + (dy)^2} = \sqrt{1 + \left(\frac{dx}{dy}\right)^2}\, dy,$$

and the length of the arc of the curve on $[c, d]$ is

$$s = \int_c^d \sqrt{1 + \left(\frac{dx}{dy}\right)^2}\, dy.$$

If x and y are functions of a parameter t, that is, $x = x(t)$ and $y = y(t)$,

Then

$$\sqrt{(dx)^2 + (dy)^2} = \sqrt{\left(\frac{dx}{dt}\right)^2 + \left(\frac{dy}{dt}\right)}\, dt,$$

and the length of the arc on $[t_1, t_2]$ is

$$s = \int_{t_1}^{t_2} \sqrt{\left(\frac{dx}{dt}\right)^2 + \left(\frac{dy}{dt}\right)^2}\, dt\,.$$

Area of a Surface of Revolution

When the arc of a curve is rotated about a line, called the axis of rotation, it forms a solid.

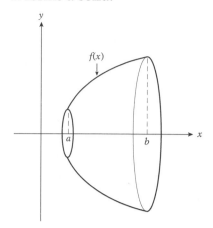

The area of the surface of revolution can be calculated by the formula

$$\text{S.A.} = \int 2\pi r \, ds,$$

where r is the distance between the curve and the line of rotation, and ds is given by one of the radical expressions given above.

If $y = f(x)$ on $[a, b]$ and the arc of the curve is rotated about the x-axis, then the surface area is given by

$$\text{S.A.} = \int_a^b 2\pi y \sqrt{1 + \left(\frac{dy}{dx}\right)^2} \, dx.$$

If the same arc is rotated about the y-axis, then the surface area is

$$\text{S.A.} = \int_a^b 2\pi x \sqrt{1 + \left(\frac{dy}{dx}\right)^2} \, dx.$$

EXAMPLE 1

Write an integral that represents the length of the arc of the graph of $y = x^2$ on $[0, 2]$.

Solution If $y = x^2$, $\dfrac{dy}{dx} = 2x$, and $s = \displaystyle\int_0^2 \sqrt{1 + 4x^2} \, dx$.

EXAMPLE 2

Write an integral that represents the length of the arc of the graph of $x = \sqrt{y^2 + 1}$ on the interval for y $[-1, 1]$.

Solution If $x = \sqrt{y^2 + 1}$, then $\dfrac{dx}{dy} = \dfrac{y}{\sqrt{y^2 + 1}}$. Then

$$s = \int_{-1}^{1} \sqrt{1 + \left(\frac{dx}{dy}\right)^2} \, dy = \int_{-1}^{1} \sqrt{1 + \frac{y^2}{y^2 + 1}} \, dy.$$

EXAMPLE 3

Write an integral in a single variable that represents the area of the surface when the arc of the graph of $y = x^2$ on $[0, 2]$ is rotated about the x-axis.

Solution S.A. $= \int_0^2 2\pi y \sqrt{1 + 4x^2}\, dx = \int_0^2 2\pi x^2 \sqrt{1 + 4x^2}\, dx.$

EXAMPLE 4

Write an integral to find the length of an arc of $x(t) = t^3$, $y(t) = t^2 + 1$, for t between -1 and 1 inclusive. Use a graphing calculator to find the value of the integral.

Solution The length of the arc is $s = \int_{-1}^1 \sqrt{9t^4 + 4t^2}\, dt = 2.879.$

Exercises

Multiple-Choice Questions

A graphing calculator is required for some questions.

1. Find the length of the part of the parabola $y = \frac{1}{2}x^2$ on the interval $[-1, 1]$.

   (A) 0.333
   (B) 1.886
   (C) 2.179
   (D) 2.296
   (E) 2.958

2. Find the length of the arc of the curve defined by the parametric equations $\begin{array}{l} x(t) = \sin t \\ y(t) = 1 - \cos t \end{array}$ for values of t in the interval $\left[-\frac{\pi}{2}, \frac{\pi}{2}\right]$.

   (A) $\frac{\pi}{2}$
   (B) π
   (C) $\pi + 1$
   (D) $\pi - 1$
   (E) 2π

3. Find the area of the surface formed when the curve $y = e^{-x}$ on the interval $[0, 1]$ is rotated about the x-axis.
   (A) 0.772
   (B) 1.212

   (C) 1.544
   (D) 2.425
   (E) 4.849

4. Find the area of the surface formed by rotating the graph of $f(x) = \sqrt[3]{x} - 1$ on the interval $[2, 3]$ about the y-axis.
   (A) 2.582
   (B) 4.056
   (C 5.164
   (D) 8.111
   (E) 16.223

Free-Response Questions

A graphing calculator is required for some questions.

1. Find the length of the ellipse given by $x^2 + 4y^2 = 4$.

2. (a) Find the length of the graph given by $f(x) = \frac{1}{x}$ on the interval $[1, 2]$.

   (b) Find the volume of the solid generated by rotating $f(x) = \frac{1}{x}$ on the interval $[1, c]$ about the x-axis.

   (c) Find the limiting value of the volume of the solid found in part (b) as $c \to \infty$.

Chapter Assessment

Multiple-Choice Questions
No calculator is allowed for these questions.

1. $\int \frac{5x^4 - 2}{3x^2} dx =$

   (A) $\frac{x^4 - 2}{x^2} + c$

   (B) $\frac{5}{9}x^3 + \frac{2}{3x} + c$

   (C) $\frac{5}{3}x^3 + \frac{2}{3x} + c$

   (D) $\frac{5}{9}x^3 + \frac{2}{9x^3} + c$

   (E) $\frac{5}{9}x^3 - \frac{2}{9x^3} + c$

2. $\int (3x + 1)^2 dx =$

   (A) $\frac{(3x + 1)^3}{9} + c$

   (B) $\frac{(3x + 1)^3}{3} + c$

   (C) $9x^2 + 6x + c$

   (D) $3x^3 + 3x^2 + c$

   (E) $(3x + 1)^3 + c$

3. $\int_2^4 e^{x-2} dx =$

   (A) e^2

   (B) $e^2 - 1$

   (C) $\frac{e^2 - 1}{2}$

   (D) $2(e^2 - 1)$

   (E) $1 - e^{-2}$

4. $\int \frac{4}{\sqrt{x}} dx =$

   (A) $8\sqrt{x} + c$

   (B) $2\sqrt{x} + c$

   (C) $4x^{-1/2} + c$

   (D) $\frac{6}{\sqrt{x}} + c$

   (E) $-2x^{-3/2} + c$

5. $\int \left(\frac{1}{x} + x\right) dx =$

   (A) $-\frac{1}{x^2} + 1 + c$

   (B) $\ln x + x + c$

   (C) $\ln x + 1 + c$

   (D) $\ln x + \frac{x^2}{2} + c$

   (E) $1 + \frac{x^2}{2} + c$

6. $f(x)$ is a continuous function on $[a, b]$. Which of the following statements are true?

   I $f(x)$ is differentiable on (a, b).

   II There is a number c in (a, b) such that $f'(c) = \frac{f(b) - f(a)}{b - a}$.

   III $f(x)$ has a maximum value on $[a, b]$.

   (A) I only

   (B) II only

   (C) III only

   (D) I and III

   (E) I, II, and III

7. $\int \frac{x}{x + 4} dx =$

   (A) -4

   (B) 1

   (C) $x - 4 \ln|x + 4| + c$

   (D) $\frac{x^2}{x^2 + 8} + c$

   (E) $x - \ln|x + 4| + c$

8. If $\int_0^a \sin x \, dx = b$, then $\int_{-a}^a \sin x \, dx =$

   (A) b

   (B) $2b$

   (C) 0

   (D) $b + 1$

   (E) $\frac{b^2}{2}$

9. $\int_{-a}^a \frac{x}{x^2 + 1} dx =$

   (A) 0

   (B) $2 \int_0^a \frac{x}{x^2 + 1} dx$

   (C) $-\frac{1}{(a^2 + 1)^2}$

   (D) $\frac{1}{a}$

   (E) $2 \ln (a^2 + 1)$

10. $\int x \cos(x^2) dx =$

    (A) $x \sin (x^2) + c$

    (B) $\sin (x^2) + c$

    (C) $2 \sin (x^2) + c$

    (D) $-2x^2 \sin (x^2) + c$

    (E) $\frac{1}{2} \sin (x^2) + c$

11. $\int x^3(x^4 + 1)^3 \, dx =$

(A) $\dfrac{(x^4 + 1)^4}{16} + c$

(B) $\dfrac{(x^4 + 1)^4}{4} + c$

(C) $(x^4 + 1)^4 + c$

(D) $\dfrac{x^4(x^4 + 1)^4}{16} + c$

(E) $9x^2(x^4 + 1)^2 + c$

12. $\int \dfrac{x}{(2x^2 + 1)^3} \, dx =$

(A) $-\dfrac{1}{(2x^2 + 1)^2} + c$

(B) $-\dfrac{1}{8(2x^2 + 1)^2} + c$

(C) $-\dfrac{1}{16(2x^2 + 1)^2} + c$

(D) $-\dfrac{1}{2(2x^2 + 1)^2} + c$

(E) $-\dfrac{1}{4(2x^2 + 1)^4} + c$

13. $\int x^2 e^{x^3} \, dx =$

(A) $e^{x^3} + c$

(B) $2x e^{x^3} + c$

(C) $\dfrac{x^3}{3} e^{x^3} + c$

(D) $\dfrac{1}{3} e^{x^3} + c$

(E) $\dfrac{1}{4} e^{x^4} + c$

14. $\int \dfrac{\ln (x + 1)}{x + 1} \, dx =$

(A) $\dfrac{(\ln (x + 1))^2}{2} + c$

(B) $\ln (x + 1) + c$

(C) $\dfrac{1}{x + 1} + c$

(D) $\dfrac{1}{(x + 1)^2} + c$

(E) $\ln\left(\dfrac{(x + 1)^2}{2}\right) + c$

15. $\int \dfrac{\ln (x^3)}{x} \, dx =$

(A) $\ln\left(\dfrac{x^4}{4}\right) + c$

(B) $\dfrac{(\ln x)^2}{2} + c$

(C) $\dfrac{3(\ln x)^2}{2} + c$

(D) $\ln (3x^2) + c$

(E) $3\ln (x^2) + c$

16. $\int e^{\ln x^2} \, dx =$

(A) $2x + c$

(B) $x^2 + c$

(C) $\dfrac{x^3}{3} + c$

(D) $e^{\ln x^2} + c$

(E) $e^{\frac{x^3}{3}} + c$

17. $\int \dfrac{\sin \sqrt{x}}{\sqrt{x}} \, dx =$

(A) $-\cos \sqrt{x} + c$

(B) $-2 \cos \sqrt{x} + c$

(C) $-\dfrac{1}{2} \cos \sqrt{x} + c$

(D) $\dfrac{1}{2} \cos \sqrt{x} + c$

(E) $2 \cos \sqrt{x} + c$

18. $\int \tan^2 x \sec^2 x \, dx =$

(A) $\dfrac{\tan^3 x}{3} + c$

(B) $\dfrac{\tan^3 x \sec^3 x}{9} + c$

(C) $\dfrac{\sec^3 x}{3} + c$

(D) $4 \tan x \sec x + c$

(E) $\tan^3 x + c$

19. $\int \tan^3 x \sec x \, dx =$

(A) $\dfrac{\tan^4 x}{4} + c$

(B) $\dfrac{\sec^2 x}{2} + c$

(C) $\dfrac{\sec^3 x}{3} - \sec x + c$

(D) $\dfrac{\tan^3 x}{3} + c$

(E) $\dfrac{\tan^4 x}{4 \sec x} + c$

20. How many points of inflection are there on the graph of $f(x) = \ln (1 + x^3)$?

(A) 0

(B) 1

(C) 2

(D) 3

(E) 4

21. $\int \cot x \csc^2 x \, dx =$

(A) $\dfrac{\cot^2 x}{2} + c$

(B) $-\dfrac{\cot^2 x}{2} + c$

(C) $2 \cot x \csc x + c$

(D) $\dfrac{\csc^3 x}{3} + c$

(E) $\cot x + c$

22. $\int \dfrac{\cos x}{\sin^4 x} \, dx =$

(A) $-\dfrac{1}{3} \csc^3 x + c$

(B) $\dfrac{1}{3 \sin^2 x} + c$

(C) $\dfrac{1}{3 \sin^3 x} + c$

(D) $\dfrac{5}{\sin^5 x} + c$

(E) $-5 \csc^5 x + c$

23. Find the area under the graph of $f(x) = e^{-2 \ln x}$ on the interval $[1, 2]$.

(A) 0.5

(B) $\dfrac{\pi}{2}$

(C) 1.5

(D) $\dfrac{5}{3}$

(E) 1.75

24. Write the equation of the line tangent to the graph of $y = \ln(1 + \sin x)$ at $x = \dfrac{\pi}{6}$.

(A) $y = -\dfrac{\sqrt{3}}{3}\left(x - \dfrac{\pi}{6}\right) + \ln \dfrac{3}{2}$

(B) $y = \dfrac{\sqrt{3}}{3}\left(x - \dfrac{\pi}{6}\right) + \ln \dfrac{3}{2}$

(C) $y = \dfrac{\sqrt{3}}{3}(x - 30) + \ln \dfrac{3}{2}$

(D) $y = \dfrac{\sqrt{3}}{3}\left(x + \dfrac{\pi}{6}\right) + \ln \dfrac{3}{2}$

(E) $y = \dfrac{\sqrt{3}}{3}\left(x - \dfrac{\pi}{6}\right) - \ln \dfrac{3}{2}$

25. $\dfrac{d}{dt}\left(\int_1^{2t^2} (1 + \sin x) \, dx\right) =$

(A) $\sin(2t^2) - \sin 1$

(B) $1 + \sin(2t^2)$

(C) $4t(1 + \cos(2t^2))$

(D) $1 + \cos(2t^2)$

(E) $4t(1 + \sin(2t^2))$

Free-Response Questions

A graphing calculator is required for some questions.

1. Find the average value of $y = \tan^2 x$ on the interval $\left[0, \dfrac{\pi}{3}\right]$, and find the value of x in that interval at which the function attains the average value.

2. Find the mean value of $y = \sqrt{1 - x^2}$ on the interval $[-1, 1]$.

3. Sketch the region enclosed by the graphs of $y = (\ln x)^2$, the x-axis, and the line $x = e$, and find:

   (a) the area of the region
   (b) the volume of the solid generated when the region is rotated about the x-axis
   (c) the volume of the solid generated when the region is rotated about the y-axis
   (d) the volume of the solid generated when the region is rotated about the line $x = e$
   (e) the volume of the solid generated when the region is rotated about the line $y = 2$
   (f) the volume of the solid whose base is the region and such that cross sections perpendicular to the x-axis are squares
   (g) the volume of the solid whose base is the region and such that cross sections perpendicular to the y-axis are squares

4. Sketch the region enclosed by the graphs of $y = x^3 + 1$, $y = 2$, and the y-axis; and find:

   (a) the area of the region
   (b) the volume of the solid generated when the region is rotated about the x-axis
   (c) the volume of the solid generated when the region is rotated about the y-axis
   (d) the volume of the solid generated when the region is rotated about the line $y = 1$
   (e) the volume of the solid generated when the region is rotated about the line $x = 1$
   (f) the volume of the solid generated when the region is rotated about the line $x = -1$
   (g) the volume of the solid whose base is the region and such that cross sections perpendicular to the x-axis are squares
   (h) the volume of the solid whose base is the region and such that cross sections perpendicular to the y-axis are squares

5. Sketch the graph of $y = \dfrac{1}{x + 1}$ on $[0, 2]$, and use 5 subintervals to approximate the area under the curve using

(a) left-hand sums
(b) right-hand sums
(c) midpoint sums
(d) the trapezoidal approximation

6. Sketch the graph of $y = \sqrt{1 - x^3}$ on the interval $[0, 1]$ and use 5 subintervals to approximate the area under the curve using

(a) left-hand sums
(b) right-hand sums
(c) midpoint sums
(d) the trapezoidal approximation

7. If the figure shows the graph of f, and $g(x) = \int_0^x f(t)\, dt$, find:

(a) $g(0), g(1), g(2),$ and $g(3)$
(b) the interval(s) where g is increasing
(c) the interval(s) where g is concave up
(d) the absolute minimum of g on $[-1, 3]$

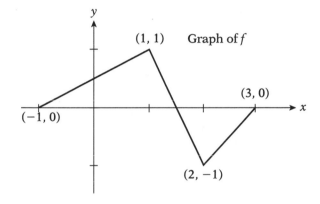

8. If the figure shows the graph of f on $[-2, 2]$ and $g(x) = \int_{-1}^x f(t)\, dt$, find:

(a) $g(-2), g(0),$ and $g(2)$
(b) the interval(s) where g is decreasing
(c) the interval(s) where g is concave down
(d) the absolute maximum of g on $[-2, 2]$

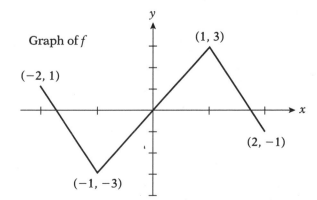

9. Car A starts at 10 ft/sec and travels for 10 seconds, while car B starts at 2 ft/sec and travels for 10 seconds. Which car travels the farther and by how many feet?

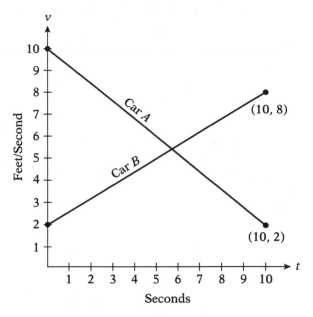

10. The velocity of an object is $v(t) = t^2 - t$ (ft/sec), and its initial position is $x(0) = 2$, $t \geq 0$.

(a) What is the acceleration of the object after 2 seconds?
(b) What is the position of the object after 2 seconds?
(c) When is the object at rest?
(d) Find the distance traveled by the object during the first 2 seconds.

BC 11. Consider the system of parametric equations

$$x(t) = t^2 + 1$$
$$y(t) = \sqrt{t + 2}$$

for values of t on the interval $[-1, 2]$.

(a) Find the length of the curve on the interval.
(b) Find the area of the surface generated when the graph is rotated about the x-axis.
(c) Find the values of t for which $x(t)$ is a minimum and for which $y(t)$ is a minimum.

CHAPTER 7
Separable Differential Equations and Slope Fields

7.1 Separable Differential Equations

A **differential equation** is an equation whose terms include the derivatives of a function with respect to an independent variable. A **separable differential equation** is a differential equation that can be separated so that one variable is on one side of the equation and the other variable is on the other side of the equation. If the variables are x and y, then separating the variables results in all the x and dx terms being on one side of the equation, and all the y and dy terms being on the other side of the equation. Separating the variables is the first step in solving a separable differential equation. The solution to a differential equation, as with any equation, is an expression that makes the equation true.

To solve a separable differential equation:

1. Separate the variables.
2. Find the antiderivative on each side of the equation.
3. Write the solution in the form y (or the dependent variable) = a function of x (or the independent variable).

EXAMPLE 1

Show that $\dfrac{dy}{dx} = xy$ is a separable differential equation.

Solution Rewrite the equation as $\dfrac{dy}{y} = x\, dx$.

EXAMPLE 2

Separate the variables in the differential equation $\frac{dP}{dt} = kPt^2$.

Solution   Rewrite the equation as $\frac{dP}{P} = kt^2\, dt$.

EXAMPLE 3

Separate the variables in the differential equation $\frac{dy}{dx} = \frac{x}{2y + 1}$.

Solution   Rewrite the differential equation as $(2y + 1)\, dy = x\, dx$.

EXAMPLE 4

Solve for y in the differential equation $\frac{dy}{dx} = xy$ from Example 1.

Solution   Separate the variables as in Example 1, and then find the antiderivative on each side:

$$\int \frac{dy}{y} = \int x\, dx.$$

The antiderivative is: $\ln|y| + c_1 = \frac{x^2}{2} + c_2$, where c_1 and c_2 are constants. Recall that the antiderivative of $\frac{1}{y}$ is $\ln|y|$. Since the domain of the ln function is the set of positive real numbers, the absolute value sign ensures that the quantity is positive.

Subtract the constant c_1 from both sides of the equation. Then combine by writing $c = c_2 - c_1$. The equation above becomes

$$\ln|y| = \frac{x^2}{2} + c.$$

We can solve for y as follows. Raise both sides of the equation to the e power:

$$e^{\ln|y|} = e^{\frac{x^2}{2} + c}.$$

Using the property that $e^{\ln|y|} = |y|$, the equation becomes

$$|y| = e^{\frac{x^2}{2} + c}.$$

Now,

$$e^{\frac{x^2}{2} + c} = e^{\frac{x^2}{2}} \cdot e^c.$$

Therefore, the equation can be rewritten as

$$y = \pm e^c \cdot e^{\frac{x^2}{2}}.$$

Further renaming $\pm e^c$ as A, the solution is

$$y = Ae^{\frac{x^2}{2}}.$$

Note: The solution $y = Ae^{\frac{x^2}{2}}$ represents a family of curves, where A is a constant.

EXAMPLE 5

Solve the differential equation $\dfrac{dP}{dt} = kPt^2$.

Solution   Separating the equation, we get

$$\frac{dP}{P} = kt^2 \, dt.$$

Integrating both sides, we get

$$\int \frac{dP}{P} = \int kt^2 \, dt.$$

$$\ln|P| = \frac{kt^3}{3} + c.$$

Solving for P,

$$|P| = \pm e^c \cdot e^{\frac{kt^3}{3}} \text{ or } P = Ae^{\frac{kt^3}{3}}, \text{ where } A \text{ is a constant.}$$

EXAMPLE 6

(a) Solve the differential equation $\dfrac{dy}{dx} = \dfrac{x}{2y+1}$ from Example 3.

(b) Find the solution for this equation that satisfies the initial condition $y(0) = 0$.

Solution   (a) Separating the variables and taking the antiderivative on each side of the equation,

$$\int (2y + 1) \, dy = \int x \, dx \quad \text{becomes}$$

$$\frac{y^2}{2} + y = \frac{x^2}{2} + c.$$

(b) Substituting the values $x = 0$ and $y = 0$ into the equation and solving for c, $c = 0$, and $\dfrac{y^2}{2} + y = \dfrac{x^2}{2}$.

Multiply both sides of the equation by 2, and the equation becomes $y^2 + 2y = x^2$. To solve for y, complete the square:

$$y^2 + 2y + 1 = x^2 + 1, \text{ and}$$

$$(y + 1)^2 = x^2 + 1.$$

Then $y + 1 = \pm\sqrt{x^2 + 1}$.
Since $y(0) = 0$,

$$y + 1 = \sqrt{x^2 + 1} \text{ and}$$

$$y = \sqrt{x^2 + 1} - 1.$$

Population Growth
Many physical situations can be modeled as separable differential equations. Population growth can be modeled as follows. Suppose that the rate of change of a population P is proportional to the population at a time t. This sentence translates into the differential equation $\frac{dP}{dt} = kP$.

Precalculus students may know the solution as $y = Ce^{kt}$. Calculus students can derive this formula. Separating the variables, and taking the antiderivative of both sides of the equation $\frac{dP}{dt} = kP$, we get

$$\int \frac{dP}{P} = \int k\,dt.$$

Solving for the antiderivative, $\ln|P| = kt + c$.
Using the techniques in the previous examples, $P = Ce^{kt}$.
Other situations that can be modeled by similar differential equations and solutions are radioactive decay of an element and bacterial growth.

EXAMPLE 7

The rate of growth of a certain bacterium is proportional to the number present. In population B, there are 200 bacteria initially, and 500 bacteria five minutes later.
(a) Write a differential equation that represents the rate of growth of the bacterial population B with respect to time t (in minutes).
(b) Solve the differential equation for B using the given conditions.
(c) Use the solution in part (b) to predict the value of B at $t = 10$.

Solution

(a) The differential equation is $\frac{dB}{dt} = kB$.

(b) The solution of the differential equation is $B = Ce^{kt}$.
   Since there are 200 bacteria initially, $B = 200$ when $t = 0$. Substituting these values into the solution gives

$$B = Ce^{kt}$$
$$200 = Ce^{k(0)}$$
$$200 = Ce^{0}$$
$$200 = C$$

Thus, the constant $C = 200$ and $B = 200e^{kt}$.
   We can find k using the other given condition. Since there are 500 bacteria present 5 minutes later, $B = 500$ when $t = 5$. Substituting these values into $B = 200e^{kt}$ and solving for k,

$$k = \frac{1}{5}\ln\left(\frac{5}{2}\right) = 0.183, \text{ and}$$

$$B = 200e^{0.183t}$$

(c) The value of k can be stored in the calculator (conveniently under the letter K), and used to predict the number of bacteria at any time t.
   Using the stored value of k, the value of B at $t = 10$ is $B = 1,250$.

Exercises

No calculator is allowed for these questions.
Solve the following differential equations by using the separation of variables method.

(a) $\dfrac{dy}{dx} = x^2 + x$

(b) $\dfrac{dy}{dx} = \dfrac{y}{x^2}$

(c) $\dfrac{dy}{dx} = y^3$ with the initial condition $y(0) = 1$

(d) $\dfrac{dy}{dx} = xy + y$

Multiple-Choice Questions
No calculator is allowed for these questions.

1. The graph of any solution to the differential equation $\dfrac{dy}{dx} = \dfrac{1}{1 + x^2}$

   (A) is monotonically increasing
   (B) is always concave up
   (C) is symmetric to the y-axis
   (D) is symmetric to the origin
   (E) lies completely above the x-axis

2. The differential equation $\dfrac{dy}{dx} = xy + 2y$ in separable form is

   (A) $\dfrac{dy}{xy + 2y} = dx$

   (B) $dy = (xy + 2y)\,dx$

   (C) $\dfrac{dy}{dx} - xy = 2y$

   (D) $dy = (x + 2)y\,dx$

   (E) $\dfrac{dy}{y} = (x + 2)\,dx$

3. A particle begins at $(0, 1)$ and moves up the y-axis so that at time t its velocity y' is double the position y. A solution to this differential equation could be
   (A) $y = 2e^{2t}$
   (B) $2y = e^{2t}$
   (C) $y = e^{2t} + 1$
   (D) $y = e^{2t}$
   (E) $y = 2t + 1$

4. A possible solution to $\dfrac{dy}{dt} = y - 5$ is

   (A) $y = 5 + Ce^t$
   (B) $y = Ce^t - 5$
   (C) $y = 5e^t$
   (D) $y^2 - 5y = t + c$
   (E) $y = Ce^{-5t}$

5. The solution to the differential equation $\dfrac{dP}{dt} = -0.02P$ with $P(0) = 5$ is

   (A) $P = 5e^{-0.02t}$
   (B) $P = 5e^{-0.002t}$
   (C) $P = 5 + e^{-0.02t}$
   (D) $P = -0.02P^2 + c$
   (E) $P = \dfrac{1}{5 - 0.02t}$

Free-Response Questions
A graphing calculator is required for some questions.

1. A radioactive element has a half-life of 1,000 years. (This means that the amount present initially will be halved after 1,000 years.)

   (a) If 100 grams of the element are present initially, how many grams remain after 5000 years?
   (b) If the rate of change of the number of grams present is proportional to the amount present, write and solve a differential equation that represents the amount y of the element remaining after t years.

2. A spherical snowball is melting so that the rate of change of the radius is 2 cm/hr.

   (a) Show that the rate of change of the volume is proportional to the surface area.

   (Volume $= \dfrac{4}{3}\pi r^3$, Surface Area $= 4\pi r^2$)

   (b) Find the constant of proportionality of the equation in part (a).

3. The slope of a curve is given by the formula $3x^2y^2$ at a point (x, y). Find the equation of the curve if the curve passes through the point $(1, -1)$.

7.2 Slope Fields

Imagine the coordinate plane and all the points (x, y). Suppose that $\frac{dy}{dx} = f(x) \, g(y)$ is a differential equation, and suppose that the value of $\frac{dy}{dx}$ is calculated at every point in the plane, and that a tiny line segment is drawn at each point with slope $\frac{dy}{dx}$. The resulting set of tiny line segments is called a **slope field,** and it is a sketch of a general solution to a differential equation. Since drawing a line segment at every point on the coordinate plane is not possible, a finite number of points is usually given, and a slope field is drawn using these points. Knowing the slopes of solutions to a differential equation at a field of points gives information as to how the solution functions are behaving near given points and helps us visualize the general shape of these curves.

EXAMPLE 1

On graph paper, draw the slope field for the differential equation $\frac{dy}{dx} = \frac{x}{y}$ at each point (x, y) where x and y are the integers $-1 \le x \le 1$ and $-1 \le y \le 1$.

Solution

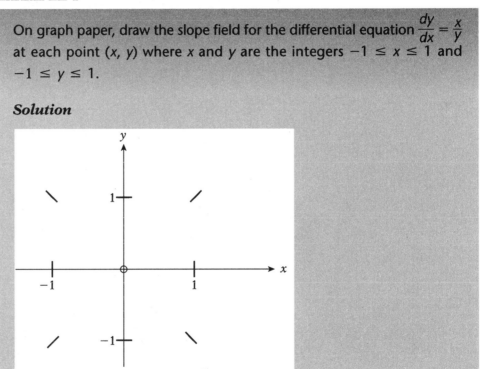

Calculator Note

The graphing calculator can be used to draw slope fields. There is a program that can be entered into the TI-83 to draw slope fields, but the TI-89 is tailor-made for drawing slope fields since it has a built-in slope fields program and a better display window than the TI-83.

    The instructions that follow are for the TI-89.

    Press MODE. On the first line, scroll right on Graph → DIFF EQUATIONS.

    Press ENTER ENTER. (Pressing ENTER the first time makes the choice, and pressing ENTER the second time locks it in.) Now press ● Y=. It is important to note that y is a function of t in the TI-89. Thus, for example, the differential equation $\frac{dy}{dx} = 2xy$ would be entered in Y= as y1' = 2t ⊠ y1.

Press Zoom 4 and the slope field will appear on the screen. To see the slope field below, press ⊙ WINDOW and set Xmin = −5 and Xmax = 5.

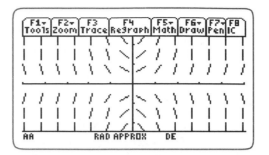

The symbol *yi*1 below *y*1' means the initial value of *y*1. You can enter one or more initial values in Y=, or you can enter them in the graph window by pressing 2nd F8 IC (which stands for Initial Conditions). This allows several solutions of the differential equation to appear on the screen. Using F8 IC, a message will appear in the window, prompting Initial Conditions? Enter a value of *t*. Use *t* = 0 by entering 0 and pressing ENTER. Then enter the corresponding *y*-value on the question mark in *y*1 = ? The calculator will then graph the solution to the differential equation with that initial condition.

More than one solution to the differential equation can be graphed by pressing F8 IC again, and entering a new initial condition. This allows you to see more than one solution to the differential equation at the same time on the graph. Graphing several *y*-values, both positive and negative, will allow you to see what properties the solutions have in common.

EXAMPLE 2

Using the example from the Calculator Note, in the Differential Equations mode of the TI-89, press ⊙ Y= and enter the differential equation $\frac{dy}{dx} = 2xy$ as *y*1' = 2*t* × *y*1. Press ⊙ GRAPH.

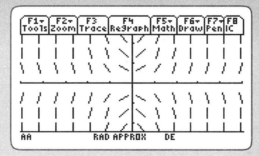

Press F8 IC and enter the initial conditions *t* = 0 and *y*1 = 2.
Repeat F8 IC and enter the initial conditions *t* = 0 and *y*1 = −1.

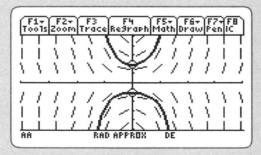

EXAMPLE 3

In the Differential Equations Mode of the TI-89, enter the differential equation $\frac{dy}{dx} = \frac{x}{y}$ into Y= as $y1' = \frac{t}{y1}$ and press ⬥ GRAPH.

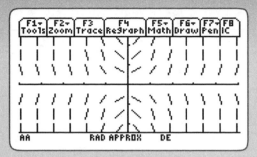

Compare the slope field in the calculator with the one drawn by hand in Example 1 for the properties of symmetry and asymptotes.
Press F8 IC and enter the initial conditions $t = 0$ and $y1 = 2$.
Repeat F8 IC and enter the initial conditions $t = 0$ and $y1 = -1$.

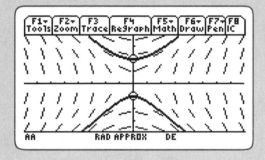

Exercises

Multiple-Choice Questions
No calculator is allowed for these questions.

1. In a slope field, the line segments are
   (A) part of the graph of the solution to the differential equation
   (B) parts of the lines tangent to the graph of the solution to the differential equation
   (C) asymptotes to the graph of the solution of the differential equation
   (D) lines of the symmetry of the graph of the solution to the differential equation
   (E) none of the above

2. Drawing a slope field
   (A) provides a way of visualizing the solution to a differential equation
   (B) can help find horizontal asymptotes to the graph of the solution of the differential equation
   (C) can serve as a check to the solution of a differential equation

   (D) can give evidence as to the symmetry of the graph of the solution to a differential equation
   (E) all of the above

3. The slope field for the differential equation $\frac{dy}{dx} = x^2$
   (A) has line segments symmetric to the y-axis
   (B) shows that the solutions to the differential equation are even functions
   (C) shows that the graphs of the solutions are increasing for increasing x
   (D) shows that the graphs of the solutions are decreasing for increasing x
   (E) shows that there are solutions that have a horizontal asymptote

4. The slope field for the differential equation $\dfrac{dy}{dx} = x$

  (A) has line segments symmetric to the y-axis
  (B) shows that the solutions to the differential equation are odd functions
  (C) shows that the solutions to the differential equation are straight lines
  (D) shows that the solutions to the differential equation are decreasing for increasing x
  (E) shows that there is a horizontal asymptote

5. The slope field for $\dfrac{dy}{dx} = y$ shows that the solutions to the differential equation

  (A) have y-intercept $(0, 1)$
  (B) have a positive y-intercept
  (C) have a horizontal asymptote
  (D) are even functions
  (E) are odd functions

Free-Response Questions

A graphing calculator is required for some questions.

For each differential equation in Questions 1–4:

  (a) Sketch a slope field for points in the plane with integer values of x and y between -2 and 2 inclusive.
  (b) Use the slope field to determine whether the solutions to the differential equation are even, odd, or neither.

  (c) Use the slope field to determine whether the solutions to the differential equation have a horizontal asymptote.
  (d) Sketch a solution on the slope field that passes through the point $(0, 1)$.
  (e) Enter the differential equation in the graphing calculator, and compare the slope field on the calculator with the one drawn by hand.

1. $\dfrac{dy}{dx} = x$

2. $\dfrac{dy}{dx} = x^2$

3. $\dfrac{dy}{dx} = y$

4. $\dfrac{dy}{dx} = 2xy$

5. Given the differential equation $\dfrac{dy}{dx} = 2xy$:

  (a) Find the value of $\dfrac{dy}{dx}$ at the points (x, y) where $-2 \le x \le 2$ and $-2 \le y \le 2$.
  (b) On graph paper, draw a tiny line segment at each of the points above with slope equal to the value of $\dfrac{dy}{dx}$ at that point.
  (c) In which quadrants is $\dfrac{dy}{dx} > 0$? In which quadrants is $\dfrac{dy}{dx} < 0$?
  (d) For what values of x and y is $\dfrac{dy}{dx} = 0$? For what values is $\dfrac{dy}{dx}$ undefined?

7.3 The Connection Between a Slope Field and Its Differential Equation

A slope field provides a visual representation of the family of solutions to a differential equation. If a solution to the differential equation is graphed on the same set of axes as the slope field, it would be apparent that some of the segments in the slope field would be lines tangent to the graph of the solution. Once a slope field is drawn, solutions to the differential equation can be drawn on the slope field using the tiny line segments as a guide. The solutions drawn on the slope field represent members of the family of curves that are solutions to the differential equation. Furthermore, when the differential equation is solved, solutions can be graphed on the slope field as a check to see if segments in the slope field are tangent to the graph of the solution.

Exercises

No calculator is allowed for these questions.

Match the differential equations 1–6 with the slope fields I–VI.

Differential Equation	Slope Field
1. $\dfrac{dy}{dx} = x + xy^2$	I
2. $\dfrac{dy}{dx} = -\dfrac{x}{y}$	II
3. $\dfrac{dy}{dx} = -y + 1$	III
4. $\dfrac{dy}{dx} = \dfrac{y^2}{x}$	IV

5. $\dfrac{dy}{dx} = x + y$

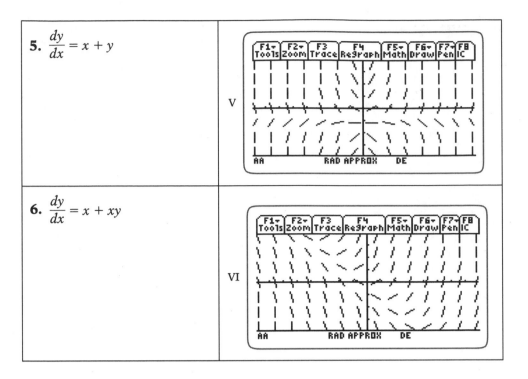

V

6. $\dfrac{dy}{dx} = x + xy$

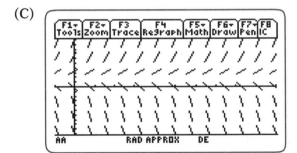

VI

Multiple-Choice Questions

A graphing calculator is required for some questions.

1. Which is the slope field for the differential equation $\dfrac{dy}{dx} = 2y - 4$?

(A)
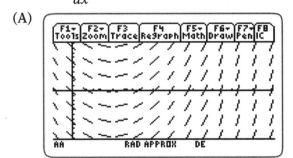

(B)
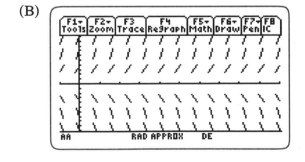

(C)
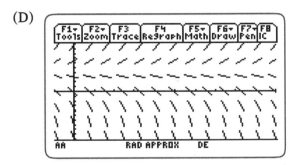

(D)
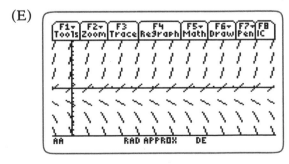

(E)

2. Which graph shows a slope field with a solution to the differential equation $\dfrac{dy}{dx} = y^2$?

(A)

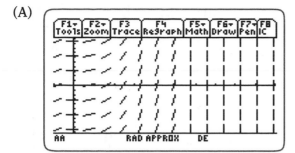

(B)

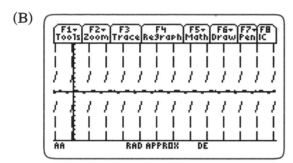

(C)

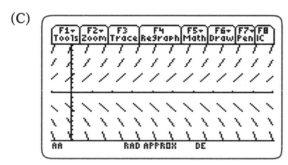

(D)

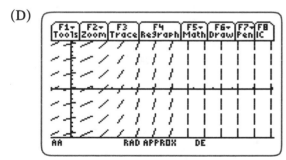

(E)

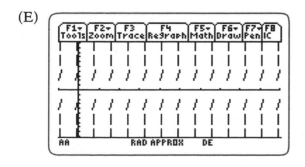

3. Of the four curves A, B, C, and D on the slope field shown, which graphs the function that is the solution to the equation $\dfrac{dy}{dx} = -\dfrac{x}{y}$ with initial condition $y(0) = 4$?

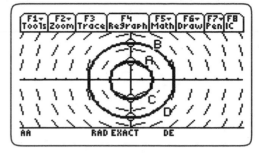

(A) A
(B) B
(C) C
(D) D
(E) none

4. The solution to $\dfrac{dy}{dx} = -x$ with initial condition $y(0) = 1$
(A) is always concave up
(B) is always concave down
(C) is undefined at $x = 0$
(D) is always increasing
(E) is always decreasing

Free-Response Questions
A graphing calculator is required for some questions.
For Questions 1–4, use the points in the plane where x *and* y *are integers and* $-2 \le$ x ≤ 2 *and* $-2 \le$ y ≤ 2.

    (a) Draw a slope field for each of the following differential equations.
    (b) Use the slope field to sketch two solutions to the differential equation.
    (c) Solve the differential equation and check to see if the sketches drawn in part (b) match the solution.

1. $\dfrac{dy}{dx} = 2x$

2. $\dfrac{dy}{dx} = 2y$

3. $\dfrac{dy}{dx} = y^2$

4. $\dfrac{dy}{dx} = -\dfrac{x}{y}$

Chapter Assessment

Multiple-Choice Questions

No calculator is allowed for Questions 1–11.

1. The differential equation $\dfrac{dy}{dx} = 2y + 50$ written in separable form is

   (A) $\dfrac{1}{2y}\dfrac{dy}{dx} = 50$

   (B) $\dfrac{dy}{y + 50} = 2dx$

   (C) $dy = (2y + 50)dx$

   (D) $\dfrac{dy}{y + 25} = 2dx$

   (E) $\dfrac{dy}{2y} = 50dx$

2. If $y = \ln(e^{-t^2} + 10)$, then $\dfrac{dy}{dx} =$

   (A) $-2t$

   (B) $\dfrac{1}{e^{-t^2} + 10}$

   (C) $\dfrac{-2te^{-t^2}}{e^{-t^2} + 10}$

   (D) $\dfrac{-2t}{e^{-t^2} + 10}$

   (E) $-2t + \dfrac{1}{10}$

3. $\displaystyle\int_{-4}^{0} \dfrac{1}{5x + 25}\,dx =$

   (A) $5 \ln 5$

   (B) $-5 \ln 5$

   (C) $-\dfrac{1}{5}\ln 5$

   (D) $\dfrac{1}{5}\ln 5$

   (E) undefined

4. $\dfrac{d^2y}{dt^2} = 2t + 10$ and $y'(0) = 9$. $\dfrac{dy}{dt} =$

   (A) 2

   (B) $t^2 + 10t$

   (C) $t^2 + 9$

   (D) $t^2 + 10t + 9$

   (E) $\ln\left(\dfrac{2t + 10}{10}\right) + 9$

5. If $y'' = e^{-2x} + x + 1$, $y'(0) = 1$, and $y(0) = 0$, then $y =$

   (A) $y = \dfrac{1}{4}e^{-2x} + \dfrac{1}{6}x^3 + \dfrac{1}{2}x^2 + \dfrac{3}{2}x - \dfrac{1}{4}$

   (B) $y = 4e^{-2x} + \dfrac{1}{6}x^3 + \dfrac{1}{2}x^2 + 3x - 4$

   (C) $y = e^{-2x} + \dfrac{1}{6}x^3 + \dfrac{1}{2}x^2 - 1$

   (D) $y = e^{-2x} + \dfrac{1}{2}x^2 - 1$

   (E) $y = \dfrac{1}{4}e^{-2x} + \dfrac{1}{6}x^3 + \dfrac{1}{2}x^2 + \dfrac{1}{2}x - \dfrac{1}{4}$

6. An acorn falls into a pond, creating a circular ripple whose area is increasing at a constant rate of 5π m²/second. When the radius of the circle is 4 m, at what rate is the diameter of the circle changing?

   (A) $\dfrac{5}{8}$ m/sec

   (B) $\dfrac{5}{4}$ m/sec

   (C) $\dfrac{5}{2}$ m/sec

   (D) 5 m/sec

   (E) $\dfrac{5}{4\pi}$ m/sec

7. Which of the following could be a solution of the differential equation with the given slope field?

   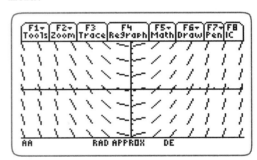

   (A) $y = x + 1$
   (B) $y = x^2 + 2$
   (C) $y = x^3 - 2$
   (D) $y = \ln(x + 1)$
   (E) $y = 2e^x$

8. Which of the following could be a solution of the differential equation $\dfrac{dy}{dx} = (1 + x^2)(1 + y^2)$?

   (A) $y = x$

   (B) $y = \tan\left(x + \dfrac{x^3}{3} + 6\right)$

   (C) $y = \sqrt[3]{x + \dfrac{x^3}{3} - \dfrac{x^3}{9}}$

   (D) $y = \arctan\left(x + \dfrac{x^3}{3}\right)$

   (E) $y = \sin\left(x + \dfrac{x^3}{3} + \pi\right)$

9. On the positive y-axis, the slope field for the differential equation $\frac{dy}{dt} = \frac{t^2}{y}$ has

   (A) horizontal segments
   (B) vertical segments
   (C) segments with positive slope
   (D) segments with negative slope
   (E) segments with slope equal to 1

10. The solution to $\frac{dy}{dx} = y \cos x$ is

   (A) $y = Ce^{\sin x}$
   (B) $y = \sin x + C$
   (C) $y = -\sin x + C$
   (D) $y = e^{\sin x} + C$
   (E) $y = Ce^{-\sin x}$

11. The solution to the differential equation $\frac{dy}{dx} = x^2\sqrt{y}$ with initial condition $y(0) = 9$ is

   (A) $y = \dfrac{9}{(x^3 + 1)^2}$

   (B) $y = \dfrac{9}{x^3 + 1}$

   (C) $y = \left(\dfrac{x^3}{6} + 3\right)^2$

   (D) $y = e^{x^3 + 1}$
   (E) $y = e^{9(x^3 + 1)^2}$

A graphing calculator is required for Questions 12–20.

12. Which of the following is the slope field for the differential equation $\frac{dy}{dx} = y^2 - 4$?

(A)

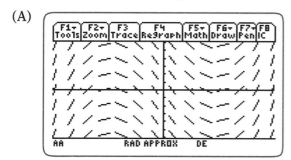

(B)

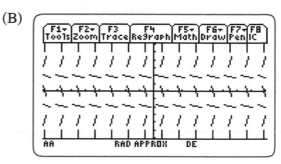

(C)

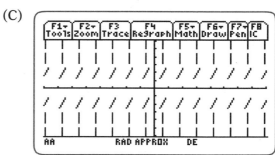

(D)

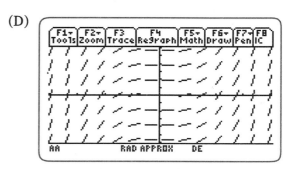

(E)

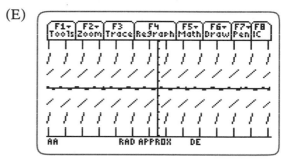

13. $x^2 - y^2 = k$ is a family of solutions to which of the following differential equations?

   (A) $\dfrac{dy}{dx} = \dfrac{x}{y}$

   (B) $x^2 \dfrac{dy}{dx} = y^2$

   (C) $x \dfrac{dy}{dx} = y$

   (D) $x \dfrac{dy}{dx} = -y$

   (E) $\dfrac{dy}{dx} = xy$

14. Which of the following is the slope field for the differential equation $x\dfrac{dy}{dx} = y - x$?

(A)

(B)

(C)

(D)

(E)

15. Which of the following differential equations has $x^2 - 4y^2 = 4$ as a solution?

(A) $\dfrac{dy}{dx} = 4xy$

(B) $y\dfrac{dy}{dx} = \dfrac{x}{4}$

(C) $\dfrac{dy}{dx} = \dfrac{4y}{x}$

(D) $\dfrac{dy}{dx} = -\dfrac{x}{4y}$

(E) $\dfrac{dy}{dx} = \dfrac{4x}{y}$

16. The value of a new car depreciates so that the rate of change of the value V at time t is proportional to the value of the car at that time. Which of the following graphs illustrates the value V of the car at time t?

(A)

(B)

(C)

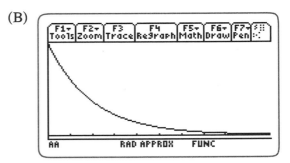

(D)

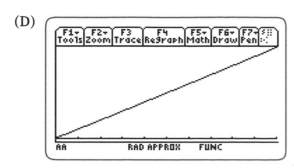

(E)

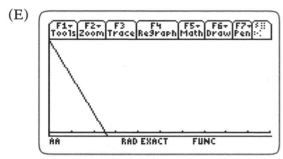

17. The rate of growth of bacteria in a Petri dish is proportional to the number of bacteria present. If there are initially 10 bacteria placed in the Petri dish and there are 100 bacteria in the dish 10 minutes later, by what factor has the bacterial population grown after another 30 minutes?
(A) 10
(B) 1,000
(C) 10,000
(D) 100,000
(E) 1 million

18. A student in an SAT verbal class learns 4 vocabulary words the first day. The student's learning curve is given by the differential equation $\frac{dw}{dt} = -0.2(w - 8)$, where w is the number of words learned. If this learning curve is correct, what is the maximum number of words the student can learn per day?
(A) 4
(B) 5
(C) 6
(D) 7
(E) 8

19. If $\frac{dy}{dt} = -\frac{ty}{\ln y}$ and $y(4) = e^2$, then $y =$

(A) $y = e^{\frac{1}{2}(20 - t^2)}$
(B) $y = e^{\sqrt{20 - t^2}}$
(C) $y = e^{\frac{1}{2}\sqrt{20 - t^2}}$
(D) $y = \ln\sqrt{20 - t^2}$
(E) $y = e^{\ln\sqrt{20 - t^2}}$

20. $\frac{dy}{dx} = x + 2xy$ and $y(0) = 1$. Find y as a function of x.
(A) $y = 3e^{x^2} - 2$
(B) $y = 3x^2 + 1$
(C) $y = \frac{3}{2}e^{x^2} - \frac{1}{2}$
(D) $y = 3\ln(x^2 + 1) + 1$
(E) $y = \frac{3}{2}e^{\frac{x^2}{2}} - \frac{1}{2}$

Free-Response Questions

A graphing calculator is required for some questions.

1. The subway fare in a metropolitan area has increased according to the table.

t Years since 1966	$f(t)$ Subway fare (in cents)
0	20
4	30
6	35
9	50
14	60
15	75
18	90
20	100
24	115
26	125
29	150

(a) Find the average rate of change of the fare $f(t)$ on the interval [20, 24].
(b) Use the trapezoidal rule on the intervals [0, 6], [6, 14], [14, 18], [18, 24], and [24, 29] to approximate the average value of the fare from $t = 0$ (1966) to $t = 29$ (1995).
(c) A statistician for the Transit Authority found a model equation for the increase in the fare to be $y = 7.012(1.07)^x$. Use the model equation to find the average value of the fare from 1966 to 1995.
(d) Find $y'(20)$, and interpret the meaning of this number in the context of the fare increase.

2. Recent data from the Air Transport Association on profit and loss in the airline industry are listed in the table.

t Years since 2000	R Profit or loss (in billions of dollars)
0	2.5
1	−7.7
2	−10
3	−6.7 (projected)

(a) Is the average rate of change for R in the interval $[0, 3]$ positive or negative? Interpret the meaning of this value. Indicate units of measure.

(b) Use the Trapezoidal Rule with three equal subintervals to approximate the average value of R from $t = 0$ to $t = 3$. Interpret the meaning of this value.

(c) Between which two consecutive years is the average rate of change of R the greatest?

(d) A model equation for the data is

$$y = 3.375x^2 - 13.115x + 2.385.$$

Use this model equation to find the average value of R on the interval $[0, 3]$. Indicate units of measure.

3. Given the differential equation $x^2\dfrac{dy}{dx} - y^2 = 1$, with initial condition $y(1) = 0$:

(a) Write the equation of the line tangent to the graph of the solution of the differential equation at $x = 1$.

(b) Is the graph of the solution to the differential equation concave up or concave down at $x = 1$? Explain your answer.

(c) Find the solution to the differential equation.

4. Fannie Mae is a federal institution that lends money for home mortgages. The outstanding debt over a ten-year period is indicated in the table.

t Years since 1990	M Debt (in billions of dollars)
0	120
1	130
2	150
3	200
4	225
5	240
6	250
7	300
8	450
9	550
10	640

(a) Find the average rate of change in M over the ten-year period. Indicate units of measure.

(b) Use the Trapezoidal Rule with five equal subintervals to approximate the total debt over the ten-year period.

(c) A model equation for the debt is calculated to be

$$y = 0.744x^3 - 5.093x^2 + 31.028x + 114.441.$$

Find the value of $y'(5)$, and explain the meaning of this value. Indicate units of measure.

(d) Use the model equation to approximate the total amount of funding over the ten-year period.

BC Topics

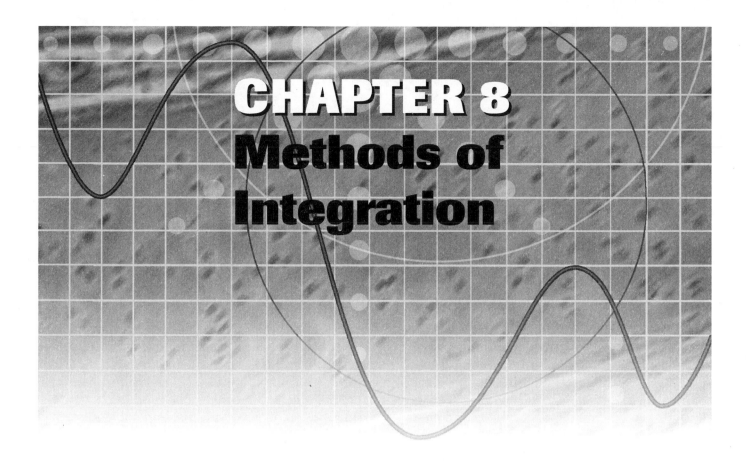

CHAPTER 8
Methods of Integration

Introduction

Since the introduction of symbolic graphing calculators, such as the TI-89, which can find antiderivatives, the Calculus BC course outline has changed. The topic of methods of integration now includes AB topics, simple integration by parts, and the method of partial fractions (for linear factors only). The elimination of other methods of integration corresponds to the general changes in AP Calculus. The emphasis is on understanding relationships and using theory to justify conclusions, rather than on extensive algebraic manipulation.

8.1 Integration by Parts

Integration by parts is a method of transforming an integral that is impossible to evaluate into an integral that is possible to evaluate. The method of integration by parts comes from the product rule for derivatives. If u and v are functions of x, then the derivative of uv is

$$\frac{d(uv)}{dx} = u\,\frac{dv}{dx} + v\,\frac{du}{dx}, \text{ or } d(uv) = u\,dv + v\,du.$$

Thus,

$$u\,dv = d(uv) - v\,du.$$

Taking the antiderivative of both sides, we get

$$\int u \, dv = uv - \int v \, du,$$

which is the formula for integration by parts.

> **To apply the formula for integration by parts:**
>
> 1. Identify the two parts, u and dv, in the integrand.
> 2. Integrate dv to find v and differentiate u to find du.
> 3. Substitute v and du into the integration by parts formula.

Skillful use of integration by parts can change a difficult problem into an easy one. An integral that cannot be found is traded for an integral that can be found. If the correct trade is made, then the integration by parts method works.

Integration by parts is often effective when the integrand is the product of two functions that are unrelated, such as a polynomial and an exponential function, a polynomial and a logarithmic function, a trigonometric and an exponential function, or a polynomial and a trigonometric function.

EXAMPLE 1

Find the antiderivative $\int x \sin x \, dx$.

Solution Since the integrand is the product of a polynomial and a trigonometric function, integration by parts is a possible method of solution.

Use the formula for integration by parts: $\int u \, dv = uv - \int v \, du$.
Let

$$u = x \text{ and } dv = \sin x \, dx.$$

Then

$$du = dx \text{ and } v = \int \sin x \, dx = -\cos x.$$

By the formula, the integrand becomes

$$\int x \sin x \, dx = -x \cos x - \int -\cos x \, dx = -x \cos x + \sin x + c.$$

The method of integration by parts traded $\int x \sin x \, dx$ for $\int \cos x \, dx$, which is an antiderivative that can be found more easily.

Note: It is not necessary to add a constant of integration in finding v, the antiderivative of dv, as long as one constant of integration, c, is included at the end.

EXAMPLE 1 REVISITED

Find the antiderivative $\int x \sin x \, dx$ by letting $u = \sin x$ and $dv = x \, dx$. Then $du = \cos x \, dx$ and $v = \frac{x^2}{2}$.

By the formula for integration by parts,

$$\int x \sin x \, dx = \frac{x^2}{2} \sin x - \int \frac{x^2}{2} \cos x \, dx.$$

In this case, the $\int x \sin x \, dx$, which cannot be found, was traded for $\int \frac{x^2}{2} \cos x \, dx$, which also cannot be found. This was not a good trade since it led to an integrand with a higher power of x, which cannot be solved by elementary methods.

EXAMPLE 2

Find the antiderivative $\int \ln x \, dx$.

Solution The integrand is the product of $\ln x$ and dx.

Use the formula for integration by parts: $\int u \, dv = uv - \int v \, du$.
Let

$$u = \ln x \text{ and } dv = dx.$$

Then

$$du = \frac{1}{x} \, dx \text{ and } v = x.$$

By the formula,

$$\int \ln x \, dx = x \ln x - \int dx = x \ln x - x + c.$$

Hint: If a term with ln (function of x) is in the integrand, try integration by parts with $u =$ the term with ln (function of x).

EXAMPLE 3

Find the antiderivative $\int \arctan x \, dx$.

Solution Use the formula for integration by parts: $\int u \, dv = uv - \int v \, du$.

Let $u = \arctan x$ and $dv = dx$. Then $du = \frac{1}{1 + x^2} \, dx$ and $v = x$. By the formula,

$$\int \arctan x \, dx = x \arctan x - \int \frac{x}{1 + x^2} \, dx =$$

$$x \arctan x - \frac{1}{2} \ln|1 + x^2| + c.$$

Exercises

Find the following antiderivatives by the most direct method. (Note: Not all the exercises require integration by parts.)

1. $\int \arcsin x \, dx$

2. $\int x \ln x \, dx$

3. $\int x e^{x^2} \, dx$

Multiple-Choice Questions
No calculator is allowed for these questions.

1. $\int x^3 e^{x^2} \, dx =$

   (A) $\frac{1}{2} e^{x^2}(x^2 - 1) + c$

   (B) $\frac{1}{2} e^{x^2}(x^2 + 1) + c$

   (C) $3x^2 e^{x^2} + c$

   (D) $x^2 e^{x^2}(2x^2 + 3) + c$

   (E) $\frac{x^4}{4} e^{x^2} + c$

2. $\int \arcsin x \, dx =$

   (A) $(1 - x^2)^{-1/2} + c$

   (B) $x \arcsin x + \sqrt{1 - x^2} + c$

   (C) $x \arcsin x + \frac{1}{2}\sqrt{1 - x^2} + c$

   (D) $x \arcsin x - \sqrt{1 - x^2} + c$

   (E) $x \arcsin x + \frac{1}{2} \ln\left|1 - x^2\right| + c$

3. $\int x \cos (x^2) \, dx =$

   (A) $x \sin (x^2) + c$

   (B) $\frac{1}{2} \sin (x^2) + c$

   (C) $-\frac{1}{2} \sin (x^2) + c$

   (D) $\cos (x^2) + c$

   (E) $\sin (x^2) + c$

4. $\int_{1}^{e^2} x^2 \ln (x^2) \, dx =$

   (A) $\frac{e^6 - 2}{9}$

   (B) $\frac{e^6 + 2}{9}$

   (C) $\frac{10e^6 - 2}{9}$

   (D) $\frac{10e^6 + 2}{9}$

   (E) $\frac{10e^6 + 1}{9}$

Free-Response Question
A graphing calculator is required for this question.

Let R be the region bounded by $y = \ln x$, the x-axis, and the line $x = e$.
(a) Find the volume of the solid generated when R is rotated about the x-axis.
(b) Find the volume of the solid formed with R as base and such that cross sections perpendicular to the y-axis are squares.
(c) A line $x = k$ divides region R into two equal parts. Find the value of k.

8.2 Integration by the Method of Partial Fractions

Adding fractions involves finding the least common denominator, rewriting the fractions as equivalent fractions with the same denominator, and then adding the numerators. The **method of partial fractions** uses the same understanding of fractions to transform an integrand that is a rational function into an integrand that is easier to evaluate. The objective of this method is to find the factors of the denominator, and rewrite the rational function as a sum of fractions in which each denominator is a factor of the given denominator. The antiderivative is then found by finding the antiderivatives of the individual, simpler fractions. Breaking a rational function down into its component fractions can be a tedious algebraic process. Thus, the method of partial fractions, as described in the Calculus BC topic outline, is applied only to a fraction whose denominator is the product of linear factors.

EXAMPLE 1

Rewrite $\dfrac{1}{x^2 - x}$ as a sum of its component fractions.

Solution   The denominator $x^2 - x = x(x - 1)$. Thus the fraction $\dfrac{1}{x^2 - x}$ can be written as the sum of $\dfrac{A}{x}$ and $\dfrac{B}{x - 1}$, where A and B are constants.

$$\frac{1}{x^2 - x} = \frac{A}{x} + \frac{B}{x - 1}.$$

To find the values of A and B, multiply the equation by $x^2 - x$:

$$(x^2 - x)\,\frac{1}{x^2 - x} = \frac{A}{x} + \frac{B}{x - 1}\,(x^2 - x)$$

$$1 = A(x - 1) + Bx.$$

To solve for A and B, choose appropriate values of x and substitute into the equation above. The values of x chosen in this example are $x = 1$ and $x = 0$. They are the most appropriate since one of the terms in the equation is equal to zero for these values of x. They are values for which the original equation is undefined.

When $x = 1$, the equation $1 = A(x - 1) + Bx$ becomes

$$1 = A(1 - 1) + B(1)$$
$$1 = B$$

Thus, $B = 1$.

When $x = 0$, the equation $1 = A(x - 1) + Bx$ becomes

$$1 = A(0 - 1) + B(0)$$
$$1 = A(-1)$$

Thus, $A = -1$.

Using these values of A and B, the fraction can be written

$$\frac{1}{x^2 - x} = \frac{-1}{x} + \frac{1}{x - 1}.$$

EXAMPLE 2

Find the antiderivative $\displaystyle\int \frac{1}{x^2 - x}\,dx$.

Solution   Using the fractions found in Example 1,

$$\int \frac{1}{x^2 - x}\,dx = \int \left(\frac{-1}{x} + \frac{1}{x - 1} \right) dx$$

$$= -\ln|x| + \ln|x - 1| + c.$$

Furthermore, using the properties of the ln function, $-\ln|x| + \ln|x - 1|$ may be rewritten as $\ln\left|\dfrac{x - 1}{x}\right|$, and the antiderivative is $\ln\left|\dfrac{x - 1}{x}\right| + c$.

EXAMPLE 3

Find the antiderivative $\int \dfrac{1}{x^3 - x}\, dx$.

Solution Find the factors of the denominator, and use them to rewrite the fraction $\dfrac{1}{x^3 - x}$ as the sum of its component fractions. The factors of $x^3 - x$ are x, $x + 1$, and $x - 1$. Find the values of A, B, and C so that

$$\frac{1}{x^3 - x} = \frac{A}{x} + \frac{B}{x + 1} + \frac{C}{x - 1}.$$

Multiply this equation by $x^3 - x$ to get

$$1 = A(x + 1)(x - 1) + Bx(x - 1) + Cx(x + 1).$$

Choose values of x that make the factors x, $x + 1$, and $x - 1$ equal to zero.

$$x = 0: 1 = A(1)(-1), \text{ and } A = -1$$

$$x = -1: 1 = B(-1)(-2), \text{ and } B = \frac{1}{2}$$

$$x = 1: 1 = C(1)(2), \text{ and } C = \frac{1}{2}$$

Thus, $\dfrac{1}{x^3 - x} = \dfrac{-1}{x} + \dfrac{\frac{1}{2}}{x + 1} + \dfrac{\frac{1}{2}}{x - 1}$, and for the antiderivative we have

$$\int \frac{1}{x^3 - x}\, dx = \int \left(\frac{-1}{x} + \frac{\frac{1}{2}}{x + 1} + \frac{\frac{1}{2}}{x - 1} \right) dx$$

$$= -\ln|x| + \frac{1}{2} \ln|x + 1| + \frac{1}{2} \ln|x - 1| + c.$$

The answer may also be rewritten by combining the ln terms:

$$\frac{1}{2} \ln|(x + 1)(x - 1)| - \ln|x| + c$$

$$= \frac{1}{2} \left[\ln|(x + 1)(x - 1)| - 2 \ln|x| \right] + c$$

$$= \frac{1}{2} \left[\ln|x^2 - 1| - \ln|x^2| \right] + c$$

$$= \frac{1}{2} \ln \left| \frac{x^2 - 1}{x^2} \right| + c$$

If the integrand is a rational function for which the degree of the numerator is greater than or equal to the degree of the denominator, then we must use long division to rewrite the integrand as the quotient $+ \dfrac{\text{remainder}}{\text{divisor}}$. Then, if necessary, proceed to rewrite the term with $\dfrac{\text{remainder}}{\text{divisor}}$ as the sum of its component fractions.

EXAMPLE 4

Find the antiderivative $\displaystyle\int \dfrac{x^2 - x + 1}{x^2 - x}\, dx$.

Solution Since the degree of the numerator is greater than or equal to the degree of the denominator, we must use long division.

$$
\begin{array}{r}
1 \\
x^2 - x \overline{\smash{)}\, x^2 - x + 1} \\
\underline{-x^2 - x} \\
1
\end{array}
$$

We find that the quotient $= 1$ and the remainder $= 1$. Thus,

$$\dfrac{x^2 - x + 1}{x^2 - x} = 1 + \dfrac{1}{x^2 - x}.$$

The antiderivative $\displaystyle\int \dfrac{x^2 - x + 1}{x^2 - x}\, dx = \int \left(1 + \dfrac{1}{x^2 - x} \right) dx$ and, using the solution from Example 1,

$$\int \dfrac{x^2 - x + 1}{x^2 - x}\, dx = x + \ln \left| \dfrac{x - 1}{x} \right| + c.$$

Exercises

Find the following antiderivatives:

1. $\displaystyle\int \dfrac{1}{x^2 - 1}\, dx$

2. $\displaystyle\int \dfrac{x}{x^2 - 1}\, dx$

3. $\displaystyle\int \dfrac{x^3}{x^2 - 1}\, dx$

4. $\displaystyle\int \dfrac{x^2}{x^2 - 1}\, dx$

5. $\displaystyle\int \dfrac{x}{x^2 - 5x + 6}\, dx$

Multiple-Choice Questions
No calculator is allowed for these questions.

1. $\displaystyle\int_2^3 \dfrac{1}{x^2 - 1}\, dx =$

   (A) $\dfrac{1}{2} \ln \dfrac{2}{3}$

   (B) $\dfrac{1}{2} \ln \dfrac{3}{2}$

   (C) $\ln \dfrac{3}{2}$

   (D) $\ln \dfrac{2}{3}$

   (E) $2 \ln \dfrac{3}{2}$

2. Find the area bounded by $f(x) = \dfrac{1}{x(2-x)}$ and the x-axis on the interval $[3, 5]$.

(A) $\dfrac{1}{2} \ln \dfrac{5}{9}$

(B) $\ln \dfrac{5}{9}$

(C) $\dfrac{1}{2} \ln \dfrac{9}{5}$

(D) $\ln \dfrac{9}{5}$

(E) $\dfrac{1}{2} \ln 12$

3. $\displaystyle\int_4^6 \dfrac{x-1}{x^2-4}\, dx =$

(A) $\dfrac{7 \ln 2 + 3 \ln 3}{4}$

(B) $\dfrac{7 \ln 2 - 3 \ln 3}{4}$

(C) $\dfrac{7}{4} \ln \dfrac{3}{2}$

(D) $\dfrac{4}{7} \ln \dfrac{3}{2}$

(E) $\dfrac{7 \ln 2 - 2 \ln 3}{4}$

4. $\displaystyle\int \dfrac{x^2 + 5x}{x^2 + 5x + 6}\, dx =$

(A) $-6 \ln \left| \dfrac{x+2}{x+3} \right| + c$

(B) $x - 6 \ln \left| \dfrac{x+2}{x+3} \right| + c$

(C) $-5 \ln \left| \dfrac{x+2}{x+3} \right| + c$

(D) $-\ln \left| \dfrac{x+2}{x+3} \right| + c$

(E) $\dfrac{1}{6} x + c$

5. $\displaystyle\int \dfrac{(x+2)^3}{x^2 + 2x}\, dx =$

(A) $4 \ln |x| + c$

(B) $\dfrac{1}{2} x^2 + 4x + \ln |x| + c$

(C) $\dfrac{1}{2} x^2 + 2x + 4 \ln |x| + c$

(D) $\dfrac{1}{2} x^2 + 4x + 4 \ln |x| + c$

(E) $\dfrac{1}{2} x^2 + 4 \ln |x| + c$

Free-Response Questions
A graphing calculator is required for some questions.

1. The region R is bounded by $y = \dfrac{1}{e^x + 1}$, the x-axis, the y-axis, and the line $x = 1$. Find the volume of the solid with base the region R and with cross sections perpendicular to the x-axis that are semicircles.

2. (a) $\displaystyle\int \dfrac{3u^2 - 4}{u^3 - 4u}\, du =$

(b) $\displaystyle\int \dfrac{3u^2 + 1}{u^3 - 4u}\, du =$

8.3 **Improper Integrals**

There are two cases in which integrals are called **improper integrals:**

Case 1. One or both of the limits of the integral are ∞ or $-\infty$. The interval of integration is $[a, +\infty)$, $(-\infty, c]$, or $(-\infty, +\infty)$.

Case 2. The integrand is not continuous on the interval defined by the limits of the integration.

Improper integrals are evaluated by finding the antiderivative of the integrand and taking the limit(s) of the antiderivative expression. If the limit exists, the integral is said to *converge* to that number. If no limit exists, the integral is said to *diverge*.

In Case 1, if one or both of the limits of the integral are ∞ or $-\infty$, then we have either $\int_a^\infty f(x)\, dx$ or $\int_{-\infty}^c f(x)\, dx$, or $\int_{-\infty}^\infty f(x)\, dx$.

$$\int_a^\infty f(x)\, dx \text{ means } \lim_{b \to \infty} \int_a^b f(x)\, dx.$$

$$\int_{-\infty}^{c} f(x)\,dx \text{ means } \lim_{b \to -\infty} \int_{b}^{c} f(x)\,dx.$$

$$\int_{-\infty}^{\infty} f(x)\,dx \text{ means for some } b, \ -\infty < b < \infty,$$

$$\lim_{a \to -\infty} \int_{a}^{b} f(x)\,dx + \lim_{c \to \infty} \int_{b}^{c} f(x)\,dx.$$

In Case 2, if the integrand is undefined at the left endpoint of $[a, b]$,

$$\int_{a}^{b} f(x)\,dx = \lim_{c \to a^{+}} \int_{c}^{b} f(x)\,dx.$$

If the integrand is undefined at the right endpoint of $[a, b]$,

$$\int_{a}^{b} f(x)\,dx = \lim_{c \to b^{-}} \int_{a}^{c} f(x)\,dx.$$

If the integrand is undefined at a point c in the interval $[a, b]$,

$$\int_{a}^{b} f(x)\,dx = \lim_{d \to c^{-}} \int_{a}^{d} f(x)\,dx + \lim_{e \to c^{+}} \int_{e}^{b} f(x)\,dx.$$

EXAMPLE 1

Find the value of $\int_{0}^{\infty} e^{-x}\,dx$, if it exists.

Solution   This is an example of Case 1. The interval of integration is $[0, +\infty)$. By definition,

$$\int_{0}^{\infty} e^{-x}\,dx = \lim_{b \to \infty} \int_{0}^{b} e^{-x}\,dx.$$

The integral in the limit is

$$\int_{0}^{b} e^{-x}\,dx = \left[-e^{-x} \right]_{0}^{b} = -e^{b} - (-e^{0}) = -e^{-b} + 1.$$

Therefore,

$$\int_{0}^{\infty} e^{-x}\,dx = \lim_{b \to \infty} (-e^{-b} + 1) = 1.$$

EXAMPLE 2

Find the value of $\int_{-\infty}^{-1} \frac{1}{x^2}\,dx$.

Solution   This is another example of Case 1. The interval of integration is $(-\infty, -1]$. By definition,

$$\int_{-\infty}^{-1} \frac{1}{x^2}\,dx = \lim_{b \to -\infty} \int_{b}^{-1} \frac{1}{x^2}\,dx.$$

The integral in the limit is

$$\int_b^{-1} \frac{1}{x^2}\, dx = \left[-\frac{1}{x} \right]_b^{-1} = 1 - \left(-\frac{1}{b} \right) = 1 + \frac{1}{b}.$$

Therefore,

$$\int_{-\infty}^{-1} \frac{1}{x^2}\, dx = \lim_{b \to -\infty} \left(1 + \frac{1}{b} \right) = 1.$$

EXAMPLE 3

Find the value of $\int_0^1 \frac{1}{\sqrt{x}}\, dx$, if it exists.

Solution   This is an example of Case 2. The integrand is not continuous at $x = 0$, the left endpoint of the interval $[0, 1]$. By definition,

$$\int_0^1 \frac{1}{\sqrt{x}}\, dx = \lim_{b \to 0^+} \int_b^1 \frac{1}{\sqrt{x}}\, dx.$$

The integral in the limit is

$$\int_b^1 \frac{1}{\sqrt{x}}\, dx = \int_b^1 x^{-1/2}\, dx = 2\, x^{1/2} \Big|_b^1 = 2 - 2b^{1/2}.$$

Therefore,

$$\int_0^1 \frac{1}{\sqrt{x}}\, dx = \lim_{b \to 0^+} (2 - 2b^{1/2}) = 2.$$

Exercises

Evaluate the following improper integrals, if they exist. If the integral does not exist, state so.

1. $\int_1^\infty \frac{1}{\sqrt{x}}\, dx$

2. $\int_0^{\frac{\pi}{2}} \tan x\, dx$

3. $\int_1^2 \frac{2}{x-1}\, dx$

4. $\int_{-1}^1 \frac{1}{x^2}\, dx$

Multiple-Choice Questions
No calculator is allowed for these questions.

1. $\int_1^\infty \frac{2}{\sqrt[3]{x}}\, dx =$

   (A) $-\infty$

   (B) $-\frac{2}{3}$

   (C) 0

   (D) $\frac{2}{3}$

   (E) ∞

2. $\int_0^1 \frac{dx}{\sqrt[3]{x-1}} =$

   (A) $-\infty$

   (B) $-\frac{3}{2}$

   (C) 0

   (D) $\frac{3}{2}$

   (E) ∞

3. When r is a real number greater than 1, $\int_1^r \dfrac{1}{x \ln x} dx =$

   (A) 0

   (B) 1

   (C) $\ln r$

   (D) $-\infty$

   (E) ∞

4. When n is an integer greater than 1, $\int_0^1 \dfrac{1}{x^n} dx =$

   (A) 0

   (B) $\dfrac{1}{-n+1}$

   (C) 1

   (D) $-\infty$

   (E) ∞

5. When n is an integer greater than 1, $\int_1^\infty \dfrac{1}{x^n} dx =$

   (A) 0

   (B) 1

   (C) $\dfrac{1}{n-1}$

(D) $-\infty$

(E) ∞

Free-Response Questions
A graphing calculator is required for some questions.

1. $f(x) = e^{-2x}$ for $x \geq 0$.
   (a) Find the area under the curve.
   (b) Find the volume when the region under the curve is rotated about the x-axis.
   (c) Find the volume when the region under the curve is rotated about the y-axis.
   (d) Find the length of the curve.

2. For what value of p does each of the following integrals converge?

   (a) $\int_0^1 \dfrac{1}{x^p} dx$

   (b) $\int_1^\infty \dfrac{1}{x^p} dx$

   (c) $\int_0^1 \dfrac{1}{(\ln x)^p} dx$

   (d) $\int_1^\infty \dfrac{1}{(\ln x)^p} dx$

Chapter Assessment

For Questions 1–3, find the integrals:

1. $\int xe^x \, dx$

2. $\int (\ln x)^3 \, dx$

3. $\int \dfrac{1}{x^2 - 4} dx$

4. Find the area bounded by $y = \ln x$ and the x-axis on the interval $[b, 1]$ for $0 < b < 1$.

5. Find the limit, if it exists, of the area in Question 4 as $b \to \infty$.

6. Find the volume of the solid generated by rotating $y = e^{-x}$ on the interval $[b, 0]$ for $b < 0$ about the x-axis.

7. Find the limit, if it exists, of the volume in Question 6 as $b \to -\infty$.

Multiple-Choice Questions
No calculator is allowed for these questions.

1. $\int_1^3 x^3 \ln x \, dx =$

   (A) $27 \ln 3 - 12$

   (B) $27 \ln 3 - \dfrac{27}{2}$

   (C) $\dfrac{81}{4} \ln 3 - \dfrac{81}{16}$

   (D) $\dfrac{81}{4} \ln 3 - 5$

   (E) $27 \ln 3$

2. $\int_0^{\frac{\pi}{4}} x \sec^2 x \, dx =$

(A) $\frac{\pi}{4}$

(B) $\frac{\pi}{4} + 1$

(C) $\frac{\pi}{4} - \frac{3}{2} \ln 2$

(D) $\frac{\pi}{4} - \frac{1}{2} \ln 2$

(E) $\frac{\pi}{4} - \ln 2$

3. $\int_1^2 \frac{x^3}{\sqrt{x^2 - 1}} \, dx =$

(A) 0

(B) $\sqrt{3}$

(C) $2\sqrt{3}$

(D) $4\sqrt{3}$

(E) ∞

4. $\int_1^2 \frac{x^4 + 1}{x^3 + x^2} \, dx =$

(A) $\ln \frac{9}{8} + 1$

(B) $\ln \frac{8}{9} + 1$

(C) $\ln \frac{9}{8} + \frac{1}{2}$

(D) $\ln \frac{8}{9} + \frac{1}{2}$

(E) $\ln \frac{9}{8}$

5. Find the area under the curve $f(x) = \frac{1}{x^2 - x}$

for $x \geq 2$.

(A) $-\ln 2$
(B) $\ln 2$
(C) 1.25
(D) e^2
(E) ∞

6. Find $\lim_{n \to \infty} \int_0^2 \frac{1}{\sqrt[n]{x}} \, dx$, for $n > 1$.

(A) 0
(B) 1
(C) 2
(D) $2\sqrt{2}$
(E) ∞

7. The region bounded by the graph of $y = \tan x$, the x-axis, and the line $x = \frac{\pi}{4}$ is the base of a solid. Find the volume of the solid if cross sections perpendicular to the x-axis are squares.

(A) 1

(B) $1 - \frac{\pi}{4}$

(C) $4 - \pi$

(D) $4 - \frac{\pi}{4}$

(E) $\sqrt{3} - \frac{\pi}{3}$

8. If $f(x) = \frac{1}{\sqrt{x^2 - 1}}$, then $\int_1^2 x \, f(x) \, dx =$

(A) $\sqrt{3}$

(B) $\sqrt{3} - 1$

(C) $\frac{1}{\sqrt{3}}$

(D) 1

(E) ∞

9. $\int x^3 f''(x^2) \, dx =$

(A) $\frac{1}{2} (x^2 f(x^2) - f(x^2)) + c$

(B) $\frac{1}{2} (x^2 f'(x^2) - f(x^2)) + c$

(C) $x^2 f'(x^2) - f(x^2) + c$

(D) $2(x^2 f'(x^2) - f(x^2)) + c$

(E) $\frac{1}{2} (x^2 f''(x^2) - f'(x^2)) + c$

10. Find the area between the x-axis and the curve $f(x) = \frac{1}{x^2 + x - 6}$ on the interval $[-2, 0]$.

(A) $\ln \frac{3}{2}$

(B) $\frac{1}{5} \ln \frac{3}{2}$

(C) $\frac{1}{5} \ln 6$

(D) $\ln 6$

(E) undefined

11. $f(x) = 2x^2$, $g(x) = \csc x$. Find $\displaystyle\int_{\frac{\pi}{4}}^{\frac{\pi}{2}} f(g(x))\, dx$.

(A) -2
(B) -1
(C) 1
(D) $\sqrt{3}$
(E) 2

12. $\displaystyle\int \frac{1}{5 + 5\cos x}\, dx =$

(A) $5x + 5\sin x + c$

(B) $\dfrac{1}{5x + 5\sin x} + c$

(C) $\dfrac{1}{5}(\csc x - \cot x) + c$

(D) $\ln(5 + 5\cos x) + c$

(E) $\dfrac{1}{5}(x + \ln|\sec x + \tan x|) + c$

13. $\displaystyle\int_{1}^{\infty} \frac{1}{x(\ln x + 1)^2}\, dx =$

(A) $\dfrac{1}{2}$
(B) 1
(C) 2
(D) 3
(E) ∞

14. $\displaystyle\int_{0}^{2} \frac{1}{\sqrt[5]{1 - x}}\, dx =$

(A) 0

(B) $\dfrac{5}{6}$

(C) $\dfrac{5}{4}$

(D) $\dfrac{5}{2}$

(E) undefined

15. Find the y-intercept of the line tangent to the graph of $xy^2 + \ln x = y + 6$ at the point $(1, 3)$.

(A) $-\dfrac{23}{5}$

(B) -2

(C) 1

(D) $\dfrac{7}{5}$

(E) 5

Free-Response Questions

A graphing calculator is required for some questions.

1. The graphs of $f(x) = e^x$ and $g(x) = \sec^2 x$ intersect at two points with x-coordinates p and q (with $p < q$) in the interval $[0, 1]$.
   (a) Find the values of p and q.
   (b) Find the average value of $f(x) - g(x)$ in the interval $[p, q]$.
   (c) Is there a value of x in the interval $[p, q]$ where the tangent lines to $f(x)$ and $g(x)$ are parallel? Explain your answer.
   (d) Let R be the region bounded by $f(x)$ and $g(x)$ on the interval $[p, q]$. Find the volume of the solid whose base is the region R and such that cross sections perpendicular to the x-axis are squares.

2. In recent years, many U.S. companies have cut back on employee travel. The table below lists the annual cost per traveler, in thousands of dollars, beginning in the year 1992 ($t = 0$).

t Years since 1992	y Cost per Traveler
0	10
2	9.5
4	8
6	9.1
8	10
10	6.8

   (a) Find the average rate of change of the cost per traveler from 1992 to 2002. Indicate the units in your answer.
   (b) In which two-year period was the rate of change the greatest? Explain your answer.
   (c) Approximate the total cost per traveler over the ten-year period using the trapezoidal rule with five equal subintervals.
   (d) Approximate the instantaneous rate of change at $t = 10$.

3. $f(x) = \ln|1 + x^3|$.

(a) Find the domain of $f(x)$.

(b) Find the equations of the vertical and horizontal asymptotes.

(c) On what interval(s) is $f(x)$ increasing? Explain your answer.

(d) On what interval(s) is $f(x)$ concave down? Explain your answer.

4. $g(x) = \sin x + \cos 2x$.

(a) Find the critical values of $g(x)$ in the interval $\left[-\dfrac{\pi}{2}, \dfrac{3\pi}{2}\right]$.

(b) Find the value of $\displaystyle\int_0^{\frac{\pi}{4}} g'(x)\, dx$.

(c) Find the area enclosed by the graph of $g(x)$ and the line tangent to $g(x)$ at $x = 0$.

CHAPTER 9
Polynomial Approximations and Infinite Series

9.1 Introduction

The algebra of polynomials—adding, subtracting, multiplying, and dividing—is straightforward. Finding derivatives of polynomial functions consists of repeated application of a few simple rules. If only all functions were polynomials! This is the wish that is answered by Taylor polynomials. Any function that has derivatives of a certain order can be approximated by a polynomial of that order. This includes logarithmic, exponential, trigonometric, and many other functions. There is also a formula that gives an upper bound on the error in using a Taylor polynomial of a certain degree to approximate a function.

The tangent line to the graph of a function $f(x)$ at a point $(a, f(a))$ is the first-degree Taylor polynomial for the function at that point. As we have seen, the tangent line provides a linear approximation of the function at values close to the given point. The slope of the tangent line is $f'(a)$. Thus, the equation of the tangent line in point-slope form is

$$y - f(a) = f'(a)(x - a) \text{ or}$$

$$y = f(a) + f'(a)(x - a),$$

which is a first-degree polynomial.

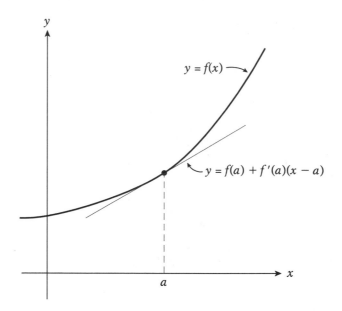

We know that zooming in at a point on the graph of a function gives a picture of the graph of the function that looks like the tangent line. By local linearity, we know that the tangent line approximates f near values of x close to a. As the tangent line (y) moves farther away from the point of tangency $(a, f(a))$, the linear approximation becomes less accurate. Extend this idea to the Taylor polynomials: as the degree of a Taylor polynomial increases, the interval where the polynomial is a good approximation of the function also increases.

If the degree of the Taylor polynomial increases without bound, the polynomial becomes a **Taylor series.** A Taylor polynomial *approximates* the function on a particular interval, while a Taylor series *equals* the function on a particular interval.

Exercises

Multiple-Choice Questions
No calculator is allowed for these questions.

1. $f(x) = x^4 - 2x^2$ has three zeros. Find the slope of the first-degree Taylor polynomial for $f(x)$ at the largest zero.
   (A) 1
   (B) $\sqrt{2}$
   (C) 2
   (D) $2\sqrt{2}$
   (E) $4\sqrt{2}$

2. The linear approximation function for $f(x) = \sqrt{x} - 1$ at $x = 2$ is
   (A) $x - 2y = 0$
   (B) $y - 2 = \frac{1}{2}(x - 1)$
   (C) $y - 1 = \frac{1}{2\sqrt{2}}(x - 2)$
   (D) $y - 1 = \frac{2}{3}(x - 2)$
   (E) $x - 2y = 1$

Free-Response Question
No calculator is allowed for this question.

For $f(x) = x^3 - x + 1$:
(a) Find the equation of the tangent line at the point of inflection.
(b) Use the tangent line found in part (a) to approximate $f(0.1)$.

9.2 Sigma Notation

Sums with many terms can be expressed concisely in **sigma notation,** in which the Greek letter capital sigma stands for summation.

The last value of n

$$\sum_{n=1}^{5} n^2$$

Sigma tells us to add → $\sum$ n^2 ← What to add up

$n = 1$

The first value of n

Therefore, the symbol $\displaystyle\sum_{n=1}^{5} n^2$ denotes that n starts as 1 and takes on the values of consecutive integers ending with 5. The expression n^2 tells us to take the sum of the squares, $1^2 + 2^2 + 3^2 + 4^2 + 5^2$, which equals 55. *Note:* There is no unique way of expressing a sum in sigma notation. For example, the sum above can also be written as $\displaystyle\sum_{n=0}^{4} (n + 1)^2$ or $\displaystyle\sum_{n=2}^{6} (n - 1)^2$.

There are three basic rules for working with sigma notation. If c is any constant, then:

1. $\displaystyle\sum_{k=m}^{n} ca_k = c \sum_{k=m}^{n} a_k$

2. $\displaystyle\sum_{k=m}^{n} (a_k + b_k) = \sum_{k=m}^{n} a_k + \sum_{k=m}^{n} b_k$

3. $\displaystyle\sum_{k=m}^{n} (a_k - b_k) = \sum_{k=m}^{n} a_k - \sum_{k=m}^{n} b_k$

EXAMPLE 1

Evaluate $\displaystyle\sum_{k=2}^{4} (2k + 1)$.

Solution Starting with $k = 2$, find the terms through $k = 4$ and then add.

$$(2 \cdot 2 + 1) + (2 \cdot 3 + 1) + (2 \cdot 4 + 1)$$
$$= 5 + 7 + 9 = 21$$

The sum is 21.

EXAMPLE 2

Write the sum $\dfrac{1}{2} + \dfrac{1}{3} + \dfrac{1}{4} + \cdots + \dfrac{1}{10}$ in sigma notation.

Solution In sigma notation, the sum may be represented by $\displaystyle\sum_{n=2}^{10} \dfrac{1}{n}$.

EXAMPLE 3

Write the sum $\frac{1}{2} + \frac{1}{4} + \frac{1}{8} + \frac{1}{16} + \cdots + \frac{1}{128}$ in sigma notation.

Solution   The denominators of the fractions above are all powers of 2. Thus, the sum can be written in sigma notation as $\displaystyle\sum_{n=1}^{7} \frac{1}{2^n}$.

EXAMPLE 4

Find $\displaystyle\sum_{i=1}^{n} \left(i^2 + 1 \right)$.

Solution   Starting at $i = 1$, begin to evaluate the terms.

$$(1^2 + 1) + (2^2 + 1) + (3^2 + 1) + \cdots + (n^2 + 1)$$
$$= n + (1^2 + 2^2 + 3^2 + \cdots + n^2)$$

EXAMPLE 5

Find $\displaystyle\sum_{k=2}^{5} \frac{1}{10} (k^3 - k^2)$.

Solution   Rewrite the sum using rules 1 and 3:

$$\frac{1}{10}\sum_{k=2}^{5} k^3 - \frac{1}{10}\sum_{k=2}^{5} k^2.$$

Evaluating the terms, we get:

$$\frac{1}{10}(2^3 + 3^3 + 4^3 + 5^3) - \frac{1}{10}(2^2 + 3^2 + 4^2 + 5^2)$$
$$= \frac{1}{10}(8 + 27 + 64 + 125) - \frac{1}{10}(4 + 9 + 16 + 25)$$
$$= \frac{1}{10}(224 - 54) = 17.$$

Exercises

Multiple-Choice Questions

A graphing calculator is required for some questions.

1. Written in sigma notation, the sum $1 + \frac{1}{4} + \frac{1}{9} + \cdots + \frac{1}{100}$ is

(A) $\displaystyle\sum_{n=1}^{10} \frac{1}{n^2}$

(B) $\displaystyle\sum_{n=0}^{10} \frac{1}{n^2}$

(C) $\displaystyle\sum_{n=0}^{100} \frac{1}{n^2}$

(D) $\displaystyle\sum_{n=1}^{10} n^2$

(E) $\displaystyle\sum_{n=1}^{100} n^2$

2. The sum $\displaystyle\sum_{n=1}^{\infty} \frac{n+1}{n}$ represents which of the following expressions?

(A) $2 + \frac{3}{2} + \frac{4}{3} + \frac{5}{4} + \cdots$

(B) $\frac{3}{2} + \frac{4}{3} + \frac{5}{4} + \cdots$

(C) $2 + 1 + \frac{1}{2} + \frac{1}{4} + \cdots$

(D) $\frac{3}{2} - \frac{4}{3} + \frac{5}{4} - \cdots$

(E) $1 - \frac{1}{2} + \frac{1}{3} - \frac{1}{4} + \cdots$

3. $1 + \frac{1}{2} + \frac{1}{6} + \frac{1}{24} + \frac{1}{120} =$

(A) $\displaystyle\sum_{n=0}^{4} \frac{1}{2^n}$

(B) $\displaystyle\sum_{n=1}^{5} \frac{1}{2^n}$

(C) $\displaystyle\sum_{n=1}^{5} \frac{1}{2n}$

(D) $\displaystyle\sum_{n=1}^{5} \frac{1}{n!}$

(E) $\displaystyle\sum_{n=1}^{\infty} \frac{1}{n!}$

4. Expressed in sigma notation, the sum $2 - \frac{1}{2} + \frac{1}{8} - \frac{1}{32} + \cdots$ is

(A) $\displaystyle\sum_{n=0}^{\infty} \frac{1}{2^n}$

(B) $\displaystyle\sum_{n=0}^{\infty} (-1)^n \frac{1}{2^n}$

(C) $\displaystyle\sum_{n=1}^{4} (-1)^n \frac{1}{2^n}$

(D) $\displaystyle\sum_{n=0}^{\infty} (-1)^n \frac{2}{4^n}$

(E) $\displaystyle\sum_{n=0}^{\infty} \frac{(-1)^n}{2^{2n-1}}$

Free-Response Questions

A graphing calculator is required for some questions.

1. (a) Evaluate the following sums:

   i. $\displaystyle\sum_{n=1}^{5} (n^2 + 1)$

   ii. $\displaystyle\sum_{n=1}^{5} n(n + 1)$

   iii. $\displaystyle\sum_{n=2}^{6} n(n - 1)$

   iv. $\displaystyle\sum_{n=0}^{4} (n^2 + 3n + 2)$

   (b) Explain why one of the sums in part (a) is NOT equal to the others.

2. (a) Write each sum in sigma notation.
   (b) Evaluate each sum.

   i. $\left(1 - \frac{1}{2}\right) + \left(1 - \frac{1}{3}\right) + \left(1 - \frac{1}{4}\right)$
   $+ \cdots + \left(1 - \frac{1}{10}\right)$

   ii. $\left(1 - \frac{1}{2}\right) + \left(\frac{1}{2} - \frac{1}{3}\right) + \left(\frac{1}{3} - \frac{1}{4}\right)$
   $+ \cdots + \left(\frac{1}{9} - \frac{1}{10}\right)$

   iii. $\left(1 - \frac{1}{3}\right) + \left(\frac{1}{3} - \frac{1}{5}\right) + \left(\frac{1}{5} - \frac{1}{7}\right)$
   $+ \cdots + \left(\frac{1}{9} - \frac{1}{11}\right)$

   iv. $\left(1 - \frac{1}{3}\right) + \left(1 - \frac{1}{5}\right) + \left(1 - \frac{1}{7}\right)$
   $+ \cdots + \left(1 - \frac{1}{11}\right)$

9.3 Derivation of the Taylor Polynomial Formula

If a function $f(x)$ is approximated by a polynomial so that

$$f(x) \approx a_0 + a_1 x + a_2 x^2 + a_3 x^3 + \cdots + a_n x^n,$$

Then

$$f(0) \approx a_0$$
$$f'(0) \approx a_1$$
$$f''(0) \approx 2a_2$$
$$f'''(0) \approx 6a_3, \text{ and so on.}$$

It follows from this that,

$$f(x) \approx f(0) + f'(0)x + \frac{f''(0)}{2}x^2 + \frac{f'''(0)}{6}x^3 + \cdots + \frac{f^{(n)}(0)}{n!}.$$

Using sigma notation, $f(x) \approx \sum_{k=0}^{n} \frac{f^{(k)}(0)}{k!}x^k.$

Since this polynomial is centered at 0, it is a special case of a Taylor polynomial called a **Maclaurin polynomial.**

The Taylor Polynomial Formula

A Taylor polynomial can be centered at any value, call it c, in the domain of the function. In that case, the function is approximated by

$$f(x) \approx f(c) + f'(c)(x - c) + \frac{f''(c)}{2}(x - c)^2 + \frac{f'''(c)}{6}(x - c)^3$$

$$+ \cdots + \frac{f^{(n)}(c)}{n!}(x - c)^n.$$

In sigma notation, $f(x) \approx \sum_{k=0}^{n} \frac{f^{(k)}(c)}{k!}(x - c)^k.$

An equivalent formula is $f(x) \approx \sum_{k=0}^{n} a_k (x - c)^k$, where the coefficients are $a_k = \frac{f^{(k)}(c)}{k!}.$

Note: The order of the highest derivative is the *order* of the Taylor polynomial.

EXAMPLE 1

(a) Find a third-degree Taylor polynomial centered at 1 for $f(x) = \sqrt{x}$, and use the polynomial to approximate $\sqrt{1.2}$.
(b) Use the calculator to graph $f(x)$ and the Taylor polynomial on the same axes.

Solution   Note that $f(x) = \sqrt{x} = x^{1/2}$; the function is not polynomial since polynomials have positive integer exponents.

$$f(1) = \sqrt{1} \qquad\qquad f(1) = 1 \qquad\qquad a_0 = 1$$

$$f'(x) = \frac{1}{2\sqrt{x}} \qquad\qquad f'(1) = \frac{1}{2} \qquad\qquad a_1 = \frac{1}{2}$$

$$f''(x) = -\frac{1}{4}x^{-3/2} \qquad f''(1) = -\frac{1}{4} \qquad a_2 = -\frac{1}{8}$$

$$f'''(x) = \frac{3}{8}x^{-5/2} \qquad f'''(1) = \frac{3}{8} \qquad a_3 = \frac{1}{16}$$

The third-degree Taylor polynomial centered at 1 for $f(x) = \sqrt{x}$ is

$$P_3 = 1 + \frac{1}{2}(x - 1) - \frac{1}{8}(x - 1)^2 + \frac{1}{16}(x - 1)^3,$$

and the approximate value of $\sqrt{x}$ at $x = 1.2$ is

$$\sqrt{1.2} \approx 1 + \frac{1}{2}(1.2 - 1) - \frac{1}{8}(1.2 - 1)^2 + \frac{1}{16}(1.2 - 1)^3$$

$$\sqrt{1.2} \approx 1.0955.$$

(b)

EXAMPLE 2

Find a Maclaurin polynomial of degree 4 for $f(x) = \dfrac{1}{1-x}$.

Solution A Maclaurin polynomial is a Taylor polynomial centered at 0. The value of $\dfrac{1}{1-x}$ at $x = 0$ is $f(0) = 1$, and $a_0 = 1$.

$$f'(x) = \frac{1}{(1-x)^2} \qquad f'(0) = 1 \qquad a_1 = 1$$

$$f''(x) = \frac{2}{(1-x)^3} \qquad f''(0) = 2 \qquad a_2 = \frac{2}{2!} = 1$$

$$f'''(x) = \frac{6}{(1-x)^4} \qquad f'''(0) = 6 \qquad a_3 = \frac{6}{3!} = 1$$

$$f^{(4)}(x) = \frac{24}{(1-x)^5} \qquad f^{(4)}(0) = 24 \qquad a_4 = \frac{24}{4!} = 1$$

Thus, the Maclaurin polynomial of degree 4 for $f(x) = \dfrac{1}{1-x}$ is $1 + x + x^2 + x^3 + x^4$. In sigma notation, $\dfrac{1}{1-x} \approx \displaystyle\sum_{n=0}^{4} x^n$.

While the Taylor polynomial can be derived for any function $f(x)$ by using the formula (provided that the derivatives are of a certain order), the AP Calculus exam emphasizes knowing and applying the Taylor polynomials for commonly used functions like those given in the table:

Function	Taylor Polynomial	Sigma Notation	Center
e^x	$1 + x + \dfrac{x^2}{2!} + \dfrac{x^3}{3!} + \dfrac{x^4}{4!} + \cdots + \dfrac{x^n}{n!}$	$\displaystyle\sum_{k=0}^{n} \dfrac{x^k}{k!}$	0
$\ln x$	$(x-1) - \dfrac{(x-1)^2}{2} + \dfrac{(x-1)^3}{3} - \dfrac{(x-1)^4}{4} + \cdots + \dfrac{(-1)^{n+1}(x-1)^n}{n}$	$\displaystyle\sum_{k=1}^{n} \dfrac{(-1)^{k+1}(x-1)^k}{k}$	1
$\sin x$	$x - \dfrac{x^3}{3!} + \dfrac{x^5}{5!} - \dfrac{x^7}{7!} + \cdots + \dfrac{(-1)^n x^{2n+1}}{(2n+1)!}$	$\displaystyle\sum_{k=0}^{n} \dfrac{(-1)^k x^{2k+1}}{(2k+1)!}$	0
$\cos x$	$1 - \dfrac{x^2}{2!} + \dfrac{x^4}{4!} - \dfrac{x^6}{6!} + \cdots + \dfrac{(-1)^n x^{2n}}{(2n)!}$	$\displaystyle\sum_{k=0}^{n} \dfrac{(-1)^k x^{2k}}{(2k)!}$	0
$\dfrac{1}{1-x}$	$1 + x + x^2 + x^3 + \cdots + x^n$	$\displaystyle\sum_{k=0}^{n} x^k$	0

EXAMPLE 3

(a) Find the first-, third-, and fifth-degree Taylor polynomials for the function $f(x) = \sin x$ at $x = 0$.

(b) Use a graphing calculator to graph $f(x)$ with each of the polynomials. Determine which polynomial is the best approximation to $\sin x$ at $x = 0$.

Solution   First find the derivatives:

$$f(x) = \sin x \qquad\qquad f(0) = 0$$

$$f'(x) = \cos x \qquad\qquad f'(0) = 1$$

$$f'''(x) = -\cos x \qquad\qquad f'''(0) = -1$$

$$f^{(5)}(x) = \cos x \qquad\qquad f^{(5)}(0) = 1$$

Using the derivatives, we can write the polynomials:

$$P_1 = x$$

$$P_3 = x - \frac{x^3}{3!}$$

$$P_5 = x - \frac{x^3}{3!} + \frac{x^5}{5!}$$

(b)

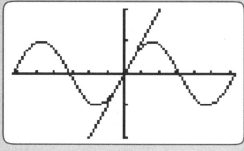

$\sin x$ and P_1

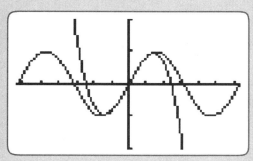

$\sin x$ and P_3

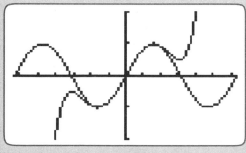

$\sin x$ and P_5

Observing the graphs, it is apparent that the fifth-degree polynomial P_5 is the best approximation to $\sin x$ at $x = 0$.

Exercises

Multiple-Choice Questions

A graphing calculator is required for some questions.

1. There is no Taylor polynomial for $f(x) = \sqrt[3]{x}$ centered at $x = 0$ because
   - (A) $f(x)$ is not continuous at $x = 0$
   - (B) $f(x)$ is not differentiable at $x = 0$
   - (C) $f(0)$ does not exist
   - (D) $\lim\limits_{x \to 0^+} f(x) \neq \lim\limits_{x \to 0^-} f(x)$
   - (E) $f'(0) = 0$

2. Use the formula for the sum of a finite geometric series to find an expression for $1 + x + x^2 + \cdots + x^{n-1}$.
   - (A) $\dfrac{1}{1-x}$
   - (B) $n\left(\dfrac{1 + x^{n-1}}{2}\right)$
   - (C) $\dfrac{1 - x^n}{1 - x}$
   - (D) $\dfrac{1 + x^n}{1 - x}$
   - (E) $\dfrac{1 + x^n}{1 + x}$

3. If $P(x)$ is the third-degree Taylor polynomial for $f(x) = \ln x$ centered at $x = 1$, then $P(1.2) =$
   - (A) 0.181
   - (B) 0.182
   - (C) 0.183
   - (D) 0.2
   - (E) 0.223

4. Use the fourth-degree Taylor polynomial for $\cos x$ centered at $x = 0$ to approximate $\cos\left(\dfrac{\pi}{6}\right)$.
   - (A) 0.5
   - (B) 0.866
   - (C) 0.882
   - (D) 1.140
   - (E) 1.156

Free-Response Questions

1. (No calculator)
   - (a) Write the fifth-degree Taylor polynomial for $f(x) = \ln x$ centered at $x = 1$.
   - (b) Use the Taylor polynomial in part (a) to approximate $\ln 2$.
   - (c) Would the tenth-degree Taylor polynomial for $f(x) = \ln x$ centered at $x = 1$ give a better approximation to $\ln 2$? Explain.

2. (Calculator required)
   - (a) Use the Taylor polynomial for $f(x) = \sin x$ to approximate $\sin(0.6)$ to four decimal places.
   - (b) Use the Taylor polynomial for $g(x) = \cos x$ to approximate $\cos(0.6)$ to four decimal places.
   - (c) Using your answers to parts (a) and (b), approximate the value of
     $$\sin^2(0.6) + \cos^2(0.6).$$

9.4 Finding New Polynomials from Old

Once a Taylor polynomial is found that approximates a function, this polynomial can be used to find other polynomials that approximate a variety of similar functions. For example, the Maclaurin polynomial for $\dfrac{1}{1-x}$ in Section 9.3 Example 2 can be used to find the Maclaurin polynomial of degree 4 for $\dfrac{1}{1 - 2x}$ by substituting $2x$ for x. Thus, the Maclaurin polynomial for $\dfrac{1}{1 - 2x}$ is

$$1 + (2x) + (2x)^2 + (2x)^3 + (2x)^4 = 1 + 2x + 4x^2 + 8x^3 + 16x^4.$$

This procedure of using known polynomial approximations of functions to find polynomial approximations of similar functions often appears in AP questions on Taylor polynomials and Taylor series. Look closely at the next few examples where Maclaurin polynomials are found for $\frac{1}{1-3x}$, $\frac{1}{1+x}$, $\frac{1}{1+x^2}$, and $\frac{x}{1+x^2}$ using the Maclaurin polynomial for $\frac{1}{1-x}$.

EXAMPLE 1

Find the Maclaurin polynomial of degree 4 for $\frac{1}{1-3x}$ and write it in sigma notation.

Solution   Replace x by $3x$ in the Maclaurin polynomial of degree 4 for $\frac{1}{1-x}$. Thus the Maclaurin polynomial of degree 4 for $\frac{1}{1-3x}$ is

$$1 + (3x) + (3x)^2 + (3x)^3 + (3x)^4 = 1 + 3x + 9x^2 + 27x^3 + 81x^4$$

$$= \sum_{n=0}^{4} (3x)^n.$$

EXAMPLE 2

Find the Maclaurin polynomial of degree 4 for $\frac{1}{1+x}$ and write the polynomial in sigma notation.

Solution   Replace x with $-x$ in the Maclaurin polynomial of degree 4 for $\frac{1}{1-x}$. Thus the Maclaurin polynomial of degree 4 for $\frac{1}{1+x}$ is

$$1 + (-x) + (-x)^2 + (-x)^3 + (-x)^4 = 1 - x + x^2 - x^3 + x^4$$

$$= \sum_{n=0}^{4} (-1)^n x^n.$$

EXAMPLE 3

Find the Maclaurin polynomial of degree 8 for $\frac{1}{1+x^2}$ and write the polynomial in sigma notation.

Solution   Replace x by $-x^2$ in the Maclaurin polynomial of degree 4 for $\frac{1}{1-x}$. Thus the Maclaurin polynomial of degree 8 for $\frac{1}{1+x^2}$ is

$$1 + (-x^2) + (-x^2)^4 + (-x^2)^6 + (-x^2)^8 = 1 - x^2 + x^4 - x^6 + x^8$$

$$= \sum_{n=0}^{4} (-1)^n x^{2n}.$$

EXAMPLE 4

Find the Maclaurin polynomial of degree 9 for $\dfrac{x}{1 + x^2}$.

Solution   Using the Maclaurin polynomial for $\dfrac{1}{1 + x^2}$ in Example 3, multiply each term by x. Thus the Maclaurin polynomial of degree 4 for $\dfrac{x}{1 + x^2}$ is

$$x(1 - x^2 + x^4 - x^6 + x^8) = x - x^3 + x^5 - x^7 + x^9$$

$$= \sum_{n=0}^{4} (-1)^n x^{2n+1}.$$

EXAMPLE 5

Find the Maclaurin polynomial of degree 4 for $\dfrac{1}{2 - x}$ and write the polynomial in sigma notation.

Solution   Rewrite $\dfrac{1}{2 - x}$ as $\dfrac{1}{2\left(1 - \dfrac{x}{2}\right)} = \dfrac{1}{2} \cdot \dfrac{1}{1 - \dfrac{x}{2}}$. Using the Maclaurin series for $\dfrac{1}{1 - x}$, replace x by $\dfrac{x}{2}$ and multiply the resulting polynomial by $\dfrac{1}{2}$. Thus, the Maclaurin series of degree 4 for $\dfrac{1}{2 - x}$ is

$$\frac{1}{2} \cdot \left(1 + \frac{x}{2} + \left(\frac{x}{2}\right)^2 + \left(\frac{x}{2}\right)^3 + \left(\frac{x}{2}\right)^4\right)$$

$$= \frac{1}{2} \cdot \left(1 + \frac{x}{2} + \frac{x^2}{4} + \frac{x^3}{8} + \frac{x^4}{16}\right)$$

$$= \frac{1}{2} + \frac{x}{4} + \frac{x^2}{8} + \frac{x^3}{16} + \frac{x^2}{32}$$

$$= \sum_{n=0}^{4} \frac{x^n}{2^{n+1}}.$$

EXAMPLE 6

Find the Taylor polynomial of degree 4 for $\dfrac{1}{2 - x}$ centered at 1 and write the polynomial in sigma notation.

Solution   Rewrite $\dfrac{1}{2 - x}$ as $\dfrac{1}{1 - (x - 1)}$, and use the Maclaurin series for $\dfrac{1}{1 - x}$ with x replaced by $x - 1$. Then the Taylor polynomial of degree 4 for $\dfrac{1}{2 - x}$ centered at 1 is

$$1 + (x - 1) + (x - 1)^2 + (x - 1)^3 + (x - 1)^4$$

$$= \sum_{n=0}^{4} (x - 1)^n.$$

Exercises

1. Use the Maclaurin polynomial for $f(x) = \dfrac{1}{1-x}$ in Section 9.3 Example 2 to find the following polynomials. Then write the polynomial in sigma notation.
   (a) A Maclaurin polynomial of degree 8 for $\dfrac{1}{1-x^2}$
   (b) A Maclaurin polynomial of degree 4 for $\dfrac{1}{1+2x}$
   (c) A Maclaurin polynomial of degree 4 for $\dfrac{1}{3-x}$
   (d) A Taylor polynomial of degree 4 centered at 2 for $\dfrac{1}{3-x}$
   (e) An eleventh-degree Maclaurin polynomial for $\dfrac{x^2}{1+x^3}$

2. Find a Maclaurin polynomial of degree 8 for $\dfrac{x^2}{1-x^2}$ in the following three ways:
   (a) Use the Maclaurin polynomial for $f(x) = \dfrac{1}{1-x}$ in Section 9.3 Example 2.
   (b) Show that $\dfrac{x^2}{1-x^2} = \dfrac{1}{1-x^2} - 1$, using the polynomial for $\dfrac{1}{1-x^2}$ in Exercise 1(a) above.
   (c) Show that $\dfrac{1}{1-x^2} = \dfrac{1}{2}\left(\dfrac{1}{1+x} + \dfrac{1}{1-x}\right)$, using the polynomials for $\dfrac{1}{1-x}$ and $\dfrac{1}{1+x}$.

3. Use the Taylor polynomials for e^x, $\ln x$, $\sin x$, and $\cos x$ to find a Taylor polynomial for each of the following functions. Write each polynomial in sigma notation, and state the center for each polynomial.
   (a) e^{-x}
   (b) $\sin(2x)$
   (c) $\ln(x+1)$
   (d) $\sin^2 x$ $\left(\text{Hint: Use the identity } \sin^2 x = \dfrac{1-\cos 2x}{2}.\right)$

Multiple-Choice Questions
No calculator is allowed for these questions.

1. The fourth-degree Taylor polynomial for e^{2x} centered at $x = 0$ is

(A) $1 + 2x + \dfrac{2x^2}{2!} + \dfrac{2x^3}{3!} + \dfrac{2x^4}{4!}$

(B) $2 + 2x + \dfrac{2x^2}{2!} + \dfrac{2x^3}{3!} + \dfrac{2x^4}{4!}$

(C) $1 + 2x + \dfrac{4x^2}{2!} + \dfrac{8x^3}{3!} + \dfrac{16x^4}{4!}$

(D) $1 - 2x + \dfrac{2x^2}{2!} - \dfrac{2x^3}{3!} + \dfrac{2x^4}{4!}$

(E) $1 - 2x + \dfrac{4x^2}{2!} - \dfrac{8x^3}{3!} + \dfrac{16x^4}{4!}$

2. Find the fourth-degree Taylor polynomial centered at $x = 0$ for $f(x) = 1 - \cos x$.

(A) $1 - \dfrac{x^2}{2!} + \dfrac{x^4}{4!}$

(B) $1 + \dfrac{x^2}{2!} + \dfrac{x^4}{4!}$

(C) $-\dfrac{x^2}{2!} + \dfrac{x^4}{4!}$

(D) $\dfrac{x^2}{2!} - \dfrac{x^4}{4!}$

(E) $1 - \dfrac{x^2}{2!} + \dfrac{x^4}{4!} - \dfrac{x^6}{6!}$

3. Which of the following is the third-degree Maclaurin polynomial for $f(x) = \ln(1-x)$?

(A) $-x - \dfrac{x^2}{2} - \dfrac{x^3}{3}$

(B) $-x - \dfrac{x^2}{2!} - \dfrac{x^3}{3!}$

(C) $(1-x) - \dfrac{(1-x)^2}{2} + \dfrac{(1-x)^3}{3}$

(D) $-x + \dfrac{x^2}{2!} - \dfrac{x^3}{3!}$

(E) $-x + \dfrac{x^2}{2} - \dfrac{x^3}{3}$

4. Use the fifth-degree Taylor polynomial for $\sin x$ to find the fifth-degree Taylor polynomial for $\sin \dfrac{1}{2}x$.

(A) $\dfrac{x}{2} - \dfrac{x^3}{2(3)} + \dfrac{x^5}{2(5)}$

(B) $\dfrac{x}{2} - \dfrac{x^3}{2(3!)} + \dfrac{x^5}{2(5!)}$

(C) $\dfrac{x}{2} + \dfrac{x^3}{2^3(3!)} + \dfrac{x^5}{2^5(5!)}$

(D) $\dfrac{x}{2} - \dfrac{x^3}{2^3(3!)} + \dfrac{x^5}{2^5(5!)}$

(E) $\dfrac{x}{2} + \dfrac{x^3}{2(3!)} + \dfrac{x^5}{2(5!)}$

Free-Response Questions

1. (No calculator)
   (a) Write the fourth-degree Taylor polynomial for $f(x) = \dfrac{1}{1-x}$ centered at $x = 0$.

(b) Use the Taylor polynomial in part (a) to write a fourth-degree Taylor polynomial for $g(x) = \dfrac{1}{5 - x}$. State the center.

(c) Use the Taylor polynomial in part (a) to write a fourth-degree Taylor polynomial for $h(x) = \dfrac{1}{5 - x^2}$. State the center.

2. (Calculator required)
   (a) Write the Taylor polynomial of degree four for $f(x) = e^x$.
   (b) Use the Taylor polynomial in part (a) to write an expression for $f(\ln x)$.
   (c) Using TABLE in the calculator, make a table of five values of x and $f(\ln x)$.
   (d) Write a sentence drawing a conclusion based on the values of x and $f(\ln x)$ in the table.

9.5 Error Formula for Taylor Polynomial Approximation

The Taylor polynomial approximation of degree n to a function $f(x)$ centered at c is

$$f(x) \approx \sum_{k=0}^{n} \frac{f^{(k)}(c)}{k!} (x - c)^k.$$

If this polynomial is used to approximate the function at a particular value of x, then the error formula gives an upper estimate of the difference between the actual value of the function and the approximated value.

$$\text{Error } E \leq \left| \frac{f^{(n+1)}(z)}{(n + 1)!} (x - c)^{n+1} \right|, \text{ where } z \text{ is between } x \text{ and } c.$$

To assist in remembering this formula, note that it is remarkably similar to the absolute value of the $(n + 1)$st term in the Taylor polynomial, except that z replaces the variable x.

EXAMPLE 1

In Example 1 of Section 9.3, $\sqrt{1.2}$ was approximated using a third-degree Taylor polynomial centered at 1 for $\sqrt{x}$, giving the approximate value of 1.0955. Calculate the error of that approximation.

Solution The error $E \leq \left| \dfrac{f^{(4)}(z)}{4!} (1.2 - 1)^4 \right|$, where z is between 1 and 1.2.

If $f(x) = \sqrt{x}$, then the fourth derivative is $-\dfrac{15}{16 \, x^{7/2}}$. To maximize the error E at z, choose the value of z between 1 and 1.2 that will make the denominator the smallest; that is, $z = 1$. Then the error formula becomes

$$\text{error } E \leq \left| \frac{-\dfrac{15}{16}}{4!} (0.2)^4 \right| = 0.0000625.$$

This error estimate is close to the actual error: $\sqrt{1.2} - 1.0955 \approx 0.0000549$.

EXAMPLE 2

How many terms are needed to approximate ln 1.5 with an error less than 0.001 by using a Taylor polynomial centered at $x = 1$?

Solution The error E for ln x using a Taylor polynomial of degree n centered at 1 is

$$E \leq \left| \frac{f^{(n+1)}(z)}{(n+1)!} (x-c)^{n+1} \right|$$

Since $f^{(n+1)}(z) = \frac{(-1)^n n!}{z^{n+1}}$, using $x = 1.5$ and $c = 1$,

$$E \leq \left| \frac{\frac{(-1)^n n!}{z^{n+1}}}{(n+1)!} (x-1)^{n+1} \right|$$

$$E \leq \left| \frac{1}{z^{n+1}(n+1)} (x-1)^{n+1} \right|.$$

Since z is between 1 and 1.5, to maximize the error, choose the smallest value for z, that is, $z = 1$. Now the error in estimating ln 1.5 $\leq$ $\frac{0.5^{n+1}}{n+1}$.

To find the value of n that makes $\frac{0.5^{n+1}}{n+1} \leq 0.001$, solve the inequality using a calculator. One method is simply to choose bigger values of n until the quantity $\frac{0.5^{n+1}}{n+1}$ is less than 0.001.

Another method is to enter into $\boxed{Y=}$, $Y_1 = \frac{0.5^{x+1}}{x+1}$ and make a table of values for increasing integer values of x. You can also graph the function in Y_1 and $\boxed{TRACE}$ to find the smallest integral value of x that makes the function less than 0.001.

The answer is $n + 1 = 7$, or $n = 6$. Therefore by adding 6 terms of the Taylor polynomial, the approximation of ln 1.5 will have an error less than 0.001.

Calculator Note

On the TI-89, press $\boxed{F3}$: 9 and the symbol taylor(will appear. This command has the following syntax: taylor(function, variable, degree, center). Using this command, the sum of the first 6 terms in Example 2 can be found by entering taylor(ln (x), x, 6, 1) | $x = 1.5$. This gives an approximation to ln 1.5 of 0.4046875. The error between this value and the actual value of ln 1.5 is less than 0.001. If an error calculation is required on an AP Calculus exam, all work must be shown. The calculator may be used only as a check.

Exercises

1. Use the error formula to estimate the error if $\sin^2(0.2)$ is approximated with a Taylor polynomial of degree 4 centered at $x = 0$ for $\sin^2 x$.

2. Find the estimate for the error if $e^{-1.5}$ is approximated using a Taylor polynomial of degree 4 centered at $x = 0$ for e^x.

3. How many terms are needed to approximate $e^{-1.5}$ using a Taylor polynomial centered at $x = 0$ so that the error is less than 0.001?

Multiple-Choice Questions

A graphing calculator is required for some questions.

1. Using the formula for the error E, what is the maximum value of the error in approximating ln 1.2 with a Taylor polynomial of degree 3 centered at $x = 1$?
   (A) 0.000345
   (B) 0.0004
   (C) 0.00666
   (D) 0.1813
   (E) 0.1827

2. What is the degree of the Taylor polynomial needed to approximate $\sqrt{e}$ with error < 0.001?
   (A) 3
   (B) 4
   (C) 5
   (D) 6
   (E) 7

3. A Taylor polynomial of degree n approximates the value of cos (0.5) with error < 0.001. Find the smallest value of n.
   (A) 0
   (B) 2
   (C) 4
   (D) 6
   (E) 8

Free-Response Questions

No calculator is allowed for these questions.

1. (a) Derive a second-degree Taylor polynomial for $f(x) = \sqrt[3]{x}$, centered at $x = 1$.
   (b) Use the Taylor polynomial in part (a) to approximate $\sqrt[3]{2}$.
   (c) Find the error in the approximation in part (b).

2. (a) Use division to find a Taylor polynomial of degree n for $f(x) = \dfrac{1 + 2x}{1 + x}$.
   (b) Write the Taylor polynomial in part (a) in sigma notation.

9.6 Sequences and Series

In the study of series of numbers, the major goal is to determine whether a series has a limit, that is, whether the sum of the terms approaches a finite number. If the series has a limit, it is said to **converge** to that value. If the series does not have a limit, it is said to **diverge.**

Consider a square with a side length of 1 unit. Draw a line through the center of the square and shade one side. That represents $\frac{1}{2}$. Next, divide the unshaded portion in half and shade half of that. The shaded portion now represents $\frac{1}{2} + \frac{1}{4}$. If we repeat the procedure, the shaded portion will represent $\frac{1}{2} + \frac{1}{4} + \frac{1}{8}$.

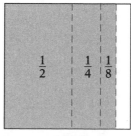

1 Unit

We see that we can go on indefinitely and that the following series results:

$$\frac{1}{2} + \frac{1}{4} + \frac{1}{8} + \cdots + \frac{1}{2^n} + \cdots = 1.$$

This is an example of an infinite series. Notice that although the number of terms in the series is infinite, the series does have a finite sum. If we look at the *partial sums* of the series, we see that they appear to converge to 1.

$$S_1 = \frac{1}{2} = 0.50$$

$$S_2 = \frac{1}{2} + \frac{1}{4} = 0.75$$

$$S_3 = \frac{1}{2} + \frac{1}{4} + \frac{1}{8} = 0.875$$

$$S_4 = \frac{1}{2} + \frac{1}{4} + \frac{1}{8} + \frac{1}{16} = 0.9375$$

Geometric Series   In a geometric sequence, the first term is denoted a_1 and succeeding terms are each multiplied by a constant r. The geometric series formed by adding successive terms of a geometric sequence has a limit when $|r| < 1$. The sum of the terms of a convergent geometric series is given by the formula $S = \frac{a_1}{1 - r}$. What makes a geometric series special is that we know not only whether the series converges, but also the value to which it converges.

Notice that the Taylor polynomial $1 + x + x^2 + x^3$ looks like part of a geometric series where $r = x$. This series would converge if $|x| < 1$. Applying the formula for the sum of the series produces $S = \frac{1}{1 - x}$, which is the sum of the series $1 + \frac{1}{2} + \frac{1}{4} + \frac{1}{8} + \cdots$.

EXAMPLE 1

Find the sum of the series formed by adding successive terms of the sequence $1, \frac{1}{2}, \frac{1}{4}, \frac{1}{8}, \cdots$

Solution   Since this is a geometric sequence with $r = \frac{1}{2}$ and $a_1 = 1$, it converges. The sum of the terms of the series is $S = \dfrac{1}{1 - \frac{1}{2}} = 2$.

EXAMPLE 2

Find the sum of the series $3 + 1 + \frac{1}{3} + \frac{1}{9} + \cdots$

Solution   This is a geometric series with $r = \frac{1}{3}$ and $a_1 = 3$. The sum of the series is

$$S = \frac{3}{1 - \frac{1}{3}} = \frac{9}{2} = 4.5.$$

EXAMPLE 3

Find the value of $\sum_{n=0}^{\infty} (0.5^n - 0.2^n)$.

Solution This series can be split into two geometric series as $\sum_{n=0}^{\infty} 0.5^n - \sum_{n=0}^{\infty} 0.2^n$. In the first series, $a_1 = 1$ and $r = 0.5$, and the sum is $S = \frac{1}{1 - 0.5} = 2$.

In the second series, $a_1 = 1$ and $r = 0.2$, and the sum is $S = \frac{1}{1 - 0.2} = \frac{5}{4} = 1.25$. Therefore, the value of $\sum_{n=0}^{\infty} (0.5^n - 0.2^n)$ is $2 - 1.25 = 0.75$.

The *p*-Series The *p*-series, like the geometric series, is easy to test for convergence.

> The *p*-series $\sum_{n=1}^{\infty} \frac{1}{n^p} = \frac{1}{1^p} + \frac{1}{2^p} + \frac{1}{3^p} + \cdots$ converges for $p > 1$.
>
> The *p*-series diverges for $p \leq 1$.

In the case of a *p*-series, we can determine if the series converges, but not the value to which it converges.

EXAMPLE 4

Test the convergence of $\sum_{n=1}^{\infty} \frac{1}{n^2}$.

Solution This is a *p*-series with $p = 2$. Since $p > 1$, the series converges.

EXAMPLE 5

Test the convergence of $\sum_{n=1}^{\infty} \frac{1}{n^{0.99}}$.

Solution This is a *p*-series with $p = 0.99$. Since $p \leq 1$, the series diverges.

EXAMPLE 6

Does the series $\sum_{n=1}^{\infty} \left(\frac{1}{n^3} - 0.9^n \right)$ converge?

Solution Split the series into two parts: $\sum_{n=1}^{\infty} \frac{1}{n^3} - \sum_{n=1}^{\infty} 0.9^n$.

The first part is a *p*-series with $p = 3$. Since $p > 3$, the *p*-series converges. The second part is a geometric series with $r = 0.9$. Since $|r| < 1$, the geometric series converges. Thus, the series $\sum_{n=1}^{\infty} \left(\frac{1}{n^3} - 0.9^n \right)$ converges.

Telescoping Series   A third series whose convergence is easily tested is the telescoping series. One example of a telescoping series is

$$\sum_{n=1}^{\infty} \left(\frac{1}{n} - \frac{1}{n+1} \right) = \left(1 - \frac{1}{2} \right) + \left(\frac{1}{2} - \frac{1}{3} \right) + \left(\frac{1}{3} - \frac{1}{4} \right) + \cdots$$

Notice that the terms of this series cancel in pairs: $-\frac{1}{2}$ and $\frac{1}{2}$, $-\frac{1}{3}$ and $\frac{1}{3}$, etc. This causes the sum to "collapse" like a telescope.

The sequence of even-numbered partial sums S_{2n} is as follows:

$$S_2 = \frac{1}{2},$$

$$S_4 = \frac{2}{3},$$

$$S_6 = \frac{3}{4}, \dots$$

Thus, $S_{2n} = \dfrac{n}{n+1}$, and the sum of the series $S = \lim\limits_{n \to \infty} S_{2n} = \lim\limits_{n \to \infty} \dfrac{n}{n+1} = 1$.

EXAMPLE 7

Determine whether the series $\displaystyle\sum_{n=1}^{\infty} \left(\frac{3}{n} - \frac{3}{n+2} \right)$ converges and, if possible, find its sum.

Solution   This series may be rewritten as

$$3 \sum_{n=1}^{\infty} \left(\frac{1}{n} - \frac{1}{n+2} \right).$$

The first few terms of the series are

$$3 \left[\left(1 - \frac{1}{3} \right) + \left(\frac{1}{2} - \frac{1}{4} \right) + \left(\frac{1}{3} - \frac{1}{5} \right) + \left(\frac{1}{4} - \frac{1}{6} \right) + \cdots \right].$$

The sum of the series can be found by taking two sums: the sum of the 1st, 3rd, 5th,... parentheses, which is 1, and the sum of the 2nd, 4th, 6th,... parentheses, which is $\frac{1}{2}$. Thus the sum of the series is

$$3 \left[1 + \frac{1}{2} \right] = \frac{9}{2} = 4.5.$$

The Harmonic Series   The harmonic series has the form

$$\sum_{n=1}^{\infty} \frac{1}{n} = 1 + \frac{1}{2} + \frac{1}{3} + \frac{1}{4} + \frac{1}{5} + \cdots$$

We can observe partial sums to determine whether the harmonic series converges or diverges:

$$S_1 = 1$$

$$S_2 = 1 + \frac{1}{2}$$

$$S_4 = 1 + \frac{1}{2} + \left(\frac{1}{3} + \frac{1}{4} \right)$$

Notice that in S_4, $\left(\frac{1}{3} + \frac{1}{4}\right) > 2\left(\frac{1}{4}\right)$, or $\frac{1}{2}$.

$$S_8 = 1 + \frac{1}{2} + \left(\frac{1}{3} + \frac{1}{4}\right) + \left(\frac{1}{5} + \frac{1}{6} + \frac{1}{7} + \frac{1}{8}\right)$$

Again, notice that in S_8, $\left(\frac{1}{5} + \frac{1}{6} + \frac{1}{7} + \frac{1}{8}\right) > 4\left(\frac{1}{8}\right)$, or $\frac{1}{2}$.

By increasing n, it is possible to make the harmonic series arbitrarily large. As $n \to \infty$, the partial sum $\to \infty$, or $\lim\limits_{n \to \infty} S_n = \infty$. Since the sequence of partial sums diverges, the harmonic series diverges, or $\sum\limits_{n=1}^{\infty} \frac{1}{n} = \infty$. The harmonic series is an important example of a series that diverges, yet has terms that approach zero.

Strategy for Testing Series The geometric series, the p-series, the telescoping series, and the harmonic series are easily tested for convergence. Series other than these can also be tested for convergence. The convergence tests for a series of positive terms are:

> The Ratio Test
> The Limit Comparison Test
> The Direct Comparison Test
> The Integral Test
> The nth-Root Test

Additionally, the Alternating Series Test applies specifically to a series in which the terms alternate in sign. Aside from the special case of alternating series, there is no best or right test for convergence of a series. The convergence tests can be applied effectively in the order in which they appear on the list. After some practice, however, the best method is probably the one that is the easiest to do.

Before testing for convergence of a series $\sum\limits_{n=1}^{\infty} a_n$, always use the Divergence Test.

Divergence Test

If

$$\lim_{n \to \infty} a_n \neq 0,$$

Then

$$\sum_{n=1}^{\infty} a_n \text{ diverges.}$$

Keep in mind that the Divergence Test is *inconclusive* if $\lim\limits_{n \to \infty} a_n = 0$. Be careful not to use the converse of the statement.

The Ratio Test

1. **If** $\quad \lim\limits_{n \to \infty} \left| \dfrac{a_{n+1}}{a_n} \right| < 1,$

   Then $\quad$ the series $\sum\limits_{n=1}^{\infty} a_n$ converges.

2. **If** $\quad \lim\limits_{n \to \infty} \left| \dfrac{a_{n+1}}{a_n} \right| > 1,$

   Then $\quad$ the series $\sum\limits_{n=1}^{\infty} a_n$ diverges.

3. **If** $\quad \lim\limits_{n \to \infty} \left| \dfrac{a_{n+1}}{a_n} \right| = 1,$

   Then $\quad$ the test is inconclusive.

EXAMPLE 8

Does the series $\sum\limits_{n=1}^{\infty} \dfrac{n}{n+1}$ converge or diverge?

Solution By the Divergence Test, $\lim\limits_{n \to \infty} \dfrac{n}{n+1} = 1 \neq 0$. Therefore, the series diverges.

EXAMPLE 9

Does the series $\sum\limits_{n=1}^{\infty} \dfrac{2^n}{n^2}$ converge or diverge?

Solution By the Ratio Test,

$$\lim_{n \to \infty} \left| \frac{a_{n+1}}{a_n} \right| = \lim_{n \to \infty} \frac{\dfrac{2^{n+1}}{(n+1)^2}}{\dfrac{2^n}{n^2}} = \lim_{n \to \infty} \frac{2n^2}{(n+1)^2} = 2 > 1.$$

Therefore, the series diverges.

EXAMPLE 10

Does the series $\sum\limits_{n=1}^{\infty} \dfrac{n^3}{n!}$ converge or diverge?

Solution   By the Ratio Test,

$$\lim_{n\to\infty}\left|\frac{\frac{(n+1)^3}{(n+1)!}}{\frac{n^3}{n!}}\right| = \lim_{n\to\infty}\left(\frac{(n+1)^3 n!}{(n+1)! n^3}\right) = \lim_{n\to\infty}\left(\frac{(n+1)^3}{(n+1)n^3}\right)$$

$$= \lim_{n\to\infty}\frac{(n+1)^2}{n^3} = 0 < 1.$$

Therefore, the series converges.

In both the Limit Comparison Test and the Direct Comparison Test, a series whose convergence is being tested, say $\sum_{n=1}^{\infty} a_n$, is compared with a series whose convergence is known, say $\sum_{n=1}^{\infty} b_n$. The Limit Comparison Test is easier to use since it involves taking the limit of the ratio of the terms of the two series, while the Direct Comparison Test involves establishing an inequality between the terms of the two series.

The Limit Comparison Test

1. **If** $\sum a_n$ and $\sum b_n$ are series of positive terms, and $\lim_{n\to\infty}\frac{a_n}{b_n}$ is a positive finite number,

   Then the series $\sum_{n=1}^{\infty} a_n$ and $\sum_{n=1}^{\infty} b_n$ either both converge or both diverge.

The Direct Comparison Test

1. **If** $0 \le a_n \le b_n$ and the series $\sum_{n=1}^{\infty} a_n$ diverges,

   Then $\sum_{n=1}^{\infty} b_n$ diverges.

2. **If** $0 \le a_n \le b_n$ and the series $\sum_{n=1}^{\infty} b_n$ converges,

   Then $\sum_{n=1}^{\infty} a_n$ converges.

EXAMPLE 11

Test $\displaystyle\sum_{n=2}^{\infty} \frac{1}{n^2 - 1}$ for convergence.

Solution Use the Limit Comparison test and compare $\displaystyle\sum_{n=2}^{\infty} \frac{1}{n^2 - 1}$ with $\displaystyle\sum_{n=1}^{\infty} \frac{1}{n^2}$:

$$\lim_{n \to \infty} \frac{\dfrac{1}{n^2 + 1}}{\dfrac{1}{n^2}} = \lim_{n \to \infty} \frac{n^2}{n^2 - 1} = 1.$$

Since the limit is a positive finite number and the series $\displaystyle\sum_{n=1}^{\infty} \frac{1}{n^2}$ converges (p-series, $p = 2$), the series $\displaystyle\sum_{n=2}^{\infty} \frac{1}{n^2 - 1}$ converges.

EXAMPLE 12

Test $\displaystyle\sum_{n=1}^{\infty} \frac{1}{n + 1}$ for convergence.

Solution Use the Limit Comparison Test and compare $\displaystyle\sum_{n=1}^{\infty} \frac{1}{n + 1}$ with $\displaystyle\sum_{n=1}^{\infty} \frac{1}{n}$:

$$\lim_{n \to \infty} \frac{\dfrac{1}{n + 1}}{\dfrac{1}{n}} = \lim_{n \to \infty} \frac{n}{n + 1} = 1.$$

Since the limit is a positive finite number and the series $\displaystyle\sum_{n=1}^{\infty} \frac{1}{n}$ diverges (p-series, $p = 1$), the series $\displaystyle\sum_{n=1}^{\infty} \frac{1}{n + 1}$ diverges.

EXAMPLE 13

Test the series $\displaystyle\sum_{n=1}^{\infty} \frac{1}{3^n}$ using the Direct Comparison Test with the series $\displaystyle\sum_{n=1}^{\infty} \frac{1}{n^2}$.

Solution In using the Direct Comparison test, we need to establish one of two inequalities. In this case, we think that $\displaystyle\sum_{n=1}^{\infty} \frac{1}{3^n}$ converges, and since $\displaystyle\sum_{n=1}^{\infty} \frac{1}{n^2}$ converges (p-series, $p = 2$), we need to show that $\dfrac{1}{3^n} \leq \dfrac{1}{n^2}$.

Alternatively, we can determine if $3^n \geq n^2$. Taking successive values of n beginning with $n = 1$, the inequality is true and since the values of 3^n are increasing faster than the values of n^2, the inequality is true for all positive integers n. In general, an exponential function with a base > 1 will always eventually exceed any polynomial function.

Another way to verify the inequality in Example 13 is to use the graphing calculator either to graph the two functions 3^x and x^2, or to make a table of values for positive integers. Entering $Y_1 = 3^x$ and $Y_2 = x^2$, we see that the graphs do not intersect for positive values of x, and that 3^x is always greater than x^2, thus verifying the inequality.

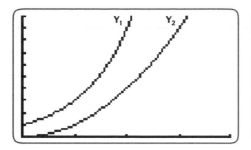 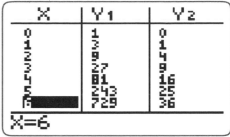

EXAMPLE 14

Test the series $\displaystyle\sum_{n=1}^{\infty} \frac{1}{2^n}$ using the Direct Comparison Test with the series $\displaystyle\sum_{n=1}^{\infty} \frac{1}{n^2}$.

Solution Since $\displaystyle\sum_{n=1}^{\infty} \frac{1}{n^2}$ converges (*p*-series, $p = 2$), we need to show that $\dfrac{1}{2^n} \leq \dfrac{1}{n^2}$.

Alternatively, show that $2^n \geq n^2$. The inequality is true for $n = 1$, but taking successive values of n, we see that the inequality is true for $n = 2$, but not for $n = 3$. It is true again for $n = 4$. For values of $n > 4$, the inequality remains true. Again, an exponential function with a base > 0 will always eventually exceed a polynomial function. Thus, the series $\displaystyle\sum_{n=1}^{\infty} \frac{1}{2^n}$ converges.

Another way to verify the inequality in Example 14 is to graph 2^x and x^2 or make a table of values for positive integers. On the graphing calculator, enter $Y_1 = 2^x$ and $Y_2 = x^2$.

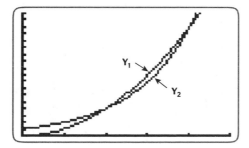

In this case, the graphs intersect twice for positive values of x, at $x = 2$ and at $x = 4$. For values of x greater than 4, the graph of 2^x is above the graph of x^2, so the inequality holds for positive integers greater than 4.

Example 14 illustrates several strategies that can be helpful in working with inequalities:

- Check a few successive values of n. When an inequality is true for one value of n, it is not automatically true for all larger values of n.
- Use the graphing calculator to graph the functions or to make a table of values to help in verifying the inequality.
- Remember that the inequality does not have to be true for all positive integers n. It is sufficient that the inequality be true for n greater than some positive integer.

The Integral Test

A series $\sum_{n=1}^{\infty} a_n$ can be thought of as a function $f(x)$ whose domain is the positive integers and where $f(n) = a_n$. The existence of the sum of the series $\sum_{n=1}^{\infty} a_n$ is related to $\int_1^{\infty} f(x)\,dx$ as follows:

1. **If** $\int_1^{\infty} f(x)\,dx$ converges,

   Then $\sum_{n=1}^{\infty} a_n$ converges.

2. **If** $\int_1^{\infty} f(x)\,dx$ diverges,

   Then $\sum_{n=1}^{\infty} a_n$ diverges.

EXAMPLE 15

Test the series $\sum_{n=1}^{\infty} \dfrac{n}{n^2 + 1}$ for convergence.

Solution

METHOD 1   By the Integral Test, $\int_1^{\infty} \dfrac{x}{x^2 + 1}\,dx =$

$$\lim_{b \to \infty} \int_1^b \frac{x}{x^2 + 1}\,dx = \lim_{n \to \infty} \frac{(n+1)^2}{n^3} = 0 < 1 = \lim_{b \to \infty}$$

$$= \lim_{b \to \infty} \frac{1}{2} \ln (x^2 + 1) \Big|_1^b$$

$$= \lim_{b \to \infty} = \left(\frac{1}{2} \ln (b^2 + 1) - \frac{1}{2} \ln 2 \right) = \infty.$$

Since the integral $\int_1^{\infty} \dfrac{x}{x^2 + 1}\,dx$ diverges, $\sum_{n=1}^{\infty} \dfrac{n}{n^2 + 1}$ diverges.

METHOD 2   By the Limit Comparison Test with $\sum_{n=1}^{\infty} \dfrac{1}{n}$,

$$\lim_{n \to \infty} \frac{\dfrac{n}{n^2 + 1}}{\dfrac{1}{n}} = \lim_{n \to \infty} \frac{n^2}{n^2 + 1} = 1,$$

which is a positive finite number.

Since $\displaystyle\sum_{n=1}^{\infty} \frac{1}{n}$ diverges (p-series, $p = 1$), so does $\displaystyle\sum_{n=1}^{\infty} \frac{n}{n^2 + 1}$.

EXAMPLE 16

Test for convergence $\displaystyle\sum_{n=2}^{\infty} \frac{1}{n \ln n}$.

Solution The integral $\displaystyle\int_{2}^{\infty} \frac{1}{x \ln x} \, dx$ works well for this series.

$$\int_{2}^{\infty} \frac{1}{x \ln x} \, dx = \lim_{b \to \infty} \int_{2}^{b} \frac{1}{x \ln x} \, dx$$

$$= \lim_{b \to \infty} \ln (\ln x) \Big|_{2}^{b}$$

$$= \lim_{b \to \infty} (\ln (\ln b) - \ln(\ln 2)) = \infty.$$

Since $\displaystyle\int_{2}^{\infty} \frac{1}{x \ln x} \, dx$ diverges, $\displaystyle\sum_{n=2}^{\infty} \frac{1}{n \ln n}$ diverges.

Alternating Series An **alternating series** is of the form $a_1 - a_2 + a_3 - a_4 + \cdots = \displaystyle\sum_{n=1}^{\infty} (-1)^{n+1} a_n$.

(Note that in the alternating series, the term a_n does not include the + or − sign that precedes it.)

Alternating Series Test

If

1. $\displaystyle\lim_{n \to \infty} a_n = 0$, and
2. $a_{n+1} \leq a_n$,

Then

$\displaystyle\sum_{n=1}^{\infty} (-1)^{n+1} a_n$ converges.

EXAMPLE 17

Does the alternating series $\displaystyle\sum_{n=1}^{\infty} (-1)^{n+1} \frac{1}{n}$ converge or diverge?

Solution By the Alternating Series Test,

1. $\displaystyle\lim_{n \to \infty} \frac{1}{n} = 0$, and
2. $\displaystyle\frac{1}{n+1} \leq \frac{1}{n}$.

Therefore, $\displaystyle\sum_{n=1}^{\infty} (-1)^{n+1} \frac{1}{n}$ converges.

Error Formula for an Alternating Series

If

an alternating series $\sum\limits_{n=1}^{\infty}(-1)^{n+1}a_n$ converges,

Then

its sum can be approximated by the sum of the first n terms of the series, and the error in the approximation is less than the $(n+1)$st term.

EXAMPLE 18

If the first 5 terms of the series $\sum\limits_{n=1}^{\infty}(-1)^{n+1}\dfrac{1}{n}$ are used to approximate the sum, what is the error estimate on this approximation?

Solution The estimate for the error in approximating $\sum\limits_{n=1}^{\infty}(-1)^{n+1}\dfrac{1}{n}$ using the first five terms is less than or equal to the sixth term; that is,

error $\leq \dfrac{1}{6} \approx 0.167$.

Absolute and Conditional Convergence

If an alternating series $a_1 - a_2 + a_3 - a_4 + \cdots = \sum\limits_{n=1}^{\infty}(-1)^{n+1}a_n$ converges and the series of positive terms $\sum\limits_{n=1}^{\infty}a_n$ converges, then the alternating series $\sum\limits_{n=1}^{\infty}(-1)^{n+1}a_n$ is said to be *absolutely convergent*.

If an alternating series $a_1 - a_2 + a_3 - a_4 + \cdots = \sum\limits_{n=1}^{\infty}(-1)^{n+1}a_n$ converges and the series of positive terms $\sum\limits_{n=1}^{\infty}a_n$ diverges, then the alternating series $\sum\limits_{n=1}^{\infty}(-1)^{n+1}a_n$ is said to be *conditionally convergent*.

To expedite the process of deciding if an alternating series is absolutely or conditionally convergent, first test the series of positive terms. If the series of positive terms converges, then the alternating series must converge as well, and the alternating series is absolutely convergent.

On the other hand, if the series of positive terms diverges, then use the alternating series test to test the convergence of the alternating series. If the alternating series converges, then the alternating series is conditionally convergent. Otherwise, the alternating series diverges.

EXAMPLE 19

Is the series $\sum\limits_{n=1}^{\infty}(-1)^{n+1}\dfrac{1}{n}$ absolutely or conditionally convergent?

Solution First test the series of positive terms for convergence: $\sum\limits_{n=1}^{\infty}\dfrac{1}{n}$ is a p-series with $p = 1$. For $p \leq 1$, the p-series diverges. Therefore, the series of positive terms diverges.

Now use the Alternating Series Test to test the alternating series for convergence.

1. $\lim\limits_{n \to \infty} a_n = \lim\limits_{n \to \infty} \dfrac{1}{n} = 0$

2. $\dfrac{1}{n+1} \leq \dfrac{1}{n}$

Therefore, the alternating series $\sum\limits_{n=1}^{\infty} (-1)^{n+1} \dfrac{1}{n}$ converges and the series is conditionally convergent.

EXAMPLE 20

Is the series $\sum\limits_{n=1}^{\infty} (-1)^{n+1} \dfrac{1}{n\sqrt{n}}$ absolutely convergent?

Solution Testing the series of positive terms, $\sum\limits_{n=1}^{\infty} \dfrac{1}{n\sqrt{n}} = \sum\limits_{n=1}^{\infty} \dfrac{1}{n^{3/2}}$, which is a p-series with $p = \dfrac{3}{2}$. Since a p-series converges for $p > 1$, this series converges and the series $\sum\limits_{n=1}^{\infty} (-1)^{n+1} \dfrac{1}{n\sqrt{n}}$ is absolutely convergent.

EXAMPLE 21

Test the series $\sum\limits_{n=0}^{\infty} \dfrac{(-1)^n}{e^n}$ for absolute convergence.

Solution First test the series of positive terms $\sum\limits_{n=0}^{\infty} \dfrac{1}{e^n}$. This is a geometric series with $r = \dfrac{1}{e}$. Since $|r| < 1$, this series converges. Therefore, the series $\sum\limits_{n=0}^{\infty} \dfrac{(-1)^n}{e^n}$ is absolutely convergent.

EXAMPLE 22

Is the series $\sum\limits_{n=1}^{\infty} (-1)^{n+1} \dfrac{n}{e^{n^2}}$ absolutely convergent?

Solution The series of positive terms $\sum\limits_{n=1}^{\infty} \dfrac{n}{e^{n^2}}$ can be tested for convergence using the Integral Test:

$$\int_1^{\infty} \dfrac{x}{e^{x^2}}\, dx = \lim_{b \to \infty} \int_1^b x e^{-x^2}\, dx = \lim_{b \to \infty} \left. -\dfrac{1}{2} e^{-x^2} \right|_1^b$$

$$= \lim_{b \to \infty} \left(-\dfrac{1}{2} e^{-b^2} + \dfrac{1}{2} e^{-1} \right) = \dfrac{1}{2} e^{-1}.$$

Since the integral $\int_1^{\infty} \dfrac{x}{e^{x^2}}\, dx$ converges, so does the series $\sum\limits_{n=1}^{\infty} \dfrac{n}{e^{n^2}}$. Therefore, the series $\sum\limits_{n=1}^{\infty} (-1)^{n+1} \dfrac{n}{e^{n^2}}$ is absolutely convergent.

Exercises

Test the following series for convergence.

1. $\sum_{n=1}^{\infty} n^2$

2. $\sum_{n=1}^{\infty} \frac{2n^2 - 1}{n^2 + 1}$

3. $\sum_{n=0}^{\infty} \left(\frac{3^n}{4^n}\right)$

4. $\sum_{n=1}^{\infty} \frac{1}{n^n}$

5. $\sum_{n=1}^{\infty} \frac{kn^2}{n!}$, k constant

6. $\sum_{n=2}^{\infty} \frac{1}{n^2 - 3}$

7. $\sum_{n=2}^{\infty} (-1)^n \frac{1}{\ln n}$

8. $\sum_{n=0}^{\infty} \frac{3^{n+1}}{4^n}$

9. $\sum_{n=0}^{\infty} \frac{1}{2^{n^2}}$

10. $\sum_{n=2}^{\infty} (-1)^n \frac{1}{(\ln n)^3}$

11. $\sum_{n=3}^{\infty} \frac{1}{n - 2}$

12. $\sum_{n=0}^{\infty} 6^{-n}$

13. Do the following series converge absolutely, converge conditionally, or diverge?

   (a) $\sum_{n=2}^{\infty} (-1)^n \frac{1}{\ln n}$

   (b) $\sum_{n=0}^{\infty} (-1)^n \left(\frac{x}{2}\right)^n$, when $x = 1$? $x = 2$? $x = 3$?

   (c) $\sum_{n=2}^{\infty} (-1)^n \left(\frac{n + 1}{n^3}\right)$

Multiple-Choice Questions

No calculator is allowed for these questions.

1. Find the value of r (if it exists) in the series

   $3 - \frac{9}{2} + \frac{27}{4} - \cdots$

   (A) $-\frac{3}{2}$

   (B) $-\frac{2}{3}$

   (C) $\frac{2}{3}$

   (D) $\frac{3}{2}$

   (E) no r exists

2. How many terms of the series $\sum_{n=1}^{\infty} (-1)^{n+1} \frac{1}{n^4}$ are needed to approximate the sum of the series with error <0.001?

   (A) 3
   (B) 4
   (C) 5
   (D) 6
   (E) 7

3. If the series $\sum_{n=1}^{\infty} \frac{1}{n^{1.01}}$ converges, which of the following series also converges by the Direct Comparison Test?

   (A) $\sum_{n=1}^{\infty} \frac{1}{n}$

   (B) $\sum_{n=1}^{\infty} \frac{1}{\sqrt{n}}$

   (C) $\sum_{n=1}^{\infty} (-1)^{n+1} \frac{1}{n^{1.01}}$

   (D) $\sum_{n=1}^{\infty} \frac{1}{n^{0.9}}$

   (E) $\sum_{n=1}^{\infty} \frac{1}{n^{0.01}}$

4. Find the sum of the series $\left(1 - \frac{1}{3}\right) + \left(\frac{1}{3} - \frac{1}{5}\right) + \left(\frac{1}{5} - \frac{1}{7}\right) + \cdots$.

   (A) $\frac{2}{3}$

   (B) $\frac{4}{5}$

   (C) $\frac{6}{7}$

   (D) 1

   (E) does not exist

5. Which of the following series is absolutely convergent?

   (A) $\sum_{n=1}^{\infty} \frac{(-1)^{n+1}}{n^{0.99}}$

   (B) $\sum_{n=1}^{\infty} \frac{(-1)^{n+1}}{n^2}$

   (C) $\sum_{n=1}^{\infty} \frac{(-1)^{n+1}}{n}$

   (D) $\sum_{n=1}^{\infty} (-1)^{n+1} 3^n$

   (E) $\sum_{n=2}^{\infty} \frac{(-1)^{n+1}}{\ln n}$

6. Of the following, which series is conditionally convergent?

(A) $\displaystyle\sum_{n=1}^{\infty} \frac{(-1)^{n+1}}{n^2}$

(B) $\displaystyle\sum_{n=1}^{\infty} \frac{(-1)^{n+1}}{\sqrt{n}}$

(C) $\displaystyle\sum_{n=1}^{\infty} \frac{(-1)^{n+1}}{n^3}$

(D) $\displaystyle\sum_{n=1}^{\infty} \frac{(-1)^{n+1}}{n!}$

(E) $\displaystyle\sum_{n=1}^{\infty} (-1)^{n+1} e^n$

7. $\displaystyle\sum_{n=0}^{\infty} \left(\frac{2}{5}\right)^n =$

(A) $\dfrac{2}{5}$

(B) $\dfrac{2}{3}$

(C) 1

(D) $\dfrac{5}{3}$

(E) $\dfrac{5}{2}$

8. If $\displaystyle\sum_{n=1}^{\infty} \frac{1}{n}$ diverges, which of the following series also diverges?

(A) $\displaystyle\sum_{n=1}^{\infty} \frac{1}{n^2}$

(B) $\displaystyle\sum_{n=1}^{\infty} \frac{(-1)^{n+1}}{n}$

(C) $\displaystyle\sum_{n=1}^{\infty} \frac{0.5}{n}$

(D) $\displaystyle\sum_{n=1}^{\infty} \frac{10^6}{n^2}$

(E) $\displaystyle\sum_{n=1}^{\infty} \frac{1}{n^n}$

9. A student states: "If a series $\displaystyle\sum_{n=1}^{\infty} a_n$ converges, then $\displaystyle\sum_{n=1}^{\infty} |a_n|$ converges." Which of the following series makes this statement false?

(A) $\displaystyle\sum_{n=1}^{\infty} \frac{(-1)^{n+1}}{n^3}$

(B) $\displaystyle\sum_{n=1}^{\infty} \frac{(-1)^{n+1}}{n}$

(C) $\displaystyle\sum_{n=1}^{\infty} \frac{\cos n\pi}{n^2}$

(D) $\displaystyle\sum_{n=1}^{\infty} \frac{(-1)^{n+1}}{n^{1.5}}$

(E) $\displaystyle\sum_{n=1}^{\infty} \frac{(-1)^{n+1}}{n!}$

10. A student uses the Ratio Test to determine the convergence of the series $\displaystyle\sum_{n=1}^{\infty} a_n$. Which value of the limit will ensure that the series converges?

(A) 1

(B) 2

(C) $\dfrac{\pi}{2}$

(D) $\sqrt{e}$

(E) $\dfrac{1}{2}$

Free-Response Questions
A graphing calculator is required for some questions.

1. Consider the series $\displaystyle\sum_{n=1}^{\infty} \frac{(-1)^{n+1}}{n^p}$.

  (a) Determine the values of p for which the series converges.

  (b) Find the maximum value of the error if k terms are used to approximate the sum of the series.

2. (a) Find the sum $\displaystyle\sum_{n=1}^{10} \frac{(-1)^{n+1}}{n^n}$.

  (b) What is the maximum value of the error if the sum $\displaystyle\sum_{n=1}^{\infty} \frac{(-1)^{n+1}}{n^n}$ is approximated by the answer to part (a)?

  (c) If the sum of the first twenty terms was used instead in part (a), would the error in part (b) be increased or decreased? Explain your answer.

3. (a) Find the sum of the series $\displaystyle\sum_{n=1}^{\infty} \frac{1}{n^2}$ correct to three decimal places, and state the number of terms needed to arrive at this answer.

    Calculator Note: Use the sum and seq commands found in CATALOG.

  (b) Find the sum of the series $\displaystyle\sum_{n=1}^{\infty} \frac{1}{n!}$ correct to three decimal places and state the number of terms needed to arrive at this answer.

(c) Describe in a sentence or two your conclusions about the convergence of each of the two series in parts (a) and (b).

4. (a) Find the error when the alternating series $\sum\limits_{n=0}^{\infty} (-0.25)^n$ is approximated by the first four terms of the series.

(b) Find the exact sum of the series and use it to find the actual error between exact sum and the approximation using the first four terms of the series. Compare your answer to the answer in part (a).

9.7 Power Series

A power series centered at c is a series of the form

$$a_0 + a_1(x - c) + a_2(x - c)^2 + a_3(x - c)^3 + \cdots = \sum_{n=0}^{\infty} a_n(x - c)^n,$$

where a_n are constants. For each value of x, the power series is a series of constants that can be tested for convergence. A power series may converge for some values of x and diverge for others.

Note: A Taylor series is a special case of a power series. The series in Section 9.3 for $\dfrac{1}{1 - x}, \dfrac{1}{2 - x}, \dfrac{1}{1 + x}$, and so on, are power series, as are the series given for $\sin x$, $\cos x$, $\ln x$, and e^x.

Each power series has an **interval of convergence,** that is, the set of values of x for which the power series converges. In general, there are three possible cases for the convergence of a power series $\sum\limits_{n=0}^{\infty} a_n(x - c)^n$:

Case 1. The series converges only when $x = c$. The radius of convergence is 0.

Case 2. The series converges for all values of x. The radius of convergence is ∞.

Case 3. The series converges if $|x - c| < R$; the series diverges if $|x - c| > R$. The radius of convergence is R.

In geometric series, the interval of convergence is determined by the condition that $|r| < 1$. For a general power series, the interval of convergence is determined by using the Ratio Test as shown in the examples that follow. The endpoints of the interval must be checked individually using one of the tests for convergence in Section 9.6.

EXAMPLE 1

Find the values of x for which the series $\sum\limits_{n=0}^{\infty} (3x)^n$ converges. State the radius of convergence.

Solution

METHOD 1 Use the Ratio Test to find the limit.

$$\lim_{n \to \infty} \left| \frac{(3x)^{n+1}}{(3x)^n} \right| = \lim_{n \to \infty} |3x| = |3x|$$

The series converges if $|3x| < 1$. Therefore, the interval of convergence is $|x| < \frac{1}{3}$, or $-\frac{1}{3} < x < \frac{1}{3}$, and the radius of convergence is $R = \frac{1}{3}$.

To check the endpoints, substitute $x = -\frac{1}{3}$ and $x = \frac{1}{3}$ into the series. Both $\sum_{n=0}^{\infty} (-1)^n$ and $\sum_{n=0}^{\infty} (1)^n$ diverge. Therefore, the interval of convergence of $\sum_{n=0}^{\infty} (3x)^n$ is $-\frac{1}{3} < x < \frac{1}{3}$.

METHOD 2 $\sum_{n=0}^{\infty} (3x)^n$ is a geometric series with $r = 3x$. Therefore, the interval of convergence is $-\frac{1}{3} < x < \frac{1}{3}$ or $-1 < r < 1$. The radius of convergence is $R = \frac{1}{3}$. There is no need to check endpoints here since the condition for convergence of a geometric series is $-1 < r < 1$.

EXAMPLE 2

Find the interval of convergence for the series $\sum_{n=1}^{\infty} \frac{(x-1)^n}{n}$.

Solution   Use the Ratio Test to find the limit.

$$\lim_{n \to \infty} \left| \frac{\dfrac{(x-1)^{n+1}}{n+1}}{\dfrac{(x-1)^n}{n}} \right| = \lim_{n \to \infty} \left| \frac{n}{n+1}(x-1) \right| = |x-1|$$

The interval of convergence is $|x - 1| < 1$ or $0 < x < 2$.

To check the endpoints, substitute $x = 0$ and $x = 2$ into the series.

At $x = 0$, the series becomes $\sum_{n=1}^{\infty} \frac{(-1)^n}{n}$. This alternating series converges by the Alternating Series Test.

At $x = 2$, the series becomes $\sum_{n=1}^{\infty} \frac{1}{n}$. This is a p-series with $p = 1$. Since $p \leq 1$, this series diverges.

Thus, the interval of convergence for the series $\sum_{n=1}^{\infty} \frac{(x-1)^n}{n}$ includes 0 but excludes 2. The interval of convergence is $0 \leq x < 2$.

EXAMPLE 3

Test the series $\sum_{n=0}^{\infty} \frac{(x-3)^n}{3^n}$ for convergence.

Solution

METHOD 1   Use the Ratio Test to find the limit.

$$\lim_{n \to \infty} \left| \frac{\dfrac{(x-3)^{n+1}}{3^{n+1}}}{\dfrac{(x-3)^n}{3^n}} \right| = \lim_{n \to \infty} \left| \frac{x-3}{3} \right| = \left| \frac{x-3}{3} \right|$$

The series converges if $\left|\dfrac{x-3}{x}\right| < 1$, or $|x - 3| < 3$, or $0 < x < 6$.

Checking the endpoints, at $x = 0$ the series becomes $\displaystyle\sum_{n=0}^{\infty} (-1)^n$, which diverges by the Divergence Test.

At $x = 6$, the series becomes $\displaystyle\sum_{n=0}^{\infty} 1$, which diverges by the Divergence Test. Thus, the interval of convergence is $0 < x < 6$.

METHOD 2   The series $\displaystyle\sum_{n=0}^{\infty} \dfrac{(x-3)^n}{3^n} = \sum_{n=0}^{\infty} \left(\dfrac{x-3}{3}\right)^n$, and is a geometric series with $r = \dfrac{x-3}{3}$. Thus, the series converges when $-1 < r < 1$, or $-1 < \dfrac{x-3}{3} < 1$. The interval of convergence is $0 < x < 6$.

The Derivative and Antiderivative of a Power Series

The derivative and the antiderivative of a power series are again power series. The intervals of convergence of the derivative and the antiderivative of a power series have the same center and radius as the interval of convergence of the original power series, but the endpoints may differ. *The interval of convergence of the derivative of a power series may lose endpoints, while the antiderivative of a power series may gain endpoints.*

> The derivative of $\displaystyle\sum_{n=0}^{\infty} a_n(x-c)^n$ is $\displaystyle\sum_{n=1}^{\infty} na_n(x-c)^{n-1}$.
>
> The antiderivative of $\displaystyle\sum_{n=0}^{\infty} a_n(x-c)^n$ is $k + \displaystyle\sum_{n=0}^{\infty} a_n \dfrac{(x-c)^{n+1}}{n+1}$, k constant.

In other words, the derivative and the antiderivative of a power series are obtained by integrating and differentiating, respectively, each individual term in the original series.

EXAMPLE 4

(a) Write the series for e^x centered at $x = 0$, and find its interval of convergence.

(b) Find the series for the derivative of e^x, and the series for the antiderivative of e^x, and state the interval of convergence for each.

Solution

(a) The series for e^x is $\displaystyle\sum_{n=0}^{\infty} \dfrac{x^n}{n!}$. The interval of convergence is found using the Ratio Test:

$$\lim_{n\to\infty} \left|\dfrac{\dfrac{x^{n+1}}{(n+1)!}}{\dfrac{x^n}{n!}}\right| = \lim_{n\to\infty} \left|\dfrac{x}{n+1}\right| = 0.$$

Since this limit is less than 1 for all values of x, the interval of convergence is all real numbers, that is, $-\infty < x < \infty$.

(b) The derivative of $\displaystyle\sum_{n=0}^{\infty} \frac{x^n}{n!} = 1 + x + \frac{x^2}{2!} + \frac{x^3}{3!} + \cdots =$

$$\sum_{n=1}^{\infty} \frac{x^{n-1}}{(n-1)!} = 1 + x + \frac{x^2}{2!} + \frac{x^3}{3!} + \cdots,$$

showing once more that the derivative of e^x is e^x.

The antiderivative of $\displaystyle\sum_{n=0}^{\infty} \frac{x^n}{n!} = 1 + x + \frac{x^2}{2!} + \frac{x^3}{3!} + \cdots$ is

$$k + x + \frac{x^2}{2!} + \frac{x^3}{3!} + \cdots = k + \sum_{n=0}^{\infty} \frac{x^{n+1}}{(n+1)!}.$$

Since the antiderivative of e^x is e^x, $e^x = k + x + \frac{x^2}{2!} + \frac{x^3}{3!} + \cdots$.

Let $x = 0$, and the equation becomes $1 = k$. Thus the series for the antiderivative of e^x is

$$1 + x + \frac{x^2}{2!} + \frac{x^3}{3!} + \cdots,$$

which is identical with the series for e^x.

Thus, the derivative and the antiderivative of e^x have the same series as e^x, and all three have the same interval of convergence, $-\infty < x < \infty$.

EXAMPLE 5

(a) Write the power series for $\ln x$ centered at $x = 1$, and find its interval of convergence.

(b) Find the power series for the derivative of $\ln x$ and for the antiderivative of $\ln x$. State the interval of convergence for each power series.

Solution

(a) The power series for $\ln x$ centered at $x = 1$ is

$$(x-1) - \frac{(x-1)^2}{2} + \frac{(x-1)^3}{3} - \cdots = \sum_{n=1}^{\infty} (-1)^{n+1} \frac{(x-1)^n}{n}.$$

The interval of convergence is found by using the Ratio Test.

$$\lim_{n\to\infty} \left| \frac{\dfrac{(x-1)^{n+1}}{n+1}}{\dfrac{(x-1)^n}{n}} \right| = \lim_{n\to\infty} \left| \frac{n}{n+1}(x-1) \right| = |x-1|$$

Thus, the interval of convergence is $|x - 1| < 1$ or $0 < x < 2$.

Checking the endpoints, we find that $\ln x$ is not defined at $x = 0$, so this point is not in the interval of convergence. If this value is substituted into the series, the result is

$$\sum_{n=1}^{\infty} (-1)^{n+1} \frac{(-1)^n}{n} = \sum_{n=1}^{\infty} \frac{(-1)^{2n+1}}{n} = \sum_{n=1}^{\infty} \frac{-1}{n},$$

which diverges.

At $x = 2$, the series becomes $\displaystyle\sum_{n=1}^{\infty} (-1)^{n+1} \frac{1}{n}$, which is a convergent alternating series. Therefore, the interval of convergence of the series for $\ln x$ is $0 < x \le 2$.

(b) The power series for the derivative of ln x centered at $x = 1$ is

$$\sum_{n=1}^{\infty} (-1)^{n+1} (x - 1)^{n-1}.$$

Since the interval of convergence of the series for the derivative can only lose an endpoint, it is sufficient to check the convergence at $x = 2$.

At $x = 2$, the series is $\sum_{n=1}^{\infty} (-1)^{n+1}$, which diverges. Therefore the interval of convergence of the series for the derivative of ln x is $0 < x < 2$. The power series for the antiderivative of ln x is

$$\sum_{n=1}^{\infty} (-1)^{n+1} \frac{(x - 1)^{n+1}}{n(n + 1)}.$$

Since the interval of convergence of the antiderivative of ln x can only gain an endpoint, it is sufficient to check for convergence at $x = 0$. The antiderivative of ln x is x ln $x - x$, which is not defined at $x = 0$. Therefore, the interval of convergence of the antiderivative is $0 < x \leq 2$.

Taylor Series   A Taylor polynomial $P_n(x)$ of degree n can be written for any function $f(x)$ that has derivatives up to order n. As the degree of the polynomial increases, the quantity $|f(x) - P_n(x)|$ approaches zero. The Taylor series is a power series extension of the Taylor polynomial. The Taylor series is a power series where the coefficients a_n are found using the formula

$$a_n = \frac{f^{(n)}(c)}{n!}.$$

Thus, given a function $f(x)$,

$$f(x) \sum_{n=0}^{\infty} a_n(x - c)^n.$$

AP Calculus exam questions on Taylor series often involve using series that are known, such as the Taylor series for e^x, ln x, sin x, and cos x. The questions may require you to create new series from these known series, or to find a series for an unknown function given the values of its derivatives. Using the derivatives, find the coefficients a_n and write the Taylor series for the function.

Exercises

1. Use the Ratio Test to find the interval of convergence of the following series. Be sure to check the endpoints of the interval.

    (a) $\displaystyle\sum_{n=0}^{\infty} \left(\frac{x}{3}\right)^n$

    (b) $\displaystyle\sum_{n=0}^{\infty} \frac{(x - 1)^n}{n!}$

    (c) $\displaystyle\sum_{n=1}^{\infty} \frac{(3x)^n}{\sqrt{n}}$

    (d) $\displaystyle\sum_{n=1}^{\infty} \frac{(3x)^n}{n}$

2. Find the power series for $\dfrac{1}{(1 - x)^2}$ using the power series for $\dfrac{1}{1 - x}$, and state its interval of convergence.

3. Find the power series for $\dfrac{1}{(1 - x)^3}$ using the power series for $\dfrac{1}{1 - x}$, and state its interval of convergence.

4. Use the power series for e^x to find the exact value of $\displaystyle\sum_{n=0}^{\infty} \frac{(0.5)^n}{n!}$.

5. Use the power series for sin x to find the exact value of $\displaystyle\sum_{n=0}^{\infty} (-1)^n \frac{\left(\dfrac{\pi}{2}\right)^{2n+1}}{(2n + 1)!}$.

Multiple-Choice Questions
No calculator is allowed for these questions.

1. The interval of convergence of the series
$\displaystyle\sum_{n=1}^{\infty}\frac{(x-1)^n}{n}$ is
   (A) $0 \le x < 2$
   (B) $0 < x < 2$
   (C) $0 < x \le 2$
   (D) $0 \le x \le 2$
   (E) all real numbers

2. The series $\displaystyle\sum_{n=0}^{\infty}\frac{(2x-1)^n}{n!}$ converges for which
   of the following values of x?
   (A) all real numbers
   (B) $0 < x < 1$
   (C) $0 < x \le 1$
   (D) $0 \le x \le 1$
   (E) no values of x

3. For which of the following values of x does
   the series $\displaystyle\sum_{n=0}^{\infty}\left(\frac{5x}{3}\right)^n$ converge?
   (A) all real numbers
   (B) $|x| \le \dfrac{3}{5}$
   (C) $|x| < \dfrac{3}{5}$
   (D) $|x| \le \dfrac{5}{3}$
   (E) $|x| \le 1$

4. The power series for $f(x) = \dfrac{3}{3-x}$ centered at
   $x = 0$ is
   (A) $\displaystyle\sum_{n=0}^{\infty}\left(\frac{x}{3}\right)^n$
   (B) $3\displaystyle\sum_{n=0}^{\infty}\left(\frac{x}{3}\right)^n$
   (C) $9\displaystyle\sum_{n=0}^{\infty}\left(\frac{x}{3}\right)^n$
   (D) $\dfrac{1}{3}\displaystyle\sum_{n=0}^{\infty}\left(\frac{x}{3}\right)^n$
   (E) $\displaystyle\sum_{n=1}^{\infty}\left(\frac{x}{3}\right)^n$

5. The number e can be represented by which
   of the following power series?
   (A) $\displaystyle\sum_{n=0}^{\infty}\frac{(-1)^n}{n!}$
   (B) $\displaystyle\sum_{n=1}^{\infty}\frac{(-1)^n}{n!}$
   (C) $\displaystyle\sum_{n=0}^{\infty}\frac{1}{n!}$
   (D) $\displaystyle\sum_{n=1}^{\infty}\frac{1}{n!}$
   (E) $\displaystyle\sum_{n=0}^{\infty}\frac{e^n}{n!}$

6. The power series $\displaystyle\sum_{n=1}^{\infty}\frac{(-1)^{n+1}(3x-1)^n}{n}$ is
   equivalent to $f(x) =$
   (A) e^{3x-1}
   (B) $\ln(3x-1)$
   (C) $\ln(3x)$
   (D) $\ln(3x) - 1$
   (E) $e^{3x} - 1$

7. For values of x in the interval $-5 < x < 5$, the
   sum of the series $\displaystyle\sum_{n=1}^{\infty}\left(\frac{x}{5}\right)^n$ is equal to
   (A) $\dfrac{x}{5-x}$
   (B) $\dfrac{5}{5-x}$
   (C) $\dfrac{1}{5-x}$
   (D) $\dfrac{5}{x-5}$
   (E) $\dfrac{x}{x-5}$

8. On the interval $(-3, 3)$, the sum of the series
   $\displaystyle\sum_{n=1}^{\infty}n\left(\frac{x}{3}\right)^{n-1}$ can be represented by
   (A) $f(x) = \dfrac{9}{(3-x)^2}$
   (B) $f(x) = \dfrac{3}{(3-x)^2}$
   (C) $f(x) = -\dfrac{3}{(3-x)^2}$
   (D) $f(x) = \dfrac{x}{3-x}$
   (E) $f(x) = \dfrac{3}{3-x}$

Free-Response Questions
A graphing calculator is required for some questions.

1. (a) Write a power series for $f(x) = e^{2x} - 1$
   and state its interval of convergence.
   (b) Find the power series for $f'(x)$ by differentiating the power series found in part (a).
   (c) Use the power series for $f(x)$ to find the
   power series for $f'(x)$ by a method other
   than taking the derivative.
   (d) Write an expression for $f'(0.5)$ in sigma
   notation.

2. Consider the series $\frac{x^3}{2!} - \frac{x^5}{4!} + \frac{x^7}{6!} - \cdots$.

   (a) Find a function $f(x)$ to which the series converges.

   (b) If $F'(x) = f(x)$, find a power series representation for $F(x)$.

3. (a) Find a function $f(x)$ that represents the sum of the series $\sum\limits_{n=0}^{\infty} \left(\frac{x}{3}\right)^n$, and state the domain of $f(x)$.

   (b) Find a function $g(x)$ where $g'(x) = f(x)$.

   (c) Write the power series for $g(x)$, and state the values of x for which the power series converges to $g(x)$.

   (d) Approximate $g(1)$ to 3 decimal places.

4. If $f(x)$ is a function with $f(1) = 1$, $f'(1) = 2$, $f''(1) = 3$, and $f'''(1) = -2$:

   (a) Write a third-degree Taylor polynomial $P_3(x)$ for $f(x)$ centered at $x = 1$.

   (b) Use the polynomial in part (a) to approximate $f(0.9)$.

   (c) Explain why $P_3(0.9) \neq f(0.9)$.

5. Given a function $f(x)$ with $f(2) = \frac{1}{2}$, $f'(2) = -\frac{1}{4}$, $f''(2) = \frac{1}{4}$, and $f'''(2) = -\frac{3}{8}$:

   (a) Write a Taylor polynomial of degree 3 for $f(x)$ centered at $x = 2$.

   (b) Write a Taylor polynomial of degree 2 for $f'(x)$ centered at $x = 2$.

   (c) Write a Taylor polynomial of degree 4 for $\int f(x)\,dx$ centered at $x = 2$.

6. Rewrite $\frac{1}{x}$ as $\frac{1}{1 + (x - 1)}$ to

   (a) Write a Taylor series for $\frac{1}{x}$ centered at $x = 1$.

   (b) Find the interval of convergence for the series in part (a).

   (c) Find the Taylor series centered at $x = 1$ for the derivative of $\frac{1}{x}$, and find the interval of convergence.

   (d) Find the Taylor series centered at $x = 1$ for $\int \frac{1}{x}\,dx$, and find the interval of convergence.

Chapter Assessment

1. Find the error estimate in approximating $\sum\limits_{n=1}^{\infty}(-1)^n\frac{1}{n}$ with the first ten terms of the series.

2. What is the least positive integer n that will make the error estimate of $\sum\limits_{n=1}^{\infty}(-1)^{n+1}\frac{1}{n^3}$ less than 0.001?

3. Find the error for estimating $\sin(0.5)$ by the third-degree Taylor polynomial for $\sin x$.

4. For each series, state the type of series and state the test for convergence or divergence that is most appropriate to show the convergence or divergence of the series.

   (a) $\sum\limits_{n=1}^{\infty} \frac{1}{\sqrt{n}}$

   (b) $\sum\limits_{n=1}^{\infty} \frac{1}{n^4}$

   (c) $\sum\limits_{n=1}^{\infty} \frac{1}{4^n n^4}$

   (d) $\sum\limits_{n=0}^{\infty} \left(\frac{2}{5}\right)^n$

   (e) $\sum\limits_{n=2}^{\infty} \left(\frac{1}{n-1} - \frac{1}{n}\right)$

   (f) $\sum\limits_{n=1}^{\infty} \frac{(-1)^{n+1}}{\sqrt{n}}$

   (g) $\sum\limits_{n=1}^{\infty} \frac{n}{\sqrt{n^2 + 1}}$

   (h) $\sum\limits_{n=0}^{\infty} \frac{2^n}{n!}$

   (i) $\sum\limits_{n=0}^{\infty}(-1)^n$

   (j) $\sum\limits_{n=1}^{\infty} \frac{(-1)^{n+1}n!}{n^n}$

   (k) $\sum\limits_{n=0}^{\infty} \cos n$

   (l) $\sum\limits_{n=1}^{\infty} \left(\left(\frac{2}{3}\right)^n - \frac{1}{n^3}\right)$

   (m) $\sum\limits_{n=0}^{\infty}(2.5)^n$

5. Which of the series in Exercise 4 converge? Justify your answer.

6. (a) For which of the series in Exercise 4 above can the sum of the series be found?

   (b) For each answer in part (a), find the sum of the series.

7. Find each of the following sums:

(a) $\displaystyle\sum_{n=1}^{5} \frac{1}{n}$

(b) $\displaystyle\sum_{k=3}^{6} \frac{1}{k^2}$

(c) $\displaystyle\sum_{n=0}^{8} \sin(n\pi)$

(d) $\displaystyle\sum_{n=1}^{10} \left(\frac{1}{n} - \frac{1}{n+1}\right)$

8. Use the series $1 + x + x^2 + x^3 + x^4 + \cdots = \dfrac{1}{1-x}$ for $|x| < 1$ to find the exact value of each of the following series:

(a) $1 + \dfrac{7}{8} + \left(\dfrac{7}{8}\right)^2 + \left(\dfrac{7}{8}\right)^3 + \cdots$

(b) $\displaystyle\sum_{n=1}^{\infty} 7\left(\frac{1}{4}\right)^n$

(c) $\displaystyle\sum_{n=2}^{\infty} (0.4)^n$

9. Use the series $1 - x + x^2 - x^3 + x^4 - \cdots = \dfrac{1}{1+x}$ for $|x| < 1$ to find the exact value of each of the following series:

(a) $1 - \dfrac{1}{2} + \dfrac{1}{4} - \dfrac{1}{8} + \cdots$

(b) $\displaystyle\sum_{n=0}^{\infty} (-1)^n \left(\frac{1}{3}\right)^n$

(c) $\displaystyle\sum_{n=1}^{\infty} (-1)^{n+1}(0.7)^n$

10. Find the interval of convergence for the following series. (Be sure to check the endpoints!)

(a) $\displaystyle\sum_{n=1}^{\infty} \frac{(2x)^n}{n^2}$

(b) $\displaystyle\sum_{n=0}^{\infty} \frac{(x-5)^{n+1}}{n+1}$

(c) $\displaystyle\sum_{n=1}^{\infty} (-1)^{n+1}\frac{(2x-3)^n}{n^{\frac{3}{2}}}$

11. Use the series for the family of curves of e^x, $\dfrac{1}{1-x}$, $\ln x$, $\sin x$, and $\cos x$ to find an exact expression for each of the following series:

(a) $2 + \dfrac{2^2}{2!} + \dfrac{2^3}{3!} + \cdots$

(b) $\displaystyle\sum_{n=1}^{\infty} \frac{(-1)^{n+1}}{n}$

(c) $1 - 2(0.1) + 3(0.1)^2 - 4(0.1)^3 + 5(0.1)^4 - \cdots$

(d) $1 - 2x + 2x^2 - 2x^3 + \cdots$

(e) $1 - \dfrac{1}{2!} + \dfrac{1}{4!} - \dfrac{1}{6!} + \cdots$

(f) $x - \dfrac{x^3}{3} + \dfrac{x^5}{5} - \dfrac{x^7}{7} + \cdots$

Multiple-Choice Questions
No calculator is allowed for these questions.

1. $\displaystyle\sum_{n=1}^{\infty} \left(-\frac{1}{5}\right)^n$

(A) converges to $-\dfrac{1}{6}$

(B) converges to $-\dfrac{1}{5}$

(C) converges to $-\dfrac{1}{4}$

(D) converges to 0

(E) diverges

2. For what values of x does $\displaystyle\sum_{n=0}^{\infty} (2x)^{2n}$ converge?

(A) for no values of x

(B) $|x| < \dfrac{1}{2}$

(C) $|x| \le \dfrac{1}{2}$

(D) $|x| < 2$

(E) for all real numbers

3. The series $1 - \dfrac{1}{2} + \dfrac{1}{3} - \dfrac{1}{4} + \cdots$

(A) converges to $\dfrac{2}{3}$

(B) converges to $\ln 2$

(C) converges to 2

(D) converges to e

(E) diverges

4. Find the sum $\displaystyle\sum_{n=1}^{\infty} n\left(\frac{1}{4}\right)^{n-1}$.

(A) $\dfrac{9}{16}$

(B) $\dfrac{16}{25}$

(C) $\dfrac{3}{4}$

(D) $\dfrac{4}{3}$

(E) $\dfrac{16}{9}$

5. The series $\displaystyle\sum_{n=0}^{\infty} \frac{(-1)^n \pi^{2n+1}}{(2n+1)!}$ has a sum of

(A) -1

(B) 0

(C) 1

(D) π

(E) no value

6. $\displaystyle\sum_{n=1}^{\infty} \frac{(-1)^n \left(\frac{\pi}{3}\right)^{2n}}{(2n)!} =$

(A) $-\frac{1}{2}$

(B) $\frac{1}{2}$

(C) $\frac{3}{3 - \pi}$

(D) $\frac{3}{3 + \pi}$

(E) no value

7. The series $\displaystyle\sum_{n=0}^{\infty} \left(\frac{2^n}{3^n} - 1\right)$

(A) converges to $\frac{2}{3}$

(B) converges to 2

(C) converges to 3

(D) converges to 0

(E) diverges

8. Determine the sum of the series $\frac{1}{2} - \frac{1}{6} + \frac{1}{24} - \cdots$

(A) 1

(B) 2

(C) $\frac{1}{e}$

(D) e

(E) $\frac{3}{2}$

9. The error in estimating e^{-2} using five terms of the Taylor series for e^{-x} is not greater than

(A) $\frac{2^4}{4!}$

(B) $\frac{2^5}{5!}$

(C) $\frac{2^6}{6!}$

(D) $\frac{2^5}{5}$

(E) $\frac{2^6}{6}$

10. The interval of convergence of the series $\displaystyle\sum_{n=0}^{\infty} \frac{3^n(x - 2)^n}{n!}$ is

(A) $(-\infty, \infty)$

(B) $[2, \infty)$

(C) $(-\infty, 2]$

(D) $\left(\frac{5}{3}, \frac{7}{3}\right)$

(E) $x = 2$ only

11. Find the values of x for which the series $\displaystyle\sum_{n=0}^{\infty} \frac{5^n}{2^n}(x + 1)^n$ converges.

(A) no values of x

(B) $-\frac{7}{5} < x < -\frac{3}{5}$

(C) $-\frac{5}{2} < x < \frac{5}{2}$

(D) $x = 0$ only

(E) $x = -1$ only

12. For what value(s) of p does $\displaystyle\sum_{n=2}^{\infty} \frac{(-1)^n}{(\ln n)^p}$ converge?

(A) $p \neq 0$

(B) $p < 0$

(C) $p > 0$

(D) $p \geq 1$

(E) $p > 1$

13. The series represented by $\displaystyle\sum_{n=0}^{\infty} \left(\frac{1}{5}\right)^n$ is

(A) an alternating series

(B) a p-series

(C) a geometric series

(D) a telescoping series

(E) a power series

14. $\displaystyle\sum_{n=1}^{\infty} \frac{2^n}{n}$ can be described as a series that is

(A) geometric and convergent

(B) not geometric but convergent

(C) alternating

(D) a power series

(E) divergent

15. The series $\displaystyle\sum_{n=1}^{\infty} \left(1 + \frac{1}{n}\right)^n$

(A) converges to 1

(B) diverges

(C) converges to e

(D) is geometric with $r > 1$

(E) is alternating

16. The fourth-degree Taylor polynomial for $\frac{1}{1 - x}$ centered at $x = -1$ is

(A) $\displaystyle\sum_{n=0}^{4} x^n$

(B) $\displaystyle\sum_{n=0}^{4} (x + 1)^n$

(C) $\displaystyle\sum_{n=0}^{4} \frac{(x + 1)^n}{2^{n+1}}$

(D) $\displaystyle\sum_{n=0}^{4} \frac{(x + 1)^n}{2^n}$

(E) $\displaystyle 2\sum_{n=0}^{4} (x + 1)^n$

17. What is the sum of the series $\sum_{n=0}^{\infty} \frac{\left(\frac{\pi}{6}\right)^{2n}}{n!}$, if it exists?

(A) $\frac{6}{6 - \pi}$

(B) $\frac{1}{2}$

(C) $\frac{\sqrt{3}}{2}$

(D) $e^{\pi^2/36}$

(E) does not exist

18. $\dfrac{d}{dx}\left(\displaystyle\sum_{n=1}^{\infty} \frac{x^{2n}}{n!}\right) =$

(A) $-\sin(x^2)$
(B) $-2x\sin(x^2)$
(C) $\cos(x^2)$
(D) e^{x^2}
(E) $2xe^{x^2}$

19. The series $\displaystyle\sum_{n=0}^{\infty}\left(\frac{2^n - n^2}{3^n}\right)$

(A) converges to 0

(B) converges to $\dfrac{32}{81}$

(C) converges to $\dfrac{7}{243}$

(D) converges but the sum can only be approximated

(E) diverges

20. What does the series $\dfrac{\pi}{2}\displaystyle\sum_{n=0}^{\infty} \cos n\pi \frac{\left(\frac{\pi}{2}\right)^{2n}}{(2n + 1)!}$ converge to?

(A) -1

(B) 0

(C) 1

(D) $\dfrac{2}{2 - \pi}$

(E) It diverges.

Free-Response Questions

A graphing calculator is required for some questions.

1. $f(x)$ is continuous for all real numbers. The Taylor polynomial $P_4(x)$ for $f(x)$ centered at $x = 2$ is

$$P_4(x) = 1 + 2(x - 2) + 3(x - 2)^2 + 4(x - 2)^3 + 5(x - 2)^4.$$

(a) Write the equation of the line tangent to $f(x)$ at $x = 2$.

(b) Express $P_4(x)$ in sigma notation.

(c) Find the value of $\displaystyle\int_2^3 P_4(x)\,dx$.

(d) Is $\displaystyle\int_2^3 f(x)\,dx$ equal to the answer in part (c)? Explain.

2. (a) Derive the Taylor series $T(x)$ for $f(x) = e^x$ centered at $x = 2$. State its interval of convergence.

(b) Write the answer to part (a) in sigma notation and show that it is equal to e^x.

(c) Find $T'(x)$.

3. (a) Find $\displaystyle\int_1^2 \ln x\,dx$ and write a sentence describing what the value of the integral represents.

(b) Use the Trapezoidal Rule with five equal subintervals to approximate the area under the curve $y = \ln x$ on the interval $[1, 2]$.

(c) Using the answer to part (a), find the average value of $y = \ln x$ on the interval $[1, 2]$.

(d) Write an integral that represents the volume of the solid obtained by rotating the region bounded by $y = \ln x$, the x-axis, and the line $x = 2$ about the line $x = 2$. Do not evaluate.

4. (a) Sketch the graph of the region R bounded by $y = \sqrt{x} - 1$, the x-axis, and the line $x = 2$.

(b) Write an integral in terms of a single variable that represents the volume of the solid generated when the region R is rotated about the y-axis.

(c) A line $y = k$ divides R into two regions R_1 and R_2 so that the volumes of the solids generated when R_1 and R_2 are rotated about the y-axis are equal. Write an equation that can be used to solve for k.

Calculator Note: Use the solve command on the calculator to find the value of k.

On the TI-83, enter [2nd] CATALOG and scroll to solve.

Then enter solve(expression, variable, guess).

On the TI-89, find solve in CATALOG or in toolbar under [F2]: Algebra.

Then enter solve(equation, variable).

5. Consider the functions $f(x) = \sqrt[3]{x} - 1$ and $g(x) = \ln x$.
   (a) Find the points of intersection of $f(x)$ and $g(x)$.
   (b) Find the area bounded by $f(x)$ and $g(x)$ on the interval $[1, 6]$.
   (c) Write the equation of the lines tangent to $f(x)$ and $g(x)$ at $x = 1$.
   (d) $h(x) = f(g(x))$. For what values of x is $h(x)$ increasing?

6. $f(x)$ is continuous for all real numbers. The number lines for $f'(x)$ and $f''(x)$ are shown below:

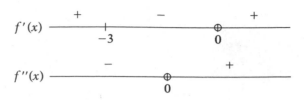

   (a) Use the number lines to determine the relative extrema of $f(x)$. Explain how you arrived at your answer.
   (b) Use the number lines to determine the x-coordinate(s) of the point(s) of inflection of $f(x)$. Explain how you arrived at your answer.
   (c) Is it possible for $f(x)$ to be an odd function? Is it possible for $f(x)$ to be an even function? Explain your conclusions.
   (d) If $f(0) = 0$, use the information in parts (a)–(c) to sketch a graph of $f(x)$.

CHAPTER 10
Logistic Growth, Euler's Method, and Other BC Topics

10.1 The Logistic Growth Model

Chapter 7 describes types of separable differential equations. In one kind of separable differential equation, the rate of change of the variable y at time t is proportional to the value of the variable y at time t; that is, $\frac{dy}{dt} = ky$.

For the growth model $\frac{dy}{dt} = ky$:

If $k > 0$, this model describes the growth of the variable y.
If $k < 0$, this model describes the decay of the variable y.

This model has a wide range of applications, the most common of which are problems involving population or bacterial growth and radioactive decay. It is possible, however, for y to represent the number of fish in an artificial pond or the number of people in a town who are infected with a contagious disease. In these cases, the growth is *restricted*; the value of the variable y has a limiting value M. The number of fish in the pond is limited due to the amounts of food and oxygen available. The number of people infected with the disease cannot exceed the population of the town. This type of restricted growth is called **logistic growth.** In the differential equation for logistic growth, the rate of change of the variable y is proportional not only to the value of y itself, but also to the difference between y and the limiting value M, $M > y$.

The Logistic Growth Model

$$\frac{dy}{dt} = ky(M - y)$$

This differential equation can be solved by separating the variables,

$$\frac{dy}{y(M - y)} = k\, dt,$$

and then using the method of partial fractions (see Section 8.2):

$$\frac{1}{y(M - y)} = \frac{1}{M}\left(\frac{1}{y} + \frac{1}{M - y}\right).$$

Taking the antiderivative on both sides of

$$\int \frac{1}{M}\left(\frac{1}{y} + \frac{1}{M - y}\right)dy = \int k\, dt$$

results in

$$\frac{1}{M}\left(\ln|y| - \ln|M - y|\right) = kt + c.$$

It now remains to solve this equation for y:

$$y = \frac{M}{1 + Ae^{-Mkt}}.$$

When $t = 0$, let $y = y_0$. Substituting these values into the equation above,

$$y_0 = \frac{M}{1 + A}, \text{ or } A = \frac{M}{y_0} - 1.$$

The graph of the solution to a logistic growth model has a horizontal asymptote $y = M$.

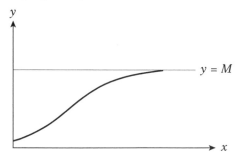

EXAMPLE 1

Show that the value of y at the point of inflection of $y = \dfrac{M}{1 + Ae^{-Mkt}}$ is $y = \dfrac{M}{2}$.

Solution To find the point of inflection, find $\frac{d^2y}{dt^2}$.

Since $\frac{dy}{dt} = ky(M - y) = kMy - ky^2$,

$$\frac{d^2y}{dt^2} = kM\frac{dy}{dt} - 2ky\frac{dy}{dt} = k\frac{dy}{dt}(M - 2y) = k^2y(M - y)(M - 2y).$$

The solutions to $\frac{d^2y}{dt^2} = 0$ are $y = 0$, $y = M$, and $y = \frac{M}{2}$. Since the range of y is between y_0 and M, the only value of y that is a possible point of inflection is $y = \frac{M}{2}$.

EXAMPLE 2

Which of the following differential equations are separable? Which equations are examples of the logistic growth model?

(a) $\frac{dy}{dt} + y = 5$

(e) $\frac{1}{y}\frac{dy}{dt} = 2t$

(b) $y\frac{dy}{dt} = 2t + 7$

(f) $\frac{dy}{dt} = 2t(10 - t)$

(c) $\frac{dy}{dt} = y^2 + t^2$

(g) $\frac{1}{y}\frac{dy}{dt} = 4(10 - y)$

(d) $\frac{dy}{dt} = 2y$

Solution

(a) $\frac{dy}{dt} + y = 5$ is a separable differential equation. It can be rewritten as

$$\frac{dy}{dt} = 5 - y, \qquad \frac{dy}{5 - y} = dt.$$

(b) $y\frac{dy}{dt} = 2t + 7$ is a separable differential equation. It can be rewritten as

$$y\, dy = (2t + 7)dt.$$

(c) $\frac{dy}{dt} = y^2 + t^2$ is not a separable differential equation.

(d) $\frac{dy}{dt} = 2y$ is a separable differential equation. It can be rewritten as

$$\frac{dy}{y} = 2\, dt.$$

(e) $\frac{1}{y}\frac{dy}{dt} = 2t$ is a separable differential equation. It can be rewritten as

$$\frac{1}{y}dy = 2t\, dt.$$

(f) $\dfrac{dy}{dt} = 2t(10 - t)$ is a separable differential equation. It can be rewritten as

$$dy = 2t(10 - t)dt.$$

(g) $\dfrac{1}{y}\dfrac{dy}{dt} = 4(10 - y)$ is a separable differential equation and the only one in this example that fits the logistic growth model since $\dfrac{dy}{dt} = 4y(10 - y)$ is an equivalent form. Separating the variables, the equation can be rewritten as

$$\dfrac{dy}{y(10 - y)} = 4\,dt.$$

Exercises

1. Solve the differential equation in Example 2(a), with the initial condition $y(0) = 1$.

2. Solve the differential equation in Example 2(b), with the initial condition $y(1) = 4$.

3. Solve the differential equation in Example 2(d), with the initial condition $y(0) = 10$.

4. Solve the differential equation in Example 2(e), with the initial condition $y(0) = 2$.

5. Solve the differential equation in Example 2(f), with the initial condition $y(3) = 0$.

6. Solve the differential equation in Example 2(g), with the initial condition $y(0) = 1$.

7. In the logistic growth model

$$y = \dfrac{M}{1 + Ae^{-Mkt}},$$

the y-value of the inflection point of the graph is $y = \dfrac{M}{2}$. Find the value of t at the inflection point.

Multiple-Choice Questions
No calculator is allowed for these questions.

1. Which of the following differential equations is an example of the logistic growth model?

   (A) $\dfrac{dy}{dx} = 10x(5 - x)$

   (B) $\dfrac{dy}{dx} = 10y(50 - y)$

   (C) $\dfrac{dV}{dt} = 2V(5 - t)$

   (D) $\dfrac{dR}{dt} = t(R - t)$

   (E) $\dfrac{ds}{dt} = 4s(10 + s)$

2. Which of the following differential equations is separable, but NOT an example of the logistic growth model?

   (A) $\dfrac{dy}{dx} = x + y$

   (B) $\dfrac{dy}{dx} = 2y(10 - y)$

   (C) $\dfrac{dy}{dx} = 21 - y$

   (D) $\dfrac{dy}{dx} = x^2 + y^2$

   (E) $\dfrac{1}{y}\dfrac{dy}{dt} = 100 - y$

3. The solution to the equation $\dfrac{dy}{dx} = 2y^2$ with $y(1) = 2$ is

   (A) $y = 2e^{x-1}$

   (B) $y = \sqrt{4 + e^{2x-2}}$

   (C) $y = \sqrt{4 + e^{2x} - e^2}$

   (D) $y = \sqrt[3]{\dfrac{3x + 13}{2}}$

   (E) $y = \dfrac{2}{5 - 4x}$

4. The solution to the equation $\dfrac{dy}{dt} = 2y(10 - y)$ with $y(0) = 1$ is

   (A) $y = \dfrac{10}{1 - 9e^{-20t}}$

   (B) $y = \dfrac{10}{1 + 9e^{20t}}$

(C) $y = \dfrac{10}{1 + 9e^{-20t}}$

(D) $y = \dfrac{20}{11 + 9e^{-20t}}$

(E) $y = \dfrac{10}{1 + 9e^{-10t}}$

Free-Response Questions

1. (No calculator) Consider the differential equation $\dfrac{dy}{dt} = 2y(1 - t)$.

   (a) Sketch the graph of the solution to the differential equation on the slope field provided below with $y(0) = 5$.

   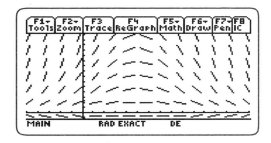

   (b) Solve the differential equation with $y(0) = 5$.
   (c) Find the coordinates of the points where the rate of change of y with respect to t is the greatest.

2. (Calculator required) Two dogs infected with a virus were admitted to a veterinary clinic, which holds a maximum of fifty dogs. The virus spread among the animals, and two days later ten dogs were infected.

   (a) Assuming the logistic growth model for the spread of the virus $\dfrac{dy}{dt} = ky(M - y)$, find the values of M and k, and find y as a function of t.
   (b) If spread of the virus is not halted, after how many days will 25 dogs be infected?

3. (Calculator required) The rate of growth of the fish population in an artificial pond is given by the differential equation $\dfrac{dy}{dt} = 0.003y(500 - y)$, where y is the number of fish in the pond after t days.

   (a) What is the maximum number of fish that the fish pond can hold?
   (b) Write the solution y to the differential equation if the pond is populated initially with 50 fish.
   (c) What is the y-value at the point of inflection?
   (d) Use a graphing calculator to draw a slope field of the differential equation, and draw a graph of the solution on the same set of axes.
   (e) Find the number of fish in the pond after 1 day; 2 days; 3 days; 4 days; 5 days.

10.2 Euler's Approximation Method

In Sections 7.2 and 7.3, we found graphical solutions to differential equations by using slope fields. Euler's method is a simple but powerful method, based on tangent line approximation, by which we can find numerical approximations to solutions to differential equations. Euler's method uses a point on the graph of the function and the differential equation for which the function is a solution to approximate values of a solution to the differential equation

Given a differential equation with an initial value (x_0, y_0), we know that since $y = y_0$ when $x = x_0$, the solution y is known at only the initial point (x_0, y_0), while the derivative is known at all points (x, y).

To begin applying Euler's method, draw a line through (x_0, y_0) with slope equal to $\dfrac{dy}{dx}$. This is the line tangent to the graph of the function $f(x)$ at the point (x_0, y_0).

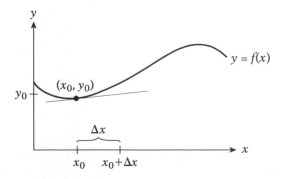

Use the tangent line to approximate the value of the function at (x_1, y_1), one small step Δx away from the initial value x_0. This is the process of linear approximation using the derivative of a function; that is, to approximate the value of the function at $x_1 = x_0 + \Delta x$, use the expression

$$f(x_0 + \Delta x) \approx f(x_0) + \frac{dy}{dx}\Delta x.$$

Thus, $y_1 \approx y_0 + \frac{dy\,\Delta x}{dx}$. This gives us an approximate value for y one step away from the initial point (x_0, y_0).

To continue the process, take one more step Δx away from x_0 to $x_0 + 2\Delta x$. To approximate the value of the function at (x_2, y_2) when $x_2 = x_0 + 2\Delta x$, draw a line through (x_1, y_1) on the tangent line with x-coordinate $x_1 = x_0 + \Delta x$, using the slope formula $\frac{dy}{dx}$ at that point. This line is no longer tangent to the graph of the original function, but it does have the same slope as the tangent line at $x = x_i$. Use this line to approximate the value of the function at $x_2 = x_0 + 2\Delta x$.

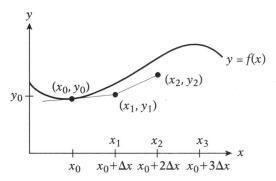

This process may be continued, but for each iteration the error in the approximation becomes greater. For small Δx, though, the approximation is quite close to the value of the function.

EXAMPLE 1

Given the differential equation $\frac{dy}{dx} = 2x$ with the initial point $(0, 1)$, use Euler's method with a step size of 0.1 to approximate the value of y at $x = 0.3$.

Solution Since $\frac{dy}{dx} = 2x$, the slope of the tangent line at the point $(0, 1)$ is zero. Thus, the equation of the tangent line at $(0, 1)$ is $y = 1$.

Taking a step $\Delta x = 0.1$ away from $x = 0$, the new value $x_1 = x_0 + \Delta x = 0.1$.

The new value y_1 is found by using the equation of the tangent line, $y = 1$. Thus, $y_1 = 1$ (which is the same as y_0). The point (x_1, y_1) is $(0.1, 1)$.

Now take another step Δx to $x_2 = 0.2$. To find the approximate value of y_2 at $x_2 = 0.2$, draw a line from $(0.1, 1)$ with slope equal to $\dfrac{dy}{dx}$; that is, the slope is $2(0.1) = 0.2$. The approximate value of y_2 at $x_2 = 0.2$ is calculated by taking the y-value at $(0.1, 1)$ and adding the change in y, Δy, where $\Delta y = \dfrac{dy}{dx} \Delta x = 2x_0 \Delta x$. Thus, $\Delta y = 2(0.1)(0.1) = 0.02$, the value of y_2 is 1.02, and the point (x_2, y_2) is $(0.2, 1.02)$.

Before iterating a third time, it will be useful to organize the data into a table:

Old Point (x, y)	Equation of Tangent Line at (x, y) $\left(\text{Slope} = \dfrac{dy}{dx}\right)$	New Point (x, y)
$(0, 1)$	$y - 1 = 2(0)(x - 0)$ $y = 1$	$(0.1, 1)$
$(0.1, 1)$	$y - 1 = 2(0.1)(x - 0.1)$ $y = 0.2x + 0.98$	$(0.2, 1.02)$
$(0.2, 1.02)$	$y - 1.02 = 2(0.2)(x - 0.2)$ $y = 0.4x + 0.94$	$(0.3, 1.06)$

Thus $f(0.3) \approx 1.06$.

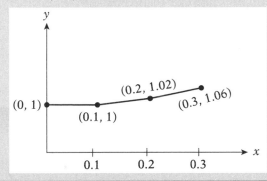

EXAMPLE 2

Given the differential equation $\dfrac{dy}{dx} = x^2$ with the initial condition $y(0) = 1$, use Euler's method with a step size of 0.1 to approximate the value of y at $x = 0.2$.

Solution

Old Point (x, y)	Equation of Tangent Line at (x, y) $\left(\text{Slope} = \dfrac{dy}{dx}\right)$	New Point (x, y)
$(0, 1)$	$y - 1 = 0^2(x - 0)$ $y = 1$	$(0.1, 1)$
$(0.1, 1)$	$y - 1 = 0.1^2(x - 0.1)$ $y = 0.1x + 0.999$	$(0.2, 1.001)$

Thus $f(0.2) \approx 1.001$.

Exercises

1. Given the differential equation $\frac{dy}{dx} = x + 2$ with the initial point $(0, 1)$, use Euler's method with a step size of 0.1 to approximate the value of $f(0.2)$.

2. Given the differential equation $\frac{dy}{dx} = 3x$ with the initial condition $f(1) = 1$, use Euler's method with a step size of 0.1 to approximate the value of $f(1.2)$.

Multiple-Choice Questions
No calculator is allowed for these questions.

1. $\frac{dy}{dx} = \frac{x}{1 + x^2}$ and $y(0) = 0$. Using Euler's method with step $\Delta x = 0.2$, $y(0.2)$ is approximately
   (A) 0
   (B) 0.0196
   (C) 0.192
   (D) 0.2
   (E) 0.888

2. $\frac{dy}{dx} = x + y$ and $y(0) = 1$. Using Euler's method with step $\Delta x = 0.5$, approximate the value of $y(0.5)$.
   (A) 0
   (B) 1
   (C) 1.5
   (D) 1.797
   (E) 2

3. $x^2 \frac{dy}{dx} = y - 1$ and $y(1) = 2$. Use Euler's method with step $\Delta x = 0.1$ to approximate $y(1.2)$.
   (A) 2
   (B) 2.091
   (C) 2.1
   (D) 2.181
   (E) 2.191

4. $(x^2 + 1) \frac{dy}{dx} = y - 1$ and $y(0) = 3$. What is the approximate value of $y(0.1)$ using Euler's method with step $\Delta x = 0.1$?
   (A) −0.891
   (B) 3
   (C) 3.2
   (D) 3.21
   (E) 3.418

Free-Response Questions
A graphing calculator is required for some questions.

1. $\frac{dy}{dx} = \frac{1}{x}$ and $y(1) = 0$.
   (a) Use Euler's method with step $\Delta x = 0.2$ to complete the table.

x	y (approximate)
1	0 (actual value)
1.2	
1.4	

   (b) Find the equation of the lines tangent to the graph of $y(x)$ at each of the points in the table above using slope $= \frac{dy}{dx}$.
   (c) Graph a segment of the first tangent line on the interval $[1, 1.2)$, the second tangent line on the interval $[1.2, 1.4)$, and the third tangent line on the interval $[1.4, 1.6)$.
   (d) Solve the differential equation $\frac{dy}{dx} = \frac{1}{x}$ and then write a third-degree Taylor polynomial centered at $x = 1$ for the solution to the differential equation. Find the error in using this polynomial to approximate $y(1.4)$.

2. $\frac{dy}{dx} = \frac{1}{2 + 2x^2}$ with $y(0) = 0$.
   (a) Use Euler's method with step $\Delta x = 0.2$ to complete the table below. State the approximate value of $y(0.6)$.

x	y (approximate)
0	0 (actual value)
0.2	
0.4	
0.6	

   (b) Solve the differential equation $\frac{dy}{dx} = \frac{1}{2 + 2x^2}$ for y, and use the first three terms of the Taylor series for y centered at $x = 0$ to approximate $y(0.6)$.

(c) Using the Taylor series in part (b), find the error in using the first three terms to approximate $y(0.6)$.

(d) Is the approximation to $y(0.6)$ by Euler's method greater than or less than the approximation to $y(0.6)$ using the Taylor series? Use the graph of y to explain your answer.

10.3 Logarithmic Differentiation

While there are formulas to find the derivatives of x^n and a^x, there are no formulas to find the derivative of functions of the form x^x, $(\ln x)^{\cos x}$, or $(1 - x)^x$, where the base and the exponent are both variables. Logarithmic differentiation is the process used to find the derivative of functions of this type.

Logarithmic functions are used to transform multiplication to addition, division to subtraction, and powers to multiplication. For example, if $y = x^x$, taking the natural logarithm on both sides of the equation gives

$$\ln y = \ln x^x.$$

Applying the ln property for exponents, the equation becomes

$$\ln y = x \ln x.$$

Now using the process of implicit differentiation, the equation becomes

$$\frac{1}{y} \frac{dy}{dx} = x \cdot \frac{1}{x} + \ln x \quad \text{or} \quad \frac{dy}{dx} = y(1 + \ln x).$$

Writing the derivative in terms of x,

$$\frac{dy}{dx} = x^x(1 + \ln x).$$

EXAMPLE 1

Find the derivative of $y = (\ln x)^{\cos x}$ and use it to find the value of $y'(e)$.

Solution   The first step in logarithmic differentiation is to take the natural logarithm of both sides of the equation:

$$\ln y = \ln(\ln x)^{\cos x}.$$

This equation becomes

$$\ln y = \cos x \cdot \ln(\ln x).$$

Taking the derivative implicitly produces the following result:

$$\frac{1}{y} \frac{dy}{dx} = \cos x \cdot \frac{1}{\ln x} \cdot \frac{1}{x} + \ln(\ln x)(-\sin x).$$

Thus,

$$\frac{dy}{dx} = y\left(\frac{\cos x}{x \ln x} - (\sin x) \ln(\ln x)\right), \quad \text{or}$$

$$\frac{dy}{dx} = (\ln x)^{\cos x}\left(\frac{\cos x}{x \ln x} - (\sin x) \ln(\ln x)\right).$$

Substituting $x = e$,

$$y'(e) = \frac{dy}{dx}\bigg|_{x=e} = (\ln e)^{\cos e}\left(\frac{\cos e}{e \ln e} - (\sin e) \ln(\ln e)\right),$$

and $y'(e) = \dfrac{\cos e}{e} = -0.3354.$

EXAMPLE 2

Find the derivative of $y = (1 - x)^x$ and use it to find the slope of the line tangent to the graph of y at $x = -\dfrac{1}{e}$.

Solution To find y', take ln of both sides of the equation:

$$\ln y = \ln(1 - x)^x \quad \text{or} \quad \ln y = x \ln(1 - x).$$

Now, using implicit differentiation,

$$\frac{1}{y}\frac{dy}{dx} = x \cdot \frac{-1}{1 - x} + \ln(1 - x).$$

Thus,

$$\frac{dy}{dx} = y\left(\frac{x}{x - 1} + \ln(1 - x)\right), \quad \text{or}$$

$$\frac{dy}{dx} = (1 - x)^x\left(\frac{x}{x - 1} + \ln(1 - x)\right).$$

The slope of the line tangent to the graph of y at $x = -\dfrac{1}{e}$ is

$$\frac{dy}{dx}\bigg|_{x=-\frac{1}{e}} = \left(1 + \frac{1}{e}\right)^{-\frac{1}{e}}\left(\frac{1}{e + 1} + \ln\left(1 + \frac{1}{e}\right)\right) \approx 0.5188$$

Exercises

Multiple-Choice Questions
No calculator is allowed for these questions.

1. Find the derivative of $f(x) = x^{\sin x}$.

   (A) $(\sin x) x^{\sin x - 1}$

   (B) $x^{\sin x}\left(\dfrac{\cos x}{x}\right)$

   (C) $x^{\sin x} \cos\left(\dfrac{1}{x}\right)$

   (D) $x^{\sin x}\left(\cos x \cdot \ln x + \dfrac{\sin x}{x}\right)$

   (E) $x^{\sin x}\left(\dfrac{\cos (\ln x)}{x}\right)$

2. If $f(x) = \left(1 + \frac{1}{x}\right)^x$, find $f'(1)$.

   (A) $\ln 2 - \frac{1}{2}$

   (B) $2 - \frac{e}{2}$

   (C) $e \ln 2 - \frac{e}{2}$

   (D) $2 \ln 2 - 1$

   (E) $2 \ln 2 + 1$

3. The derivative of $y = (\sin x)^{\ln x}$ is

   (A) $(\sin x)^{\ln x}(\tan x)$

   (B) $(\sin x)^{\ln x}(-\csc^2 x)$

   (C) $x \cos x + \sin x$

   (D) $(\sin x)^{\ln x}\left(\dfrac{\ln x}{\sin x} + \dfrac{\ln(\sin x)}{x}\right)$

   (E) $(\sin x)^{\ln x}\left(\ln x \cot x + \dfrac{\ln(\sin x)}{x}\right)$

4. $f(x) = x^{\frac{1}{x}}$. Find $f'(x)$.

   (A) 1

   (B) $x^{\frac{1}{x} - 2}$

   (C) $\dfrac{1}{x^2}(1 - \ln x)$

   (D) $x^{\frac{1}{x} - 2}(1 - \ln x)$

   (E) $\dfrac{1 + \ln x}{x^{2 - \frac{1}{x}}}$

Free-Response Questions

A graphing calculator is required for some questions.

1. Consider the function $f(x) = (\ln x)^{\cos x}$.
   (a) Is $f(x)$ a periodic function? Explain your answer.
   (b) Find the coordinates of the relative maxima of $f(x)$ on the interval $[0, 6\pi)$. Justify your answer.
   (c) On what curve do the points found in part (b) seem to fit? Explain your reasoning.

2. If $y = x^{1/x}$,
   (a) For what values of x is y continuous?
   (b) What are the coordinates of the relative maximum value of y for the domain in part (a)? Explain your reasoning.

10.4 L'Hôpital's Rule

When evaluating limits, the result may be an indeterminate form such as

$$\frac{0}{0}, \quad \frac{\infty}{\infty}, \quad -\frac{\infty}{\infty}, \quad 0 \cdot \infty, \quad \text{or} \quad \infty - \infty.$$

There are also some exponential indeterminate forms such as 1^{∞}, 0^0, or ∞^0. L'Hôpital's Rule is a method of evaluating limits of indeterminate forms. The proof of L'Hôpital's Rule comes from the Extended Mean Value Theorem.

L'Hôpital's Rule

 If

$$\lim_{x \to a}\frac{f(x)}{g(x)} = \frac{0}{0}, \frac{\infty}{\infty}, \text{ or } -\frac{\infty}{\infty},$$

Then

$$\lim_{x \to a}\frac{f(x)}{g(x)} = \lim_{x \to a}\frac{f'(x)}{g'(x)}.$$

The rule applies when a is a finite number or when $a = \pm\infty$.

> ### Tips for Using L'Hôpital's Rule
>
> - Apply L'Hôpital's Rule ONLY when taking the limit of a quotient. If the expression is an indeterminate form, but not in the form of a quotient, it must first be rewritten in quotient form.
> - Remember to take the derivative of the numerator and the derivative of the denominator when applying L'Hôpital's Rule. DO NOT USE THE QUOTIENT RULE!
> - Be sure to recheck each time L'Hôpital's Rule is applied to see if the result is still indeterminate. L'Hôpital's Rule may be applied more than once, but only if the limit results in an indeterminate form each time.

EXAMPLE 1

Evaluate $\lim\limits_{x \to 5} \dfrac{x^2 - 5x}{x - 5}$.

Solution   There are two methods of evaluating this limit.

METHOD 1   Factor the numerator and reduce the expression to $\lim\limits_{x \to 5} x$. The value of the limit is 5.

METHOD 2   Use L'Hôpital's Rule:

$$\lim_{x \to 5} \frac{x^2 - 5x}{x - 5} = \frac{0}{0}.$$

Since this is an indeterminate form, apply L'Hôpital's Rule. The result is $\lim\limits_{x \to 5} \dfrac{2x - 5}{1} = 5$.

EXAMPLE 2

Find the value of $\lim\limits_{x \to 0} \dfrac{2e^x - 2}{x}$.

Solution   Substituting the value $x = 0$ gives the result $\dfrac{0}{0}$. Since this is an indeterminate form, L'Hôpital's Rule may be applied. Taking the derivative of the numerator and the derivative of the denominator, we have

$$\lim_{x \to 0} \frac{2e^x - 2}{x} = \lim_{x \to 0} \frac{2e^x}{1} = 2.$$

EXAMPLE 3

Evaluate the limit of $\lim\limits_{x \to \infty} \dfrac{\ln x}{x}$, if it exists.

Solution   Since both $\ln x$ and x approach ∞ as $x \to \infty$, the limit has the indeterminate form $\dfrac{\infty}{\infty}$. Thus, L'Hôpital's Rule may be applied, and the result is

$$\lim_{x \to \infty} \frac{\ln x}{x} = \lim_{x \to \infty} \frac{\frac{1}{x}}{1} = 0.$$

EXAMPLE 4

Find $\lim\limits_{x \to 0^+} x^x$.

Solution In this case, the indeterminate form is 0^0. In order to apply L'Hôpital's Rule, the limit must be rewritten in the form of a quotient. The method here is to use the fact that $x^x = e^{\ln x^x} = e^{x \ln x}$. Then

$$\lim_{x \to 0^+} x^x = \lim_{x \to 0^+} e^{x \ln x} = e^{\lim\limits_{x \to 0^+} x \ln x}.$$

The second step in this equality uses the fact that e^x is a continuous function. Next rewrite $\lim\limits_{x \to 0^+} x \ln x$ as a quotient:

$$\lim_{x \to 0^+} x \ln x = \lim_{x \to 0^+} \frac{\ln x}{\frac{1}{x}}.$$

Check to see if the limit results in an indeterminate form:

$$\lim_{x \to 0^+} \frac{\ln x}{\frac{1}{x}} = \frac{-\infty}{\infty}.$$

Since this is an indeterminate form, apply L'Hôpital's Rule:

$$\lim_{x \to 0^+} \frac{\ln x}{\frac{1}{x}} = \lim_{x \to 0^+} \frac{\frac{1}{x}}{-\frac{1}{x^2}} = \lim_{x \to 0} (-x) = 0.$$

Thus, the limit is $e^0 = 1$.

EXAMPLE 5

Find $\lim\limits_{x \to \infty} \dfrac{x}{\sqrt{x^2 - 1}}$.

Solution $\lim\limits_{x \to \infty} \dfrac{x}{\sqrt{x^2 - 1}}$ gives the indeterminate form $\frac{\infty}{\infty}$. Apply L'Hôpital's Rule and the result is:

$$\lim_{x \to \infty} \frac{x}{\sqrt{x^2 - 1}} = \lim_{x \to \infty} \frac{1}{\frac{x}{\sqrt{x^2 - 1}}} = \lim_{x \to \infty} \frac{\sqrt{x^2 - 1}}{x}.$$

In this case, applying L'Hôpital's Rule does not yield an answer. Instead, the result is the limit of the reciprocal of the original expression. Applying L'Hôpital's Rule a second time will only result in returning to the original expression. In this case, the limit must be evaluated algebraically by dividing both numerator and denominator by x:

$$\lim_{x \to \infty} \frac{x}{\sqrt{x^2 - 1}} = \lim_{x \to \infty} \frac{1}{\frac{\sqrt{x^2 - 1}}{x}} = \lim_{x \to \infty} \frac{1}{\sqrt{\frac{x^2 - 1}{x^2}}} = \lim_{x \to \infty} \frac{1}{\sqrt{1 - \frac{1}{x^2}}} = 1.$$

This example demonstrates that L'Hôpital's Rule does not give an answer for every indeterminate form. Other methods can be used in such cases.

Exercises

Multiple-Choice Questions

No calculator is allowed for these questions.

1. Evaluate $\lim\limits_{x \to 2} \dfrac{2x^2 - 8}{x - 2}$.
   - (A) 0
   - (B) 2
   - (C) 4
   - (D) 8
   - (E) 16

2. Find $\lim\limits_{x \to 1} \dfrac{x - 1}{1 - \sqrt{x}}$.
   - (A) -2
   - (B) $-\dfrac{1}{2}$
   - (C) $\dfrac{1}{2}$
   - (D) 2
   - (E) ∞

3. Find the value of $\lim\limits_{x \to \infty} \dfrac{\sin x}{x}$.
   - (A) 0
   - (B) 1
   - (C) 2π
   - (D) ∞
   - (E) does not exist

4. If $f(x) = x^{1/x}$, find $\lim\limits_{x \to \infty} f(x)$.
   - (A) 0
   - (B) 1
   - (C) e
   - (D) ∞
   - (E) does not exist

Free-Response Questions

A graphing calculator is required for some questions.

1. (a) Evaluate each of the following limits:
   - i. $\lim\limits_{x \to \infty} \dfrac{x^{100}}{e^x}$
   - iii. $\lim\limits_{x \to \infty} \dfrac{\ln(100x)}{x}$
   - ii. $\lim\limits_{x \to \infty} \dfrac{e^x}{4^x}$
   - iv. $\lim\limits_{x \to \infty} \dfrac{x}{\sqrt{e^x}}$

   (b) Use the values of the limits in part (a) to write a conclusion about the relative "strengths" of the logarithmic, exponential, and polynomial functions as $x \to \infty$.

2. (a) Find the area under the graph of $f(x) = \dfrac{x}{e^x}$ for $x \geq 0$, if it exists.

   (b) Find the area under the graph of $g(x) = \dfrac{\ln x}{x}$ for $x \geq 1$, if it exists.

   (c) For what values of p does the $\displaystyle\int_1^\infty \dfrac{\ln x}{x^p}\, dx$ have a finite value?

3. (a) Find the area under the graph of $y = \dfrac{1}{\sqrt{x}}$ for $x \geq 1$, if it exists.

   (b) Find the volume when the region under the graph of $y = \dfrac{1}{\sqrt{x}}$ for $x \geq 1$ is rotated about the x-axis, if it exists.

   (c) For what values of p do the area under the graph of $y = \dfrac{1}{x^p}$ for $x \geq 1$ AND the volume when the region under the graph of $y = \dfrac{1}{x^p}$ for $x \geq 1$ is rotated about the x-axis both have a finite value?

10.5 Polar Curves

The **polar coordinate system** in the plane consists of points (r, θ), where r is the distance of the point from the pole (the origin of the rectangular coordinate system) and θ is the angle formed with the polar axis (the positive x-axis). An essential difference between the polar coordinate system and the rectangular coordinate system is that a point in the polar coordinate system does not have a unique representation; that is, a point can be represented in multiple ways with more than one set of coordinates. This is because r and θ may not be unique. It is important to remember this when working with polar equations. In some cases, it may make it difficult to identify all the points of intersection of polar graphs. The graphs may intersect at a point, but for different values of r or θ, or both.

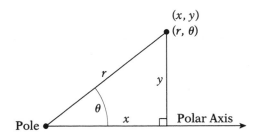

When r is positive, as in the figure above, the point is on the ray that is the terminal side of angle θ. When r is negative, the point is in the opposite direction from the ray that is the terminal side of θ. Therefore, as the following figure shows, the point $(-r, \theta)$ is the same as the point $(r, \theta + \pi)$.

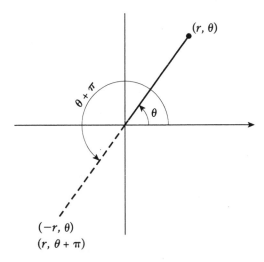

In some situations, it is very useful to locate points using polar coordinates. For example, some important curves have equations in the polar coordinate system that are much simpler than in the rectangular coordinate system. For this reason, it can be useful to convert rectangular coordinates (and vice versa).

Converting Polar Coordinates to Rectangular Coordinates

If a point has polar coordinates (r, θ), then the rectangular coordinates of the point are $(r \cos \theta, r \sin \theta)$. In other words, since

$\cos \theta = \frac{x}{r}$ and $\sin \theta = \frac{y}{r}$,

$\qquad x = r \cos \theta$, and

$\qquad y = r \sin \theta.$

> **Converting Rectangular Coordinates to Polar Coordinates**
> If a point has rectangular coordinates (x, y), then the polar coordinates of the point are (r, θ) where
>
> $$r^2 = x^2 + y^2, \text{ or}$$
>
> $$r = \sqrt{x^2 + y^2}$$
>
> and
>
> $$\theta = \arctan\left(\frac{y}{x}\right), \text{ or}$$
>
> $$\theta = \tan^{-1}\left(\frac{y}{x}\right), \text{ or}$$
>
> $$\tan\theta = \frac{y}{x}.$$
>
> *Note:* Use the positive square root of $x^2 + y^2$ for r if $x > 0$, and the negative square root if $x \leq 0$.

EXAMPLE 1

(a) Find the polar equation for the curve represented by the rectangular coordinate equation $x\sqrt{x^2 + y^2} = 2y$.

(b) Find the rectangular coordinate equation for the curve represented by the polar equation $r = 3\cos 2\theta$.

Solution

(a) Use the relationships given to convert both sides of the equation:

$$x\sqrt{x^2 + y^2} = (r\cos\theta)r, \text{ and}$$
$$2y = 2r\sin\theta.$$

Thus,

$$(r\cos\theta)r = 2r\sin\theta$$

$$r = \frac{2r\sin\theta}{r\cos\theta}$$

$$r = 2\tan\theta.$$

The resulting polar equation is much simpler than the original rectangular coordinate equation.

(b) Begin by applying the double-angle formula to get

$$r = 3\cos^2\theta - 3\sin^2\theta.$$

Multiply both sides by r^2:

$$r^3 = 3(r\cos\theta)^2 - 3(r\sin\theta)^2.$$

Now use the relationships given to convert both sides of the equation. Working on the right side, we get

$$r^3 = \left(\sqrt{x^2 + y^2}\right)^3, \quad \text{or}$$

$$r^3 = (x^2 + y^2)^{3/2}.$$

Working on the left side, we get

$$3(r\cos\theta)^2 - 3(r\sin\theta)^2 = 3(x)^2 - 3(y)^2, \text{ or}$$

$$3(r\cos\theta)^2 - 3(r\sin\theta)^2 = 3(x^2 - y^2).$$

Thus, the rectangular coordinate equation is

$$(x^2 + y^2)^{3/2} = 3(x^2 - y^2), \quad \text{or}$$

$$(x^2 + y^2)^3 = 9(x^2 - y^2)^2.$$

Again, we see that the polar equation is much simpler than the rectangular coordinate equation.

Although the equations presented, which relate x, y, r, and θ, may be useful, the focus in Calculus BC is not on translating polar coordinates into rectangular coordinates (or vice versa). Rather, the focus is on graphing polar curves, investigating their properties, and finding points of intersection, enclosed areas, and arc lengths.

Polar Curves A polar curve is represented by an equation of the form $r = f(\theta)$. The following are some curves and their equations that you should become familiar with and be able to sketch by hand. Note that curves that have a term with cosine are symmetric to the polar axis, while curves that have a term with sine are symmetric to the line perpendicular to the polar axis.

Circle with Its Center on the Polar Axis

$r = a\cos\theta$

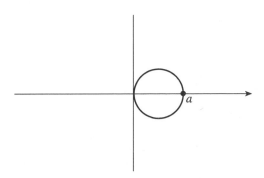

Circle With Its Center on the Line Perpendicular to the Polar Axis

$$r = a \sin \theta$$

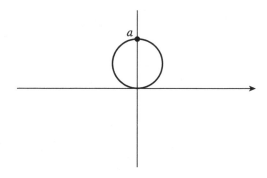

Note: These circles are completely drawn for $0 \leq \theta \leq \pi$.

Limaçon

$$r = a \pm b \cos \theta \quad \text{or} \quad r = a \pm b \sin \theta$$

If $a < b$, the limaçon has an inner loop.

If $a = b$, the limaçon is called a **cardioid.**

If $a > b$, the limaçon has a flattened end.

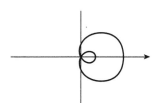

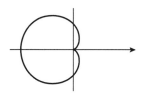

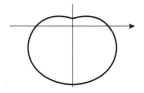

Petal Curves

$$r = a \cos n\theta \quad \text{or} \quad r = a \sin n\theta$$

If n is a positive even integer, the curve has $2n$ petals.

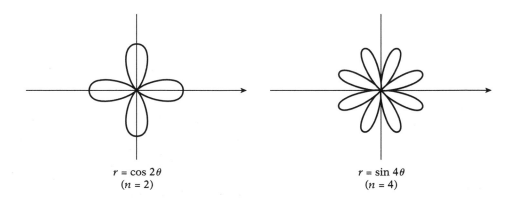

$r = \cos 2\theta$
$(n = 2)$

$r = \sin 4\theta$
$(n = 4)$

If n is a positive odd integer, the curve has n petals.

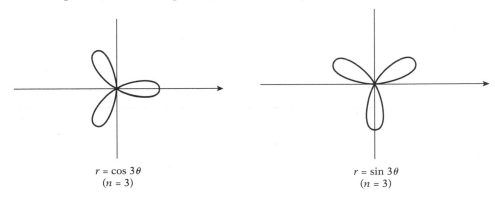

$r = \cos 3\theta$
$(n = 3)$

$r = \sin 3\theta$
$(n = 3)$

If n is not an integer, then the petals overlap.

 Calculator Note

To graph a polar curve on the TI-83

Press MODE and scroll down and right to Pol. Press ENTER.

Press Y= and enter the equation in r_1.

Press GRAPH and adjust the window (if necessary) to see the entire graph.

Note: ZOOM 4 is a good window for most polar curves.

Notice the values of θ in WINDOW. Some polar curves are traced from $\theta = 0$ to $\theta = \pi$. Other curves are traced from $\theta = 0$ to $\theta = 2\pi$.

After graphing the curve, press TRACE to see coordinates. To change to polar coordinates (r, θ), press 2nd ZOOM (FORMAT), scroll right to PolarGC, and press ENTER.

To graph a polar curve on the TI-89

Press MODE. Go to Graph. Go to Polar. Press ENTER ENTER. Proceed as above.

Note: The graphing calculator does not find points of intersection in polar mode.

Points of Intersection of Polar Curves

Since each point in the plane has multiple representations in polar coordinates, solving for the points of intersection of two polar curves may require more than solving an equation.

EXAMPLE 2

Find the points of intersection of $r = 2 \sin \theta$ and $r = 2 + 2 \cos \theta$.

Solution Begin by solving the equations simultaneously.

$$2 \sin \theta = 2 + 2 \cos \theta$$

Dividing by 2 and squaring both sides:

$$\sin^2 \theta = (1 + \cos \theta)^2$$

$$\sin^2 \theta = 1 + 2 \cos \theta + \cos^2 \theta$$

Now use the Pythagorean Identity to replace $\sin^2 \theta$ with $1 - \cos^2 \theta$:

$1 - \cos^2 \theta = 1 + 2 \cos \theta + \cos^2 \theta$, which becomes

$$2 \cos^2 \theta + 2 \cos \theta = 0.$$

Factoring the equation, $2 \cos \theta(\cos \theta + 1) = 0$. Thus, either $2 \cos \theta = 0$ or $\cos \theta + 1 = 0$.

The solutions are $\theta = \dfrac{\pi}{2}$ and $\theta = \pi$.

The only solution for $2 \cos \theta = 0$ is $\theta = \dfrac{\pi}{2}$ since the domain for the circle $r = 2 \sin \theta$ is $0 \le \theta \le \pi$. Furthermore, the solution $\theta = \pi$ makes $r = 0$, and thus the point of intersection is at the pole. When $r = 0$ on both curves, for *any* value of θ, the pole is a point of intersection. Thus, the points of intersection are $\left(2, \dfrac{\pi}{2} \right)$ and the pole.

Looking at the graph, we see that these are the only two points of intersection.

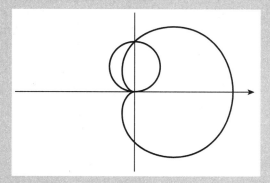

EXAMPLE 3

Find the points of intersection of $r = \sin \theta$ and $r = 1 + 2 \sin \theta$.

Solution Solving the equation $\sin \theta = 1 + 2 \sin \theta$, the equation becomes

$$\sin \theta = -1.$$

Thus $\theta = \dfrac{3\pi}{2}$ is the solution and appears to be the only solution.

When $\theta = \dfrac{3\pi}{2}$, $r = -1$, and the point of intersection is $\left(-1, \dfrac{3\pi}{2} \right)$.

On the polar graph, the point $\left(-1, \dfrac{3\pi}{2} \right)$ is equivalent to the point $\left(1, \dfrac{\pi}{2} \right)$. Furthermore, there is another point of intersection, the pole.

When both graphs have $r = 0$ for *any* value of θ, the curves go through the pole, and the pole is a point of intersection. Thus, the two points of intersection are $\left(-1, \frac{3\pi}{2}\right)$ and the pole.

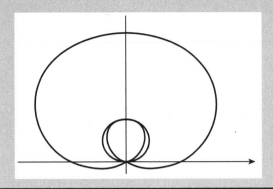

Area in Polar Coordinates

The formula for the area inside a polar curve is

$$\text{Area} = \int \frac{1}{2} r^2 \, d\theta,\ \text{where the limits of the integral are values of } \theta.$$

EXAMPLE 4

Write an integral that represents the area inside the circle $r = 2 \cos\theta$ from $\theta = 0$ to $\theta = \frac{\pi}{4}$. Find the value of the integral using a calculator.

Solution $\text{Area} = \frac{1}{2} \int_0^{\frac{\pi}{4}} (2\cos\theta)^2 \, d\theta = 1.285.$

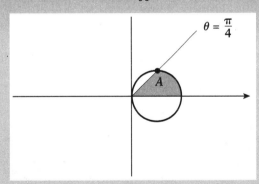

EXAMPLE 5

Find the area common to the curves $r = 2 \cos\theta$ and $r = 2 + 2 \sin\theta$.

Solution   First find the points of intersection by solving the equation $2 \cos\theta = 2 + 2 \sin\theta$.

The solutions are $\theta = 0$ and $\theta = \frac{3\pi}{2}$.
The points of intersection are $(2, 0)$ and the pole.

The area in common is the sum of the upper semicircle and the part of the cardioid from $\theta = \dfrac{3\pi}{2}$ to $\theta = 2\pi$. Thus, the area is the sum of two integrals:

$$\frac{1}{2}\int_0^{\frac{\pi}{2}} (2\cos\theta)^2\,d\theta + \frac{1}{2}\int_{\frac{3\pi}{2}}^{2\pi} (2 + 2\sin\theta)^2\,d\theta = 2.283.$$

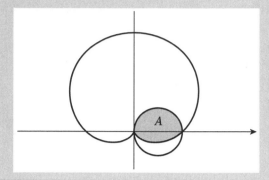

Other Polar Curve Formulas   The following two formulas for polar curves are used infrequently, but are given here for reference.

> ### Slope of the Tangent Line to a Polar Curve
>
> $$\frac{dy}{dx} = \frac{r\cos\theta + \dfrac{dr}{d\theta}\sin\theta}{-r\sin\theta + \dfrac{dr}{d\theta}\cos\theta}$$

> ### Arc Length of a Polar Curve from $\theta = a$ to $\theta = b$
>
> $$s = \int_a^b \sqrt{r^2 + \left(\frac{dr}{d\theta}\right)^2}\,d\theta$$

EXAMPLE 6

Find the perimeter of the polar curve $r = 2 - 2\cos\theta$.

Solution   Since the graph of $r = 2 - 2\cos\theta$ is traced out once for values of θ between 0 and 2π, use the arc length formula with $a = 0$ and $b = 2\pi$.

$$s = \int_0^{2\pi} \sqrt{r^2 + (r')^2}\,d\theta = 16.$$

Calculator Note

To make the computation of the arc length easier, in Polar mode enter the equation $r = 2 - 2\cos\theta$ into r_1 and $2\sin\theta$ into r_2. Then go to the Home Screen and press MATH 9 and enter

$$\text{fnInt}\left(\sqrt{r_1^2 + r_2^2}, \theta, 0, 2\pi\right).$$

EXAMPLE 7

Find the perimeter of the inner loop of the graph of $r = 2 - 4 \cos \theta$.

Solution The first step is to find the values of θ that make $r = 0$. These are the values of θ where the curve intersects the pole. These values can be found algebraically by solving the equation:

$$2 - 4 \cos \theta = 0$$

$$-4 \cos \theta = -2$$

$$\cos \theta = \frac{1}{2}.$$

Therefore, $\theta = \frac{\pi}{3}$ and $\frac{5\pi}{3}$.

Graphing and tracing the curve on the calculator, we can see that the bottom half of the inner loop is traced out from $\theta = 0$ to $\theta = \frac{\pi}{3}$.

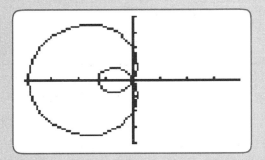

Thus, the perimeter of the inner loop can be found by doubling the arc length from $\theta = 0$ to $\theta = \frac{\pi}{3}$:

$$s = 2 \int_0^{\frac{\pi}{3}} \sqrt{r^2 + (r')^2} \, d\theta = 5.365.$$

EXAMPLE 8

At what point(s) on the graph of $r = 2 - 4 \cos \theta$ is the tangent line
(a) vertical
(b) horizontal

Solution The formula for $\frac{dy}{dx}$ gives the slope of the tangent line to a polar curve.

(a) To find points at which the tangent line is vertical, set the denominator equal to zero and solve for θ. Thus,

$$-\sin \theta (2 - 4 \cos \theta) + 4 \sin \theta \cos \theta = 0, \text{ or}$$

$$2 \sin \theta (4 \cos \theta - 1) = 0.$$

There are four solutions: $\theta = 0$, π, 1.318, and 4.965.
The four points at which the tangent line is vertical are $(-2, 0)$, $(6, \pi)$, $(1, 1.318)$, and $(1, 4.965)$.

(b) To find the points at which the tangent line is horizontal, set the numerator of $\frac{dy}{dx}$ equal to zero. Thus,

$$2\cos\theta - 4\cos^2\theta + 4\sin^2\theta = 0.$$

Using a Pythagorean identity, the equation becomes

$$4\cos^2\theta - \cos\theta - 2 = 0.$$

Using the quadratic formula to solve, we get

$$\cos\theta = \frac{1 + \sqrt{33}}{8}.$$

There are four solutions: $\theta = 0.568, 2.205, 4.078,$ and $5.715.$ The four points at which the tangent line is horizontal are $(-1.372, 0.568), (4.372, 2.205), (4.372, 4.078),$ and $(-1.372, 5.715).$

Exercises

1. Identify each polar equation by matching it with one of the descriptions:
   (a) $r = 2\cos 3\theta$
   (b) $r = 4 + \sin\theta$
   (c) $r = 4\sin 2\theta$
   (d) $r = 3\cos\theta$
   (e) $r = 3 + 3\cos\theta$
   (f) $r = 1 + 3\cos\theta$
   (g) $r = 2\sin\theta$

      i. circle symmetric to the polar axis
      ii. circle symmetric to the line ⊥ the polar axis
      iii. petal with three leaves
      iv. petal with four leaves
      v. limaçon with an inner loop
      vi. limaçon with a flattened loop
      vii. cardioid

2. Find the number of points of intersection of the polar curves $r = \cos 2\theta$ and $r = 1 + 2\sin\theta$.

3. Find the points of intersection of $r = 2\cos\theta$ and $r = 3 + 3\cos\theta$.

Multiple-Choice Questions
No calculator is allowed for these questions.

1. The graph of $r = 4\cos\theta$ is
   (A) a circle with radius 4
   (B) a circle with radius 2
   (C) a four-petal rose
   (D) an eight-petal rose
   (E) a cardioid

2. The graphs of $r = \cos\theta$ and $r = 2\cos 2\theta$ intersect in how many points?
   (A) 1
   (B) 2
   (C) 3
   (D) 4
   (E) 5

3. The graph of $r = 2 + 4\sin\theta$ is symmetric to
   (A) the polar axis
   (B) the line $\theta = \frac{\pi}{2}$
   (C) the line $\theta = \frac{\pi}{4}$
   (D) the line $\theta = \frac{\pi}{6}$
   (E) The graph has no symmetry.

4. The graph of the equation $r = \frac{2}{\cos\theta}$
   (A) intersects the polar axis at one point
   (B) intersects the polar axis at two points
   (C) does not intersect the polar axis
   (D) intersects the line $\theta = \frac{\pi}{2}$ at one point
   (E) intersects the line $\theta = \frac{\pi}{2}$ at two points

Free-Response Questions
A graphing calculator is required for some questions.

1. (a) Sketch a graph of the polar curves and find their points of intersection.

$$r = 2(1 - \cos\theta)$$
$$r = 2\cos\theta$$

(b) Find an expression for the slope of the tangent to the graph of $r = 2\cos\theta$ in terms of θ.
(c) Find the slope of the tangent to the graph of $r = 2\cos\theta$ at each of the points of intersection in part (a).

2. Consider the polar curves $r = 1 - \sin\theta$ and $r = 2\cos\theta$.

(a) Identify each polar graph.
(b) Find the points of intersection of the two graphs.
(c) Sketch the graphs and shade the region common to both curves.
(d) Find the area of the region common to both curves.

Chapter Assessment

Multiple-Choice Questions
No calculator is allowed for Questions 1–15.

1. Find the number of points of intersection of the polar curves $r = 2\cos\theta$ and $r = 1 + 2\sin\theta$.
   (A) 0
   (B) 1
   (C) 2
   (D) 3
   (E) 4

2. The points of intersection of $r = \cos\theta$ and $r = \cos 2\theta$ are
   (A) $(1, 0)$ and the pole
   (B) $\left(\frac{1}{2}, \frac{5\pi}{3}\right)$, $(1, 0)$, and the pole
   (C) $\left(-\frac{1}{2}, \frac{2\pi}{3}\right)$ and $(1, 0)$
   (D) $\left(-\frac{1}{2}, \frac{2\pi}{3}\right)$, $\left(-\frac{1}{2}, \frac{4\pi}{3}\right)$, $(1, 0)$, and the pole
   (E) There are no points of intersection.

3. The graph of the polar curve $r = 3 + 4\cos\theta$ is a
   (A) circle
   (B) cardioid
   (C) petal curve
   (D) limaçon with an inner loop
   (E) limaçon with a flattened loop

4. The area of the right half of the polar curve $r = 1 + \sin\theta$ is equal to
   (A) $\frac{1}{2}\pi$
   (B) $\frac{3\pi}{4}$
   (C) π
   (D) $\frac{3\pi}{2}$
   (E) 2π

5. Which integral expression represents the area common to the graphs of both $r = \cos\theta$ and $r = 1 + \sin\theta$?
   (A) $\int_0^{2\pi} \frac{1}{2}(1 + \sin\theta)^2\, d\theta$
   (B) $\int_0^{\pi} \frac{1}{2}\cos^2\theta\, d\theta + \int_\pi^{2\pi} \frac{1}{2}(1 + \sin\theta)^2\, d\theta$
   (C) $\int_0^{\frac{\pi}{2}} \frac{1}{2}\cos^2\theta\, d\theta + \int_{\frac{3\pi}{2}}^{2\pi} \frac{1}{2}(1 + \sin\theta)^2\, d\theta$
   (D) $\int_0^{\frac{\pi}{2}} \frac{1}{2}\cos^2\theta\, d\theta + \int_\pi^{2\pi} \frac{1}{2}(1 + \sin\theta)^2\, d\theta$
   (E) $\int_0^{\frac{\pi}{2}} \cos^2\theta\, d\theta + \int_\pi^{2\pi} \frac{1}{2}(1 + \sin\theta)^2\, d\theta$

6. Find the solution of the differential equation $\frac{dP}{dt} = 4P^2$ with $P(1) = 2$.
   (A) $P = 4e^{t^2} - 2$
   (B) $P = 2e^{4t^2}$
   (C) $P = 2e^{2t-2}$
   (D) $P = \dfrac{2}{9 - 8t}$
   (E) $P = 2(e^{2t} - e^2 + 1)$

7. Water pours into a tank at the rate of 10 ft³/min. The tank is a cylinder with radius of 4 feet and a height of 10 feet. At what rate is the depth of the water changing when the water is 5 feet deep?
   (A) $\dfrac{5}{16\pi}$ ft/min
   (B) $\dfrac{5}{16}$ ft/min
   (C) $\dfrac{5}{4\pi}$ ft/min
   (D) $\dfrac{5}{8\pi}$ ft/min
   (E) $\dfrac{5}{8}\pi$ ft/min

8. Find the slope of the line tangent to $y = \arcsin x$ at $x = -0.5$.

(A) $\dfrac{\sqrt{3}}{2}$

(B) $-\dfrac{\sqrt{3}}{2}$

(C) $\dfrac{\pi}{6}$

(D) $\dfrac{5\pi}{6}$

(E) $\dfrac{2\sqrt{3}}{3}$

9. Water rises in a conical paper cup of radius 3 inches and height 5 inches so that at a certain instant the rate of change of the area of the surface is twice the rate of change of the radius of the surface. What is the length of the radius at that instant?

(A) 1 in.

(B) $\dfrac{1}{\pi}$ in.

(C) $\dfrac{2}{\pi}$ in.

(D) $\dfrac{\pi}{2}$ in.

(E) 2 in.

10. Find the function $y = f(x)$ if $y(1) = 0$ and the derivative $\dfrac{dy}{dx} = 1 + y^2$.

(A) $y = x + \dfrac{x^3}{3} - \dfrac{4}{3}$

(B) $y + \dfrac{y^3}{3} = t - 1$

(C) $y = \sin(x - 1)$

(D) $y = \tan(x - 1)$

(E) $y^2 = e^{x-1} - 1$

11. $\ln y + \ln x = -x^2 + 1$. Find $\lim\limits_{x \to \infty} y'$.

(A) $-\infty$

(B) -2

(C) 0

(D) 2

(E) ∞

12. Evaluate $\lim\limits_{x \to \infty} x^{\frac{1}{\ln x}}$.

(A) 0

(B) $\dfrac{1}{e}$

(C) 1

(D) e

(E) does not exist

13. $\displaystyle\int_{-2}^{2} \arctan x \, dx =$

(A) 0

(B) $\dfrac{2}{5}$

(C) $4 \arctan 2$

(D) $4 \arctan 2 - \ln 5$

(E) $\ln 5$

14. The region in the first quadrant bounded by the graphs of $y = x^3$, $y = 2x + 4$, and the y-axis has area A. Which of the following is the best estimate of the value of A?

(A) 4

(B) 6

(C) 12

(D) 16

(E) 24

15. What is the maximum value of $y = (\sin x)^{1/x}$ on $(0, \pi)$?

(A) 0.5

(B) 1

(C) $\dfrac{\pi}{2}$

(D) $\dfrac{\sqrt{2}}{2}$

(E) There is no maximum value.

A graphing calculator is required for Questions 16–25.

16. A solid is formed by rotating the graph of $y = \sqrt{\ln x}$ on the interval $[1, 2]$ around the x-axis. For what value of k does the line $x = k$ divide the solid into two parts with equal volumes?

(A) 0.094

(B) 0.193

(C) 0.607

(D) 1.255

(E) 1.683

17. Region R is in the first quadrant bounded by the graphs of $y = \sqrt{x} + 1$, $y = -\dfrac{1}{2}x + 5$, and $x = 0$. Region R is the base of a solid for which each cross section perpendicular to the x-axis is a semicircle. Find the volume of the solid.

(A) 6.074

(B) 11.519

(C) 12.147

(D) 16

(E) 23.038

18. The region bounded by the graph of $y = x^3$, the y-axis, and the line $y = r^3, (r > 0)$ is rotated about the y-axis forming a solid. Find the value of r if the volume of the solid is 20π.
(A) 1.503
(B) 2.016
(C) 2.535
(D) 2.714
(E) 8.198

19. For what values of p does the series $\displaystyle\sum_{n=1}^{\infty} \frac{n^{0.01}}{n^p}$ converge?
(A) $p \geq 1$
(B) $p > 1$
(C) $p > 0.99$
(D) $p > 1.01$
(E) $p < 1.01$

20. The curve of a road is modeled by the vector $<\cos t, \tan t>$. Find the length of the road from $t = 0$ to $t = \frac{\pi}{3}$.
(A) 1.42
(B) 1.809
(C) 1.817
(D) 4.619
(E) 8.923

21. The function $f(x)$ has a continuous derivative for all values of x in the interval $[a, b]$. Which of the following must be true?
(A) $f'(c) = \dfrac{f(b) - f(a)}{b - a}$ where c is any value of x in the interval $[a, b]$.
(B) $f''(x)$ is continuous on the interval $[a, b]$.
(C) $f(a) = f(b)$.
(D) There is a value of c in the interval (a, b) such that $f'(c) = 0$.
(E) There is a value of c in the interval $[a, b]$ such that $f'(c) = \dfrac{1}{b - a}\displaystyle\int_a^b f'(x)\, dx$.

22. Find the sum of the series $\displaystyle\sum_{n=1}^{\infty} \left(\frac{1}{2n} - \frac{1}{2^n} \right)$, if it exists.
(A) -1
(B) 0
(C) 1
(D) 2
(E) does not exist

23. Find the x-coordinate of the point on the graph of $y = x^3 + 1$ closest to $(0, 2)$.
(A) 0
(B) 0.348
(C) 0.5
(D) 0.846
(E) 1

24. Consider the graph of the derivative of f.

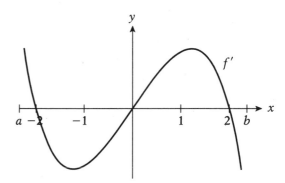

Which of the following can be concluded about the function f?
  I f has exactly one relative maximum and exactly one relative minimum on the interval $[a, b]$.
  II f has exactly one point of inflection on the interval $[a, b]$.
  III f is concave up on the interval $(-1, 1)$.
(A) II only
(B) III only
(C) I and III
(D) II and III
(E) I, II, and III

25. Which of the following series converge conditionally?
  I $\displaystyle\sum_{n=1}^{\infty} (-1)^{n+1} \frac{n+1}{n^2}$
  II $\displaystyle\sum_{n=2}^{\infty} \frac{(-1)^n}{n \ln n}$
  III $\displaystyle\sum_{n=0}^{\infty} 3\left(-\frac{3}{4} \right)^n$
(A) III only
(B) I and II
(C) I and III
(D) II and III
(E) I, II, and III

Free-Response Questions
No calculator is allowed for Questions 1–4.

1. A highly infectious strain of smallpox invades a town of 2,000 people. On the first day, 20 people are infected. Town officials immediately contact a team of doctors and mathematicians. The doctors treat infected patients, while the mathematicians analyze the data and conclude that the rate of growth of the infection is modeled by the differential equation $\frac{dP}{dt} = 0.0004P(2{,}000 - P)$, where P is the number of people infected after t days. Use this differential equation to do the following:
   (a) Find the solution to the differential equation.
   (b) Find the day on which the rate of growth is fastest.
   (c) Predict the number of people infected after 2 days and after 4 days.

2. Use Euler's method to approximate $y(0.2)$ with $\Delta x = 0.1$, if $\frac{dy}{dx} = x + y$ and $y(0) = 0$.

3. (a) If $f'(x) = \arctan x$ and $f(0) = 1$, find $f(x)$.
   (b) Use the fact that $f''(x) = \frac{1}{1 + x^2}$ to find a Taylor series for $f(x)$ centered at $x = 0$.
   (c) Find the sum of the series $\sum_{n=1}^{\infty} \frac{(-1)^{n+1}}{2n(2n - 1)}$ using the results of parts (a) and (b).

4. Consider the function $f(x) = \frac{e^x + e^{-x}}{2}$.
   (a) Show that $f(x)$ is a solution to the differential equation $y'' = y$.
   (b) Find the equation of the line tangent to $f(x)$ at $x = \ln 10$.
   (c) Find $f'(x)$, and show that $(0, 0)$ is on the graph of $f'(x)$ and that $f'(x)$ is an odd function.

A graphing calculator is required for Questions 5 and 6.

5. Consider the functions $f(x) = \cos x$ and $g(x) = \frac{1}{1 + x^2}$ on the interval $[-2, 2]$.
   (a) Find the area of the region R bounded by $f(x)$ and $g(x)$.
   (b) Find the perimeter of region R.
   (c) Find the value of x such that the difference between the y-coordinates of $f(x)$ and $g(x)$ is a maximum.

6. Consider the graph of f shown, and the given $g(x) = \int_0^x f(t)\, dt$.

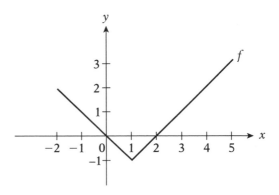

   (a) Find the relative extrema of $g(x)$. Justify your answer.
   (b) Find the value(s) of x in the interval $[-2, 5]$ such that $g(x) = g(0)$.
   (c) Find $g''(x)$.
   (d) Use the information in parts (a)–(c) to sketch a graph of $g(x)$ on the interval $[-2, 5]$.

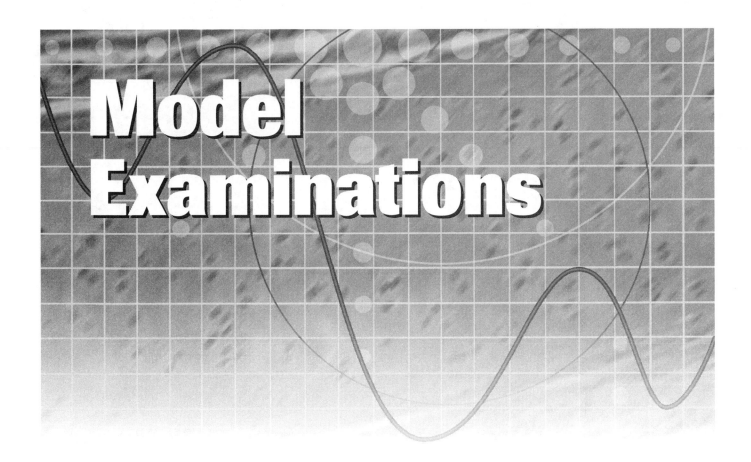

Model Examinations

Section I

Part A

No calculator is allowed for these questions.

1. If $xy - y = 2x + 4$, $\dfrac{dy}{dx}$ is

   (A) $\dfrac{y-2}{x-1}$

   (B) $\dfrac{2-y}{x-1}$

   (C) $\dfrac{y-6}{x-1}$

   (D) $\dfrac{2}{x-1}$

   (E) $\dfrac{y-2}{x+1}$

2. Let $f(x)$ be an odd function and $g(x)$ be even. Which of the following statements are true?

   I $\displaystyle\int_{-2}^{2} f(x)\,dx = 0$

   II $\displaystyle\int_{-2}^{2} g(x)\,dx = 0$

   III $\displaystyle\int_{-2}^{2} f(x)g(x)\,dx = 0$

   (A) II

   (B) III

   (C) I and II

   (D) I and III

   (E) I, II, and III

3. $\displaystyle\lim_{x \to 0} \dfrac{\sin 3x}{5x} =$

   (A) $\dfrac{3}{5}$

   (B) $\dfrac{5}{3}$

   (C) 3

   (D) 5

   (E) no limit exists

4. For which of the following x-values on the graph of $y = 2x - x^2$ is $\dfrac{dy}{dx}$ the largest?

   (A) -2.7

   (B) -2.2

   (C) 0

   (D) 1

   (E) 2.7

5. If $y = e^{2x} + \tan 2x$, then $y'(\pi) =$

   (A) $2e^{2\pi}$

   (B) $e^{2\pi} + 1$

   (C) $2e^{2\pi} + 2$

   (D) $2e^{\pi} - 2$

   (E) 0

6. Write the equation of the line tangent to $y = e^{x+1}$ at $x = 0$.

   (A) $y = ex + e$

   (B) $y = x$

   (C) $y = x + 1$

   (D) $y = x + e$

   (E) $y = ex + 1$

7. If the acceleration of a particle is given by $a(t) = 2e^t$ and at $t = 1$ the velocity is 2, then $v(0)$ is

   (A) 0

   (B) $2 - 2e$

   (C) $2 - \dfrac{1}{2}e$

   (D) $4 - 2e$

   (E) 2

8. If $3xy + 2y^2 = 5$, find $\dfrac{dy}{dx}$ at $(1, 1)$.

   (A) $-\dfrac{3}{7}$

   (B) 0

   (C) $\dfrac{3}{7}$

   (D) 7

   (E) undefined

9. The graph of $y = \dfrac{\ln(1 - x)}{x + 1}$ has vertical asymptote(s) at

   (A) $x = 1$

   (B) $x = 0$

   (C) $x = \pm 1$

   (D) $x = -1$

   (E) no vertical asymptote

10. $\dfrac{d}{dt}\displaystyle\int_t^{t^2} \dfrac{1}{x}\, dx =$

   (A) $\dfrac{1}{t^2}$

   (B) $\ln(t)$

   (C) $\ln(t^2)$

   (D) $\dfrac{1}{t}$

   (E) $\ln\dfrac{1}{t}$

11. $\displaystyle\lim_{h \to 0} \dfrac{\cos\left(\dfrac{\pi}{4} + h\right) - \cos\dfrac{\pi}{4}}{h} =$

   (A) $-\dfrac{\sqrt{3}}{2}$

   (B) $-\dfrac{\sqrt{2}}{2}$

   (C) 0

   (D) $\dfrac{\sqrt{2}}{2}$

   (E) 1

12. $\displaystyle\int (3x^2 - \cos x)\, dx =$

   (A) $6x + \sin(x) + C$

   (B) $x^3 + \sin(x) + C$

   (C) $x^3 - \sin(x) + C$

   (D) $6x - \sin(x) + C$

   (E) $3x^3 - \sin(x) + C$

13. Find the area under the curve $y = x^2 + 1$ on the interval $[1, 2]$.

   (A) $\dfrac{7}{3}$

   (B) 3

   (C) $\dfrac{10}{3}$

   (D) 4

   (E) 7

14. $\displaystyle\int_{-1}^{2} \dfrac{x}{x^2 + 1}\, dx =$

   (A) $\ln\dfrac{2}{5}$

   (B) 0

   (C) $\dfrac{1}{2}\ln\dfrac{5}{2}$

   (D) $\dfrac{1}{2}\ln 3$

   (E) undefined

15. $\displaystyle\int_0^1 e^{3x+2}\, dx =$

   (A) $\dfrac{1}{3}e^5$

   (B) $\dfrac{1}{3}(e^5 - e^2)$

   (C) $\dfrac{1}{3}(e^5 - 1)$

   (D) $e^5 - 1$

   (E) $e^5 - e^2$

16. If $y = \sin^2 5x$, $\dfrac{dy}{dx} =$

(A) $5 \sin 10x$

(B) $5 \cos 5x$

(C) $5 \sin 5x$

(D) $10 \sin 10x$

(E) $10 \sin^2 5x$

17. For what values of x is $f(x) = 2x^3 - x^2 + 2x$ concave up?

(A) $x < \dfrac{1}{6}$

(B) $x < 0$

(C) $x > 0$

(D) $x > \dfrac{1}{6}$

(E) $x > 6$

Questions 18 and 19 refer to the graph of the velocity v(t) of an object at time t shown below.

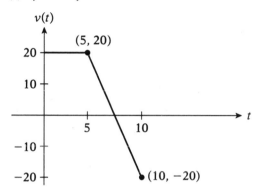

18. If $x(t)$ is the position of the object at time t, and $a(t)$ is the acceleration of the object at time t, which of the following is true?

(A) $v(5) > v(2)$

(B) $x(5) > x(2)$

(C) $a(6) > a(2)$

(D) $x(10) < x(5)$

(E) $a(9) > a(6)$

19. $\displaystyle\int_0^{10} v(t)\, dt =$

(A) 0

(B) 5

(C) 50

(D) 75

(E) 100

20. If $f(1) = 2$ and $f'(1) = 5$, use the equation of the line tangent to the graph of f at $x = 1$ to approximate $f(1.2)$.

(A) 1

(B) 1.2

(C) 3

(D) 5.4

(E) 9

21. The equation of the line tangent to $y = \tan^2(3x)$ at $x = \dfrac{\pi}{4}$ is

(A) $y = -12x + 3\pi - 1$

(B) $y = -12x + 3\pi + 1$

(C) $y = -6x + \dfrac{3\pi}{2} + 1$

(D) $y = -12x + 3\pi + 3$

(E) $y = -12x + \pi + 3$

22. The graph of $f'(x)$ is shown below.

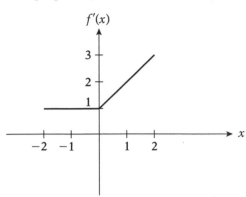

Which of the following could be the graph of f?

(A)

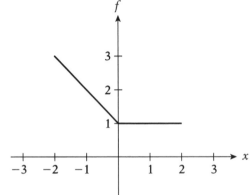

(B)

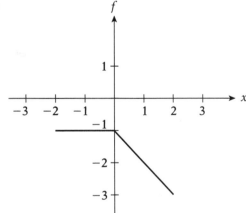

(C)

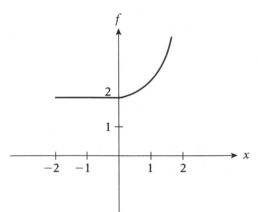

(D)

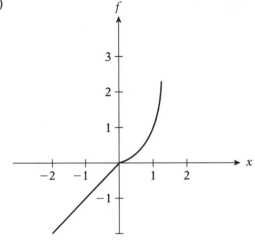

(E)

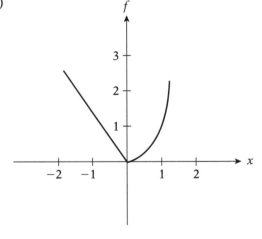

23. At what value of x is the line tangent to the graph of $y = x^2 + 3x + 5$ perpendicular to the line $x - 2y = 5$?

(A) $-\dfrac{5}{2}$

(B) -2

(C) $-\dfrac{1}{2}$

(D) $\dfrac{1}{2}$

(E) $\dfrac{5}{2}$

24. The function $f(x)$ graphed here is called a sawtooth wave. Which of the following statements about this function is true?

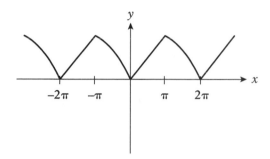

(A) $f(x)$ is continuous everywhere.
(B) $f(x)$ is differentiable everywhere.
(C) $f(x)$ is continuous everywhere but $x = n\pi$
(D) $f(x)$ is is an even function.
(E) $f(x)$ is a one-to-one function.

25. Find the derivative of $y = x^2 e^{x^2}$.

(A) $2xe^{x^2}(x^2 + 1)$

(B) $2xe^{x^2}$

(C) $2x^3 e^{x^2}$

(D) $4x^2 e^{x^2}$

(E) $x^4 e^{x^2}$

26. $\displaystyle\int_0^{\frac{\pi}{2}} e^{2-\cos x} \sin x \, dx =$

(A) $e^2 - e$

(B) 1

(C) 0

(D) e^2

(E) does not exist

27. The average value of $f(x) = -\dfrac{1}{x^2}$ on $\left[\dfrac{1}{2}, 1\right]$ is

(A) -2

(B) -1

(C) $-\dfrac{1}{2}$

(D) 2

(E) undefined

28. $f(x) = |x^2 - 3x|$. Find $f'(1)$.

(A) -3

(B) -1

(C) 1

(D) 3

(E) does not exist

Section I

Part B

A graphing calculator is required for some questions.

1. Which of the following statements is true about the figure?

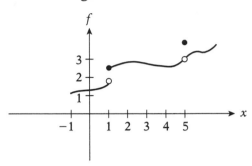

   (A) $\lim_{x \to 5} f(x)$ exists

   (B) $\lim_{x \to 1} f(x)$ exists

   (C) $\lim_{x \to 5} f(x) = f(5)$

   (D) $\lim_{x \to 1} f(x) = f(1)$

   (E) $\dfrac{f(5) - f(1)}{5 - 1} = f'(c)$

2. How many points of inflection are there for the function $y = x + \cos 2x$ on the interval $[0, \pi]$?

   (A) 0

   (B) 1

   (C) 2

   (D) 3

   (E) 4

3. The graph of the function $f(x)$ is shown below.

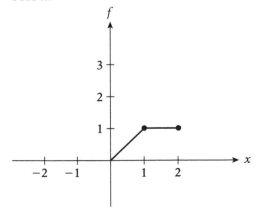

If $F'(x) = f(x)$, and $F(0) = -3$, then $F(2) =$

   (A) -4.5

   (B) -1.5

   (C) 1.5

   (D) 3

   (E) 4.5

4. If $\lim_{h \to 0} \dfrac{f(3 + h) - f(3)}{h} = 0$, then which of the following must be true?

   I f has a derivative at $x = 3$.
   II f is continuous at $x = 3$.
   III f has a critical value at $x = 3$.

   (A) I only

   (B) II only

   (C) I and II

   (D) I and III

   (E) I, II, and III

5. Consider the function $y = x^3 - x^2 - 1$. For what value(s) of x is the slope of the tangent equal to 5?

   (A) -1 only

   (B) $\dfrac{5}{3}$ only

   (C) -1 and $\dfrac{5}{3}$

   (D) $\dfrac{1}{3}$

   (E) 2.219

6. A pebble thrown into a pond creates circular ripples such that the rate of change of the circumference is 12π cm/sec. How fast is the area of the ripple changing when the radius is 3 cm?

   (A) 6π cm²/sec

   (B) 2π cm²/sec

   (C) 12π cm²/sec

   (D) 36π cm²/sec

   (E) 6 cm²/sec

7. If $y = x^2 + 1$, what is the smallest positive value of x such that $\sin y$ is a relative maximum?

(A) 0.756

(B) 0.841

(C) 1

(D) 1.463

(E) 1.927

8. Find the area in the first quadrant bounded by $y = 2 \cos x$, $y = 3 \tan x$, and the y-axis.

(A) 0.347

(B) 0.374

(C) 0.432

(D) 0.568

(E) 1.040

9. In the following figure, region R bounded by $x = y^2$ and the line $x = 4$ is the base of a solid. Cross sections of the solid perpendicular to the x-axis are semicircles with diameters in the plane of the region.

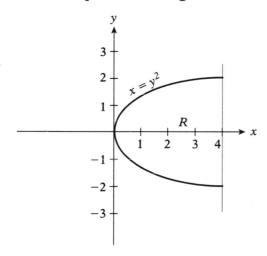

Which of the following represents the volume of the solid?

(A) π

(B) 4π

(C) 8π

(D) $\dfrac{32}{3}\pi$

(E) 16π

10. $f'(x) = x^3(x-2)^4(x-3)^2$. $f(x)$ has a relative maximum at $x =$

(A) 0

(B) 2

(C) 2 and 3

(D) 0 and 3

(E) There is no relative maximum.

11. Find the average rate of change of $f(x) = \sec x$ on the interval $\left[0, \dfrac{\pi}{3}\right]$.

(A) 0.396

(B) 0.955

(C) 1.350

(D) 1.910

(E) undefined

12. $a(t) = \dfrac{5t^2 + 1}{5t}$ and $v(1) = 1$. Find $v(2)$.

(A) 1.139

(B) 2.10

(C) 2.139

(D) 2.639

(E) undefined

13. Use the table shown to approximate the area under the curve of $y = f(x)$ using trapezoids.

x	y
0	1
1	2
3	4
4	1

(A) 5.5

(B) 8

(C) 10

(D) 11

(E) 20

14. In the figure shown, which of the following is true?

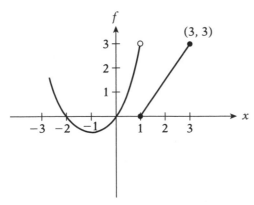

(A) $\lim\limits_{x \to 1} f(x) = 3$

(B) $\lim\limits_{x \to 1^+} f(x) = 3$

(C) $f'(1) = 1$

(D) $f(1) = 3$

(E) The average rate of change of $f(x)$ on $[1, 3]$ equals $f'(2)$.

15. The region enclosed by the graphs of $y = \sqrt{x}$, $y = 2$, and the y-axis is rotated about the line $y = 4$. Write an integral that represents the volume of the solid generated.

(A) $2\pi \int_0^2 \sqrt{x}\, dx$

(B) $\pi \int_0^2 \left(4 - \sqrt{x}\right) dx$

(C) $\pi \int_0^4 \left(\left(4 - \sqrt{x}\right)^2 - 4\right) dx$

(D) $\pi \int_0^2 \left(\left(4 - \sqrt{x}\right)^2 - 4\right) dx$

(E) $\pi \int_0^4 \left(4 - \sqrt{x}\right)^2 dx$

16. The position of a particle on a line is given by $x(t) = t^3 - t, t \geq 0$. Find the distance traveled by the particle in the first two seconds.

(A) 0.385

(B) 3.385

(C) 6

(D) 6.385

(E) 6.770

17. $\int_a^b |f(x)|\, dx = p$ and $\left|\int_a^b f(x)\, dx\right| = q$. Which of the following must be true?

(A) $p = q$

(B) $p \geq q$

(C) $p \leq q$

(D) $p > q$

(E) $p < q$

Section II

Part A

A graphing calculator is required for some questions.

1. A rocket is launched with an initial velocity of zero, and with acceleration in feet per second per second defined by

$$a(t) = \begin{cases} 20e^{-t/2}, \text{ for } 0 \leq t \leq 10 \text{ seconds} \\ -16, \quad \text{ for } t > 10 \text{ seconds} \end{cases}$$

   (a) At what time does the rocket begin to descend?

   (b) How high does the rocket reach?

   (c) What is the velocity when the rocket impacts the earth?

   (d) Write a formula for the position of the rocket with respect to time for $t > 10$ seconds.

2. A leaky cylindrical oilcan has a diameter of 4 inches and a height of 6 inches. The can is full of oil and is leaking at the rate of 2 in.³/hr. The oil leaks into an empty conical cup with a diameter of 8 inches and a height of 8 inches.

   (a) At what rate is the depth of the oil in the conical cup rising when the oil in the cup is 3 inches deep?

   (b) When the oilcan is empty, what is the depth of the oil in the conical cup?

3. Consider the graph of the derivative of f.

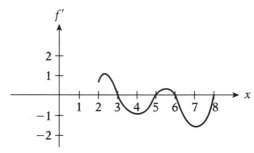

   (a) At what value(s) of x does f have a relative maximum? Justify your answer.

   (b) On what intervals is f concave up?

   (c) At what value(s) of x does f have a point of inflection? Justify your answer.

   (d) Is $f(3) > f(2)$? Justify your answer.

Section II

Part B

No calculator is allowed for these questions.

4. Region R is bounded by the graph of $y = x^{2/3}$, the x-axis, and the line $x = 8$.

   (a) For what value of k, $0 < k < 8$, does the line $x = k$ divide region R into two parts equal in area?

   (b) Region R is rotated about the x-axis. Find the value of p if the lines $x = p$ and $x = q$ $(p < q)$ divide the solid into three parts that have the same volume.

5. Consider the graph of $f(x)$ shown, which consists of four straight line segments.

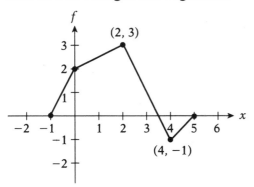

   If $h(x) = \displaystyle\int_1^x f(t)\, dt$,

   (a) Find $h(2)$ and $h(-1)$.

   (b) On what interval(s) is $h(x)$ decreasing? Justify your answer.

   (c) What are the critical values of h? Justify your answer.

   (d) What are the points of inflection of h? Justify your answer.

   (e) Find the absolute maximum and the absolute minimum of h. Justify your answer.

6. (a) Draw a slope field for the differential equation
   $$\frac{dy}{dx} = x(y - 1)$$
   for $0 \le x \le 2$ and $0 \le y \le 3$.

   (b) On the slope field drawn in part (a), sketch a solution to the differential equation with initial condition $y(0) = 2$.

   (c) Solve the differential equation with initial condition $y(0) = -1$.

1. $f(x) = 2x^3 - 6x^2 + 6x - 1$ has a point of inflection located at

   (A) $(0, -1)$

   (B) $(1, 1)$

   (C) $(2, 3)$

   (D) $(1, 0)$

   (E) $(-1, 1)$

2. Find the average value of $f(x)$ on the interval $[-1, 4]$ in the figure shown.

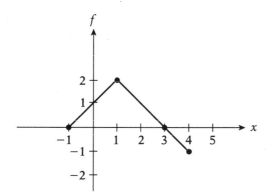

   (A) $-\dfrac{1}{5}$

   (B) $\dfrac{7}{10}$

   (C) $\dfrac{9}{10}$

   (D) $\dfrac{7}{2}$

   (E) $\dfrac{35}{2}$

3. $\displaystyle\int_{\frac{\pi}{2}}^{\pi} \sin x \cos x \, dx =$

   (A) -1

   (B) $-\dfrac{\sqrt{2}}{2}$

   (C) $-\dfrac{1}{2}$

   (D) 0

   (E) $\dfrac{1}{2}$

4. A function $f(x)$ is continuous on the closed interval $[a, b]$. Which of the following must be true?

   (A) $f(x)$ has a maximum on $[a, b]$.

   (B) $f(x)$ has a point of inflection on $[a, b]$.

   (C) $f'(c) = \dfrac{f(b) - f(a)}{b - a}$ for at least one c in the interval $[a, b]$.

   (D) $f'(c) = 0$ for at least one c in the interval $[a, b]$.

   (E) $f(x)$ has a critical value on the interval $[a, b]$.

5. Find the slope of the tangent to the graph of $3xy - 2x + 3y^2 = 5$ at the point $(2, 1)$.

   (A) $-\dfrac{1}{3}$

   (B) $-\dfrac{1}{12}$

   (C) $\dfrac{1}{12}$

   (D) 1

   (E) undefined

6. If $f(x) = \big(g(x)\big)^5$, $g(2) = -1$, and $f'(2) = 5$, find $g'(2)$.

   (A) -5

   (B) 0

   (C) $\dfrac{1}{5}$

   (D) 1

   (E) 5

7. $\dfrac{d}{dx}\left(\dfrac{x+1}{x+2}\right) =$

(A) 0

(B) 1

(C) $\dfrac{1}{x+2}$

(D) $\dfrac{1}{(x+2)^2}$

(E) $-\dfrac{1}{(x+2)^2}$

8. What is the instantaneous rate of change of $f(x) = \ln(\tan^2 x)$ at $x = \dfrac{\pi}{4}$?

(A) 0

(B) 1

(C) $\dfrac{\sqrt{3}}{2}$

(D) 4

(E) undefined

9. Consider the function
$$f(x) = \begin{cases} 2x^2 - x^3, & x < 2 \\ e^{2x-4}, & x \ge 2 \end{cases}.$$
Find $\displaystyle\lim_{x \to 2} f(x)$.

(A) 0

(B) 1

(C) 2

(D) 8

(E) does not exist

10. $f(x) = e^{\sin^2 x}$. $f'(x) =$

(A) $e^{\sin^2 x}$

(B) $2 \sin x e^{\sin^2 x}$

(C) $2 \sin x \cos x e^{\sin^2 x}$

(D) $e^{2\cos x}$

(E) $e^{\cos^2 x}$

11. $\displaystyle\int_0^{\frac{\pi}{3}} \sec x \tan x \, dx =$

(A) 0

(B) 1

(C) $\sqrt{2} - 1$

(D) $\sqrt{3} - 1$

(E) undefined

12. The position function for a particle's motion on a line is $x(t) = t^3 - t^2 - t + 1, t \ge 0$. At what value(s) of t is the particle at rest?

(A) $t = 0$

(B) $t = 1$

(C) $t = -1$ and $t = 1$

(D) $t = \dfrac{1}{3}$

(E) no value of t

13. At which value(s) of x on $[-3, 3]$ is $f(x)$ discontinuous?

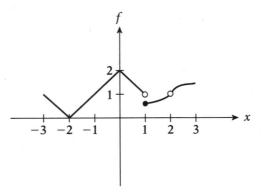

(A) $x = -2$

(B) $x = -2$ and $x = 1$

(C) $x = 1$

(D) $x = 1$ and $x = 2$

(E) $x = -2, x = 1$, and $x = 2$

14. $\displaystyle\int_0^1 \dfrac{x^2 - 1}{x^2 + 1} \, dx =$

(A) -1

(B) $1 - \dfrac{\pi}{2}$

(C) $1 - \dfrac{\pi}{3}$

(D) $1 - \dfrac{\pi}{4}$

(E) 1

15. $\dfrac{d}{dx}\left(\displaystyle\int_2^{2x} \sqrt[3]{1 + t} \, dt\right) =$

(A) $\sqrt[3]{1 + 2x} - \sqrt[3]{3}$

(B) $2\sqrt[3]{1 + 2x} - \sqrt[3]{3}$

(C) $2\sqrt[3]{1 + 2x}$

(D) $\sqrt[3]{1 + 4x^2}$

(E) $\sqrt[3]{1 + 2x}$

16. Consider the graph of f shown.

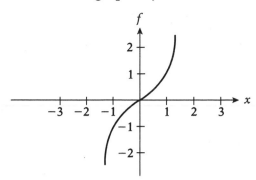

Which of the following is the graph of f'?

(A)

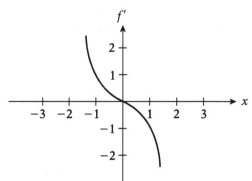

(B)

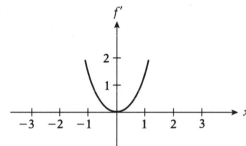

(C)

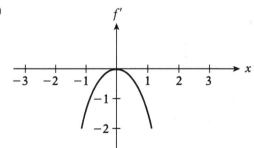

(D)

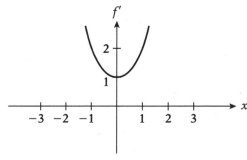

(E)

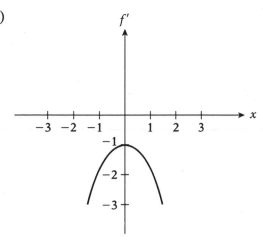

17. Find the equation of the line tangent to $y = \tan^2 x$ at $x = \frac{\pi}{3}$.

(A) $y - 3 = 8\sqrt{3}\left(x - \frac{\pi}{3}\right)$

(B) $y - 3 = 4\sqrt{3}\left(x - \frac{\pi}{3}\right)$

(C) $y - 3 = 2\sqrt{3}\left(x - \frac{\pi}{3}\right)$

(D) $y - 1 = 4\left(x - \frac{\pi}{3}\right)$

(E) $y - 1 = 4\sqrt{3}\left(x - \frac{\pi}{3}\right)$

18. $f'(x) = 2x(x + 1)(x + 2)^2$. $f(x)$ has

(A) a relative maximum at $x = -1$ and a relative minimum at $x = 0$

(B) relative maxima at $x = -1$ and $x = -2$, and a relative minimum at $x = 0$

(C) a relative maximum at $x = -2$ and a relative minimum at $x = 0$

(D) only a relative minimum at $x = 0$

(E) only a relative maximum at $x = -2$

19. The area under the graph of $y = \frac{1}{x}$ from $x = 1$ to $x = a$ (where $a > 1$) is equal to the area under the curve from $x = p$ (where $p < 1$) to $x = 1$. Express p in terms of a.

(A) $p = \frac{1}{a}$

(B) $p = -a$

(C) $p = \frac{1}{a^2}$

(D) $p = \frac{1}{\ln a}$

(E) $p = -\ln a$

20. $\frac{dy}{dt} = ky$ and $y(1) = 1$. Find $y(t)$ in terms of k and t.

   (A) $y = kt^2$

   (B) $y = k\sqrt{t}$

   (C) $y = e^{-kt}$

   (D) $y = e^{k(t-1)}$

   (E) $y = e^{kt} + 1$

21. Consider the function $f(x) = x^4 + 2x^2 + 1$. On what interval is $f(x)$ increasing?

   (A) $(-\infty, \infty)$

   (B) $(-\infty, 0)$

   (C) $(0, \infty)$

   (D) $(1, \infty)$

   (E) $(-\infty, 1)$

22. $a(t) = 6t - 12$ for $0 \le t \le 4$. If $v(0) = 18$, find the maximum velocity on the interval $[0, 4]$.

   (A) 0

   (B) 2

   (C) 4

   (D) 6

   (E) 18

23. $f(x) = \frac{1}{2}(2x + 5)^3$. $f'(x) =$

   (A) $\frac{3}{2}(2x + 5)^2$

   (B) $3(2x + 5)^2$

   (C) $3(2x + 5)$

   (D) $\frac{3}{2}(2x + 5)$

   (E) $6(2x + 5)$

24. The area enclosed by the curves $y = x^2 - 4$ and $y = 2x - 4$ can be represented by the integral

   (A) $\int_{-4}^{0}(x^2 - 2x)\,dx$

   (B) $\int_{0}^{2}(2x - x^2)\,dx$

   (C) $\int_{-4}^{0}(2x - x^2)\,dx$

   (D) $\int_{0}^{2}(x^2 - 2x)\,dx$

   (E) $\int_{-4}^{2}(x^2 - 2x)\,dx$

25. $\lim\limits_{x \to -\infty} \dfrac{2x}{\sqrt{x^2 + 1}} =$

   (A) -2

   (B) -1

   (C) 1

   (D) 2

   (E) undefined

26. $g(x)$ is a differentiable function on the closed interval $[a, b]$. Which of the following must be true?

   (A) For every x in $[a, b]$, $g(x)$ is between $g(a)$ and $g(b)$.

   (B) For every k between $g(a)$ and $g(b)$, there is a value c in $[a, b]$ such that $g(c) = k$.

   (C) There is at least one x in $[a, b]$ such that $g'(x) = 0$.

   (D) $\lim\limits_{x \to \infty} g(x)$ does not exist.

   (E) $g''(0) = 0$

27. The region enclosed by the graphs of $y = x^{2/3}$, $y = 4$, and the y-axis is rotated about the line $y = 4$. The volume of the solid generated can be represented by the integral

   (A) $2\pi \int_{0}^{8}(4 - x^{2/3})^2\,dx$

   (B) $\pi \int_{0}^{8}(4 - x^{2/3})^2\,dx$

   (C) $2\pi \int_{0}^{4}(4 - x^{2/3})^2\,dx$

   (D) $\pi \int_{0}^{4}(16 - x^{4/3})\,dx$

   (E) $\pi \int_{0}^{8}(16 - x^{4/3})\,dx$

28. On what interval(s) is the graph of $f(x) = \dfrac{x}{x^2 + 1}$ concave down?

   (A) $\left(0, \sqrt{3}\right)$

   (B) $\left(-\sqrt{3}, 0\right)$

   (C) $(0, \infty) \cup \left(-\sqrt{3}, 0\right)$

   (D) $\left(-\infty, -\sqrt{3}\right) \cup \left(0, \sqrt{3}\right)$

   (E) $\left(\sqrt{3}, \infty\right)$

Section I

Part B

A graphing calculator is required for some questions.

1. Find $\dfrac{dy}{dx}$ when $y = 0$ if $x \cos y - \sin x - 2 = 0$.

  (A) 0

  (B) 0.637

  (C) 1

  (D) 2.554

  (E) undefined

2. If $v(t) = \ln(t^2 + t + 1)$, then $a(1) =$

  (A) $\dfrac{1}{3}$

  (B) $\dfrac{2}{3}$

  (C) 1

  (D) $\dfrac{4}{3}$

  (E) 3

3. $y = \sec^2(2x + \pi)$. Find $y'\left(\dfrac{\pi}{2}\right)$.

  (A) 0

  (B) 2

  (C) 4

  (D) 8

  (E) undefined

4. $y = \dfrac{e^{2x-1}}{x}$ has

  I a relative minimum at $x = \dfrac{1}{2}$

  II a horizontal asymptote $y = 0$

  III a vertical asymptote $x = 0$

  (A) I only

  (B) I and II

  (C) I and III

  (D) II and III

  (E) I, II, and III

5. Find the shortest distance from $(3, 0)$ to a point on the curve $y = x^2 - 2x$.

  (A) 0.908

  (B) 1.0

  (C) 2.165

  (D) 2.20

  (E) 3.0

6. A solid is formed that has the region R as its base and cross sections perpendicular to the x-axis that are squares. Find the value of k so that the volume of the solid on the interval $[0, k]$ is half the total volume of the solid.

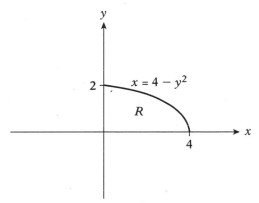

  (A) 0.568

  (B) 1.172

  (C) 2.201

  (D) 3.2

  (E) 3.567

7. $\dfrac{d}{dx}\left(\lim\limits_{h \to 0} \dfrac{\ln(x + h) - \ln x}{h}\right) =$

  (A) $-\dfrac{1}{x^2}$

  (B) $\dfrac{1}{x}$

  (C) -1

  (D) 0

  (E) undefined

8. Assuming that the function graphed here behaves like the function e^{-x} outside of the domain shown, which of the following is false?

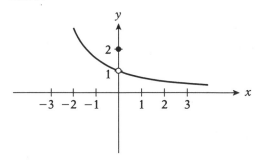

(A) $\lim\limits_{x \to 0} g(x) = 1$

(B) $\lim\limits_{x \to \infty} g(x) = 0$

(C) $g'(x) < 0$ for $x \neq 0$

(D) $g'(0) = 2$

(E) $g''(x) > 0$ for $x \neq 0$

9. For what value(s) of x are the lines tangent to $f(x) = \frac{1}{3}x^3 + 5$ and $g(x) = 4 + 2x - \frac{x^2}{2}$ parallel?

(A) $x = -2$ and $x = 1$

(B) $x = -2$ only

(C) $x = 1$ only

(D) $x = -3.475$ only

(E) $x = 4$ only

10. The equation of the line normal to $y = \frac{x^2}{x^2 + 1}$ at $x = 1$ is

(A) $y = -2x$

(B) $y = -2x - 1$

(C) $y = -2x + 2.5$

(D) $y = \frac{1}{2}x$

(E) $y = \frac{1}{2}x + 1$

11. A contractor is building a rectangular house that is 3,000 ft². What dimensions will require the least amount of building materials?

(A) $w = 31.65228$ ft, $l = 94.8683$ ft

(B) $w = 109.5445$ ft, $l = 27.3861$ ft

(C) $w = 54.7723$ ft, $l = 54.7723$ ft

(D) $w = 38.7298$ ft, $l = 77.4597$ ft

(E) $w = 98.9867$ ft, $l = 30.3071$ ft

12. $f(x) = \sin x$. Which of the following are true?

I $\int_{-a}^{a} f(x)\, dx = 2\int_{0}^{a} f(x)\, dx$

II $\int_{-a}^{a} f(x)\, dx = 0$

III $\int_{a}^{c} f(x)\, dx + \int_{c}^{b} f(x)\, dx = \int_{a}^{b} f(x)\, dx$, for $a < c < b$.

(A) I only

(B) II only

(C) III only

(D) I and III

(E) II and III

13. The derivative of $y(x) = \arcsin \frac{x}{2}$ on $-1 < x < 1$ is

(A) $y = \dfrac{1}{2\sqrt{1 - \frac{x^2}{4}}}$

(B) $y = \dfrac{1}{2\sqrt{1 - \sin(x)}}$

(C) $y = \dfrac{1}{2\cos\left(\arcsin \frac{x}{2}\right)}$

(D) $y = \dfrac{\arccos \frac{x}{2}}{2}$

(E) $y = -\dfrac{\arccos \frac{x}{2}}{2}$

14. In the graph shown, at which point is $\dfrac{dy}{dx} > 0$ and $\dfrac{d^2y}{dx^2} < 0$?

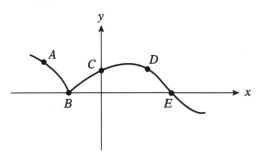

(A) A

(B) B

(C) C

(D) D

(E) E

15. If $f(x) = \begin{cases} x^2 + 2, & x < 1 \\ 2x + 1, & x \geq 1 \end{cases}$, which of the following is true about $f(x)$?

(A) The function is not continuous and not differentiable at $x = 1$.

(B) The function is continuous, but not differentiable at $x = 1$.

(C) The function is differentiable, but not continuous at $x = 1$.

(D) The function is both continuous and differentiable at $x = 1$.

(E) The function is not integratable.

16. If $f(x) = 3x^2 - 4$, then $\lim\limits_{x \to a} \dfrac{f'(x) - f'(a)}{x - a} =$

(A) $3a^2 - 4$

(B) $6a$

(C) 6

(D) 0

(E) does not exist

17. Find the area of the region enclosed by the semicircle $y = \sqrt{16 - x^2}$ and the line $y = 2$.

(A) 0.913

(B) 3.653

(C) 4.913

(D) 7.306

(E) 9.827

Section II

Part A

A graphing calculator is required for some questions.

1. The velocity, $v(t)$, of an object is a differentiable function of t. The table shows values of the velocity for integral values of t on the interval $[0, 4]$:

t	$v(t)$
0	5
1	8
2	15
3	10
4	5

(a) Show that the acceleration equals zero at least once in the interval $[0, 4]$. Justify your answer.

(b) Find the average rate of change of the velocity on the interval $[1, 4]$.

(c) If $x(t) = \int v(t)\, dt$ and $x(0) = 2$, use the Trapezoidal Rule with four equal subintervals on $[0, 4]$ to estimate $x(4)$.

2. Consider the function $y = \dfrac{kx}{x - k}$.

(a) Show that y is symmetric with respect to the line $y = x$.

(b) Write the equations of the horizontal and vertical asymptotes of y.

(c) Find the point(s) of intersection of y with the line $x - y = -2k$, and find the slope of the tangent line at the point(s) of intersection.

3. A line tangent to $y = x^2 + 1$ at $x = a, a > 0$, intersects the x-axis at point P.

(a) Write an expression for the area of the triangle formed by the tangent line, the x-axis, and the line $x = a$.

(b) For what value of a is the area of the triangle a minimum? Justify your answer.

Section II

Part B

No calculator is allowed for these questions.

4. Food is being poured into Fluffy the cat's bowl at the constant rate of 10 grams per day. Simultaneously, Fluffy is consuming the food at the rate of $\ln(t + 1)$ grams per day. At time $t = 0$, there are two grams of food in the bowl.

   (a) Find an expression for $B(t)$, the amount of food in the bowl at time t.

   (b) After four days, Joe, a dog who eats cat food, chases Fluffy away. How much food is in the bowl for Joe?

   (c) At what point is the bowl at its fullest?

   (d) At what point is the bowl empty?

5. Consider the function $f(x) = \frac{\sin(2x)}{x}$.

   (a) Find the domain of f.

   (b) State the interval(s) where f is increasing on $0 \le x \le 2\pi$. Justify your answer.

   (c) State the interval(s) where f is concave down on $0 \le x \le 2\pi$. Justify your answer.

   (d) Find $\lim_{x \to 0} f(x)$.

6. A spherical object with initial velocity 20 cm/sec is rolled down a smooth surface. The velocity of the object is described by the differential equation $\frac{dv}{dt} = -2v + 8$.

   (a) Find the velocity v of the object as a function of time t.

   (b) Find $\lim_{t \to \infty} v(t)$, the limiting velocity of the object.

Section I

Part A

No calculator is allowed for these questions.

1. If $f(x) = 2 \sin^2 5x$, $f'(x) =$
(A) $10 \sin 10x$
(B) $20 \sin 5x$
(C) $10 \sin 5x$
(D) $4 \cos 5x$
(E) $20 \cos 5x$

2. Find the x-intercept of the line tangent to $y = \ln(\ln(x))$ at $x = e$.
(A) $x = -1$
(B) $x = 0$
(C) $x = 1$
(D) $x = e$
(E) $x = -\dfrac{1}{e}$

3. $a(t) = 2e^t$ and $v(1) = 2$. Find $v(t)$.
(A) $2(e^t - e + 1)$
(B) $2(e^{t-1} + 1)$
(C) $2t + 1$
(D) $2e^t + e$
(E) $2e^t$

4. $\displaystyle \lim_{x \to -\infty} \dfrac{\ln(1-x)}{x^2+1} =$
(A) $-\infty$
(B) -1
(C) 0
(D) 1
(E) ∞

5. $y = \dfrac{e^{2x-1}}{x}$ has

  I   a relative minimum at $x = \dfrac{1}{2}$
  II a horizontal asymptote $y = 0$
  III a vertical asymptote $x = 0$

(A) I only
(B) I and II
(C) I and III
(D) II and III
(E) I, II, and III

6. For $f(x) = \begin{cases} x^2 + 2, & x < 1 \\ 2x + 1, & x \geq 1 \end{cases}$, which of the following is true?
(A) $f(x)$ is not continuous at $x = 1$.
(B) $f(x)$ is continuous but not differentiable at $x = 1$.
(C) $f(x)$ is differentiable but not continuous at $x = 1$.
(D) $f(x)$ is continuous and differentiable at $x = 1$.
(E) $f(2) = 6$

7. $\displaystyle \int_1^e x \ln x \, dx =$
(A) $\dfrac{e^2 + 1}{4}$
(B) $2e^2 - 1$
(C) $\dfrac{e^2 - e - 1}{2}$
(D) $2e^2 + 1$
(E) undefined

8. Find the area under the curve of $\frac{14x + 16}{x^2 + x - 20}$ on the interval [5, 10].

(A) $4 \ln\left(\frac{2}{3}\right) + 3 \ln(5)$

(B) $-40 \ln(5) + 54 \ln\left(\frac{3}{2}\right)$

(C) $8 \ln(6) + 6 \ln\left(\frac{3}{2}\right)$

(D) $9 \ln\left(\frac{4}{32}\right)$

(E) $2 \ln + \ln(7)$

9. Write an integral that represents the length of one arch of $y = \sin x$.

(A) $\int_0^{\frac{\pi}{2}} \sqrt{1 + \cos^2 x}\, dx$

(B) $\int_0^{\pi} \sqrt{1 + \cos^2 x}\, dx$

(C) $\int_0^{\frac{\pi}{2}} (1 + \cos x)\, dx$

(D) $\int_0^{\frac{\pi}{2}} \sin^2 x\, dx$

(E) $\int_0^{\frac{\pi}{2}} \sqrt{1 + \sin^2 x}\, dx$

10. For what values of a and c is the function $f(x) = \begin{cases} x + c, & x > 2 \\ ax^2, & x \le 2 \end{cases}$ differentiable at $x = 2$?

(A) $a = \frac{1}{2}, c = 0$

(B) $a = \frac{1}{4}, c = -1$

(C) $a = 1, c = 6$

(D) $a = 0, c = -2$

(E) no solution

11. The slope field below depicts a certain differential equation. Which of the following choices could be a solution to that equation?

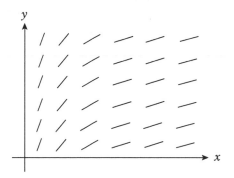

(A) $y = \ln(x)$

(B) $y = e^{-x}$

(C) $y = \sin(x)$

(D) $y = e^x$

(E) $y = x^2 \sin(x)$

12. The motion of a particle is given by the parametric equations $x = t^2 + t$ and $y = 3t - 2$. The speed of the particle at $t = 2$ is

(A) $2\sqrt{2}$

(B) $\sqrt{26}$

(C) $\sqrt{34}$

(D) 6

(E) $2\sqrt{13}$

13. $h(x) = \frac{f(x)}{(g(x))^2}$. If $f'(x) = g(x)$, $g'(x) = \frac{1}{f(x)}$, and $g(x) > 0$ for all real x, then $h'(x) =$

(A) $\frac{2}{(g(x))^3} - \frac{1}{g(x)}$

(B) $\frac{1}{g(x)} - \frac{2}{(g(x))^3}$

(C) $(g(x))^2 - 2$

(D) $\frac{1}{g(x)} - \frac{2f(x)}{(g(x))^3}$

(E) 0

14. Which of the following series converge?

I $\sum_{1}^{\infty} \frac{k}{n^2}$, where k is a constant

II $\sum_{1}^{\infty} \frac{(-1)^n}{\sqrt{n}}$

III $\sum_{1}^{\infty} (0.4)^{n-1}$

(A) I only
(B) II only
(C) III only
(D) I and III
(E) I, II, and III

15. The maximum value of $f(x) = \frac{\sqrt{x-3}}{x}$ occurs at $x =$

(A) -6
(B) $\frac{\sqrt{3}}{3}$
(C) 3
(D) 6
(E) 7

16. $y' = 2y + 5$. Find y'' in terms of y.

(A) 0
(B) 2
(C) $4y + 5$
(D) $4y + 10$
(E) $4y + 20$

17. For what value of c does $y = cx + \frac{3}{x}$ have a relative minimum at $x = 2$?

(A) $-\frac{2}{3} \ln 2$
(B) 0
(C) $\frac{3}{8}$
(D) $\frac{1}{2}$
(E) $\frac{3}{4}$

18. $f(x) = 3(x - 2)^2 + 6(x - 2) + 1$. Find the equation of the line tangent to $f(x)$ at $x = 2$.

(A) $6x - y = 11$
(B) $y = 0$
(C) $6x - y = 12$
(D) $6x - y = 13$
(E) $7x - y = 13$

19. Which of the following formulas could be used to calculate the average rate of change of $f(x)$ on the closed interval $[0, 4]$?

(A) $\frac{f(4) - f(0)}{2}$
(B) $\frac{f(0) + f(4)}{2}$
(C) $\frac{f(4) - f(0)}{4}$
(D) $\frac{f(0) + f(4)}{4}$
(E) $\frac{f'(4) - f'(0)}{4}$

20. $f(x) = \frac{x}{x - 3}$. If $f^{-1}(x)$ is the inverse of $f(x)$, find the derivative of f^{-1} at $x = -2$.

(A) -3
(B) $-\frac{1}{3}$
(C) $\frac{1}{3}$
(D) 1
(E) 3

21. An ellipse with equation $x^2 + 9y^2 = 9$ is the base of a solid in which each cross section perpendicular to the x-axis is a square. Find the volume of the solid.

(A) 4
(B) 8
(C) 16
(D) 32
(E) 64

22. $f(x) = 3x^3 - 4$. Find $\lim\limits_{x \to 2} \dfrac{f(x) - f(2)}{x - 2}$.

(A) 18

(B) 20

(C) 24

(D) 32

(E) 36

23. The graph of $f(x)$ is shown.

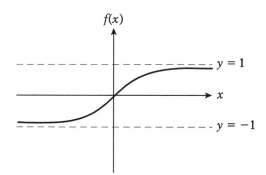

If $g(x) = f\left(\dfrac{1}{x}\right)$, find the value of $\lim\limits_{x \to 0^+} g(x)$.

(A) -1

(B) 0

(C) 1

(D) ∞

(E) does not exist

24. $y = \ln(\cos^2 x)$. $y' =$

(A) $-2 \tan x$

(B) $\sec^2 x$

(C) $2 \sec x$

(D) $2 \tan x$

(E) $-2 \sin x \cos x$

25. Write the equation of the line perpendicular to the tangent of the curve represented by the equation $y = e^{x+1}$ at $x = 0$.

(A) $y = -\dfrac{1}{e} x$

(B) $y = -\dfrac{1}{e} x + e$

(C) $y = ex + e$

(D) $y = \dfrac{1}{e} x + e$

(E) $y = ex$

26. $\displaystyle\int_1^\infty x e^{-x^2} dx$ is

(A) $\dfrac{1}{2}$

(B) 1

(C) $\dfrac{1}{2e}$

(D) 2

(E) divergent

27. Find the area bounded by the graph of $y = \dfrac{x}{x^2 - 1}$ and the x-axis on the interval $\left[-\dfrac{1}{2}, \dfrac{1}{2}\right]$.

(A) $\ln\left(\dfrac{3}{4}\right)$

(B) 0

(C) $\dfrac{1}{2} \ln\left(\dfrac{4}{3}\right)$

(D) $\ln\left(\dfrac{4}{3}\right)$

(E) $\ln 2$

28. $F(x)$ is the antiderivative of $f(x)$, $F(5) = 7$, and $\displaystyle\int_2^5 f(x)\, dx = 9$. Find $F(2)$.

(A) -16

(B) -7

(C) -2

(D) 2

(E) 16

Section I

Part B

A graphing calculator is required for some questions.

1. The region in the first quadrant bounded by $y = \sqrt[3]{x}$ and the line $x = 8$ forms the base of a solid. Cross sections of the solid perpendicular to the x-axis are squares. For what value of k does the line $x = k$ divide the solid into two solids of equal volume?

   (A) 4

   (B) 4.138

   (C) 5.278

   (D) $\frac{16}{3}$

   (E) 6.4

2. $f(x) = \cos x$. Which of the following are true?

   I $\displaystyle\int_{-a}^{a} \cos x \, dx = 2 \int_{0}^{a} \cos x \, dx$

   II $\displaystyle\int_{a}^{c} \cos x \, dx + \int_{c}^{b} \cos x \, dx = \int_{a}^{b} \cos x \, dx$

   III $\displaystyle\int_{-a}^{a} \cos x \, dx = 0$

   (A) I only

   (B) II only

   (C) I and II

   (D) II and III

   (E) I, II, and III

3. $\dfrac{d}{dt}\left(\displaystyle\int_{0}^{2t} \dfrac{1 - \cos x}{x} \, dx \right) =$

   (A) $\dfrac{1 - \cos 2t}{t}$

   (B) $\dfrac{1 - \cos 2t}{2t}$

   (C) $\sin 2t$

   (D) $2 \sin 2t$

   (E) $\dfrac{2t \sin 2t + \cos 2t}{2t^2}$

4. Find the slope of the tangent to the graph of $x \ln y + e^x = y$ at the point $(0, 1)$.

   (A) -1

   (B) 0

   (C) 1

   (D) 2

   (E) undefined

5. The graph of $f(x)$ is shown.

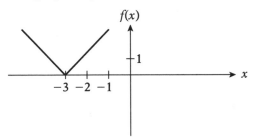

   Which of the following could be the graph of $f'(x)$?

   (A)

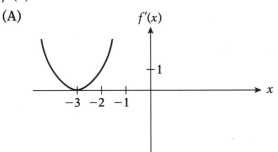

   (B)

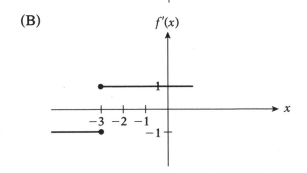

(C)

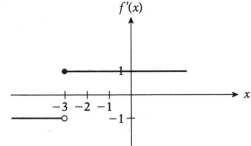

(D)

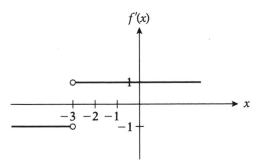

(E)

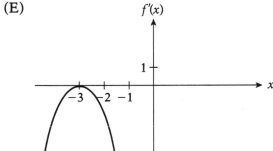

6. Let $f(x) = \sqrt{x^2 - x}$. Find $f'(1)$.

(A) $-\dfrac{1}{2}$

(B) 0

(C) $\dfrac{1}{2}$

(D) 1

(E) does not exist

7. Which of the following is NOT true about the function $f(x)$ shown?

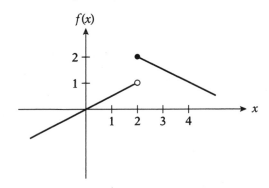

(A) $f(2) = 2$

(B) $\lim\limits_{x \to 2^-} f(x) = 1$

(C) $\lim\limits_{x \to 2} f(x) = 1$

(D) $f'(0) = \dfrac{1}{2}$

(E) $f'(x)$ does not exist at $x = 2$

8. In the figure, at which point is $\dfrac{dy}{dx}$ the smallest?

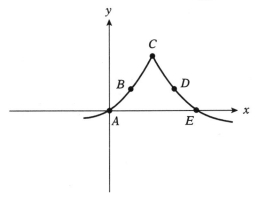

(A) A (D) D

(B) B (E) E

(C) C

9. The fourth-degree Taylor polynomial for $y = e^{\frac{1}{4}x}$, centered at $x = 0$, is

(A) $\displaystyle\sum_{n=0}^{\infty} \left(\dfrac{x}{4}\right)^n$

(B) $\displaystyle\sum_{n=1}^{\infty} \dfrac{x^n}{4^n}$

(C) $\displaystyle\sum_{n=1}^{\infty} \dfrac{x^n}{n(4^n)}$

(D) $\displaystyle\sum_{n=1}^{\infty} \dfrac{x^n}{(4^n)n!}$

(E) $\displaystyle\sum_{n=0}^{\infty} \dfrac{x^n}{n!(4^n)}$

10. $f'(x) = 0.25(x + 1)^3(2x + 5)(x - 3)^2$. The graph of $f(x)$ has

(A) no critical points

(B) one relative minimum and one relative maximum

(C) two relative minima and one relative maximum

(D) two relative minima and two relative maxima

(E) three relative minima and one relative maximum

11. Consider the function $y = \dfrac{x}{x^2 + 1}$. At what value of x is $\dfrac{dy}{dx}$ the largest?

(A) $-\sqrt{3}$

(B) -1

(C) 0

(D) 1

(E) $\sqrt{3}$

12. The acceleration a in ft/sec^2 of an object is given by the equation $a = -v$, where v is the velocity of the object in ft/sec. If the initial velocity is 1 ft/sec, then the position function could be

(A) Ce^{-t}

(B) Ce^{t}

(C) $e^{t} + c$

(D) $e^{-t} + c$

(E) $-e^{-t} + c$

13. Find the area of the region inside the limaçon $r = 2 - \cos\theta$, but outside the circle $r = \cos\theta$.

(A) $\dfrac{9}{2}\pi$

(B) $\dfrac{3}{4}\pi$

(C) $\dfrac{15}{4}\pi$

(D) $\dfrac{17}{4}\pi$

(E) 4π

14. The series $\displaystyle\sum_{n=1} \dfrac{1}{(12n + 1)(15n + 2)}$

(A) converges by the Comparison Test

(B) diverges by the p-Series Test

(C) converges by the Ratio Test

(D) diverges by the Ratio Test

(E) diverges by the Comparison Test

15. For $t \geq 0$, a particle moves along a line with position $s(t) = 2t^3 - 9t + 1$. What is the acceleration when the particle is at rest?

(A) -9

(B) -6.348

(C) 0

(D) 1

(E) 14.697

16. A taxi driver is going from LaGuardia Airport to Kennedy Airport at an average speed of v miles per hour. The distance is thirty miles and gas costs \$1.33 per gallon. The taxi consumes gas at a rate of $f(v) = 2 + \dfrac{v^2}{600}$ gallons per hour and $10 \leq v \leq 55$. What average speed will minimize the total cost of fuel?

(A) 10.0 mph

(B) 25.823 mph

(C) 54.46 mph

(D) 40.00 mph

(E) 34.641 mph

17. The series $\displaystyle\sum_{n=0}^{\infty} \left(\dfrac{4}{k}\right)^{n}$ converges to 5. Find the value of k.

(A) 1

(B) 2

(C) 4.5

(D) 5

(E) 8

Section II

Part A

A graphing calculator is required for some questions.

1. Let R be the region bounded by $y = \sin x$ and $y = \cos x$ on the interval $\left[\dfrac{\pi}{4}, \dfrac{5\pi}{4} \right]$.

   (a) Find the area of region R.

   (b) Find the volume when R is rotated about the line $y = -1$.

   (c) A solid is formed with region R as the base and such that each cross section perpendicular to the x-axis is a square. Find the volume of the solid.

2. $\dfrac{dy}{dt} = 0.03y(100 - y)$. If $y(0) = 10$,

   (a) For what values of y is y increasing?

   (b) For what value of y is y increasing the fastest?

   (c) Use Euler's method, the initial value, and a step $\Delta t = 0.1$ to approximate $y(0.2)$.

3. The motion of a particle is described by the set of parametric equations $x = \dfrac{t}{5} + 1$, $y = 2t - e^{t/2} + 1$, for $0 \le t \le 5$.

   (a) Find the coordinates of the absolute maximum and minimum. Justify your answer.

   (b) Find the x-intercept of the line tangent to the graph at $t = 2$.

   (c) Find the length of the graph from $t = 0$ to $t = 5$.

Part B

No calculator is allowed for these questions.

4. Consider the function $y = \sqrt[3]{x^3 - 1}$.

    (a) Find the coordinates of the points on the graph where the tangent line is vertical or horizontal.

    (b) Find $\lim\limits_{x \to \infty} \dfrac{\sqrt[3]{x^3 - 1}}{x}$ and $\lim\limits_{x \to -\infty} \dfrac{\sqrt[3]{x^3 - 1}}{x}$.

Interpret the end behavior of the graph of $y = \sqrt[3]{x^3 - 1}$ using the values of these limits.

    (c) Use the information in parts (a) and (b) to sketch the graph of y.

5. (a) Write the first four terms of the Maclaurin series for $f(x) = \dfrac{1}{1 + 2x}$, and express the series in sigma notation. State the interval of convergence for the series.

    (b) Use the series in part (a) to write the first four terms of the Maclaurin series for $\dfrac{1}{(1 + 2x)^2}$, and express the series in sigma notation. State the interval of convergence for the series.

    (c) Use the series in part (a) to write the Maclaurin series for $\ln(1 + 2x)$, and express the series in sigma notation. State the interval of convergence for the series.

6. The graph of the function $f(x)$ on the interval $[-2, 2]$ consists of two line segments and a semicircle.

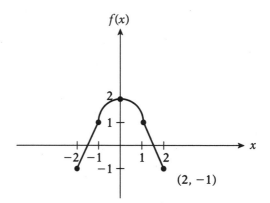

If $g(x) = \displaystyle\int_0^x f(t)\, dt$,

    (a) Find $g(0)$ and $g(2)$.

    (b) Find the relative maxima and minima of g. Justify your answer.

    (c) Find the point(s) of inflection of g. Justify your answer.

    (d) Sketch a graph of $g(x)$ on the interval $[-2, 2]$.

BC Model Examination 2

Section I

Part A

No calculator is allowed for these questions.

1. The sum $\frac{2}{5} + \frac{3}{5^2} + \frac{4}{5^3} + \cdots + \frac{n}{5^{n-1}} + \cdots$ approaches what value?
   - (A) $\frac{1}{16}$
   - (B) $\frac{1}{15}$
   - (C) $\frac{1}{2}$
   - (D) $\frac{9}{16}$
   - (E) $\frac{2}{3}$

2. Write the equation of the line tangent to the graph of $y = \frac{x+3}{x}$ at $x = 1$.
   - (A) $3x + y = 7$
   - (B) $-3x + y = 1$
   - (C) $3x + y = 13$
   - (D) $x - 3y + 11 = 0$
   - (E) $3y = 13 - x$

3. For what value of c does $y = cx + \frac{3}{x^2}$ have a relative minimum at $x = 2$?
   - (A) $-\frac{3}{4}$
   - (B) $-\frac{3}{8}$
   - (C) 0
   - (D) $\frac{3}{4}$
   - (E) 6

4. $f(x) = \frac{5x}{x-5}$. Find the average rate of change of $f'(x)$ on the closed interval $[0, 4]$.
   - (A) -12.6

   - (B) $-\frac{13}{2}$
   - (C) -6
   - (D) -5
   - (E) 6

5. $\int_0^\infty \frac{\ln(x)}{x}\, dx =$
   - (A) -1
   - (B) 0
   - (C) $\frac{1}{2}$
   - (D) 1
   - (E) diverges

6. For what values of a and c is the function $f(x) = \begin{cases} ax^2, & x \le 2 \\ x + c, & x > 2 \end{cases}$ differentiable for all real values of x?
   - (A) $a = \frac{1}{2}, c = 0$
   - (B) $a = \frac{1}{4}, c = -1$
   - (C) $a = 1, c = 6$
   - (D) $a = 0, c = -2$
   - (E) for no values of a and c

7. $\lim_{x \to \infty} \frac{\ln(\ln(x))}{\ln(x)} =$
   - (A) diverges
   - (B) 0
   - (C) $\frac{1}{2}$
   - (D) 1
   - (E) e

8. $\lim\limits_{x \to \infty} x^5 e^{-x/5} =$

   (A) $-\infty$

   (B) -1

   (C) 0

   (D) 1

   (E) ∞

9. $\dfrac{dx}{dt} = 5x^2$ and $x = 5$ when $t = 0$. Find the value of x when $t = 1$.

   (A) $-\dfrac{5}{24}$

   (B) $\dfrac{5}{24}$

   (C) $\dfrac{1}{5}e$

   (D) $\dfrac{5}{4}$

   (E) $5e$

10. A particle travels on a number line with velocity $v(t) = t \cos t$. Find the distance traveled from $t = 0$ to $t = \dfrac{\pi}{2}$.

    (A) $\dfrac{\pi}{2}$

    (B) $\dfrac{\pi}{2} - 1$

    (C) $\dfrac{\pi}{2} + 1$

    (D) 1

    (E) $1 - \dfrac{2}{\pi}$

11. Given $\dfrac{dy}{dx} = x^2 y + x^2 + y + 1$, and $y(0) = 0$, then $y =$

    (A) $e^{\frac{x^2}{2}+1} - 1$

    (B) $\dfrac{x^3}{3} + x$

    (C) $e^{\frac{x^3}{3}+x} - 1$

    (D) $e^{\frac{x^3}{3}+x-1}$

    (E) $\ln\left(\dfrac{x^3}{3} + x\right) - 1$

12. $f(x) = \ln |x^2 - 2x|$. $f'(x) =$

    (A) $\dfrac{2x - 2}{x^2 - 2x}$

    (B) $\left|\dfrac{2x - 2}{x^2 - 2x}\right|$

    (C) $\dfrac{|2x - 2|}{x^2 - 2x}$

    (D) $\dfrac{2x - 2}{|x^2 - 2x|}$

    (E) does not exist

13. Find the interval of convergence of the series $\sum\limits_{n=1}^{\infty} \left(\dfrac{x}{n}\right)^n$, where x is a real number.

    (A) $[0, \infty)$

    (B) $[-1, 0]$

    (C) $[-1, 1]$

    (D) $[0, 1]$

    (E) $(-\infty, \infty)$

14. What function is approximated by the following series?

    $$(x - 2) - \dfrac{(x - 2)^2}{2} + \dfrac{(x - 2)^3}{3} - \cdots$$

    (A) e^{x-2}

    (B) $\ln(x - 2)$

    (C) $\ln(x - 1)$

    (D) $\sin(x - 2)$

    (E) $\cos(x - 2)$

15. $\dfrac{dy}{dx} = 5e^{-y}$ and $y(0) = 0$. Find the value of $\dfrac{d^2 y}{dx^2}$ at $x = 0$.

    (A) -25

    (B) -5

    (C) 0

    (D) 5

    (E) 25

16. A company has 1,000 widgets and will be able to sell them all if the price is a dollar. The company will sell one less widget for each 10-cent increase in the price it charges. What price will maximize revenues, where revenue is the selling price times the quantity sold?

    (A) $2.50

    (B) $14.50

    (C) $22.30

    (D) $25.30

    (E) $50.50

17. $\int x^2 \sqrt{x+1}\, dx =$

(A) $\frac{2}{7}(x+1)^{7/2} - \frac{4}{5}(x+1)^{5/2}$
$+ \frac{2}{3}(x+1)^{3/2} + C$

(B) $\frac{2}{7}(x+1)^{7/2} - \frac{2}{5}(x+1)^{5/2}$
$+ \frac{4}{3}(x+1)^{3/2} + C$

(C) $\frac{10}{7}(x+1)^{7/2} - 2x^{1/2} + C$

(D) $(x+1)^{3/2}\left(\frac{4}{5}x^2 - x + 1\right) + C$

(E) $(x+1)^{3/2}\left(\frac{2}{7}x^2 - x + 1\right) + C$

18. If f is continuous for all real numbers, find
$$\lim_{h \to 0^+} \frac{\int_0^{h^2} f(t)\, dt}{h}.$$

(A) $f(h^2) - f(0)$
(B) $f(h^2)$
(C) $2h\, f(h^2)$
(D) $2h\, f(h^2) - f(0)$
(E) 0

19. Which of the following statements are true about $\displaystyle\sum_{n=3}^{\infty} \frac{1}{\sqrt[3]{n(n-1)(n-2)}}$

I converges by the p-Series Test
II diverges by Comparison Test
III grows less quickly than
$1 + \frac{1}{2} + \frac{1}{3} + \frac{1}{4} + \cdots$

(A) I only
(B) II only
(C) III only
(D) I and III
(E) II and III

20. Which of the following is the series representation for $\dfrac{1}{1+5x}$?

(A) $\displaystyle\sum_{n=0}^{\infty} (-1)^n (5x)^n$

(B) $\displaystyle\sum_{n=0}^{\infty} (-1)^{n+1} (5x)^n$

(C) $\displaystyle\sum_{n=0}^{\infty} (-1)^n \frac{(5x)^n}{n!}$

(D) $\displaystyle\sum_{n=0}^{\infty} \frac{(5x)^n}{n}$

(E) $\displaystyle\sum_{n=1}^{\infty} (-1)^n (5x)^n$

21. If the motion of a particle on a number line is described by $a(t) = 2t + 2$ and $v(1) = 4$ for $t \geq 0$, find the distance traveled by the particle in the first three seconds.

(A) 8
(B) 15
(C) 21
(D) 24
(E) cannot be determined

22. Find the equation of the line tangent to $y = (\arctan x)^2$ at $x = 1$.

(A) $y = \dfrac{\pi}{4x} + \dfrac{\pi^2}{16}$

(B) $y = \dfrac{\pi}{4x} - \dfrac{\pi^2}{16}$

(C) $y = \dfrac{\pi}{4x} + \dfrac{\pi(\pi - 4)}{16}$

(D) $y = \dfrac{\pi}{4}$

(E) does not exist

23. Find the area of the inner loop of the polar curve $r = 1 + 2\cos\theta$.

(A) 2π
(B) $2\pi - 3\sqrt{3}$
(C) 3π
(D) $\pi + \dfrac{3\sqrt{2}}{2}$
(E) $\pi - \dfrac{3\sqrt{2}}{2}$

24. $g(x) = \displaystyle\int_e^x \ln(1 + t)\, dt$. Find the derivative of $(g'(x))^2$ at $x = e - 1$.

(A) 0
(B) $\dfrac{2}{e}$
(C) 1
(D) 2
(E) does not exist

25. Find the derivative of $\ln|x^2 - 2x|$.

(A) $\dfrac{1}{|x^2 - 2x|}$

(B) $\dfrac{2x - 2}{|x^2 - 2x|}$

(C) $\left|\dfrac{2x - 2}{x^2 - 2x}\right|$

(D) $\dfrac{2x - 2}{x^2 - 2x}$

(E) $\dfrac{|2x - 2|}{x^2 - 2x}$

26. The voltage in a particular electrical circuit is $v(t) = 2\sin(3\pi t)$. The current through the circuit is $i(t) = \dfrac{dv}{dt}$. If the power consumed by the circuit is $p(t) = i(t)v(t)$, find the average power consumed for $0 < t < \pi$.

(A) 0

(B) $\dfrac{2}{\pi}\left(\sin^2(3\pi^2)\right)$

(C) $-\dfrac{2}{\pi}\left(\sin^2(3\pi^2)\right)$

(D) $\dfrac{4}{\pi}\left(\sin^2(3\pi^2)\right)$

(E) $\dfrac{2}{3\pi}\left(\sin^2(3\pi^2)\right)$

27. F is the antiderivative of $f(x) = -2x^2 + 4x$. If $F(0) = 5$, then $F(1) =$

(A) $\dfrac{4}{3}$

(B) $\dfrac{7}{3}$

(C) $\dfrac{11}{3}$

(D) $\dfrac{19}{3}$

(E) $\dfrac{23}{3}$

28. Find the linear approximation to $e^{x/2}$ at $x = 0$, and use it to approximate $\sqrt{e}$.

(A) 0.75

(B) 1.25

(C) 1.5

(D) 2

(E) $\dfrac{\sqrt{6}}{2}$

Section I

Part B

A graphing calculator is required for some questions.

1. Find the remainder when $\dfrac{1}{\sqrt{e}}$ is approximated by a third-degree MacLaurin polynomial.

(A) 0.0024

(B) 0.0208

(C) 0.2916

(D) 0.5833

(E) 1.6667

2. In the graph of g, $g = f'$ and $f(0) = 2$.

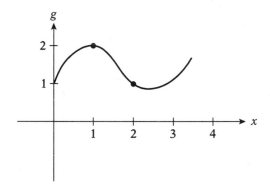

Which of the following are true?

  I $g(1) > g(2)$

 II $f(1) < f(2)$

III $f''(3) > 0$

(A) I only

(B) II only

(C) I and II

(D) I and III

(E) I, II, and III

3. Find the area in the first quadrant bounded by the graphs of $y = \dfrac{1}{x} - 1$, $y = 2x$, and the x-axis.

(A) 0.443

(B) 0.5

(C) 0.886

(D) 1

(E) does not exist

4. Find the length of the curve described by the parametric equations $x(t) = 2\sin(t)$ and $y(t) = 2\ln(\sin t)$ on $0.1 \le t \le 1.0$.

(A) 2.042

(B) 3.243

(C) 4.491

(D) 4.587

(E) undefined

5. If f is differentiable on (a, b), continuous on $[a, b]$, and $f(a) = f(b)$, which of the following statements could be false?

(A) $\lim\limits_{x \to x_0} f(x)$ exists for all $a < x_0 < b$.

(B) f has a point of inflection in $[a, b]$.

(C) f has a maximum.

(D) There exists $c > a$ and $c < b$ such that $f'(c) = 0$.

(E) There exists $c > a$ and $c < b$ such that $f(b) - f(a) = f'(c)(b - a)$.

6. Find the value of

$$\lim_{n \to \infty} \frac{1}{n}\left(\sqrt{1 - \frac{1}{n^2}} + \sqrt{1 - \frac{4}{n^2}} + \sqrt{1 - \frac{9}{n^2}} \right.$$
$$\left. + \cdots + \sqrt{1 - \left(\frac{n-1}{n}\right)^2} \right).$$

(A) π

(B) $\dfrac{\pi}{4}$

(C) $\dfrac{\pi}{2}$

(D) 2

(E) does not exist

7. $\int_0^1 \dfrac{1}{\sqrt{1-x^2}}\,dx =$

(A) $-\dfrac{\pi}{2}$

(B) $\dfrac{1}{2}$

(C) 1

(D) $\dfrac{\pi}{2}$

(E) not defined

8. The area of $r = 2 + \cos(\theta)$ on $0 \le \theta \le \pi$ is

(A) 2π

(B) $\dfrac{9\pi}{4}$

(C) π

(D) $\dfrac{5\pi}{4}$

(E) $\dfrac{3\pi}{4}$

9. $f(x) = 4x - x^3$ on the interval $[0, 2]$. Find the point of intersection of the lines tangent to the graph of f at the endpoints of the interval.

(A) $(1.333, 5.333)$

(B) $(1, 3)$

(C) $(1, 4)$

(D) $(0.75, 3.578)$

(E) $(1.155, 3.079)$

10. Let $f(x) = xe^{x^2}$. If g is the inverse of f, then $g'(e) =$

(A) 0

(B) $\dfrac{1}{4e}$

(C) $\dfrac{1}{3e}$

(D) $\dfrac{1}{e}$

(E) e

11. Use the Trapezoidal Rule with five equal subintervals to approximate $\int_0^1 \ln(x^2 + 1)\,dx$.

(A) 0.264

(B) 0.267

(C) 0.337

(D) 0.385

(E) 0.534

12. $y' = xy + 2y$ and $y(0) = 1$. What is the result when you use Euler's method with $\Delta x = 0.1$ to approximate $y(0.3)$?

(A) 1.452

(B) 1.771

(C) 1.906

(D) 2.338

(E) 2.411

13. If $h(x) = \sqrt{\sin(f(x))}$, $f(0) = \dfrac{\pi}{3}$, and $f'(0) = e$, approximate $h'(0)$.

(A) -1.6864

(B) -0.84321

(C) -0.3102

(D) 0.6409

(E) 0.73024

14. Water leaks from a storage tank at a rate $R(t) = 2te^{-0.5t}$, in thousands of gallons per day, $t \ge 0$. How many gallons have leaked at the end of the first week, to the nearest gallon?

(A) $3{,}456$ gallons

(B) $6{,}191$ gallons

(C) $6{,}407$ gallons

(D) $6{,}913$ gallons

(E) $13{,}826$ gallons

15. If $y = 2x(x - 2)^2 - p$, for how many integer values of p does y have three distinct zeros?

(A) 0

(B) 1

(C) 2

(D) 3

(E) 4

16. $g(x) = \int_0^x (\ln(1 + t))^2\,dt$. Find $g'(e - 1)$.

(A) 1

(B) $\dfrac{2}{e}$

(C) $\dfrac{2\ln(1 + e)}{e}$

(D) $\dfrac{2\ln(1 + e)}{e + 1}$

(E) $\dfrac{2}{e + 1}$

17. Which of the following series are conditionally convergent?

I $\displaystyle\sum_{0}^{\infty} \frac{(-1)^n}{n!}$

II $\displaystyle\sum_{1}^{\infty} \frac{(-1)^{n+1} n^2}{n^2 + n}$

III $\displaystyle\sum_{0}^{\infty} \frac{(-1)^{n+1} 3^n}{5^n}$

(A) none

(B) I only

(C) I and II

(D) II and III

(E) I, II, and III

Part A

A graphing calculator is required for some questions.

1. $f(x)$ has derivatives of all orders for all real numbers.

   $$f(1) = 1 \text{ and } f^{(n)}(1) = \frac{n}{2^n} \text{ for } n \geq 1.$$

   (a) Write a 3rd-degree Taylor polynomial for $f(x)$ centered at $c = 1$ and use it to approximate $f(1.2)$.

   (b) Write a 4th-degree Taylor polynomial for
   $$F(x) = \int_1^x f(t)dt \text{ centered at } c = 1. \text{ Deter-}$$
   mine the exact value of $F(2)$, or explain why it cannot be determined.

   (c) Suppose $g(x) = (x - 1) f(x)$. Use part (a) to find a 2nd-degree Taylor polynomial for $g'(x)$. Then use it to approximate $g'(2)$.

2. Given $y = \ln(x - 1)$ on the closed interval $[2, e + 1]$:

   (a) Find the average value of y on the interval.

   (b) Find the value of k so that the line $x = k$ divides the area under the curve into two regions of equal area.

   (c) Write an integral for the volume of the solid generated when the area under the curve is rotated about the line $y = 1$.

3. Consider the function $f(x) = x^2 + 2$.

   (a) Write the equation of the line tangent to $f(x)$ at point $P(a, f(a))$, where $0 < a < 4$.

   (b) Write an expression for $A(x)$ in terms of a, where $A(x)$ is the area of the triangle formed by the tangent line in part (a), the x-axis, and the line joining P and $(4, 0)$.

   (c) Find the value of a that makes $A(x)$ a minimum. Justify your answer.

Section II

Part B

No calculator is allowed for these questions.

4. Consider the differential equation $\dfrac{dy}{dt} = 5y - 5$.

   (a) Draw a slope field for the given differential equation for $-3 < t < 3$.

   (b) Solve the differential equation given that $y(0) = 5$.

   (c) Find the equation of the horizontal asymptote of the graph of the solution in part (b).

5. A water balloon is filled at a rate of 20 cubic inches per second. Assume that the balloon is a perfect sphere. Volume of sphere $= \dfrac{4}{3}\pi r^3$.

   (a) Write an equation for the change in volume as a function of the change in radius.

   (b) How fast is the radius of the balloon increasing when the radius is 10 inches?

   (c) Suppose the balloon later develops a tiny hole from which water escapes at the rate of $e^{-\frac{V}{3}}$ cubic inches/sec. Find an expression for $\dfrac{dV}{dt}$ under this condition.

   (d) How fast is the radius of the leaky balloon changing when the radius is 10 inches?

6. Consider the function $y = \dfrac{e^{2-2x^2}}{x}$.

   (a) Find y' and determine whether y' is even, odd, or neither.

   (b) On what interval(s) is y decreasing?

   (c) Find the coordinates of the point of inflection.

   (d) On what interval(s) is y concave up?

   (e) Find the range of y.

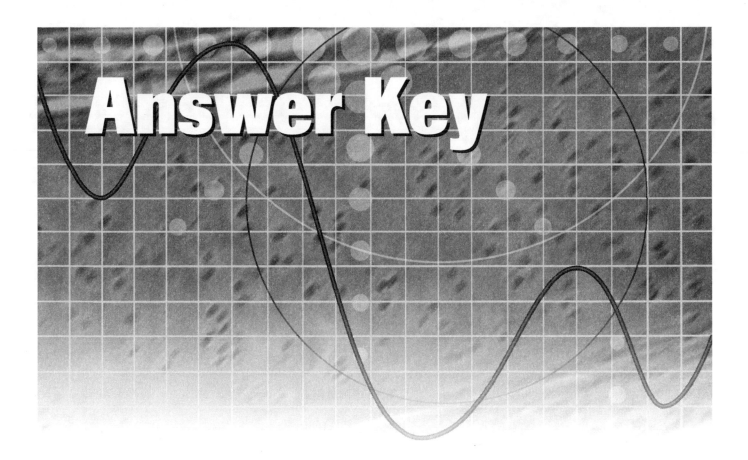

Answer Key

Chapter 2 Functions and Their Properties

2.1 A Review of Basic Functions

Exercises (pages 19–20)

Multiple-Choice Questions

1. (A) 0 and 3. $f(x) = x^4 - 3x^3 = x^3(x - 3)$

2. (D) Arctan $\sqrt{3}$ is the angle whose tangent is $\sqrt{3}$. Referring to the table, find that the angle is $\frac{\pi}{3}$.

3. (D) The equation is the same as $\cos^2 x = 1$.
   The only numbers that can be squared to produce 1 are 1 and -1.
   $\cos x = 1$ or $\cos x = -1$.
   $\cos x = 1$ at 0 and 2π in $[0, 2\pi]$.
   $\cos x = -1$ at π in $[0, 2\pi]$.
   So the solution set is $\{0, \pi, 2\pi\}$.

4. (C) $\ln 3$

5. (B) $\{y > -1\}$. $(x - 1)^2$ on $x < 1$ has range $\{y > 0\}$; $2x - 3$ on $x > 1$ has the larger range $\{y > -1\}$.

6. (E) $y = 5$. The ratio of 5 in the numerator and 1 in the denominator.

7. (C) $x = 1$. Set the denominator $(x - 1)$ equal to zero.

8. (A) $2x + 2h - 3$.
   $f(x + h) = 2(x + h) - 3 = 2x + 2h - 3$

9. (C)

10. (D)

11. (A)

12. (D)

13. (A)

14. (E)

Free-Response Questions

1.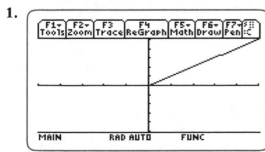

   Domain = $\{x > 0\}$, range = $\{y > 0\}$. (The log is undefined for $x \leq 0$.)

2. (a) From the vertical asymptote, we know that $2b + c = 0$, and therefore $c = -2b$. From the horizontal asymptote, we know that $\frac{a}{b} = 3$, and therefore $a = 3b$. Thus,

   $$y = \frac{ax}{bx + c} = \frac{3bx}{bx - 2b} = \frac{3x}{x - 2}.$$

   (b) Graph the function, showing the vertical and horizontal asymptotes.

   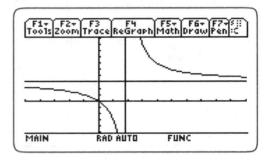

3. Answers will vary. Example:

   $$f(x) = \begin{cases} x, & x < 2 \\ 2x, & 2 \leq x \leq 4 \\ \dfrac{x}{2}, & 4 < x \end{cases}.$$

4. $\arccos \dfrac{3}{4}$

5. (a) The graphs of $\cos x$ and $\cos|x|$ are the same. $|\cos x|$ is the graph of $\cos x$ with portions below the x-axis reflected above the x-axis.

   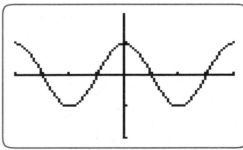

   $f(x) = \cos x$

   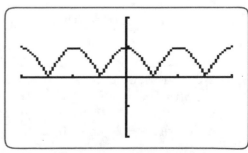

   $f(x) = |\cos x|$

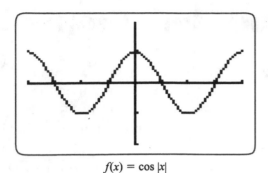

$f(x) = \cos|x|$

(b) The graph of $|\sin x|$ is the graph of $\sin x$ with portions below the x-axis reflected above the x-axis. The graph of $\sin|x|$ is the same as $y = \sin x$ for $x \geq 0$; for $x < 0$, reflect the graph of $\sin x$ ($x \geq 0$) in the y-axis.

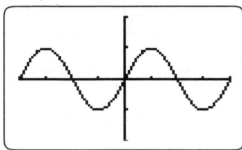

$f(x) = \sin x$

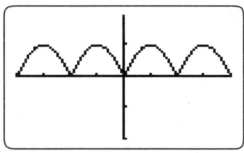

$f(x) = |\sin x|$

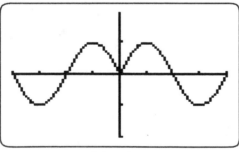

$f(x) = \sin|x|$

(c) The graph of $y = |x^2 - 2x|$ is the graph of $y = x^2 - 2x$ with portions below the x-axis reflected above the x-axis. The graph of $y = |x|^2 - 2|x|$ is the same as $x^2 - 2x$ for $x \geq 0$; for $x < 0$, reflect the graph of $x^2 - 2x$ ($x \geq 0$) in the y-axis.

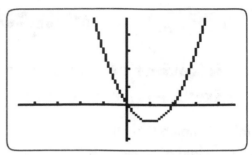

$f(x) = x^2 - 2x$

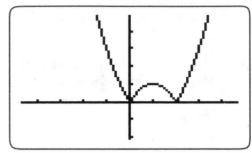

$f(x) = |x^2 - 2x|$

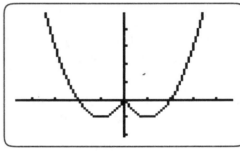

$f(x) = |x|^2 - 2|x|$

6. (a) Answers will vary. One possible solution is $y = (x - 3)^2(x^2 - 2x + 2)$.

   (b) $y = \dfrac{2(x + 1)(x - 2)}{(x + 1)(x - 1)}$

2.2 Lines

Exercises (page 22)

Multiple-Choice Questions

1. (A)

2. (C)

3. (D)

4. (C)

5. (B)

6. (C)

Free-Response Questions

1. (a) $x = 2$
   (b) Yes.
   (c) $y = \frac{1}{2}x + \frac{1}{2}$
   (d) No.

2. (a) $y - 4 = \frac{1}{5}(x - 2)$
   (b) $D(7, 5)$

2.3 Properties of Functions

Exercises (pages 27–28)

Multiple-Choice Questions

1. (B)
2. (B)
3. (C)
4. (D)
5. (E)
6. (C)
7. (C)
8. (B)
9. (A)
10. (C)

Free-Response Questions

1. $1, \dfrac{-1 \pm i\sqrt{11}}{2}$

2. (a)

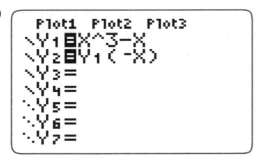

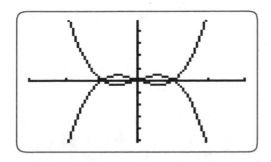

Y_2 is the opposite of Y_1 because Y_1 is odd.

(b)

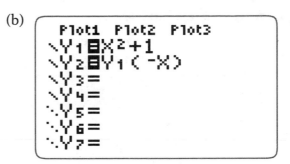

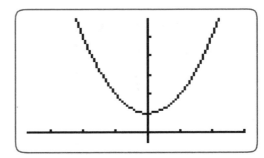

$Y_1 = x^2 + 1$; $Y_2 = Y_1(-x)$
$Y_1 = Y_2$ because Y_1 is even.

3.

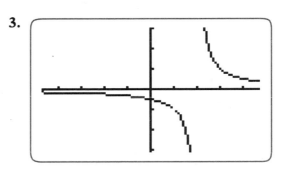

$$y = \frac{x - 1}{(x - 1)(x - 2)}$$
Vertical asymptote: $x = 2$; horizontal asymptote: $y = 0$. Hole at $x = 1$.

4. Zeros: 0, ± 1; since it is symmetric with respect to the origin, the function is odd.

2.4 Inverses

Exercises (page 30)

Multiple-Choice Questions

1. (A)
2. (C)
3. (D)
4. (D)

Free-Response Questions

1. (a) and (b) For $y = -e^{-x}$, the domain = {real numbers}, and the range = $\{y < 0\}$.

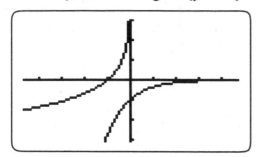

(c) The inverse of $y = -e^{-x}$ is $y = -\ln(-x)$.

(d) The graph of $y = -\ln(-x)$ matches the graph of the inverse.

2. (a) For the function $y = \sqrt{x-2} + 1$, the domain = $\{x \geq 2\}$, and the range = $\{y \geq 1\}$.

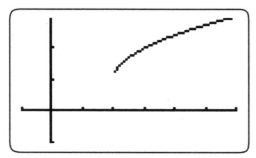

(b) For the inverse, $y = (x-1)^2 + 2$, the domain = $\{x \geq 1\}$, and the range = $\{y \geq 2\}$.

3.

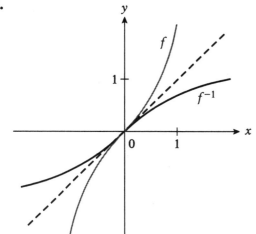

2.5 Translations and Reflections

Exercises (page 32)

1. (a)

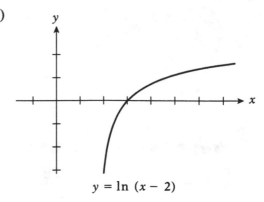

$y = \ln(x - 2)$

(b)

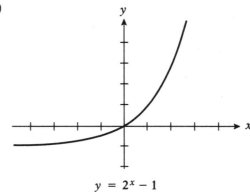

$y = 2^x - 1$

(c)

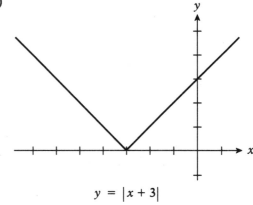

$y = |x + 3|$

(d)

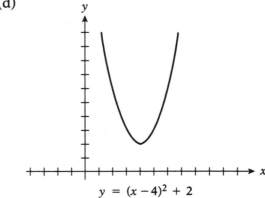

$y = (x-4)^2 + 2$

(e)

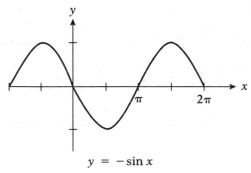

$$y = -\sin x$$

2. (a) domain $= \{x \neq 0\}$

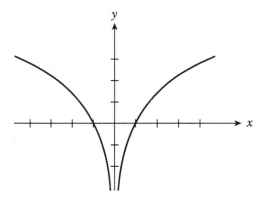

(b) domain $= \{\text{real numbers}\}$

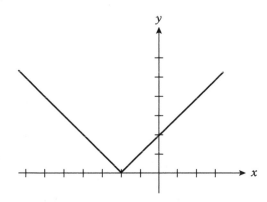

(c) domain $= \{x > 1\}$

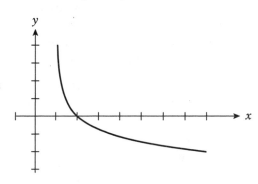

Multiple-Choice Questions

  1. (E)

  2. (B)

  3. (E)

Free-Response Questions

  1.

Graph of $y = \dfrac{1}{x}$

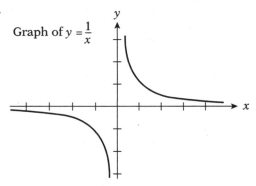

(a)

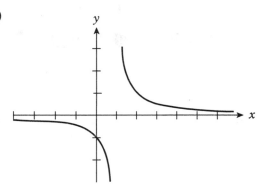

(b)

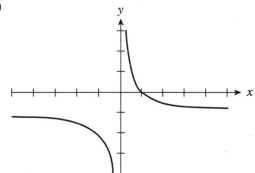

(c)

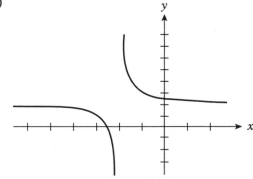

(d)

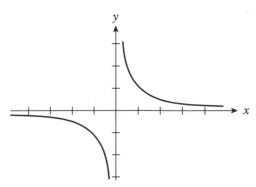

2. (a) shift up 2 units
   (b) reflection in the x-axis, shift down 3 units
   (c) reflection in the y-axis
   (d) shift to the right 1 unit, shift up 1 unit

BC 2.6 Parametric Equations

Exercises (pages 34–35)

Multiple-Choice Questions

1. (C)

2. (B)

3. (D)

4. (C)

Free-Response Questions

1.

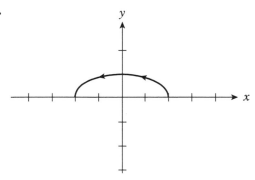

2. The curve graphs a parabola.

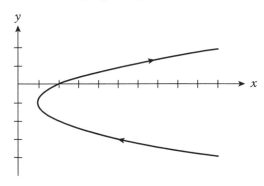

Chapter Assessment

(pages 35–38)

Multiple-Choice Questions

1. (B) $-\dfrac{2}{3}$

   $2x + 3y = 5$
   $3y = -2x + 5$
   $y = -\dfrac{2}{3}x + \dfrac{5}{3}$

2. (B) $x - 2y = 8$. The line has the form $x - 2y = k$. Substitute $2 + 6 = k$ to get $k = 8$.

3. (B) $4x - 3y = 3$. The line has the form $4x - 3y = k$. Substitute to get $3 = k$.

4. (A) 2 vertical and 1 horizontal. The denominator has two roots, and the ratio of the coefficients of highest order terms in the numerator and denominator is 1.

5. (D) The function approaches a y value of 1 as x increases.

6. (A) The function is not defined at $x = -2$, but as x approaches -2 from the right, the y-value decreases indefinitely.

7. (E) {all real numbers}

8. (E) {all real numbers}

9. (A) Since it is an even degree polynomial, the ends will behave in the same way. In this case, both increase.

10. (B) Since it is an odd degree polynomial, the ends will behave in opposite ways. Since the coefficient of the highest degree term is negative, it will behave as (B).

11. (A) Arccos 1 is the angle whose cosine is 1. In the domain of the arccosine function, this angle is 0. (Remember, arccos is a function so it has only one value.)

12. (A) $\ln(x^2) = 5$ Original equation
    $e^{\ln x^2} = e^5$
    $x^2 = e^5$ Simplify
    $(x^2)^{1/2} = \pm(e^5)^{1/2}$
    $x = \pm e^{5/2}$

13. (E) When $y = 0$, $0 = \log_2(x - 4)$.
    $2^0 = x - 4$
    $1 = x - 4$
    $5 = x$

14. (E) The y-axis is an asymptote to the graph of the function. The function $y = \ln x$ has no y-intercept.

15. (C) $\ln 2$

$$e^{2x} - e^x - 2 = 0$$
$$(e^x - 2)(e^x + 1) = 0$$
$$e^x = 2 \text{ or } -1$$
$$x = \ln 2 \ (e^x = -1 \text{ has no}$$
$$\text{real answer})$$

16. (D)

17. (D)

18. (B)

19. (A)

20. (E)

21. (B)

22. (D)

23. (C)

24. (C)

25. (B)

Free-Response Questions

1. (a)

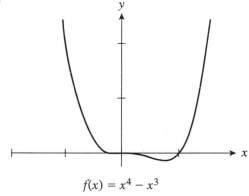

$$f(x) = x^4 - x^3$$

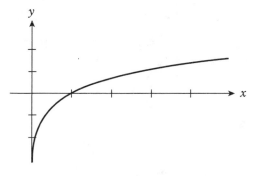

$$g(x) = \ln x$$

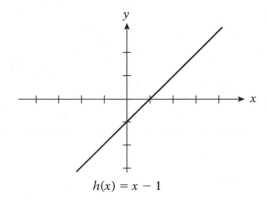

$$h(x) = x - 1$$

(b)

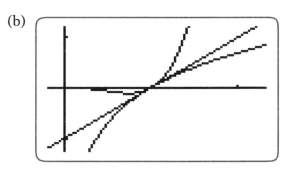

(c) The graphs of $f(x)$, $g(x)$, and $h(x)$ all intersect at $(1, 0)$, and for values of x close to 1, the values of all three functions are close to each other.

(d) The range of $f(x) = \left\{ y \ge -\dfrac{27}{256} \right\}$ or $\{ y \ge -0.105 \}$.

2. (a)

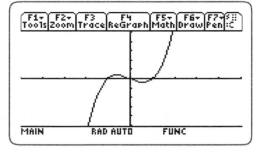

(b) $f(x)$ does not have an inverse because it does not pass the horizontal line test near $y = 0$.

(c)

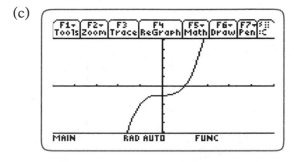

(d) Yes, it passes the horizontal line test. $g^{-1}(x) = \sqrt[3]{x + 1}$ is the inverse.

3.

Function	Domain	Range	Roots	Symmetry	Asymptotes	Graph
(a) x^2	{real numbers}	$\{y \geq 0\}$	$x = 0$	y-axis	none	
(b) $\ln x$	$\{x > 0\}$	{real numbers}	$x = 1$	none	$x = 0$	
(c) 2^x	{real numbers}	$\{y > 0\}$	none	none	$y = 0$	
(d) $\sin x$	{real numbers}	$\{-1 \leq y \leq 1\}$	$x = n\pi$, where n is an integer	origin	none	
(e) $\lvert x \rvert$	{real numbers}	$\{y \geq 0\}$	$x = 0$	y-axis	none	

4. (a)

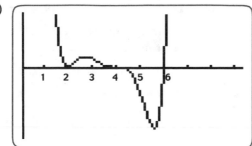

(b) degree 6; roots: 2, 4, 6
f crosses the x-axis at $x = 4$ and $x = 6$.
f bounces back at $x = 2$.

5. (a) Answers will vary.
(b) odd function: $f(-x) = -f(x)$
If $x = 0$, $f(0) = -f(0)$. Thus, $f(0) = 0$.

Chapter 3 Limits and Continuity

3.1 Functions and Asymptotes
Exercises (page 42)

Multiple-Choice Questions

1. (C)

2. (D)

3. (D)

4. (A)

Free-Response Questions

1. (a)

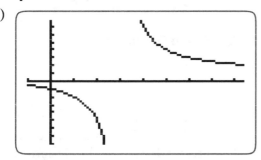

(b) The limits are $-\infty$, ∞, 1, and 1 respectively.
(c) zero: $x = -3$
vertical asymptote: $x = 3$
horizontal asymptote: $y = 1$
(d) neither
(e) Yes. The inverse is $y = \dfrac{3x + 3}{x - 1}$.

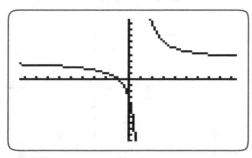

2. (a) The limits are ∞, ∞, 1, and 1 respectively.
(b) The function $f(x)$ does not have an inverse because it fails the horizontal line test.

3.2 Evaluating Limits as *x* Approaches a Finite Number *c*
Exercises (pages 45–46)

Multiple-Choice Questions

1. (C) $\dfrac{(-1)^2 - 5(-1) - 6}{(-1)^2 - 1}$ Substitute -1 for x

$\dfrac{0}{0}$ Simplify to find it is indeterminate

$\displaystyle\lim_{x \to -1} \dfrac{(x + 1)(x - 6)}{(x + 1)(x - 1)}$ Factor

$\displaystyle\lim_{x \to -1} \dfrac{x - 6}{x - 1}$ Simplify

$\dfrac{-1 - 6}{-1 - 1}$ Substitute -1 for x

$\dfrac{7}{2}$ Simplify

2. (D) $\displaystyle\lim_{x \to 0} \dfrac{x - 1}{x^2 - 1} = \dfrac{-1}{-1} = 1$

3. (C) $\displaystyle\lim_{x \to 9} \dfrac{\sqrt{x} - 3}{x - 9} = \dfrac{0}{0}$, so multiply numerator and denominator by conjugate $\left(\sqrt{x} + 3\right)$ to get
$\dfrac{x - 9}{(x - 9)\left(\sqrt{x} + 3\right)} = \dfrac{1}{\sqrt{x} + 3} = \dfrac{1}{6}$.

4. (A) $\dfrac{2-2}{\frac{1}{2}-\frac{1}{2}}$ Substitute 2 for x

$\dfrac{0}{0}$ Simplify to find it is indeterminate

$\displaystyle\lim_{x \to 2} \dfrac{(x-2)\cdot 2x}{\left(\frac{1}{x}-\frac{1}{2}\right)\cdot 2x}$ Multiply the numerator and denominator by $2x$

$\displaystyle\lim_{x \to 2} \dfrac{2x\cdot(x-2)}{2-x}$ Simplify

$\displaystyle\lim_{x \to 2} \dfrac{2x\cdot(x-2)}{2-x}\cdot\dfrac{-1}{-1}$

$\displaystyle\lim_{x \to 2} -2x$ Simplify further to $-2x$

$-2(2)$ Substitute 2 for x

-4 Simplify

Free-Response Questions

1. (a) -1
   (b) 1
   (c) -1
   (d) undefined

2.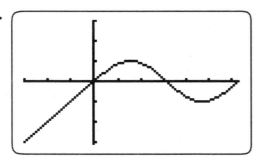

   (a) $\displaystyle\lim_{x \to -3} f(x) = -3$
   (b) $\displaystyle\lim_{x \to 0} f(x) = 0$

3.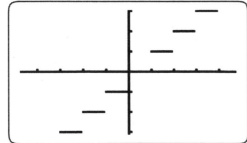

   (a) 0
   (b) $\displaystyle\lim_{x \to 1} f(x)$ is not defined since the right and left side limits are not equal.

   (c) $\displaystyle\lim_{x \to n} f(x)$ (where n is an integer) is not defined since the right and left side limits are not equal.

4. It appears that $\displaystyle\lim_{x \to 0} f(x) = 1$.

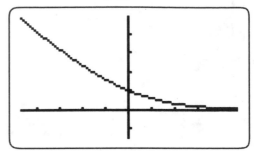

3.3 Evaluating Limits as x Approaches $\pm\infty$

Exercises (pages 47–48)

Multiple-Choice Questions

1. (B) $\dfrac{1}{2}$. $\displaystyle\lim_{x \to \infty} \dfrac{x^2-5}{2x^2+1}$ is equal to the ratio of the x^2 terms.

2. (E) ∞. Since this is a rational function and the degree of the numerator is greater than the degree of the denominator, the limit does not exist.

3. (C) 0. Since this is a rational function and the degree of the numerator is less than the degree of the denominator, the limit is 0.

4. (B)

Free-Response Questions

1. (a)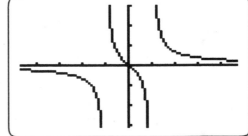

(b) • $\lim\limits_{x \to 1^+} f(x) = \infty$

  • $\lim\limits_{x \to 1^-} f(x) = -\infty$

  • $\lim\limits_{x \to -1^+} f(x) = \infty$

  • $\lim\limits_{x \to -1^-} f(x) = -\infty$

  • $\lim\limits_{x \to \infty} f(x) = 0$

  • $\lim\limits_{x \to -\infty} f(x) = 0$

2. Answers will vary.

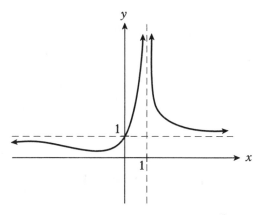

3.4 Special Limits: $\lim\limits_{x \to 0} \dfrac{\sin x}{x}$ and $\lim\limits_{x \to 0} \dfrac{1 - \cos x}{x}$

Exercises (pages 49–50)

Multiple-Choice Questions

1. (C)

2. (D) $\lim\limits_{x \to 0} \dfrac{\sin 7x}{x} = 7\left(\lim\limits_{x \to 0} \dfrac{\sin 7x}{7x}\right) = 7$

3. (B) $\lim\limits_{x \to 0} \dfrac{\sin x}{7x} = \dfrac{1}{7}\left(\lim\limits_{x \to 0} \dfrac{\sin x}{x}\right) = \dfrac{1}{7}$

4. (C)

Free-Response Questions

1. (a) 1

  (b) 0

  (c) does not exist

  (d) 0

2. $\dfrac{1 - \cos x}{x} \cdot \dfrac{1 + \cos x}{1 + \cos x}$ 　　Multiply by conjugate

$= \dfrac{1 - \cos^2 x}{x(1 + \cos x)} = \dfrac{\sin^2 x}{x(1 + \cos x)}$ 　Use Pythagorean Identity

$= \dfrac{\sin x}{x} \cdot \dfrac{\sin^2 x}{x(1 + \cos x)}$

Therefore, $\lim\limits_{x \to 0}\left(\dfrac{1 - \cos x}{x}\right) = \lim\limits_{x \to 0}\left(\dfrac{\sin x}{x} \cdot \dfrac{\sin x}{1 + \cos x}\right)$

3.5 Evaluating Limits of a Piecewise-Defined Function

Exercises (pages 51–52)

Multiple-Choice Questions

1. (D)

2. (A)

3. (E)

4. (A)

5. (C)

Free-Response Questions

1. (a)

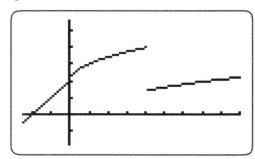

  • $f(0) = 2$
  • $\lim\limits_{x \to 0} f(x) = 2$
  • $f(4) = \ln 4$
  • $\lim\limits_{x \to 4} f(x)$ does not exist

2. Answers will vary.

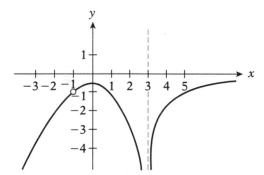

3.6 Continuity of a Function

Exercises (page 54)

Multiple-Choice Questions

1. (C)   5. (A)

2. (D)   6. (D)

3. (D)   7. (A)

4. (D)   8. (E)

Free-Response Questions

1. (a) For $f(x)$ to be continuous at $x = 1$,
$\lim\limits_{x \to 1^-} f(x) = \lim\limits_{x \to 1^+} f(x)$.
$$k(1) + 1 = (1)^2$$
$$k = 0$$

(b)
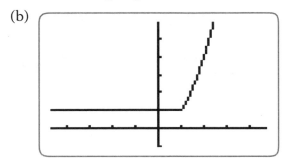

2. (a) If $g(x)$ is continuous at $x = -1$, $\lim\limits_{x \to -1^-} g(x)$
$= \lim\limits_{x \to -1^+} g(x)$. Therefore,
$$(-1)^2 + 2 = -1 - p$$
$$4 = -p$$
$$-4 = p$$

(b)
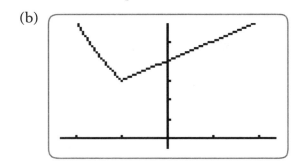

3. Redefine $f(2) = 1$ to make this function continuous.

4. (a) Answers will vary. One possibility is $f(x) = x$ for $x < 0$, $f(x) = -x$ for $x > 0$, and $f(0) = 1$.

(b) Answers will vary. One possibility is $g(x) = x$ for $x \le 1$, and $g(x) = -x$ for $x > 1$.

Chapter Assessment
(pages 54–57)

Multiple-Choice Questions

1. (E)

2. (C)

3. (C)

4. (D)

5. (D)

6. (B)

7. (D)

8. (A)

9. (D)

10. (A)

11. (E)

12. (D)

13. (D)

14. (A)

15. (C)

16. (A)

17. (B)

18. (B)

19. (A)

20. (C)

21. (C)

22. (A)

23. (B)

24. (B)

25. (C)

Free-Response Questions

1. $a = -\dfrac{1}{2}$

2. zeros: $x = 2$
holes: none
vertical asymptote: $x = -5$
horizontal asymptote: $y = 3$

3.

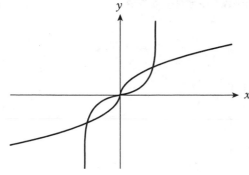

$f(f^{-1}(-1)) = -1$

4.

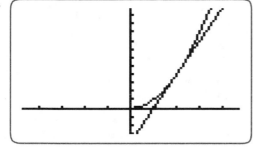

(a) Slope = 4

(b) Slope = $\frac{1}{4}$

5. • $\lim\limits_{x \to -1} f(x) = 2$

  • $\lim\limits_{x \to 1} f(x)$ does not exist

  • $\lim\limits_{x \to 2} f(x) = \infty$

6. Answers will vary.

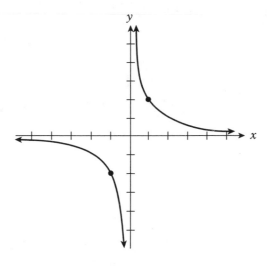

Chapter 4 The Derivative

4.1 The Derivative of a Function
Exercises (pages 62–63)

  I (C)
 II (B)
III (A)

Multiple-Choice Questions

1. (D)

2. (A)

3. (B)

4. (B)

5. (A)

6. (D)

7. (C)

Free-Response Questions

1. (a)

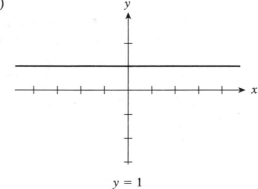

$y = 1$

(b)

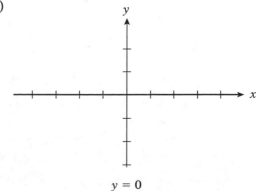

$y = 0$

2.

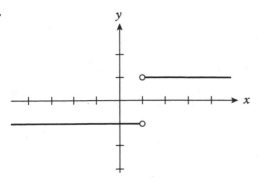

$$y = \begin{cases} 1, & x > 1 \\ -1, & x < 1 \end{cases}$$

3.

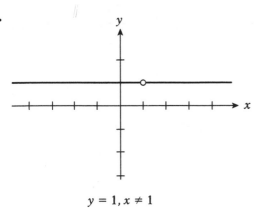

$$y = 1, x \neq 1$$

4. In Question 2, $y = |x - 1|$ is continuous for all real numbers; y' does not exist at $x = 1$.

In Question 3, $f(x)$ is continuous for $x \neq 1$; $f'(x)$ does not exist at $x = 1$.

4.2 The Average Rate of Change of a Function on an Interval

Exercises (pages 65–66)

Multiple-Choice Questions

1. (C) $\dfrac{f(3) - f(1)}{3 - 1} = \dfrac{4(3) - (3)^2 - (4(1)) - (1)^2}{2}$

$$= \dfrac{(12 - 9 - 3)}{2} = 0$$

2. (A)

3. (B)

4. (C)

Free-Response Questions

1. (a)

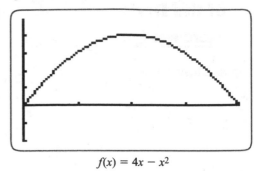

$$f(x) = 4x - x^2$$

(b) Answers will vary.

x	0	1	2	3	4
Slope	5	2	0	−2	−5

(c) Graphs will vary, but should resemble a straight line.

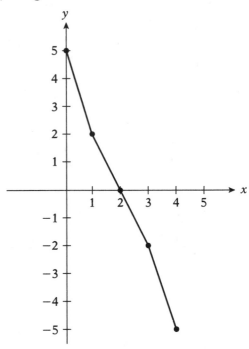

2. (a) i.   [0, 2]: average rate of change = 2
    ii. [1, 3]: average rate of change = 0
    iii. [2, 4]: average rate of change = −2

(b) Answers will vary. For each interval, the point at which the slope of the tangent line is equal to the average rate of change is somewhere in the middle of the interval. For example,
    i. $x = 1$
    ii. $x = 2$
    iii. $x = 3$

4.3 The Definition of the Derivative

Exercises (page 67)

Multiple-Choice Questions

1. (A)
2. (E)
3. (D)
4. (D)

Free-Response Questions

1. $f'(x) = 10x$
2. $f'(x) = 10x + 5$

4.4 Rules for Derivatives

Exercises (pages 72–73)

Multiple-Choice Questions

1. (C)
2. (D)
3. (B)
4. (E)
5. (A)
6. (C)
7. (C)
8. (C)
9. (E)
10. (B)
11. (E)
12. (D)
13. (C)
14. (B)

Free-Response Questions

1. (a)

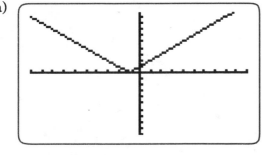

(b) $y = |x + 1|$

(c)

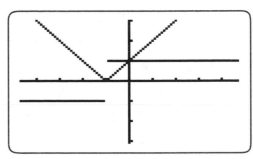

(d) On the interval $[\infty, -1]$, the graph of Y_2 is the horizontal line $y = -1$. This indicates that over the same interval, the graph of Y_1 has a constant slope of -1. On the interval $[-1, \infty]$, the graph of Y_2 is the horizontal line $y = 1$. This indicates that over the same interval, the graph of Y_1 has a constant slope of 1.

2. (a) and (b)

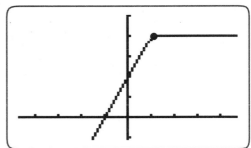

(c) No. Since $f(x)$ is not continuous at $x = 1$, $f'(x)$ does not exist at $x = 1$.

3. (a) $y' = (x^2 + 1)(3x^2) + (x^3 + 1)(2x)$
   $y' = 3x^4 + 3x^2 + 2x^4 + 2x$
   $y' = 5x^4 + 3x^2 + 2x$

   (b) $y = (x^2 + 1)(x^3 + 1)$
   $y = x^5 + x^3 + x^2 + 1$
   $y' = 5x^4 + 3x^2 + 2x$

   (c) The resulting derivatives are the same.

4.5 Recognizing the Form of the Derivative

Exercises (pages 76–78)

Multiple-Choice Questions

1. (D)

2. (B) $f'(x) = \frac{1}{x} = \frac{1}{3}; f''(x) = -\frac{1}{x^2} = -\frac{1}{9}$

3. (D) Let $f(x) = e^x$. Then $\lim_{h \to 0} \frac{e^{1+h} - e}{h}$

   $= \lim \frac{f(1 + h) - f(1)}{h} = f'(1) = e^1 = e.$

4. (E) $f'(x) = (\tan(x^2))' = 2x \sec^2(x^2)$
at $x = 1$ is $2\sec^2(1) \approx 2(3.426) = 6.851$.

5. (E) $f'(x) = \dfrac{-x\cos(x) - \sin(x)}{x^2}$ at $x = \dfrac{\pi}{2}$ is

$\dfrac{0 - 1}{\left(\dfrac{\pi}{2}\right)^2} = -\dfrac{4}{\pi^2}$.

6. (D) $f'(x) = 1 + 2e^{2x}$ at $x = 0$ is $1 + 2 = 3$.

7. (C) $\dfrac{dy}{dx} = 3(x - 2)^3 + 3x(3(x - 2)^2)$
$= (3x - 6 + 9x)(x - 2)^2$
$= (12x - 6)(x - 2)^2$

8. (B) $\dfrac{x\sin(x) + \cos(x)}{x^2}$.

$y' = \dfrac{-(-x\sin(x) - \cos(x))}{x^2}$

$= \dfrac{x\sin(x) + \cos(x)}{x^2}$

9. (D) $-2\sin(x)\cos(x)$

10. (E) $(e^x\sin(x))' = e^x\sin(x) + e^x\cos(x)$
at $x = \pi$ is $e^\pi(0) + e^\pi(-1) = -e^\pi$.

11. (B)

12. (B)

13. (A)

Free-Response Questions

1. $f'(x) = \lim\limits_{h \to 0} \dfrac{f(x + h) - f(x)}{h}$

$= \lim\limits_{h \to 0} \dfrac{(x + h)^2 + (x + h) - (x^2 + x)}{h}$

$= \lim\limits_{h \to 0} \dfrac{(x^2 + 2xh + h^2 + x + h - x^2 - x)}{h}$

$= \lim\limits_{h \to 0} (2x + h + 1) = 2x + 1$

By the Power Rule: $f'(x) = 2x + 1$.

2. $f'(x) = \dfrac{(x^2 + x)^{1/2}(2x)' - \left((x^2 + x)^{1/2}\right)'(2x)}{x^2 + x}$

$= \dfrac{2(x^2 + x)^{1/2} - (x^2 + x)^{-1/2}(2x + 1)x}{(x^2 + x)}$

$= \dfrac{2(x^2 + x) - (2x + 1)x}{(x^2 + x)^{3/2}}$

$= \dfrac{x}{(x^2 + x)^{3/2}}$

3. (a) $y' = \dfrac{x(2x) - x^2 - 4}{x^2} = \dfrac{x^2 - 4}{x^2}$

(b) $y = (x^2 - 4)\left(\dfrac{1}{x}\right)$

$y' = 2x\left(\dfrac{1}{x}\right) - (x^2 - 4)\left(\dfrac{1}{x^2}\right)$

$= 2 - \dfrac{x^2 + 4}{x^2} = \dfrac{x^2 - 4}{x^2}$

(c) $y = x + \dfrac{4}{x}$; $y' = 1 - \dfrac{4}{x^2} = \dfrac{x^2 - 4}{x^2}$

(d) $y'' = \left(1 - \dfrac{4}{x^2}\right)' = \dfrac{8}{x^3}$

4. (a)

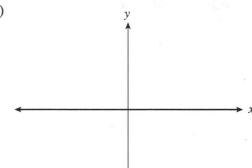

(b)

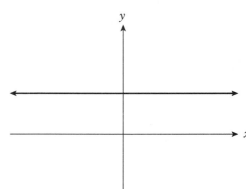

(c)

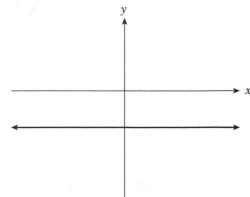

(d)

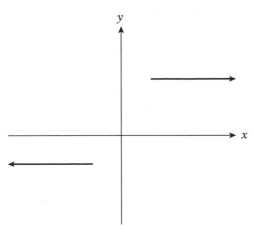

(e)

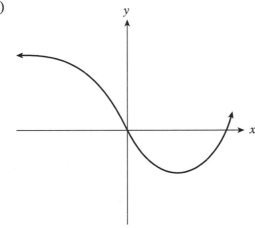

5. (a) $\left[-\dfrac{\pi}{2}, \dfrac{\pi}{2}\right]$

(b) $g(x) = \arcsin x$

domain: $[-1, 1]$ range: $\left[-\dfrac{\pi}{2}, \dfrac{\pi}{2}\right]$

(c) $g'(x) = \dfrac{1}{\sqrt{1-x^2}} = \dfrac{1}{\sin'\left(\arcsin \dfrac{1}{2}\right)}$

$= \dfrac{1}{\cos\left(\dfrac{\pi}{6}\right)} = \dfrac{2}{\sqrt{3}}$

6. (a) Yes.

(b) $g'(0) = \dfrac{1}{f'(g(0))}$

(c) $g(0) =$ the value that makes $f(x) = 0$.

$g(x) = \sqrt{\dfrac{x+3}{2}}$ $g(0) = \sqrt{\dfrac{3}{2}}$

$g'(0) = \dfrac{1}{4\sqrt{\dfrac{3}{2}}} = \dfrac{\sqrt{2}}{4\sqrt{3}} = \dfrac{1}{2\sqrt{6}}$

$g'(0) = \dfrac{1}{2\sqrt{\dfrac{0+3}{2}}} \cdot \dfrac{1}{2} = \dfrac{\sqrt{2}}{4\sqrt{3}} = \dfrac{1}{2\sqrt{6}}$

(d)

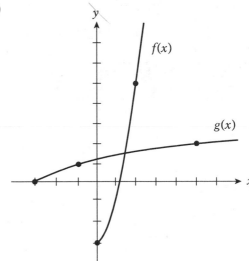

7. (a) $f'(x) = 3x^2 + 4x + 4$
$f''(x) = 6x + 4$
$f'''(x) = 6$

(b) $f'''(x)$

(c) The nth derivative of an nth-degree polynomial is a constant.

4.6 The Equation of a Tangent Line

Exercises (page 80)

Multiple-Choice Questions

1. (A)

2. (C)

3. (B)

4. (D)

Free-Response Questions

1. (a)

Zero	Tangent Line
3	$y = 4x - 12$
-1	$y = -4x - 4$

There is one point of intersection at $(1, -8)$.

(b)

Zero	Tangent Line
0	$y = x$
π	$y = -x + \pi$
2π	$y = x - 2\pi$

There are two points of intersection at $\left(\dfrac{\pi}{2}, \dfrac{\pi}{2}\right)$ and $\left(\dfrac{3\pi}{2}, -\dfrac{\pi}{2}\right)$.

2. (a)

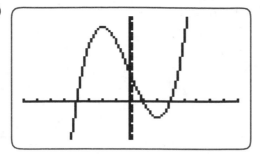

(b)

x	Equation of Tangent Line	Is Tangent Above or Below Curve?
−3	$y = 14x + 66$	above
−1	$y = -10x + 14$	above
2	$y = -x - 4$	below
3	$y = 14x - 42$	below

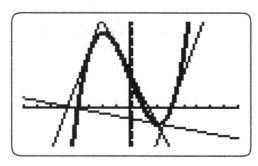

(c) The tangent line appears to change from being above the curve to being below the curve at $x = 2$.

4.7 Differentiability vs. Continuity

Exercises (pages 81–82)

Multiple-Choice Questions

1. (A)
2. (B)
3. (E)
4. (A)

Free-Response Questions

1. Answers will vary. One possible answer is $f(x) = |x - 1|$.
2. (a) $f(x)$ is continuous for $-3 \leq x \leq 4$.

   (b)

   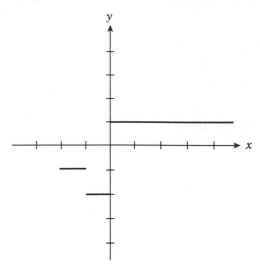

4.8 Particle Motion

Exercises (pages 84–85)

Multiple-Choice Questions

1. (D)
2. (C)
3. (C)
4. (A)
5. (D)
6. (B)
7. (A)
8. (D)

Free-Response Questions

1. (a) $v(t) = t \cos t + \sin t$

   $a(t) = -t \sin t + 2 \cos t$

   (b) The particle is at rest at $t = 2.029$ and $t = 4.913$.

   (c)

   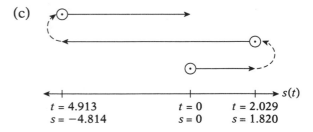

(d) Yes, distance traveled > 10.

Distance from $t = 0$ to $t = 2.029$ is 1.82.

Distance from $t = 2.029$ to $t = 4.913$ is 6.634.

Distance from $t = 4.913$ to $t = 2\pi$ is 4.814.

The total distance is 13.268.

2. (a) The particle is at rest at $t = 2$.

(b) The particle slows down as it gets closer to -4.

(c) The particle moves slowly and then faster away from -4.

(d)

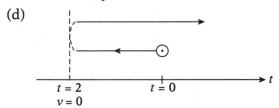

3. $X_{2T} = X'_{1T}$ represents the velocity of the particle in Question 2.

At $t = 0$, velocity $= -4$; the particle is moving to the left.

At $t = 2$, velocity $= 0$; the particle is at rest.

4.9 Motion of a Freely Falling Object

Exercises (pages 87–88)

Multiple-Choice Questions

1. (C)

2. (A)

3. (B)

4. (D)

Free-Response Questions

1. The greater the initial height, the longer it takes for the ball to hit the ground. A positive initial velocity increases the time it takes for the ball to hit the ground; a negative initial velocity decreases the time.

2. $6 = -16t^2 + v_0(t) + 80$

When $t = 3$,

$$6 = -16(9) + v_0(3) + 80$$
$$6 = -144 + v_0(3) + 80$$
$$150 = v_0(3)$$

$\dfrac{70}{3}$ ft/sec $= v_0$.

4.10 Implicit Differentiation

Exercises (pages 90–91)

1. $\dfrac{dy}{dx}$ at $(x, y) = (3, 4)$ is $-\dfrac{x}{y} = -\dfrac{3}{4}$.

2. $\dfrac{dy}{dx}$ at $(x, y) = (1, 1)$ is $-\dfrac{y}{x + 2y} = -\dfrac{1}{3}$.

3. $\dfrac{d}{dx} (x^2 + y^2 + xy = 5)$

$$2x + \frac{dy}{dx}\frac{d}{dy} y^2 + y + x \frac{dy}{dx}\frac{d}{dy} y = 0$$

$$2x + 2y \frac{dy}{dx} + y + x \frac{dy}{dx} = 0$$

$$(2y + x)\frac{dy}{dx} = -(2x + y)$$

$$\frac{dy}{dx} = -\frac{2x + y}{2y + x}$$

Multiple-Choice Questions

1. (B)

2. (A)

3. (C)

Free-Response Questions

1. (a) $\dfrac{dy}{dx} = \dfrac{2 - 2xy}{x^2 + 2y}$

(b) $(1, 1)$

(c) $(0, 0)$ and $(-2, -2)$

2. (a) $\dfrac{dy}{dx} = \dfrac{(y + 1)(1 - \ln(y + 1))}{x - y - 1}$

(b) At point $(1, 0)$, $\dfrac{dy}{dx} = \dfrac{1}{0}$, which is undefined. When the slope of a line is undefined, the line is vertical.

4.11 Related Rates

Exercises (pages 92–93)

Multiple-Choice Questions

1. (C) $\dfrac{2\pi}{3}$ ft²/sec.

Given: $\dfrac{dr}{dt} = \dfrac{1}{3}$ ft/sec; $r = 1$ ft; $A = \pi r^2$.

Find: $\dfrac{dA}{dt} = \dfrac{dA}{dr}\dfrac{dr}{dt} = 2\pi r \dfrac{dr}{dt} = \dfrac{2\pi}{3}$ ft²/sec.

2. (B) 2.4 cm²/sec

Given: $\frac{dV}{dt} = 3$ cm³/sec; $s = 5$ cm; $V = s^3$;

$A = 6s^2$.

Find: $\frac{dA}{dt}$. First find $\frac{ds}{dV}$:

$$\frac{d}{dV} V = \frac{d}{dV} s^3$$

$$1 = \frac{ds}{dV} 3s^2$$

$$\frac{ds}{dV} = \frac{1}{3s^2}.$$

$$\frac{dA}{dt} = \frac{dA}{ds}\frac{ds}{dV}\frac{dV}{dt} = \frac{12s}{3s^2}\frac{dV}{dt} = \frac{4}{s}(3 \text{ cm}^3/\text{sec})$$
$$= 2.4 \text{ cm}^2/\text{sec}$$

3. (C) $\frac{2}{3}$ ft/sec

Given: $L = 20$ ft; $\frac{dy}{dt} = -0.5$ ft/sec; $x = 12$ ft;

$x^2 + y^2 = L^2$.

Find: $\frac{dx}{dt}$. First find y: $y = 16$ ft, as it is the third side of a 12:16:20 right triangle.

Next find $\frac{dx}{dy}$: $\frac{d}{dy}(x^2 + y^2) = 0$.

$$\frac{dx}{dy} = -\frac{y}{x} = -\frac{4}{3}$$

$$\frac{dx}{dt} = \frac{dx}{dy}\frac{dy}{dt} = -\frac{4}{3}(-0.5 \text{ ft/sec}) = \frac{2}{3} \text{ ft/sec}$$

4. (A) $\frac{4}{9\pi}$ in./sec

Given: $\frac{dV}{dt} = 8$ in.³/sec; $V = 36\pi$ in.³;

$V = \frac{4}{3}\pi r^3$; $D = 2r$.

Find: $\frac{dD}{dt}$. First find r: 36π in.³ $= \frac{4}{3}\pi r^3$.

$$r^3 = 27 \text{ in.}^3$$

$$r = 3 \text{ in.}$$

Next find $\frac{dr}{dV}$: $\frac{d}{dV} V = \frac{d}{dV} \frac{4}{3}\pi r^3$.

$$1 = \frac{dr}{dV} 4\pi r^2$$

$$\frac{dr}{dV} = \frac{1}{4\pi r^2}$$

$$\frac{dD}{dt} = \frac{dD}{dr}\frac{dr}{dV}\frac{dV}{dt} = \frac{2}{4\pi r^2}\frac{dV}{dt} = \frac{8}{18\pi} \text{ in./sec}$$
$$= \frac{4}{9\pi} \text{ in./sec}$$

Free-Response Questions

1. Given: $\frac{dV}{dt} = 3$ cm³/sec; $h = 2r$; $V = \frac{1}{3}\pi r^2 h$;

$A = \pi r^2$.

(a) Given: $h = 2$ cm. Find: $\frac{dr}{dt}$.

$$r = 1$$

$$\frac{d}{dt} V = \frac{\pi}{3}\left(2rh \frac{dr}{dt} + r^2 \frac{dh}{dt}\right)$$

$$= \frac{\pi}{3}\left(2rh \frac{dr}{dt} + 2r^2 \frac{dh}{dt}\right)$$

$$\frac{dV}{dt} = \frac{\pi}{3}(4 + 2)\frac{dr}{dt} \text{ cm}^2$$

$$\frac{dr}{dt} = \frac{1}{2\pi \text{ cm}^2}\frac{dV}{dt} = \frac{3}{2\pi} \text{ cm/sec}$$

(b) Given: $h = 2$ cm. Find: $\frac{dA}{dt}$.

$$\frac{dA}{dt} = \frac{dA}{dr}\frac{dr}{dt} = (2\pi r)\frac{3}{2\pi} \text{ cm/sec}$$
$$= 3 \text{ cm}^2/\text{sec}$$

2. Given: $VF = \frac{1}{3}\pi r^2 h$; $r = 5$ cm;

$VF = 500$ cm³; $\frac{dVF}{dt} = -20$ cm³/min;

$VC = \pi r^2 y$; $\frac{dVC}{dt} = -\frac{dVF}{dt}\frac{dr}{dt} = 0$.

(a) First find $\frac{dy}{dVC}$:

$$\frac{d}{dVC} VC = 1 = \frac{d}{dVC}\pi r^2 y = \pi r^2 \frac{dy}{dVC}$$

$$\frac{dy}{dVC} = \frac{1}{\pi r^2}\frac{dy}{dt} = \frac{dy}{dVC}\frac{dVC}{dt}$$

$$= -\frac{dy}{dVC}\frac{dVF}{dt} = \frac{20 \text{ cm}^3/\text{min}}{25\pi \text{ cm}^2}$$

$$= \frac{4}{5\pi} \text{ cm/min}$$

(b) $VC = 500$ cm³ $= \pi r^2 y = 25\pi y$ cm²

$y = \frac{20}{\pi}$ cm or 6.366 cm

BC 4.12 Derivatives of Parametric Equations

Exercises (page 94)

Multiple-Choice Questions

1. (A)

2. (D)

Free-Response Question

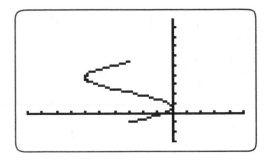

(a)

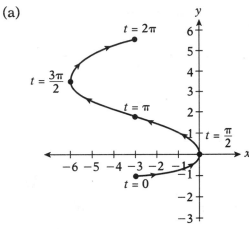

(b) position at $t = 3$: $(-2.577, 2)$
(c) velocity at $t = 3$: $\langle 3 \cos 3, 1\rangle$
(d) speed at $t = 3$: 3.134
(e) $\dfrac{dy}{dx} = \dfrac{1}{3} \cos t$. At $t = 3$, the slope is $\dfrac{1}{3} \cos 3$, which is approximately -0.337.

Chapter Assessment

(pages 94–97)

Multiple-Choice Questions

1. (B) All real numbers. $f'(x) = e^x$ is positive for all values of x.

2. (A) $\left[-\dfrac{\pi}{2}, \dfrac{\pi}{2}\right]$. $y' = -2 \cos x$, so y decreases when $\cos x$ is positive.

3. (B) $f'(x) = -2x + 2 > 0$
   $2x < 2$
   $x < 1$

4. (A) 0. The graph is the natural log reflected over the x-axis and shifted up two units. The natural log has no horizontal asymptotes.

5. (C) $\dfrac{y(2) - y(1)}{2 - 1} = \ln(4) - \ln(1)$
   $= \ln(4) \approx 1.386.$

6. (D) $\displaystyle\lim_{h \to 0} \dfrac{\tan\left(\dfrac{\pi}{4} + h\right) - \tan\left(\dfrac{\pi}{4}\right)}{h}$
   $= (\tan(x))'$ at $\dfrac{\pi}{4} = \sec^2\left(\dfrac{\pi}{4}\right)$
   $= (2)^{(1/2)(2)} = 2$

7. (A) $f(x) = x^4 - 4x$; $y = x + 1$. Then
   $\displaystyle\lim_{x \to -1} \dfrac{f(x) - f(-1)}{x + 1} = \lim_{y \to 0} \dfrac{f(y - 1) - f(-1)}{y}.$
   $f'(-1) = 4x^3 - 4$ at $-1 = -4 - 4 = -8.$

8. (E) $f'(x) = \dfrac{3}{2}(x - 1)^2$. $f'(0) = \dfrac{3}{2}.$

9. (D) $f'(x) = \dfrac{(\sin x)'}{\sin x} = \dfrac{\cos x}{\sin x}$. $f'\left(\dfrac{\pi}{4}\right) = 1.$

10. (A) $y' = 2 \cos 2x - 1.$
    $y'\left(\dfrac{\pi}{2}\right) = 2 \cos \pi - 1 = -2 - 1 = -3.$

11. (D) $y' = 6 \tan\left(\dfrac{x}{3}\right)\left(\tan\left(\dfrac{x}{3}\right)\right)'$
    $= 6 \tan\left(\dfrac{x}{3}\right) \sec^2\left(\dfrac{x}{3}\right)\left(\dfrac{x}{3}\right)'$
    $= 2 \tan\left(\dfrac{x}{3}\right) \sec^2\left(\dfrac{x}{3}\right).$
    $y'(\pi) = 2 \tan\left(\dfrac{\pi}{3}\right) \sec^2\left(\dfrac{\pi}{3}\right)$
    $= 2(3)^{1/2}(2)^2 = 8\sqrt{3}$

12. (D) $y' = \dfrac{(e^{x^2 - 1})'}{e^{x^2 - 1}} = 2x \dfrac{e^{x^2 - 1}}{e^{x^2 - 1}} = 2x.$ $y'(1) = 2.$

13. (B) $y' = (e^{x^3})' = e^{x^3}(x^3)' = 3x^2 e^{x^3}.$
    $y'(1) = 3e.$

14. (A) $x \neq 0$. $f(x)$ has a hole at $x = 0.$

15. (D) $x > 0$ and $x \neq 1$. $\sqrt{(\ln x)^2} = |\ln x|$ is not differentiable at $x = 1.$

16. (B) Find $\dfrac{d}{dx}(xy + x - y = 2).$
    $y + x \dfrac{dy}{dx} + 1 - \dfrac{dy}{dx} = 0$
    $\dfrac{dy}{dx} = -\dfrac{y + 1}{x - 1}.$ When $x = 0$, $-y = 2$,
    so $\dfrac{dy}{dx} = -2 + 1 = -1.$

17. (B) $\dfrac{ds}{dt} = \dfrac{1 - \ln t}{t^2}$ at $t = 2$ is $\dfrac{1 - \ln 2}{4}$
    $\approx 0.0767.$

18. (C) $2x - \frac{1}{x}$.

19. (A) $\left(\sqrt{(x^2 + 1)}\right)''$

$$= \left(\frac{1}{2}(x^2 + 1)^{-1/2}\,(2x)\right)'$$

$$= \left((x^2 + 1)^{-1/2}x\right)'$$

$$= (x^2 + 1)^{-1/2} + \left(-\frac{1}{2}\,(x^2 + 1)^{-3/2}\,(2x)x\right)$$

$$= (x^2 + 1)^{-3/2}\,(x^2 + 1 - x^2)$$

$$= (x^2 + 1)^{-3/2}$$

20. (D) $y'' = (x \ln x - 3x)''(1 + \ln x - 3)'$

$$= (\ln x - 2)' = \frac{1}{x}.$$

21. (C) $y' = \frac{1}{2}(x + 2)^{-1/2}$ at $x = -1$ is $\frac{1}{2}$.

22. (B) $\frac{d}{dx}\,(x = y^2 + 4)$.

$$1 = 2y\frac{dy}{dx}$$

$\frac{dy}{dx} = \frac{1}{2y}$, and at the point $(5, 1)$ is $\frac{1}{2}$.

The line through this point with this slope is $2(y - 1) = (x - 5)$ or $2y = x - 3$.

23. (A) $f'(x) = \frac{-2x}{(x^2 + 2)^2}$. At $x = 0$, $f'(x)$ is 0, so the tangent is a horizontal line with the equation $y = \frac{1}{2}$.

24. (B) $y' = \frac{1}{1 + x^2} = \frac{1}{2}$

$$y(1) = \arctan 1 = \frac{\pi}{4}$$

$$y - \frac{\pi}{4} = \frac{1}{2}\,(x - 1)$$

$$4y - 2x = \pi - 2,\text{ or}$$
$$2x - 4y = 2 - \pi$$

25. (D) $g'(2) = \frac{1}{f'(g(2))}$

$$2 = \frac{1}{(g(2))^2}$$

$$g(2) = \frac{1}{\sqrt{2}}$$

$$f' = -\frac{2}{x^3}$$

$$g'(2) = -\frac{1}{\left(\sqrt{2}\right)^3(2)} = -\frac{\sqrt{2}}{8}$$

26. (C) $\dfrac{dy}{dx} = \dfrac{\left(\dfrac{dy}{dx}\right)}{\left(\dfrac{dx}{dt}\right)} = \dfrac{4}{4t} = \dfrac{1}{t}$ and at $t = 1$ is 1.

27. (A) $y = x + 1$. $x(1) = 2$ and $y(1) = 4 - 1 = 3$, so the line is $y - 3 = x - 2$ or $y = x + 1$. More simply, (A) is the only choice with slope 1.

Free-Response Questions

1. (a)

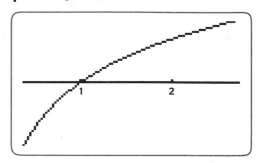

(b) $\{-1 \le y \le 1\}$

(c) $\dfrac{\ln e - \ln\left(\dfrac{1}{e}\right)}{e - \dfrac{1}{e}} = \dfrac{1 - (-1)}{e - \dfrac{1}{e}} = \dfrac{2}{e - \dfrac{1}{e}}$

$$= \frac{2e}{e^2 - 1} \approx 0.851.$$

(d) Answers will vary.

x	$\frac{1}{e}$	1	e
Slope	3	1	$\frac{1}{3}$

(e)

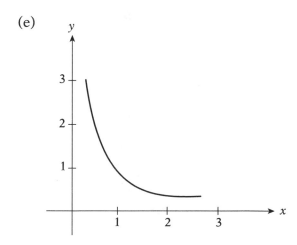

2. (a) $f'(x) = \lim\limits_{h \to 0} \dfrac{1}{h}\left(\dfrac{2}{x + h + 1} - \dfrac{2}{x + 1}\right)$

$= \lim\limits_{h \to 0} \dfrac{1}{h} \dfrac{2(x + 1) - 2(x + h + 1)}{(x + 1)(x + h + 1)}$

$= \lim\limits_{h \to 0} \dfrac{1}{h} \dfrac{-2h}{(x + 1)(x + h + 1)}$

$= \lim\limits_{h \to 0} \dfrac{-2}{(x + 1)(x + h + 1)}$

$= \dfrac{-2}{(x + 1)^2}$

(b) $f'(x) =$

$\lim\limits_{h \to 0} \dfrac{1}{h}\left((x + h)^2 - 2(x + h) - (x^2 - 2x)\right)$

$= \lim\limits_{h \to 0} \dfrac{1}{h}(2xh + h^2 - 2h)$

$= \lim\limits_{h \to 0} \dfrac{1}{h}(2x + h - 2)$

$= 2x - 2$

3. (a) $(\tan x)' = \left(\dfrac{\sin x}{\cos x}\right)'$

$= \dfrac{\cos x \cos x - \sin x\,(-\sin x)}{\cos^2 x}$

$= \dfrac{1}{\cos^2 (x)} = \sec^2 (x)$

(b) $(\cot x)' = \left(\dfrac{\cos x}{\sin x}\right)'$

$= \dfrac{\sin x\,(-\sin x) - \cos x \cdot \cos x}{\sin^2 x}$

$= \dfrac{x}{\sin^2 x}$

$= \dfrac{-1}{\sin^2 x} = -\csc^2 (x)$

(c) $(\sec x)' = \left(\dfrac{1}{\cos x}\right)'$

$= -\dfrac{-\sin x}{\cos^2 x} = \dfrac{\sin x}{\cos x} \cdot \dfrac{1}{\cos x}$

$= \sec(x)\tan(x)$

(d) $(\csc x)' = \left(\dfrac{1}{\sin x}\right)'$

$= -\dfrac{\cos x}{\sin^2 x} = \dfrac{\cos x}{\sin x} \cdot \dfrac{1}{\sin x}$

$= -\csc(x)\cot(x)$

4. Given $f(x) = \begin{cases} -x, & \text{for } x \geq 1 \\ x + k, & \text{for } x < 1 \end{cases}$:

(a) $f(x)$ at 1 is -1, but the limit from the left as $x \to 1$ is $(1 + k)$; for these two values to be equal, k must equal -2.

(b) No. The limit of $f'(x)$ as $x \to 1$ from the left is $(-x)' = -1$. The limit of $f'(x)$ as $x \to 1$ from the right is $(x - 2)' = 1$; thus, $f'(1)$ is undefined.

5. $s(t) = -16t^2 + v_0 t = 40$

$v = -32t + v_0 = 0$ when the ball reaches the top.

$\dfrac{v_0}{t} = 32$

$t = \dfrac{v_0}{32}$

$-16\left(\dfrac{v_0}{32}\right)^2 + \dfrac{(v_0)^2}{32} = 40$

$v_0 = \pm16\sqrt{10}$ ft/sec $\approx \pm50.596$ ft/sec

The initial velocity is positive since the ball is thrown upward; thus, we choose only the positive value, 50.596 ft/sec.

6. $V = \dfrac{1}{3}\pi r^2 h$

$V = \dfrac{1}{3}\pi\left(\dfrac{9}{4}h^2\right)h$

$V = \dfrac{3\pi}{4}h^3$

$\dfrac{dV}{dt} = \dfrac{3\pi}{4}(3h^2)\dfrac{dh}{dt}$

Since $h = \dfrac{2}{3}r$, $r = \dfrac{2}{3}(9) = 6$.

Thus, $5 = \dfrac{9\pi}{4}(36)\dfrac{dh}{dt}$ and $\dfrac{dh}{dt} = \dfrac{5}{81\pi}$, which is approximately 0.02 cm/sec.

Chapter 5 Applications of the Derivative

5.1 Three Theorems: The Extreme Value Theorem, Rolle's Theorem, and the Mean Value Theorem

Exercises (pages 101–102)

1. (a) The function is continuous on [1, 3], and differentiable on (1, 3). The Mean Value Theorem does apply.

   (b) $f'(c) = -\dfrac{1}{3}$

2. (a) There is a vertical asymptote at $x = 2$. The function is not continuous on [1, 3], and therefore the Mean Value Theorem does not apply.

   (b) none

3. (a) The function is not differentiable at $x = 2$. The Mean Value Theorem does not apply.

   (b) none

4. (a) The function is continuous on [0, 1], and differentiable on (0, 1). The Mean Value Theorem does apply.

   (b) $f'(c) = 1$

Multiple-Choice Questions

1. (C)

2. (E)

3. (E)

4. (A)

5. (C)

6. (E)

Free-Response Questions

1. $c = -2.029,\ 0,\ 2.029$
2. (a) $c = 0.595$

   (b)

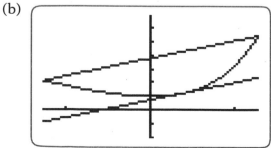

(c) The tangent line and the line joining the endpoints of the interval are parallel.

5.2 Critical Values

Exercises (pages 109–110)

Multiple-Choice Questions

1. (D)

2. (A)

3. (D)

4. (C)

5. (C)

6. (A)

7. (A)

8. (D)

Free-Response Questions

1. (a) relative maximum at $x = 2$
      relative minimum at $x = 3$

   (b) The function is increasing on the intervals $(-\infty, 2)$ and $(3, \infty)$. The function is decreasing on the interval $(2, 3)$.

2. (a) critical values: $x = \pm\dfrac{\sqrt{3}}{3}$

   (b) relative maximum at $x = -\dfrac{\sqrt{3}}{3}$; relative minimum at $x = \dfrac{\sqrt{3}}{3}$

   (c) absolute maximum = 504; absolute minimum = -0.385

3. (a) critical value: $x = 0$
   (b) relative minimum at $x = 0$
   (c) absolute minimum = -1; absolute maximum = 3

5.3 Concavity and the Second Derivative

Exercises (page 113)

Multiple-Choice Questions

1. (C)

2. (D)

3. (E)

4. (B)

Free-Response Questions

1.

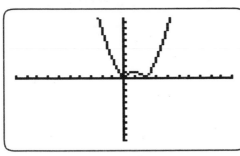

$$f(x) = |x^2 - 2x|$$

(a) critical values: $x = 0, 1, 2$

(b) relative minima at $x = 0, 2$; relative maximum at $x = 1$

(c) concave down: $(0, 2)$; concave up: $(-\infty, 0)$ and $(2, \infty)$

2.

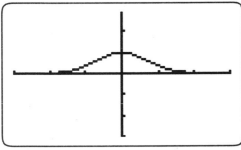

$$f(x) = e^{-x^2}$$

(a) domain = {real numbers},
range = $\{0 < y \leq 1\}$

(b) horizontal asymptote: $y = 0$

(c) even

(d) $x = 0$

(e) relative maximum = 1 at $x = 0$

(f) absolute maximum = 1 at $x = 0$;
no absolute minimum

(g) $x = \pm\dfrac{\sqrt{2}}{2}$

(h) concave up: $\left(-\infty, -\dfrac{\sqrt{2}}{2}\right)$ and $\left(\dfrac{\sqrt{2}}{2}, \infty\right)$

3. Answers will vary.

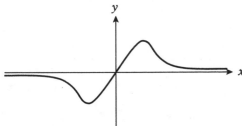

Note that at the origin, this graph is the straight line $y = x$.

5.4 Curve Sketching and the Graphing Calculator

Exercises (page 117)

Multiple-Choice Questions

1. (A)

2. (B)

3. (D)

4. (E)

Free-Response Questions

1. (a) Answers will vary.

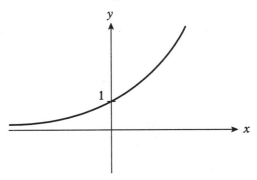

(b) Answers will vary.

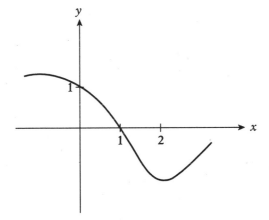

(c) Answers will vary.

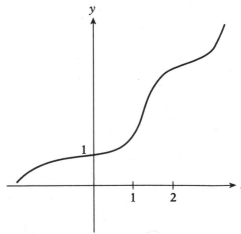

2.

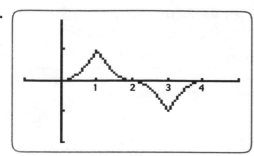

5.5 Optimization

Exercises (page 120)

Multiple-Choice Questions

1. (C)

2. (C)

3. (D)

4. (E)

Free-Response Questions

1. $A = \dfrac{4a^3 \sqrt{3}}{9} \approx 0.77a^3$

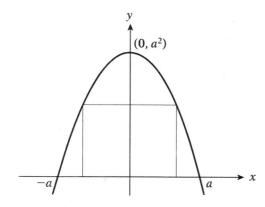

2. maximum area = 3,750 ft²

3. maximum area = 31.831 ft²

Multiple-Choice Questions

1. (A)

2. (C)

3. (A)

4. (E)

5. (B)

6. (B)

7. (C)

8. (C)

9. (D)

10. (D)

11. (C)

12. (D)

13. (D)

14. (C)

15. (B)

16. (C)

17. (B)

18. (D)

19. (E)

20. (B)

21. (E)

22. (C)

23. (A)

24. (B)

25. (C)

Free-Response Questions

1. (a) 0.690

   (b)
   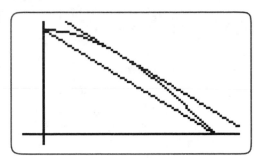

2. (a) The critical values are $x = -1$ and $x = 2$. $x = -1$ is a relative minimum. $x = 2$ is neither.

   (b) The function is increasing on the intervals $(-1, 2)$ and $(2, 3)$.

   (c) $x = 0$ and $x = 2$ are both points of inflection of f.

   (d)
   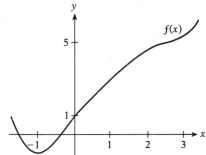

3. (a)
   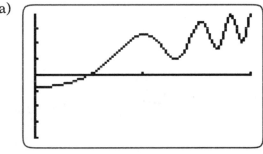

   $y = x - \sin(e^x)$ on $[0, \pi]$

   (b) critical numbers: $x = 1.159$; relative minimum

   (c) increasing: $(1.159, 2\pi)$

   (d) points of inflection: $x = 0.666, 2.475$ concave up: $(0.666, 2.475)$

   (e) range: $\{-1.341 \le y \le 5.283\}$

4. (a)
   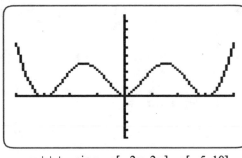

   $y = |x| + x \sin x$ $x[-2\pi, 2\pi]$ $y[-5, 10]$

   (b) $f(-x) = |-x| + (-x)\sin(-x)$
   $= |x| + x \sin x = f(x)$

   (c) Yes. f is continuous at $x = 0$; $f(0) = 0$ and $\lim\limits_{x \to 0} f(x) = 0$.

   (d) No. $f'(x) = \begin{cases} 1 + x \cos x + \sin x, & x > 0 \\ -1 + x \cos x + \sin x, & x < 0 \end{cases}$.

   $\lim\limits_{x \to 0^-} f'(x) = -1$, $\lim\limits_{x \to 0^+} f'(x) = 1$. Therefore, $\lim\limits_{x \to 0} f'(x)$ does not exist, and $f'(0)$ does not exist.

   (e) The TI-89 says $f'(0)$ does not exist. The TI-83 says that $f'(0)$ does exist. TRACE to $(0, 0)$ and ZOOM in several times. Choose a positive and a negative x-value close to 0, and find $\dfrac{dy}{dx}$.

5. The dimensions that will produce the maximum area are 25 ft by 50 ft.

6. The dimensions that will use the minimum amount of material are: length = width = height ≈ 4.642 cm.

7. (a) critical values: $x = -0.431, 3.097$

   (b) point of inflection: $x = \dfrac{4}{3}$

   (c) $c = \dfrac{2}{3}$

   (d) absolute minimum = -5.049; absolute maximum = 16

8. (a) $a = -2$

   (b) $f'(x) = \begin{cases} 2x + a, & x < 2 \\ \dfrac{1}{x - 1}, & x > 2 \end{cases}$

   (c) No. f must be continuous to be differentiable. If f is continuous, $a = -2$. When $a = -2$, $\lim\limits_{x \to 2^-} f'(x) = 2$, and $\lim\limits_{x \to 2^+} f'(x) = 1$; therefore, $f'(2)$ does not exist.

Chapter 6 Techniques and Applications of Antidifferentiation

6.1 Antiderivatives

Exercises (pages 129–130)

1. (a) $e^x + \frac{1}{2}x^2 + c$

   (b) $-\ln|1 + \sin x| + c$

2. (a) $2x^{1/2} + 3x^{1/3} + c$

   (b) $\frac{1}{3}x^3 - x + c$

Multiple-Choice Questions

1. (C)

2. (A)

3. (A)

4. (C)

5. (C)

6. (E)

7. (A)

8. (B)

9. (B)

10. (A)

6.2 Area Under a Curve: Approximation by Riemann Sums

Exercises (pages 137–138)

Multiple-Choice Questions

1. (B)

2. (C)

3. (B)

4. (B)

5. (A)

6. (E)

7. (A)

8. (B)

Free-Response Questions

1. (a) $2(1.5) + 1(2.1) + 1.5(2.4) + 2(2.8)$
   $+ 1.5(2.2) + 2.5(1.8) + 1.5(1.6)$
   $= 3 + 2.1 + 3.6 + 5.6 + 3.3 + 4.5 + 2.4$
   $= 24.5$ in.

   (b) $\frac{24.5}{12} \approx 2.042$ in./hour

2. (a) 3.7 ft/sec²
   (b) 265 feet
   (c) 4.5 ft/sec²

6.3 The Fundamental Theorem of Calculus

Exercises (pages 143–146)

1. (a) $\frac{4}{3}$

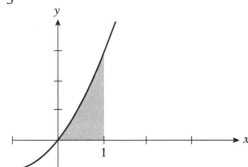

   (b) $e - 1 \approx 1.718$

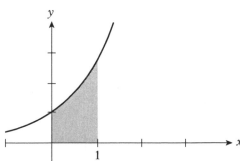

(c) 1

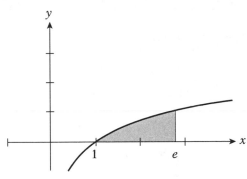

(d) 1

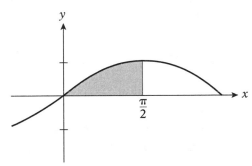

(e) $\dfrac{32}{3}$

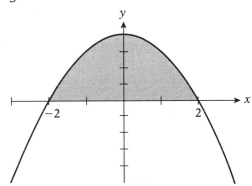

(f) $\dfrac{1}{2}\ln 2$

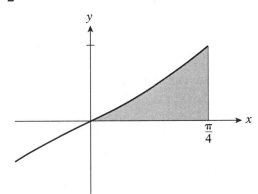

(g) $\dfrac{2}{3}$

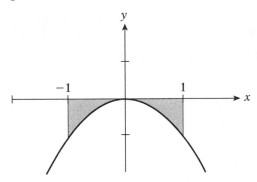

(h) 1

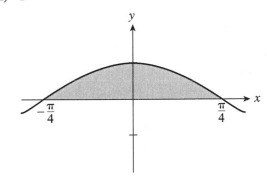

2. (a) $\displaystyle\int_{-\frac{\pi}{2}}^{\frac{\pi}{2}}\cos x\,dx = 2$

(b) $\displaystyle\int_{0}^{1}(e^x - 1)\,dx = e - 2$

(c) $\displaystyle\int_{0}^{1}\left[(4 - x^2) - (4x - x^2)\right]dx = 2$

(d) $\displaystyle\int_{-1.353}^{1}\left[(-x + 1) - (x^4 - 1)\right]dx = 4.014$

(e) $\displaystyle\int_{-1}^{1}(x^3 + 1)\,dx + \int_{1}^{3}(-x + 3)\,dx = 4$

3. (a) $\displaystyle\int_{-1}^{2}(y + 2 - y^2)\,dy$ or

$\displaystyle\int_{0}^{1}\left(\sqrt{x} - \left(-\sqrt{x}\right)\right)dx +$

$\displaystyle\int_{1}^{4}\left(\sqrt{x} - (x - 2)\right)dx = 4.5$

(b) $\displaystyle\int_{1}^{\sqrt{2}}\left(\dfrac{2}{x^2} - (x^2 - 1)\right)dx = 0.391$

(c) $\displaystyle\int_{0}^{\ln 3}e^{-2x}\,dx = \dfrac{4}{9}$

(d) $\displaystyle\int_{0}^{2\pi}(\sin x + 1)\,dx = 6.283$

(e) $\displaystyle\int_{-1}^{0}(\cos x - e^x)\,dx = 0.209$

Multiple-Choice Questions

1. (D)
2. (E)
3. (C)
4. (D)
5. (E)
6. (C)
7. (D)
8. (D)
9. (E)
10. (D)
11. (C)

Free-Response Questions

1. $k = \sqrt[3]{4}$

2. $p = \frac{6}{5}, q = \frac{3}{2}$

3. $k = 1.145$

4. Answers will vary.

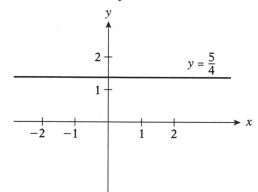

5. $18\pi + 12$

6.4 The Accumulation Function: An Application of Part Two of the Fundamental Theorem
Exercises (pages 148–149)

Multiple-Choice Questions

1. (C)
2. (A)
3. (D)
4. (B)
5. (B)
6. (A)
7. (B)
8. (E)
9. (E)
10. (D)

Free-Response Questions

1. (a) $g(-2) = -2\pi$
$g(0) = -\pi$
$g(2) = 0$
$g(4) = 4$
$g(6) = 4$
(b) $(5, 6)$
(c) $(-2, 0)$ or $(2, 4)$
(d) absolute maximum of $g = 6$
absolute minimum of $g = -2\pi$
(e) points of inflection: $x = 0, 2, 4$
(f)

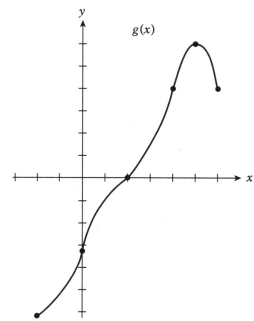

2. (a) The critical points are at $x = 2$ and $x = 4$. At $x = 2$, the sign of the derivative changes from $-$ to $+$; thus, 2 is a minimum. At $x = 4$, the sign of the derivative changes from $+$ to $-$; thus, 4 is a maximum.
(b) absolute maximum of $f = 0$
absolute minimum of $f = -2$
(c) No.
absolute maximum $= 0$ at $x = 0$
relative maximum $= -0.5$ at $x = 4$

(d) f concave up on $(1, 3)$
f concave down on $(3, 5)$

(e) Answers will vary.

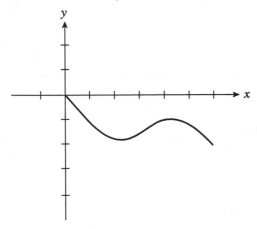

6.5 Integration by the Change of Variables or *u*-Substitution Method

Exercises (pages 153–154)

Multiple-Choice Questions

1. (B)
2. (A)
3. (B)
4. (D)
5. (E)
6. (E)
7. (B)
8. (B)
9. (B)
10. (C)

Free-Response Questions

1. 3.2926
2. $\frac{x^2}{2} + \ln|(x^2 + 5x + 6)| + c$
3. $b = -1.5, 1$

6.6 Applications of the Integral: Average Value of a Function

Exercises (pages 156–157)

Multiple-Choice Questions

1. (D)
2. (B)
3. (C)
4. (B)

Free-Response Questions

1. 56.806°F
2. (a) $\frac{-2}{3}$

    (b) $\frac{3}{4}$

    (c) $\frac{n}{n + 1}$

    (d) 1
3. 0

6.7 Volumes

Exercises (pages 166–168)

Multiple-Choice Questions

1. (A)
2. (C)
3. (A)
4. (B)
5. (E)
6. (C)
7. (C)
8. (D)
9. (B)
10. (C)

Free-Response Questions

1. (a) $4\sqrt{3}:3$

    (b) 1:2
2. (a) 1:2

    (b) 2:3

3. (a) $\frac{128\pi}{3} \approx 134.041$

(b) $\frac{32\pi}{3} \approx 33.51\,\text{oz} = 2.094\,\text{lb}$

4. (a) 49.939 in.³
(b) 0.818 liter; yes

5. (a) 4:1
(b) 8:7

6.8 The Trapezoidal Rule

Exercises (pages 171–172)

Multiple-Choice Questions

1. (B)

2. (A)

3. (A)

4. (C)

Free-Response Questions

1. (a) 4.6875
(b) 4.667

2. (a) −1.28
(b) −1.333

3. (a) 1.677
(b) 1.683

4. If the function is concave up, then all segments that connect points of subdivision are above the graph; hence the approximation is greater than the actual value. If the function is concave down, then all segments that connect points of subdivision are below the graph; hence the approximation is less than the actual value.

6.9 Arc Length and Area of a Surface of Revolution

Exercises (page 175)

Multiple-Choice Questions

1. (D)

2. (B)

3. (E)

4. (E)

Free-Response Questions

1. 9.688

2. (a) 1.132

(b) $\pi\left(1 - \dfrac{1}{c}\right)$

(c) π

Chapter Assessment

(pages 176–179)

Multiple-Choice Questions

1. (B)

2. (A)

3. (B)

4. (A)

5. (D)

6. (C)

7. (C)

8. (C)

9. (A)

10. (E)

11. (A)

12. (B)

13. (D)

14. (A)

15. (C)

16. (C)

17. (B)

18. (A)

19. (C)

20. (A)

21. (A)

22. (B)

23. (C)

24. (B)

25. (E)

Free-Response Questions

1. 0.654, $x = 0.680$

2. $\frac{\pi}{4} \approx 0.785$

3.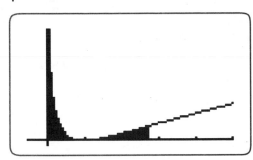

(a) 0.718
(b) 1.459
(c) 10.036
(d) 2.232
(e) 7.567
(f) 0.465
(g) 0.710

4.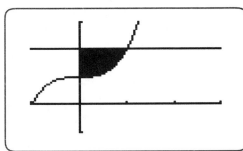

(a) 0.75
(b) 7.405
(c) 1.885
(d) 2.693
(e) 2.827

5.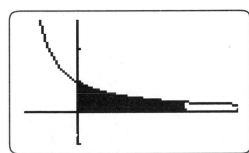

(a) 1.2436
(b) 0.9769
(c) 1.093
(d) 1.110

6.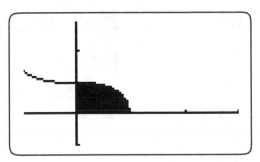

(a) 0.9095
(b) 0.7095
(c) 0.8505
(d) 0.8095

7. (a) $g(0) = 0$

$g(1) = \frac{3}{4}$

$g(2) = \frac{3}{4}$

$g(3) = \frac{1}{4}$

(b) $(-1, 1.5)$
(c) $(-1, 1)$ or $(2, 3)$
(d) The absolute minimum of $g = -\frac{1}{4}$ at $x = -1$.

8. (a) $g(-2) = 1$

$g(0) = -\frac{3}{2}$

$g(2) = 1$

(b) $(-1.75, 0)$ or $(1.75, 2)$
(c) $(-2, -1)$ or $(1, 2)$
(d) The absolute maximum of $g = \frac{9}{8}$ at $x = -1.75$ and at $x = 1.75$.

9. Car A travels 10 ft farther than car B.

10. (a) $a(2) = 3$ ft/sec^2
(b) $x(2) = \frac{8}{3}$
(c) $t = 0$ or $t = 1$
(d) 1

11. (a) 5.204
(b) 46.679
(c) x minimum $= 1$ at $t = 0$; y minimum $= 1$ at $t = -1$

Chapter 7 Separable Differential Equations and Slope Fields

7.1 Separable Differential Equations

Exercises (page 184)

(a) $y = \dfrac{x^3}{3} + \dfrac{x^2}{2} + c$

(b) $y = Ce^{-\frac{1}{x}}$

(c) $y = \dfrac{1}{\sqrt{1 - 2x}}$

(d) $y = Ce^{\frac{x^2}{2} + x}$

Multiple-Choice Questions

1. (A)

2. (E)

3. (D)

4. (A)

5. (A)

Free-Response Questions

1. (a) 3.125 g

   (b) $y = 100e^{-6.93 \times 10^{-4}t}$

2. (a) $\dfrac{dr}{dt} = 2$

   $\dfrac{dV}{dt} = kS$

   $V = \dfrac{4}{3}\pi r^3$

   $\dfrac{dV}{dt} = \dfrac{4}{3}\left(3r^2 \dfrac{dr}{dt}\right)$

   $\dfrac{dV}{dt} = 4\pi r^2(2) = kS$

   $8\pi r^2 = k(4\pi r^2)$

   (b) $\dfrac{8\pi r^2}{4\pi r^2} = \dfrac{k(4\pi r^2)}{4\pi r^2}$

   $k = 2$

3. $y = -\dfrac{1}{x^3}$

7.2 Slope Fields

Exercises (pages 187–188)

Multiple-Choice Questions

1. (B)

2. (E)

3. (C)

4. (A)

5. (C)

Free-Response Questions

1. (a)

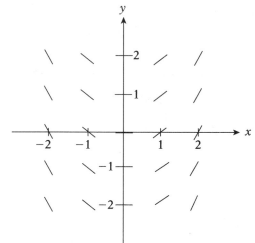

(b) even

(c) no horizontal asymptote

(d)

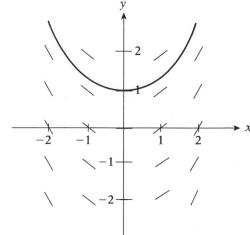

(e)

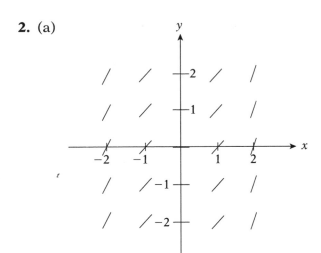

2. (a)

(b) odd

(c) no horizontal asymptote

(d)

(e)

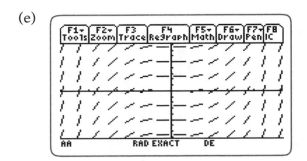

3. (a)

(b) neither

(c) horizontal asymptote $y = 0$

(d)

(e)

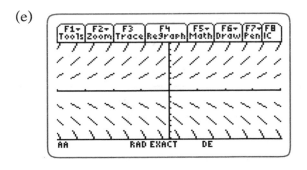

4. (a)

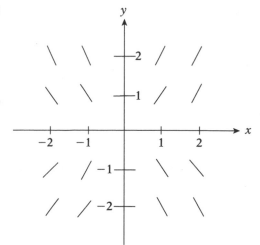

(b) even

(c) no horizontal asymptote

(d)

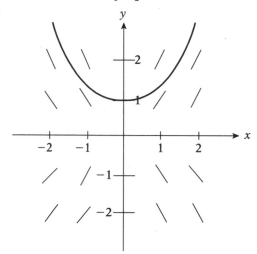

(e)

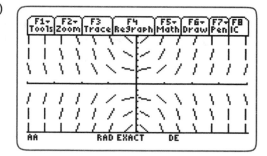

5. (a) $\dfrac{dy}{dx} = 0$ at $(0, 1)$, $(0, 2)$, $(0, -1)$, and $(0, -2)$.

$\dfrac{dy}{dx} = 2$ at $(1, 1)$, $(-1, -1)$, $(2, 2)$, and $(-2, -2)$.

$\dfrac{dy}{dx} = 4$ at $(2, 1)$ and $(-2, -1)$.

$\dfrac{dy}{dx} = 1$ at $(1, 2)$ and $(-1, -2)$.

$\dfrac{dy}{dx} = -2$ at $(2, -2)$ and $(-2, 2)$.

$\dfrac{dy}{dx}$ is undefined at $(0, 0)$.

(b)

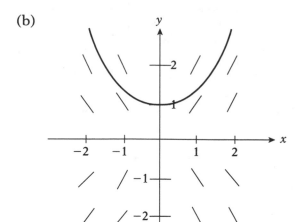

(c) $\dfrac{dy}{dx} > 0$ in Quadrants I and III.

$\dfrac{dy}{dx} < 0$ in Quadrants II and IV.

(d) $\dfrac{dy}{dx} = 0$ for $x = 0$ and $y \neq 0$.

$\dfrac{dy}{dx}$ is undefined for $y = 0$, $x \neq 0$.

7.3 The Connection Between a Slope Field and Its Differential Equation

Exercises (pages 189–191)

1. IV

2. I

3. II

4. III

5. VI

6. V

Multiple-Choice Questions

1. (C)

2. (E)

3. (B)

4. (B)

Free-Response Questions

1. (a) and (b)

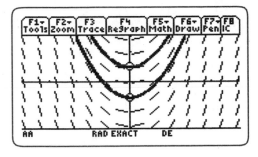

(c) $y = x^2 + c$

2. (a) and (b)

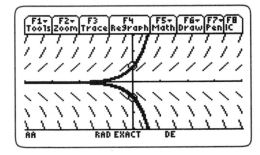

(c) $y = ce^{2x}$

3. (a) and (b)

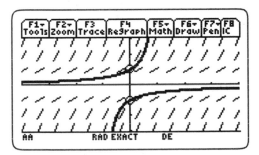

(c) $y = -\dfrac{1}{x - c}$

4. (a) and (b)

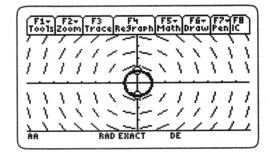

(c) $x^2 + y^2 = c$

Chapter Assessment

(pages 192–196)

Multiple-Choice Questions

1. (D)	**11.** (C)
2. (C)	**12.** (B)
3. (D)	**13.** (A)
4. (D)	**14.** (A)
5. (A)	**15.** (B)
6. (B)	**16.** (B)
7. (B)	**17.** (D)
8. (B)	**18.** (E)
9. (A)	**19.** (B)
10. (A)	**20.** (C)

Free-Response Questions

1. (a) 3.75 cents/year
 (b) 73.19 cents
 (c) 75.05 cents
 (d) 4.436 cents; rate of increase in fare in 1986

2. (a) −3.067 billion dollars/year is the rate of change of loss from 2000 to 2003.
 (b) −6.6 billion dollars is the average amount of loss per year from 2000 to 2003.
 (c) Between 2000 and 2001, the average rate of change of R was −7.986 billion dollars.
 (d) −10.200 billion dollars per year is the average rate of change of R from 2000 to 2003.

3. (a) $y = x - 1$
 (b) Since $y'' = -2$ at $x = 1$, the graph of the solution is concave down at $x = 1$.
 (c) $y = \tan\left(1 - \dfrac{1}{x}\right)$

4. (a) 52 billion dollars/year
 (b) 2,910 billion dollars
 (c) 35.898 billion dollars/year; rate of increase in debt in 1995
 (d) 2,858.143 billion dollars

Chapter 8 Methods of Integration

8.1 Integration by Parts
Exercises (page 202)

1. $x \arcsin x + \sqrt{1 - x^2} + c$

2. $\frac{x^2}{2} \ln x - \frac{x^2}{4} + c$

3. $\frac{1}{2} e^{x^2} + c$

Multiple-Choice Questions

1. (A)

2. (B)

3. (B)

4. (D)

Free-Response Question

(a) $\pi(e - 2)$

(b) $2e - \dfrac{e^2 + 1}{2}$

(c) $k = 2.156$

8.2 Integration by the Method of Partial Fractions
Exercises (pages 205–206)

1. $\frac{1}{2} \ln \left| \dfrac{x - 1}{x + 1} \right| + c$

2. $\frac{1}{2} \ln \left| x^2 - 1 \right| + c$

3. $\frac{x^2}{2} + \frac{1}{2} \ln \left| x^2 - 1 \right| + c$

4. $x + \frac{1}{2} \ln \left| \dfrac{x - 1}{x + 1} \right| + c$

5. $3 \ln \left| x - 3 \right| - 2 \ln \left| x - 2 \right| + c$

Multiple-Choice Questions

1. (B)

2. (C)

3. (B)

4. (B)

5. (D)

Free-Response Questions

1. 0.058

2. (a) $\ln \left| u^3 - 4u \right| + c$

   (b) $\frac{13}{8} \ln \left| u^2 - 4 \right| - \frac{1}{4} \ln \left| u \right| + c$

8.3 Improper Integrals
Exercises (pages 208–209)

1. diverges; ∞

2. diverges; ∞

3. diverges; ∞

4. diverges; ∞

Multiple-Choice Questions

1. (E)

2. (B)

3. (E)

4. (E)

5. (C)

Free-Response Questions

1. (a) $\frac{1}{2}$
   (b) $\frac{\pi}{4}$
   (c) $\frac{\pi}{2}$
   (d) does not exist

2. (a) $p < 1$
   (b) $p > 1$
   (c) $p < 1$
   (d) $p > 1$

Chapter Assessment
(pages 209–212)

1. $xe^x - e^x + c$

2. $x\left((\ln x)^3 - 3(\ln x)^2 + 6(\ln x) - 6\right) + c$

3. $\frac{1}{4} \ln \left| \dfrac{x - 2}{x + 2} \right| + c$

4. $1 + b \ln b - b$

5. does not exist

6. $\frac{\pi}{2}(e^{-2b} - 1)$

7. does not exist

Multiple-Choice Questions

1. (D)

2. (D)

3. (C)

4. (A)

5. (B)

6. (C)

7. (B)

8. (A)

9. (B)

10. (C)

11. (E)

12. (C)

13. (B)

14. (A)

15. (E)

Free-Response Questions

1. (a) $p = 0, q = 0.864$

(b) $e - \tan 1 - 1 \approx 0.233$

(c) Yes, $x = 0.561$. By Rolle's Theorem, since the function is continuous and differentiable and $h(p) = h(q)$; hence $h'(c) = 0$, and $f'(c) = g'(c) = 0$.

(d) 0.057

2. (a) -0.32 thousand dollars/year $= -\$320/$ year

(b) 2000–2002. The greatest change is 3.2 thousand dollars.

(c) 90 thousand dollars

(d) -1.6 thousand dollars/year

3. (a) $\{x \neq -1\}$

(b) vertical asymptote: $x = -1$
horizontal asymptote: none

(c) $(-1, \infty)$
$$f'(x) = \frac{3x^2}{1 + x^3}; f'(x) > 0; x^3 + 1 > 0;$$
$x > -1.$

(d) $(-\infty, -1) \cup (-1, 0) \cup (\sqrt[3]{2}, \infty)$
$$f''(x) = \frac{3x(2 - x^3)}{(x^3 + 1)^2}; f'' < 0; x < 0 \text{ or}$$
$x > \sqrt[3]{2}.$

4. (a) $-\frac{\pi}{2}, \frac{\pi}{2}, \frac{3\pi}{2}$, 0.2527, 2.889

(b) $\frac{\sqrt{2}}{2} - 1$

(c) 1.845

Chapter 9 Polynomial Approximations and Series

9.1 Introduction
Exercises (page 214)

Multiple-Choice Questions

1. (E)

2. (A)

Free-Response Question

(a) $y = -x + 1$

(b) 0.9

9.2 Sigma Notation
Exercises (pages 216–217)

Multiple-Choice Questions

1. (A)

2. (A)

3. (D)

4. (E)

Free-Response Questions

1. (a) i. 60
   ii. 70
   iii. 70
   iv. 70

   (b) The sum for i. is not equal to the other sums. For example, i. $\neq$ ii. since $n^2 + 1 \neq n(n + 1)$ for $n = 1$ to 5.

2. (a) i. $\displaystyle\sum_{n=2}^{10}\left(1 - \frac{1}{n}\right)$

   ii. $\displaystyle\sum_{n=1}^{9}\left(\frac{1}{n} - \frac{1}{n+1}\right)$

   iii. $\displaystyle\sum_{n=1}^{5}\left(\frac{1}{2n-1} - \frac{1}{2n+1}\right)$

   iv. $\displaystyle\sum_{n=1}^{5}\left(1 - \frac{1}{2n+1}\right)$

   (b) i. 7.071
   ii. 0.9
   iii. 0.909
   iv. 4.1218

9.3 Derivation of the Taylor Polynomial Formula

Exercises (page 221)

Multiple-Choice Questions

1. (B)   3. (C)

2. (A)   4. (B)

Free-Response Questions

1. (a) $\displaystyle\sum_{n=1}^{5}(-1)^{n+1}\frac{(x-1)^n}{n} = (x-1) - \frac{(x-1)^2}{2}$

   $+ \frac{(x-1)^3}{3} - \frac{(x-1)^4}{4} + \frac{(x-1)^5}{5}$

   (b) $\displaystyle\sum_{n=1}^{5}\frac{(-1)^{n+1}}{n} \approx 0.783$

   (c) Yes. The larger the degree, the closer the approximation is to the exact value.

2. (a) 0.5646
   (b) 0.8253
   (c) $\sin^2(0.6) + \cos^2(0.6) \approx 0.5646^2 + 0.8253^2 = 0.99989$

9.4 Finding New Polynomials from Old

Exercises (pages 224–225)

1. (a) $1 + x^2 + x^4 + x^6 + x^8 = \displaystyle\sum_{n=0}^{4}x^{2n}$

   (b) $1 - 2x + (2x)^2 - (2x)^3 + (2x)^4$
   $= \displaystyle\sum_{n=0}^{4}(-1)^n(2x)^n$

   (c) $\frac{1}{3}\left[1 + \frac{x}{3} + \left(\frac{x}{3}\right)^2 + \left(\frac{x}{3}\right)^3 + \left(\frac{x}{3}\right)^4\right]$
   $= \frac{1}{3}\displaystyle\sum_{n=0}^{4}\left(\frac{x}{3}\right)^n$

   (d) $1 + (x-2) + (x-2)^2 + (x-2)^3 +$
   $(x-2)^4 = \displaystyle\sum_{n=0}^{4}(x-2)^n$

   (e) $x^2 - x^5 + x^8 - x^{11} = \displaystyle\sum_{n=1}^{4}(-1)^{n+1}x^{3n-1}$

2. $x^2 + x^4 + x^6 + x^8 = \displaystyle\sum_{n=1}^{4}x^{2n}$

   (a) $x^2 \cdot \frac{1}{1-x^2} = x^2\displaystyle\sum_{n=0}^{3}x^{2n}$
   $= x^2(1 + x^2 + x^4 + x^6)$
   $= x^2 + x^4 + x^6 + x^8$
   $= \displaystyle\sum_{n=1}^{4}x^{2n}$

   (b) $\frac{1}{1-x^2} = 1 + x^2 + x^4 + x^6 + x^8$
   $\frac{1}{1-x^2} - 1 = x^2 + x^4 + x^6 + x^8$
   $= \displaystyle\sum_{n=1}^{4}x^{2n}$

   (c) $\frac{1}{1-x^2} = \displaystyle\sum_{n=0}^{4}x^{2n}$
   $= \frac{1}{2}\left(\displaystyle\sum_{n=0}^{4}(-x)^n + \sum_{n=0}^{4}(x^n)\right)$

3. (a) $\displaystyle\sum_{n=0}^{4}(-1)^n\frac{x^n}{n!}$; center at $x = 0$.

   (b) $\displaystyle\sum_{n=1}^{3}(-1)^{n+1}\frac{(2x)^{2n-1}}{(2n-1)!}$; center at $x = 0$.

   (c) $\displaystyle\sum_{n=1}^{4}(-1)^{n+1}\frac{x^n}{n}$; center at $x = 0$.

   (d) $\frac{1}{2}\displaystyle\sum_{n=1}^{3}(-1)^{n+1}\frac{(2x)^{2n}}{(2n)!}$; center at $x = 0$.

Multiple-Choice Questions

1. (C)
2. (D)
3. (A)
4. (D)

Free-Response Questions

1. (a) $1 + x + x^2 + x^3 + x^4$

   (b) $\frac{1}{5}\left[1 + \frac{x}{5} + \left(\frac{x}{5}\right)^2 + \left(\frac{x}{5}\right)^3 + \left(\frac{x}{5}\right)^4\right]$;
   center at $x = 0$.

   (c) $\frac{1}{5}\left[1 + \frac{x^2}{5} + \frac{x^4}{25}\right]$; center at $x = 0$.

2. (a) $1 + x + \frac{x^2}{2!} + \frac{x^3}{3!} + \frac{x^4}{4!}$

   (b) $1 + \ln x + \frac{(\ln x)^2}{2!} + \frac{(\ln x)^3}{3!} + \frac{(\ln x)^4}{4!}$

   (c) Tables will vary.

   (d) $f(\ln x)$ and x are closer the closer x is to 1.

9.5 Error Formula for Taylor Polynomial Approximations
Exercises (pages 226–227)

1. 2.844×10^{-6}

2. 0.063

3. $n = 7$

Multiple-Choice Questions

1. (B)
2. (B)
3. (C)

Free-Response Questions

1. (a) $1 + \frac{1}{3}(x - 1) - \frac{1}{9}(x - 1)^2$

   (b) 1.222

   (c) maximum error < 0.0617

2. (a) $1 + x - x^2 + x^3 - \cdots + (-1)^{n+1}x^n$

   (b) $1 + \sum_{k=1}^{n}(-1)^{k+1}x^k$

9.6 Sequences and Series
Exercises (pages 240–242)

1. diverges
2. diverges
3. converges
4. converges
5. converges
6. converges
7. converges
8. converges
9. converges
10. converges
11. diverges
12. converges
13. (a) converges conditionally
    (b) $x = 1$: converges absolutely
       $x = 2$: diverges
       $x = 3$: diverges
    (c) converges absolutely

Multiple-Choice Questions

1. (A)
2. (C)
3. (C)
4. (D)
5. (B)
6. (B)
7. (D)
8. (C)
9. (B)
10. (E)

Free-Response Questions

1. (a) $p > 0$

   (b) $\frac{1}{(k + 1)^p}$

2. (a) 0.783

   (b) 3.505×10^{-12}

   (c) The error would decrease. The error is less than $(n + 1)^{\text{st}}$ term. As the number of terms increases, the error decreases.

3. (a) 1.645; 2,304

(b) 1.718; 6

(c) $\displaystyle\sum_{n=1}^{\infty} \frac{1}{n^2}$ needs many more terms than $\displaystyle\sum_{n=1}^{\infty} \frac{1}{n!}$ to arrive at a sum correct to three decimal places. Therefore, $\displaystyle\sum_{n=1}^{\infty} \frac{1}{n!}$ converges to its sum much faster than $\displaystyle\sum_{n=1}^{\infty} \frac{1}{n^2}$.

4. (a) $\dfrac{1}{256} \approx 0.003906$

(b) exact sum = 0.8; actual error = 0.003125. The actual error is less than the estimated error.

9.7 The Power Series

Exercises (pages 246–248)

1. (a) $(-3, 3)$

(b) $(-\infty, \infty)$

(c) $\left[-\dfrac{1}{3}, \dfrac{1}{3}\right)$

(d) $\left[-\dfrac{1}{3}, \dfrac{1}{3}\right)$

2. $1 + 2x + 3x^2 + \cdots = \displaystyle\sum_{n=1}^{\infty} nx^{n-1}, (-1, 1)$

3. $1 + 3x + 6x^2 + \cdots = \displaystyle\sum_{n=2}^{\infty} \frac{n(n-1)}{2} x^{n-2}, (-1, 1)$

4. $e^{1/2} = \sqrt{e}$

5. 1

Multiple-Choice Questions

1. (A)

2. (A)

3. (C)

4. (A)

5. (C)

6. (C)

7. (A)

8. (A)

Free-Response Questions

1. (a) $\displaystyle\sum_{n=1}^{\infty} \frac{(2x)^n}{n!}, (-\infty, \infty)$

(b) $\displaystyle\sum_{n=0}^{\infty} \frac{(2x)^n}{n!} \cdot 2$

(c) $f'(x) = 2e^{2x} = 2\left[1 + 2x + \dfrac{(2x)^2}{2!} + \dfrac{(2x)^3}{3!} + \cdots\right] = 2\displaystyle\sum_{n=0}^{\infty} \frac{(2x)^n}{n!}$

(d) $\displaystyle\sum_{n=0}^{\infty} \frac{2}{n!}$

2. (a) $f(x) = x(1 - \cos x)$

(b) $F(x) = \displaystyle\sum_{n=1}^{\infty} (-1)^{n+1} \frac{x^{2n+2}}{(2n+2)(2n)!}$

3. (a) $f(x) = \dfrac{3}{3-x}, \{|x| < 3\}$

(b) $g(x) = -3 \ln|3 - x| + c$

(c) $3\displaystyle\sum_{n=0}^{\infty} \frac{\left(\dfrac{x}{3}\right)^{n+1}}{n+1} - 3\ln 3, [-3, 3)$

(d) 1.216

4. (a) $P_3(x) = 1 + 2(x - 1) + \dfrac{3}{2}(x - 1)^2 - \dfrac{1}{3}(x - 1)^3$

(b) $P_3(0.9) = 0.815$

(c) The polynomial is only an approximation. $f(x) = P_3(x) + g(x)$.

5. (a) $\dfrac{1}{2} - \dfrac{1}{4}(x - 2) + \dfrac{1}{8}(x - 2)^2 - \dfrac{1}{16}(x - 2)^3$

(b) $-\dfrac{1}{4} + \dfrac{1}{4}(x - 2) - \dfrac{3}{16}(x - 2)^2$

(c) $c + \dfrac{1}{2}(x - 2) - \dfrac{1}{8}(x - 2)^2 + \dfrac{1}{24}(x - 2)^3 - \dfrac{1}{64}(x - 2)^4$

6. (a) $1 - (x - 1) + (x - 1)^2 - (x - 1)^3 + \cdots = \displaystyle\sum_{n=0}^{\infty} (-1)^n (x - 1)^n$

(b) $(0, 2)$

(c) $\displaystyle\sum_{n=1}^{\infty} (-1)^n n(x - 1)^{n-1}, (0, 2)$

(d) $\displaystyle\sum_{n=0}^{\infty} (-1)^n \frac{(x - 1)^{n+1}}{n + 1}$ The interval of convergence is $0 < x \leq 2$.

Chapter Assessment

1. $\frac{1}{11} \approx 0.091$

2. $n = 10$

3. 0.00026

4. (a) p-series, $p = \frac{1}{2}$

   (b) p-series, $p = 4$

   (c) Direct Comparison Test with either
   $$\sum_{n=1}^{\infty} \left(\frac{1}{4}\right)^n \text{ or } \sum_{n=1}^{\infty} \frac{1}{n^4}$$

   (d) geometric series, $r = \frac{2}{5}$

   (e) telescoping series

   (f) alternating series

   (g) Test for Divergence or Integral Test

   (h) Ratio Test

   (i) Test for Divergence

   (j) alternating series

   (k) Test for Divergence

   (l) geometric series, $r = \frac{2}{3}$, and p-series, $p = 3$

   (m) geometric series, $r = 2.5$

5. (a) diverges; p-series with $p < 1$

   (b) converges; p-series with $p > 1$

   (c) converges; $0 < a_n < \frac{1}{4^n}$

   (d) converges; geometric series with $r < 1$

   (e) converges; limit can be found $= 1$

   (f) converges; alternating series with $\lim_{n \to \infty} a_n = 0$

   (g) diverges; $\lim_{n \to \infty} a_n \neq 0$

   (h) converges; $\lim \frac{a_{n+1}}{a_n} = 0$

   (i) diverges; $\lim_{n \to \infty} a_n \neq 0$

   (j) converges; $\lim_{n \to \infty} a_n = 0$ and alternating series

   (k) diverges; $\lim_{n \to \infty} a_n \neq 0$

   (l) converges; sum of two convergent series: one is geometric with $r < 1$, the other is a p-series with $p > 1$

   (m) diverges; geometric series with $r > 1$

6. (a) The sum of the series can be found for 4(d) and 4(e).

   (b) For 4(d): $\sum_{n=0}^{\infty} \left(\frac{2}{5}\right)^n = \frac{5}{3}$

   For 4(e): $\sum_{n=2}^{\infty} \left(\frac{1}{n-1} - \frac{1}{n}\right) = 1$

7. (a) 2.283

   (b) 0.241

   (c) 0

   (d) $\frac{10}{11} \approx 0.909$

8. (a) 8

   (b) $\frac{7}{3}$

   (c) 0.267

9. (a) $\frac{2}{3}$

   (b) $\frac{3}{4}$

   (c) $\frac{7}{17} \approx 0.412$

10. (a) $\left[-\frac{1}{2}, \frac{1}{2}\right]$

    (b) $[4, 6)$

    (c) $[1, 2]$

11. (a) $e^2 - 1$

    (b) $\ln 2$

    (c) $\frac{100}{121} \approx 0.826$

    (d) $\frac{1-x}{1+x}$

    (e) $\cos 1$

    (f) $\arctan x$

Multiple-Choice Questions

1. (A)

2. (B)

3. (B)

4. (E)

5. (B)

6. (A)

7. (E)

8. (C)

9. (B)

10. (A)

11. (B)

12. (C)

13. (C)

14. (E)

15. (B)

16. (C)

17. (D)

18. (E)

19. (D)

20. (C)

Free–Response Questions

1. (a) $y - 1 = 2(x - 2)$

   (b) $\displaystyle\sum_{n=1}^{5} n(x - 2)^{n-1}$

   (c) 5

   (d) No. The polynomial is only an approximation to $f(x)$.

2. (a) $T(x) = e^2 + e^2(x - 2) + \dfrac{e^2}{2!}(x - 2)^2 + \cdots$

   The interval of convergence is $(-\infty, \infty)$.

   (b) $\displaystyle\sum_{n=0}^{\infty} e^2 \frac{(x - 2)^n}{n!} = e^2 \sum_{n=0}^{\infty} \frac{(x - 2)^n}{n!}$
   $= e^2 \cdot e^{x-2} = e^x$

   (c) $T'(x) = \displaystyle\sum_{n=1}^{\infty} e^2 \frac{(x - 2)^{n-1}}{(n - 1)!}$

3. (a) $2\ln 2 - 1 \approx 0.386$. The value of the integral represents the area under $y = \ln x$ on $[1, 2]$.

   (b) 0.3846

   (c) $2\ln 2 - 1 \approx 0.386$

   (d) $\pi \displaystyle\int_0^{\ln 2} (2 - e^y)^2 \, dy$ or $2\pi \displaystyle\int_1^2 (2 - x) \ln x \, dx$

4. (a)

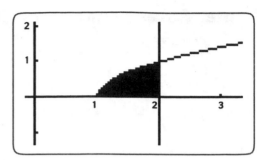

   (b) $\pi \displaystyle\int_0^1 (4 - (y^2 + 1)^2) \, dy$ or
   $2\pi \displaystyle\int_1^2 x \sqrt{x - 1} \, dx.$

   (c) $k = 0.367.$ $\displaystyle\int_0^k (4 - (y^2 + 1)^2) \, dy$
   $= \dfrac{1}{2} \displaystyle\int_0^1 (4 - (y^2 + 1)^2) \, dy$

5. (a) $x = 0.438, 1, 4.688, 1$

   (b) 0.775

   (c) tangent to $f(x)$: $x = 1$
   tangent to $g(x)$: $y = x - 1$

   (d) $\{x > 0\}$

6. (a) $f(-3)$ is a relative maximum. $f(0)$ is a relative minimum. $f'(x)$ changes from $-$ to $+$ at $x = 0$. At $x = -3$, $f'(x)$ changes from $+$ to $-$.

   (b) $x = 0$. $f''(x)$ changes from $-$ to $+$.

   (c) f cannot be odd. If f is odd and has a relative maximum at $x = -3$, then it has a relative minimum at $x = 3$.

   f cannot be even. If f is even and relative maximum at $x = -3$, then relative maximum at $x = 3$.

   (d)

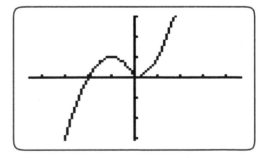

Chapter 10 Logistic Growth, Euler's Method, and Other BC Topics

10.1 The Logistic Growth Model

Exercises (pages 256–257)

1. $y = 5 - 4e^{-t}$

2. $y = \sqrt{2t^2 + 14t}$

3. $y = 10e^{2t}$

4. $y = 2e^{t^2}$

5. $y = -\frac{2}{3}t^3 + 10t^2 - 72$

6. $y = \dfrac{10}{1 + 9e^{-40t}}$

7. $t = \dfrac{\ln A}{Mk}$

Multiple-Choice Questions

1. (B)

2. (C)

3. (E)

4. (C)

Free-Response Questions

1. (a)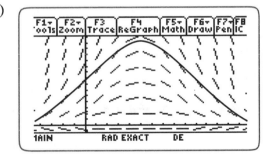

   (b) $y = 5e^{2t - t^2}$

   (c) $\left(1 \pm \dfrac{\sqrt{2}}{2}, 5\sqrt{e}\right)$

   $\approx (1.707, 8.2436), (0.293, 8.2436)$

2. (a) $M = 50, k = 0.0179, y = \dfrac{50}{1 + 24e^{-0.8959t}}$

   (b) $t = 3.547$ days

3. (a) 500

   (b) $y = \dfrac{500}{1 + 9e^{-1.5t}}$

   (c) 250

(d)

```
F1▾  F2▾  F3   F4    F5▾  F6▾ F7▾ F8
ools Zoom Trace ReGraph Math Draw Pen IC
```

```
A          RAD EXACT      DE
```

(e)

1 day	166
2 days	345
3 days	454
4 days	489
5 days	497

10.2 Euler's Approximation Method

Exercises (pages 260–261)

1. $f(0.2) \approx 1.41$

2. $f(1.2) \approx 1.63$

Multiple-Choice Questions

1. (A)

2. (C)

3. (E)

4. (C)

Free-Response Questions

1. (a)

x	y (approximate)
1	0 (actual value)
1.2	0.2
1.4	0.367

(b) At $(1, 0)$ the tangent line is $y = x - 1$.

At $(1.2, 0.2)$ the tangent line is $y = 0.833x - 0.8$.

At $(1.4, 0.367)$ the tangent line is $y = 0.714x - 0.633$.

(c)

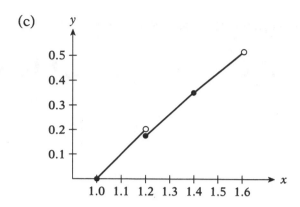

(d) $y = \ln x$

$$P(x) = (x - 1) - \frac{(x - 1)^2}{2} + \frac{(x - 1)^3}{3}$$

error ≈ 0.0049

2. (a)

x	y (approximate)
0	0
0.2	0.1
0.4	0.196
0.6	0.282

(b) $y = \frac{1}{2} \arctan x$

$y(0.6) \approx 0.3676 - 0.1646 + 0.0057$

$= 0.2087$

(c) error ≈ 0.0615

(d) The graph of y is concave down for $x > 0$. Therefore, the tangent lines are above the curve. Thus, the Euler's method approximation to $y(0.6)$ using tangent lines is greater than the actual value and is greater than the Taylor series approximation of $y(0.6)$.

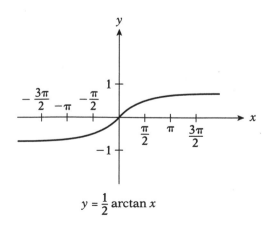

$y = \frac{1}{2} \arctan x$

10.3 Logarithmic Differentiation
Exercises (pages 262–263)

Multiple-Choice Questions

1. (D)

2. (D)

3. (E)

4. (D)

Free-Response Questions

1. (a) No; a periodic function repeats the same values.

(b) (2.031, 1.165), (6.418, 1.849), (12.6, 2.532)

(c) $y = 0.53 + 0.792 \ln x$. $\cos x$ has its maximum value of 1 at $x = 2\pi, 4\pi, 6\pi, \ldots$. When $\cos x = 1$, $f(x) = \ln x$. Therefore, the relative maxima of $f(x)$ lie on the curve $y = \ln x$.

2. (a) $x > 0$

(b) $(e, e^{1/e}) \approx (e, 1.4447)$

10.4 L'Hôpital's Rule
Exercises (page 266)

Multiple-Choice Questions

1. (D)

2. (A)

3. (A)

4. (B)

Free-Response Questions

1. (a) i. 0

ii. 0

iii. 0

iv. 0

(b) As $x \to \infty$, exponential functions are the "strongest," polynomial functions are the second "strongest," and logarithmic functions are the least "strong."

2. (a) 1

(b) undefined

(c) $p > 1$

3. (a) does not exist

(b) does not exist

(c) $p > 1$

10.5 Polar Curves

Exercises (pages 276–277)

1. (a) iii.
   (b) vi.
   (c) iv.
   (d) i.
   (e) vii.
   (f) v.
   (g) ii.

2. 4

3. 1

Multiple-Choice Questions

1. (B)

2. (E)

3. (B)

4. (A)

Free-Response Questions

1. (a)

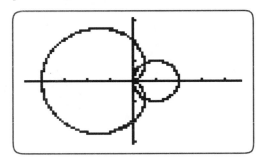

$$\text{pole}, \left(1, \frac{\pi}{3}\right), \left(1, \frac{5\pi}{3}\right) = \left(-1, \frac{2\pi}{3}\right)$$

   (b) $-\cot 2\theta$

   (c) At $\left(1, \frac{\pi}{3}\right)$ the slope $= \frac{\sqrt{3}}{3}$.

   At $\left(1, \frac{5\pi}{3}\right) = \left(-1, \frac{2\pi}{3}\right)$ the slope $= -\frac{\sqrt{3}}{3}$.

2. (a) $r = 1 - \sin\theta$: cardioid
   $r = 2\cos\theta$: circle
   (b) pole, (1.6, 5.64)
   (c)

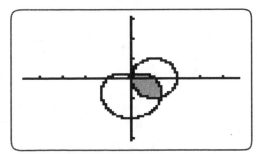

   (d) 1.188

Chapter Assessment

(pages 277–280)

Multiple-Choice Questions

1. (D)

2. (D)

3. (D)

4. (B)

5. (C)

6. (D)

7. (D)

8. (E)

9. (B)

10. (B)

11. (C)

12. (D)

13. (A)

14. (B)

15. (B)

16. (E)

17. (A)

18. (B)

19. (D)

20. (B)

21. (E)

22. (E)

23. (D)

24. (B)

25. (B)

Free-Response Questions

1. (a) $P = \dfrac{2{,}000}{1 + 99e^{-0.8t}}$
   (b) 5.744 days
   (c) after 2 days: 95
   after 4 days: 397

2. $y(0.2) \approx 0.01$

3. (a) $f(x) = x \arctan x - \frac{1}{2}\ln(1 + x^2) + 1$

(b) $1 + \frac{x^2}{2} - \frac{x^4}{12} + \frac{x^6}{30} - \cdots$

$$= 1 + \sum_{0}^{\infty}(-1)^n \frac{x^{2n+2}}{(2n+1)(2n+2)}$$

(c) $\frac{\pi}{4} - \frac{1}{2}\ln 2 \approx 0.4388$

4. (a) $f(x) = \frac{e^x + e^{-x}}{2}$

$f'(x) = \frac{e^x - e^{-x}}{2}$

$f''(x) = \frac{e^x + e^{-x}}{2}$

Since $f(x) = f''(x)$, $f(x)$ is a solution to the equation $y'' = y$.

(b) $y - 5.05 = 4.95(x - \ln 10)$

(c) $f'(x) = \frac{e^x - e^{-x}}{2}$

$x = 0$, $f'(0) = \frac{1 - 1}{2} = 0$

Thus, $(0, 0)$ is on the graph of $f'(x)$.

$f'(-x) = \frac{e^{-x} - e^x}{2}$

$-f'(x) = -\frac{e^x - e^{-x}}{2}$

Since $f'(-x) = -f(x)$, $f'(x)$ is an odd function.

5. (a) 1.1025

(b) 0.058

(c) $x = 0.687$

6. (a) relative maximum of g: $(0, 0)$; relative minimum of g: $(2, -1)$; $g'(x) = f(x)$

The critical values of g are values where $f(x) = 0$ or $f(x)$ is undefined. Thus, the critical values of $g(x)$ are $x = 0$ and $x = 2$.

Since g' changes sign at $x = 0$ from $+$ to $-$, $g(0)$ is a relative maximum.

Since g' changes sign at $x = 2$ from $-$ to $+$, $g(2)$ is a relative minimum.

(b) $x = 2 + \sqrt{2}, 0$

(c) $g''(x) = \begin{cases} -1, & x < 1 \\ 1, & x > 1 \end{cases}$

(d)

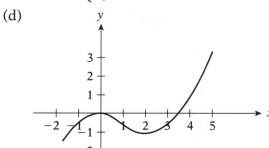

Model Examinations

AB Model Examination 1

Section I
Part A (pages 283–287)

1. (B) $\dfrac{2-y}{x-1}$

$$x \cdot \dfrac{dy}{dx} + y \cdot 1 - \dfrac{dy}{dx} = 2$$

$$x \cdot \dfrac{dy}{dx} - \dfrac{dy}{dx} = 2 - y$$

$$\dfrac{dy}{dx}(x - 1) = 2 - y$$

$$\dfrac{dy}{dx} = \dfrac{2-y}{x-1}$$

2. (D) I and III

3. (A) $\dfrac{3}{5}$

4. (A) -2.7

$\dfrac{dy}{dx} = 2 - 2x$; therefore, the lowest x-value will yield the highest value when substituted for x.

5. (C) $2e^{2\pi} + 2$

$$y' = 2 \cdot e^{2x} + \dfrac{2}{\cos^2(2x)}$$

6. (A) $y = ex + e$

$y' = e^{x+1}$

Substitute 0 for x in y' to get the slope ($m = e$).

Substitute 0 for x in y to get a point on the line $(0, e)$.

$(0, e)$ is the y-intercept (b), and $m = e$; therefore, the line has equation $y = ex + e$.

7. (D) $4 - 2e$

$$v(t) = 2 \int e^t \, dt$$
$$v(t) = 2e^t + c$$
$$v(1) = 2e^1 + c = 2$$
$$2e + c = 2$$
$$c = 2 - 2e$$
$$v(t) = 2e^t + (2 - 2e)$$

$$v(0) = 2e^0 + (2 - 2e)$$
$$= 2(1) + (2 - 2e) = 4 - 2e$$

8. (A) $\dfrac{-3}{7}$

9. (D) -1

10. (D) $\dfrac{1}{t}$

11. (B) $-\dfrac{\sqrt{2}}{2}$

12. (C) $x^3 - \sin(x) + C$

13. (C) $\dfrac{10}{3}$

14. (C) $\dfrac{1}{2} \ln \dfrac{5}{2}$

$$\int_{-1}^{2} \dfrac{x}{x^2 + 1} \, dx = \left[\dfrac{\ln(x^2 + 1)}{2} \right]_{-1}^{2}$$

$$= \dfrac{\ln(2^2 + 1)}{2} - \dfrac{\ln(1^2 + 1)}{2}$$

$$= \dfrac{1}{2} \ln \dfrac{5}{2} = 0.458$$

15. (B) $\dfrac{1}{3}(e^5 - e^2)$

16. (A) $5 \sin 10x$

$$y = \dfrac{1}{2}\left(1 - \cos 2(5x)\right) = \dfrac{1}{2}(1 - \cos 10x)$$

$$\dfrac{dy}{dx} = (10)\dfrac{1}{2}(\sin 10x) = 5 \sin 10x$$

17. (D) $x > \dfrac{1}{6}$

18. (B) $x(5) > x(2)$

19. (E) 100

$$\int_{0}^{5} 20 \, dt + \int_{5}^{10} (60 - 8t) \, dt$$

20. (C) 3. Find the equation of a line with $m = 5$ through $(1, 2)$. Then substitute 1.2 into the resulting equation to find that the answer is 3.

21. (B) $y = -12x + 3\pi + 1$

$$\frac{dy}{dx} = \frac{12 \sin 6x}{(1 + \cos 6x)^2}$$

The slope $= -12$, and the point $= \left(\frac{\pi}{4}, 1\right)$, so the line is $y = -12x + 3\pi + 1$.

22. (D)

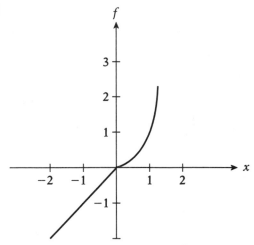

$f(x) = 1x + C_1$ from -2 to 0.

$f(x) = \frac{x^2}{2} + x + C_2$ from 0 to 2.

23. (A) $-\frac{5}{2}$. By solving $x - 2y = 5$, we can see that the slope of the line is $\frac{1}{2}$. The slope of a line perpendicular would be -2.
Take the derivative of $y = x^2 + 3x + 5$, which is $y' = 2x + 3$.
$$2x + 3 = -2; \text{ therefore, } x = -\frac{5}{2}.$$

24. (A) $f(x)$ is continuous everywhere.

25. (A) $2xe^{x^2}(x^2 + 1)$
Use the Product Rule to find the derivative.

26. (A) $e^2 - e^1$
$$\int_0^{\frac{\pi}{2}} e^{2 - \cos x} \sin x \, dx = e^{2 - \cos x} \Big|_0^{\frac{\pi}{2}}$$

27. (A) -2
$$\left(\frac{1}{1 - \frac{1}{2}}\right) \int_{\frac{1}{2}}^1 -\frac{1}{x^2} \, dx$$

28. (C) 1

Section I
Part B (pages 288–290)

1. (A) $\lim_{x \to 5} f(x)$ exists

2. (C) 2
$$f'(y) = 1 - 2 \sin(2x)$$
$$f''(y) = -4 \cos(2x)$$
$$-4 \cos(2x) = 0$$
$$x = -\frac{\pi}{4}, \frac{\pi}{4}, \frac{3\pi}{4}$$

3. (B) -1.5
$f(x) = x$ from 0 to 1. Integrate to find $F(x) = \frac{x^2}{2} + C_1$.

It follows that $F(0) = 0 + C_1 = -3$; therefore, $C_1 = -3$, and $F(x) = \frac{x^2}{2} - 3$ from 0 to 1.

$f(x) = 1$ from 1 to 2. Integrate to find $F(x) = x + C_2$.

To be continuous $\frac{1^2}{2} - 3 = 1 + C_2$; therefore, $C_2 = -3.5$.

$F(x) = x - 3.5$ from 1 to 2.

4. (E) I, II, and III

5. (C) -1 and $\frac{5}{3}$

6. (D) $36 \text{ cm}^2/\text{sec}$

$\frac{dr}{dt} = 6, r = 3$, and $A = \pi r^2$

rate of change in area$= \frac{dA}{dt} = 2\pi r \frac{dr}{dt}$

$\frac{dA}{dt} = 2\pi(6)(3) = 36 \text{ cm}^2/\text{sec}$

7. (A) $x = \sqrt{\frac{\pi}{2} - 1} \approx 0.756$

8. (D) 0.568
$$\int_0^{\frac{\pi}{6}} 2 \cdot \cos(x) - 3 \cdot \tan(x) \, dx$$

9. (B) 4π. Use the disc method.

10. (E) There is no relative maximum. Use the First Derivative Test.

11. (B) 0.955. Find the slope between $(0, 1)$ and $\left(\frac{\pi}{3}, 2\right)$, both points on the graph of $f(x) = \sec x$.

12. (D) $\int \frac{5t^2 + 1}{5t} = \frac{1}{5}\ln(|t|) + \frac{1}{2}t^2 + C = v(t)$

$\frac{1}{2}\ln(|1|) + \frac{1}{2}(1^2) + C = 1$

$C = \frac{1}{2}$

Find $v(2)$ by substituting.

13. (C) 10. Graph, connect the points, and divide the graph into trapezoids to find the area.

14. (E) The average rate of change of $f(x)$ on $[1, 3]$ equals $f'(2)$.

It is not (A) because the limit does not exist.

It is not (B) because the limit is 0.

It is not (C) because f is not differentiable at 1.

It is not (D) because $f(1) = 0$.

15. (C) $\int_0^4 \left(\left(4 - \sqrt{x}\right)^2 - 4\right)dx$

$R(x) = 4 - \sqrt{x}$ and $r(x) = 2$. The bound is $0 \le x \le 4$, so the integral is

$\int_0^4 \left(\left(4 - \sqrt{x}\right)^2 - 4\right)dx.$

16. (E) 6.770

$\int_0^2 \sqrt{1 + (3t^2 - 1)^2}\, dt$

17. (B) $p \ge q$

Section II
Part A (page 291)

1.

(a) $v(t) = \int 20e^{-t/2}dt = -40e^{-t/2} + C$	(a) 4 points
$v(0) = 0$; therefore, $C = 40$.	2: defining both integrals
$v(t) = -40e^{-t/2} + 40$ is constantly increasing. Using $v(10) \approx 39.73$, the starting point for finding the constant for the second integral:	1: limits 1: integrands
$a(t) = -16$, for $t > 10$, and	2: finding $v(t)$ for
$v(t) = -16t + C$.	$\begin{cases} a(t) = 20e^{-t/2}, 0 \le t \le 10 \\ a(t) = -16, \quad t > 10 \end{cases}$
$C \approx 199.73$, using the value $v(10) \approx 39.73$.	
$v(t) = -16t + 199.73$ for $t > 10$, is a constantly decreasing function; therefore, the rocket is descending after 10 seconds.	1: answer
(b) $x(t) = \int -40e^{-t/2} + 40\, dt = 80e^{-t/2} + 40t + C$	(b) 3 points
Since $x(0) = 0$, $C = -80$.	2: defining both integrals
$x(t) = 80e^{-t/2} + 40t - 80$, for $0 \le t \le 10$.	1: limits 1: integrands
$x(10) \approx 320.54$	
Now find the other integral and use $x(10)$.	1: answer
$x(t) = \int -16t + 199.73\, dt = -8t^2 + 199.73t + C$	
$x(10)$ is about 320.54, so $C = -876.76$.	

$x(t) = -8t^2 + 199.73t - 876.76$, for $t > 10$.

The second $x(t)$ function continues the ascent of the first, so the maximum will be found using the second $x(t)$ function. To find the maximum value, the derivative of $x(t)$ is $v(t)$, which is zero at ≈ 12.48.

$\quad x(12.48) \approx 370$

The rocket will reach a height of 370 feet.

(c) Use the second $x(t)$ function from part (b) and find where $x(t) = 0$.

$-8t^2 + 199.73t - 876.76 = 0$ when $t \approx 5.68$ and 19.28. Because 5.68 is not in the range of the function, $t = 19.28$.

$v(19.28) \approx -108.79$, meaning 108.79 ft/sec in the downward direction.

(c) 1 point

1: answer

(d) $x(t) = -8t^2 + 199.73t - 876.76$ for $t > 10$.

(d) 1 point

1: answer

2.

(a) The question asks to find the rate at which the oil is rising in the conical cup. Since the radius of the cone is 4 in. and the height of the cone is 8 in., $\frac{r}{h} = \frac{4}{8}$ or $\frac{r}{h} = \frac{1}{2}$. Thus, $r = \frac{1}{2}h$.

The volume of the cone is $V = \frac{1}{3}\pi r^2 h$. Substituting for r,

$$V = \frac{1}{3}\pi\left(\frac{1}{2}h\right)^2 h = \frac{1}{3}\pi\left(\frac{1}{4}h^2\right)h = \frac{\pi}{12}h^3.$$

Therefore, $\frac{dV}{dt} = \frac{\pi}{12}(3h^2)\frac{dh}{dt}$. Since $h = 3$ and $\frac{dV}{dt} = 2$, the equation becomes:

$$2 = \frac{3\pi}{12}(9)\frac{dh}{dt}, \text{ and } \frac{dh}{dt} = \frac{8}{9\pi} \text{ in./hr} \approx 0.283 \text{ in./hr}$$

(a) 8 points

1: finding the volume of the oil in the cone when oil in the can is 3 inches deep

1: defining radius of surface of the oil in the cone (r) in terms of the depth of the oil (h)

1: finding the height of the oil in the cone when the oil in the can is 3 inches deep

2: setting up the differential

2: implicit differentiation

1: answer

(b) The volume of the cylinder, given by $\pi r^2 h$, is 24π. (This is also the volume of the oil.)

The volume of a cone is $\frac{1}{3}\pi r^2 h$. Since we are trying to find h, we must relate h to r.

$\frac{r}{h} = \frac{1}{2}$; therefore, $r = \frac{h}{2}$.

The volume of the cone, then, is

$$\frac{1}{3}\pi\left(\frac{h}{2}\right)^2 h = \frac{h^3}{12}\pi.$$

$\frac{h^3}{12}\pi = 24\pi$; therefore, $h \approx 6.604$ in.

(b) 1 point

1: answer

3.

(a) $x = 3$ and $x = 6$ First Derivative Test 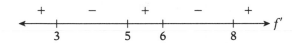 Since the f' values change from positive to negative, 3 and 6 are relative maxima.	(a) 2 points 1: answer 1: justification
(b) Second Derivative Test 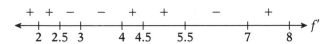 When $f''(x) > 0$ the graph of f is concave up. $\qquad 2 < x < 2.5$ $\qquad 4 < x < 5.5$ $\qquad 7 < x < 8$	(b) 3 points 1: $2 < x < 2.5$ 1: $4 < x < 5.5$ 1: $7 < x < 8$
(c) $x = 2.5, 4, 5.5, 7$ Points of inflection occur when the concavity changes. Use the Second Derivative Test to find the points of inflection. When $f''(x) < 0$ the graph of f is concave down and when $f''(x) > 0$ the graph of f is concave up. Thus, the points of inflection are 2.5, 4, 5.5, and 7.	(c) 2 points 1: answer 1: justification
(d) Yes. The slopes of the tangent lines between $f(2)$ and $f(3)$ are always positive, indicating an increasing function.	(d) 2 points 1: answer 1: justification

Section II
Part B (page 292)

4.

(a) $\displaystyle\int_0^8 x^{2/3}\,dx = \dfrac{3}{5}x^{5/3}\Big|_0^8 = \dfrac{96}{5}$
 	
 $\displaystyle\int_0^k x^{2/3}\,dx = \dfrac{1}{2}\,\text{area} = \dfrac{48}{5}.$
 	
 Thus, $\dfrac{3}{5}k^{5/3} = \dfrac{48}{5}$, $k^{5/3} = 16$ and $k = 16^{3/5}$.
	(a) 4 points
	
	 2: definite integral
	     1: limits
	     1: integrand
	 2: answer

(b) Volume $= \pi\displaystyle\int_0^8 x^{4/3}\,dx = \pi\left(\dfrac{3}{7}x^{7/3}\right)\Big|_0^8 = \dfrac{3\pi}{7}(8^{7/3}) = \dfrac{3\pi}{7}(2^7)$ $= \dfrac{384\pi}{7}.$ $\pi\displaystyle\int_0^p x^{4/3}\,dx = \dfrac{1}{3}\,\text{volume}.$ Thus, $\dfrac{3}{7}\pi x^{7/3}\Big|_0^p = \dfrac{128}{7}\pi,$ $\dfrac{3}{7}p^{7/3} = \dfrac{128}{7}$, $3p^{7/3} = 128$, and $p = \left(\dfrac{128}{3}\right)^{3/7}.$	(b) 5 points 2: volume 3: answer

5.

(a) $h(x) = \displaystyle\int_1^x f(t)\,dt$ $h(2) = \displaystyle\int_1^2 f(t)\,dt = 2.75$ $h(-1) = \displaystyle\int_1^{-1} f(t)\,dt = -\displaystyle\int_{-1}^1 f(t)\,dt$ $= -\left[\displaystyle\int_{-1}^0 f(t)\,dt + \displaystyle\int_0^1 f(t)\,dt\right] = -3.25$	(a) 1 point 1: answer

(b) $h'(x) = f(x)$
    $h(x)$ is decreasing when $h'(x) < 0$, that is, when $f(x) < 0$.
    Use the slope formula to show that $f(x) = 0$ at $x = 3.5$. If the
    x-intercept of $f(x)$ is $(x, 0)$, then $\dfrac{3 - (-1)}{2 - 4} = \dfrac{3 - 0}{2 - x}$. Then
    $-2 = \dfrac{3}{2 - x}$, $-4 + 2x = 3$, $2x = 7$, and $x = 3.5$. Therefore,
    $f(x) < 0$ on the interval $(3.5, 5)$, and $h(x)$ is decreasing on the
    interval $(3.5, 5)$.
	(b) 2 points
	 1: justification
	 1: answer

(c) The critical values of h are values of x where $h'(x) = f(x) = 0$. That is, $x = -1, 3.5$, and 5.	(c) 2 points 1: justification 1: answer

(d) Points of inflection of h are values of x where $h''(x) = 0$, or
    $h''(x)$ is undefined. That is, where $f'(x) = 0$, or $f'(x)$ is unde-
    fined.
 	
    $f'(x) = 0$ has no solution; $f'(x)$ is undefined for $x = 0$, $x = 2$,
    or $x = 4$.
	(d) 2 points
	 1: justification
	 1: answer

Since $f'(x)$ changes sign at $x = 2$ and at $x = 4$ only, these are the points of inflection.

(e) Since $h'(x) = f(x)$ changes from $+$ to $-$ at $x = 3.5$, $h(3.5)$ is a relative maximum. Since this is the only critical value of h, the absolute maximum and the absolute minimum values of h are found by examing the values of h at $x = 3.5$, and at the endpoints, $x = -1$ and $x = 5$.

From part (a), $h(-1) = -3.25$.

$$h(3.5) = \int_1^{3.5} f(t)\, dt = \int_1^2 f(t)\, dt + \int_2^{3.5} f(t)\, dt = 2.75 + 2.25 = 5.$$

$$h(5) = \int_1^5 f(t)\, dt = \int_1^{3.5} f(t)\, dt + \int_{3.5}^5 f(t)\, dt = 5 - 0.75 = 4.25.$$

Thus, the absolute maximum of h is 5 and the absolute minimum of h is -3.25.

(e) 2 points

1: justification

1: answer

6.

(a)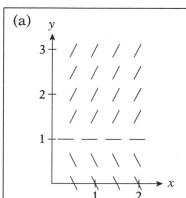

(b)

(c) $\dfrac{dy}{dx} = x(y - 1)$

$$\int \frac{dy}{y - 1} = \int x\, dx$$

$$\ln|y - 1| = \frac{x^2}{2} + c$$

$$e^{\ln|y-1|} = e^{\frac{x^2}{2} + c}$$

$$|y - 1| = Ae^{\frac{x^2}{2}} \text{ (where } A = e^c)$$

$$y = Ae^{\frac{x^2}{2}} + 1$$

$$y(0) = Ae^{\frac{0^2}{2}} + 1$$

$$-1 = Ae^0 + 1$$

$$-2 = A$$

$$y = -2e^{\frac{x^2}{2}} + 1$$

(a) 3 points

1: correct boundaries of slope field

1: zero slope at (1, 1) and (2, 1)

1: positive slope at (1, 2), (2, 2), (1, 3), and (2, 3)

(b) 3 points

3: answer

(c) 3 points

3: answer

AB Model Examination 2

Section I
Part A (pages 293–296)

1. **(B)** $(1, 1)$

$$f'(x) = 6x^2 - 12x + 6$$
$$f''(x) = 12(x - 1)$$
$$x = 1$$

2. **(B)** $\dfrac{7}{10}$

$$\frac{1}{b - a} \int_a^b f(x)\,dx$$
$$\frac{1}{4 - (-1)} \left(\left(\int_{-1}^1 x + 1 \right) + \left(\int_1^4 -x + 3 \right) \right)$$

3. **(C)** $-\dfrac{1}{2}$

$$\int_{\frac{\pi}{2}}^{\pi} \sin x \cos x\,dx = \frac{\sin^2 x}{2} \bigg|_{\frac{\pi}{2}}^{\pi} = -\frac{1}{2}$$

4. **(C)** $f'(c) = \dfrac{f(b) - f(a)}{b - a}$ for at least one c in the interval $[a, b]$.

5. **(B)** $-\dfrac{1}{12}$

$$\frac{dy}{dx} = \frac{-3y + 2}{3x + 6y}$$
$$\frac{-3(1) + 2}{3(2) + 6(1)} = -\frac{1}{12}$$

6. **(D)** 1

7. **(D)** $\dfrac{1}{(x + 2)^2}$

8. **(D)** 4

$$f(x) = \ln(\tan^2 x)$$
$$f'(x) = 2\cot(x) + 2\tan(x)$$
$$2\cot \frac{\pi}{4} + 2\tan \frac{\pi}{4}(2) = 4$$

9. **(E)** does not exist

10. **(C)** $2 \sin x \cos x\, e^{\sin^2 x}$

11. **(B)** 1

12. **(B)** 1

$$x'(t) = 3t^2 - 2t - 1$$
$$3t^2 - 2t - 1 = 0$$

$$(t - 1)(3t + 1) = 0$$
$$t = 1$$

13. **(D)** $x = 1$ and $x = 2$

14. **(C)** $1 - \dfrac{\pi}{2}$

$$\int_0^1 \frac{x^2 - 1}{x^2 + 1} = \int_0^1 \frac{x^2}{x^2 + 1} - \int_0^1 \frac{1}{x^2 + 1}$$
$$x - \arctan(x) - \arctan(x) \bigg|_0^1$$
$$= x - 2\arctan(x) \bigg|_0^1 = 1 - \frac{\pi}{2}$$

15. **(C)** $2 \sqrt[3]{1 + 2x}$

$$\int_2^{2x} \cdot (1 + t)^{1/3} = \frac{3(1 + t)^{4/3}}{4} \bigg|_2^{2x}$$
$$= \frac{3(1 + 2x)^{4/3}}{4} - \frac{3(1 + 2)^{4/3}}{4}$$
$$f'(x) = 2 \sqrt[3]{1 + 2x}$$

16. **(B)**

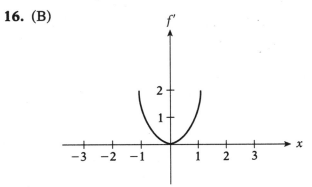

17. **(A)** $y - 3 = 8\sqrt{3}\left(x - \dfrac{\pi}{3} \right)$

$$f'(x) = \frac{4 \sin 2x}{(\cos 2x + 1)^2}$$
$$\text{slope} = 8\sqrt{3}$$
$$y - 3 = 8\sqrt{3}\left(x - \frac{\pi}{3} \right)$$

18. **(A)** A relative maximum at -1 and a relative minimum at 0. Use the First Derivative Test.

19. **(A)** $p = \dfrac{1}{a}$

$$\int_1^a \frac{1}{x}\,dx = \int_p^1 \frac{1}{x}$$
$$\ln(a) = -\ln(p)$$
$$-\ln(a) = \ln(p)$$
$$\ln\left(\frac{1}{a} \right) = \ln(p)$$

20. (D) $y = e^{k(t-1)}$

$$\frac{dt}{dy} = \frac{1}{ky}$$

$$t = \frac{1}{k}\int \frac{dy}{y}$$

$$t = \frac{1}{k}\ln(y) + C$$

$$kt - C = \ln(y)$$

$$e^{kt-C} = y(t)$$

$e^{k-C} = 1$; therefore, $C = k$.

21. (C) $(0, \infty)$

22. (E) 18

$$v(t) = 3t^2 - 12t + 18$$

$v(t) = 18$ at $t = 0$ and $t = 4$. (It reaches its minimum velocity at $t = 2$.)

23. (B) $3(2x + 5)^2$

24. (B) $\int_0^2 (2x - x^2)\, dx$

$$x^2 - 4 = 2x - 4$$

$$x = 0 \text{ or } x = 2$$

25. (A) -2

$$\lim_{x \to \infty} \frac{2x}{\sqrt{x^2 + 1}} = \lim_{x \to -\infty} \frac{\frac{2x}{x}}{\frac{\sqrt{x^2 + 1}}{-\sqrt{x^2}}}$$

$$= \lim_{x \to -\infty} \frac{2}{-\sqrt{1 + \frac{1}{x^2}}} = -2$$

26. (B) For every k between $g(a)$ and $g(b)$, there is a value c in $[a, b]$ such that $g(c) = k$.

27. (B) $\pi \int_0^8 (4 - x^{2/3})^2\, dx$

$V = \pi r^2 \Delta x$ (disc method)

$r = 4 - x^{2/3}$

$x^{2/3} = 4$ when $x = 8$

28. (D) $(-\infty, -\sqrt{3}) \cup (0, \sqrt{3})$

Section I
Part B (pages 297–299)

1. (E) undefined

2. (C) 1

$$\frac{dy}{dx} = \frac{2t + 1}{t^2 + t + 1}$$

3. (A) 0

$$y' = \frac{8\sin(4x)}{\cos^2(4x) + 1}$$

$$\frac{8\sin\left(4 \times \left(\frac{\pi}{2}\right)\right)}{\cos^2\left(4 \times \left(\frac{\pi}{2}\right)\right) + 1} = \frac{0}{4} = 0$$

4. (E) I, II, and III

5. (A) 0.908

$$D = \sqrt{(x - 3)^2 + (x^2 - 2x - 0)^2}$$

$$f(x) = x^4 - 4x^3 + 5x^2 - 6x + 9$$

$$f'(x) = 4x^3 - 12x^2 + 10x - 6$$

$$x = 2.165, y = 0.358$$

$$D = \sqrt{(2.165 - 3)^2 + (0.358 - 0)^2} = 0.908$$

6. (B) 1.172

$$y = \sqrt{4 - x}$$

$$\int_0^4 \left(\sqrt{4 - x}\right)^2 dx$$

$$= 4x - \frac{x^2}{2}\Big|_0^4 = 8$$

$$4x - \frac{x^2}{2} = 4$$

$$x = 1.172$$

7. (A) $-\dfrac{1}{x^2}$

8. (D) $g'(0) = 2$

9. (A) $x = -2$ and $x = 1$

$f'(x) = x^2$ and $g'(x) = 2 - x$

Parallel lines have equal slopes.

$$x^2 = 2 - x$$

$$x = 1 \text{ and } x = -2$$

10. (C) $y = -2x + 2.5$

11. (C) $w = 54.7723$ ft, $l = 54.7723$ ft

$A = lw$

$$l = \frac{3{,}000}{w}$$

$$P = 2w + 2\left(\frac{3{,}000}{w}\right)$$

$$P' = 2 - \left(\frac{6{,}000}{w^2}\right) = 0$$

$$w = 10\sqrt{30} = 54.7723$$

12. (E) II and III

13. (A) $y = \dfrac{1}{2\sqrt{1 - \dfrac{x^2}{4}}}$

14. (C) C

15. (D) The function is both continuous and differentiable at $x = 1$.

16. (C) 6

17. (E) 9.827

$$\int_{-2\sqrt{3}}^{2\sqrt{3}} \left(\sqrt{16 - x^2} - 2\right) dx = 9.827$$

Section II
Part A (page 300)

1.

(a) Since the function clearly rises and falls at least once, and it is differentiable, we can infer that at some point the derivative is zero.	(a) 2: points 2: justification
(b) $\dfrac{\Delta v}{\Delta t} = \dfrac{5 - 8}{4 - 1} = -1$	(b) 1: point 1: answer
(c) $x(4) - x(0) = \displaystyle\int_0^4 v(t)\,dt,\ x(4) = x(0) + \int_0^4 v(t)\,dt$ By the Trapezoidal Rule, $x(4) \approx 2 + \dfrac{1}{2}[5 + 2(8 + 15 + 10) + 5] \approx 40.$	(c) 6 points 4: for each subinterval 2: answer

2.

(a) To be symmetric about the line $y = x$, all points (x, y) must map to (y, x). Then $x = \dfrac{ky}{y - k}.$ $x(y - k) = ky$ $y = \dfrac{ky}{x} + \dfrac{kx}{x}$ Now, we must gather y. $y - \dfrac{ky}{x} = \dfrac{kx}{x}$ $y\left(1 - \dfrac{k}{x}\right) = \dfrac{kx}{x}$ $y = \dfrac{kx}{x} \cdot \dfrac{1}{1 - \dfrac{k}{x}}$ Therefore, $y = \dfrac{kx}{x - k}.$	(a) 4 points 3: inverting the equation 1: answer
(b) vertical asymptote Set the denominator equal to zero. If $x - k = 0$, we get the line $x = k$.	(b) 2 points 1: finding the vertical asymptote 1: finding the horizontal asymptote

horizontal asymptote

$\lim\limits_{x \to \infty} \dfrac{kx}{x - k} = k$, so there is a horizontal asymptote at $y = k$.

(c) Solve $\dfrac{kx}{x - k} = x + 2k$ for x.

$\quad x = \pm k\sqrt{2}$

Find y': $y' = \dfrac{-k^2}{(x - k)^2}$.

Find $y'\left(k\sqrt{2}\right)$ and $y'\left(-k\sqrt{2}\right)$.

$y'\left(-k\sqrt{2}\right) = \dfrac{-k^2}{k(\sqrt{2} - k)^2} = \dfrac{-k^2}{k^2(\sqrt{2} - 1)^2} = \dfrac{-1}{(\sqrt{2} - 1)^2} = 5.828$

$y'\left(-k\sqrt{2}\right) = \dfrac{-k^2}{(-k\sqrt{2} - k)^2} = \dfrac{-k^2}{(-k)^2(\sqrt{2} + 1)^2} = \dfrac{-1}{(\sqrt{2} + 1)^2}$
$\quad = -0.1716$

(c) 4 points
1: solving for x
1: finding y'
2: finding y' at each point of intersection

3.

(a) In a triangle, $A = \frac{1}{2}bh$.

$h = a^2 + 1$, so we need only find b.

$y' = 2x$, then substitute a for x to find the slope at that point, $y' = 2a$.

We know the point where the tangent line meets the parabola is $(a, a^2 + 1)$.

Use slope $2a$ and point $(a, a^2 + 1)$ to find the y-intercept of the tangent line to be $1 - a^2$.

Find the x intercept of the tangent line.

$\quad 0 = 2ax - a^2 + 1$

$\quad x = \dfrac{a^2 - 1}{2a}$

Therefore, the base of the triangle $b = a - \dfrac{a^2 - 1}{2a}$.

Then $A = \dfrac{1}{2}\left(a - \dfrac{a^2 - 1}{2a}\right)(a^2 + 1) = \dfrac{(a^2 + 1)^2}{4a}$.

(a) 4 points
3: find the value of the base
1: answer

(b) The minimum will occur where $\dfrac{dA}{da} = 0$.

$\quad \dfrac{dA}{da} = \dfrac{3a^4 + 2a^2 - 1}{4a^2} = 0$

$\quad\quad 3a^4 + 2a^2 - 1 = 0$

$\quad (3a^2 - 1)(a^2 + 1) = 0$

Then $a^2 = \dfrac{1}{3}$ and $a = \dfrac{\sqrt{3}}{3}$. (The solution -1 can be eliminated because $a > 0$.)

(b) 5 points
2: justification
2: differential
1: answer

4.

(a) $\int 10 + \ln(t + 1) = 11t - (t + 1)\ln(t + 1)$
    $B(0) = 2$
    $B(t) = 11t - (t + 1)\ln(t + 1) + 2$
	(a) 3 points
	    1: setting up the integral
	    1: solving the integral
	    1: answer

(b) $44 - 5\ln(5)$	(b) 1 point 1: answer

(c) $10 - \ln(t + 1) = 0$
    $t = e^{10} - 1$
	(c) 2 points
	    2: answer

(d) $11t - (t + 1)\ln(t + 1) + 2 = 0$
    $t = 5.98631 \times 10^4$
	(d) 3 points
	    1: setting up the equation
	    2: answer

5.

(a) $(-\infty, 0)$ and $(0, \infty)$	(a) 1 point 1: answer

(b) $f'(x) = \dfrac{2\cos(2x)}{x} - \dfrac{\sin(2x)}{x^2} = 0$
 	
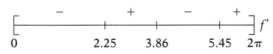
 	
The positive f' values indicate that the interval is increasing. The intervals that are increasing are
    $2.25 < x < 3.86$ and $5.45 < x < 2\pi$.
	(b) 2 points
	    1: justification
	    1: answer

(c) Second Derivative Test

Where $f''(x) < 0$, the graph of f is concave down. The intervals where f is concave down are $0 < x < 1.04$ and $2.97 < x < 4.60$.
	(c) 2 points
	    1: justification
	    1: answer

(d) Substituting 0 returns an indeterminate form, so use L'Hôpital's Rule.
    $\lim\limits_{x \to 0} \dfrac{2\cos(2x)}{1} = 2$
	(d) 4 points
	    1: defining the limit
	    2: solving the limit
	    1: answer

6.

(a) $\frac{dv}{dt} = -2v + 8$ $\frac{dv}{dt} = -2(v - 4)$ Separating the variables, we have $\frac{dv}{v - 4} = -2dt$. Finding the antiderivative of each side, we have $\ln\|v - 4\| = -2t + c$, and $\|v - 4\| = e^{-2t + c}$. Substituting A for e^c, we have $\|v - 4\| = Ae^{-2t}$. Since $v = 20$ when $t = 0$, $A = 16$. Thus $v - 4 = 16e^{-2t}$, and $v = 16e^{-2t} + 4$. (b) $\lim\limits_{t \to \infty} v = \lim\limits_{t \to \infty}(16e^{-2t} + 4) = 4$	(a) 7 points 　　2: defining both integrals 　　2: solving the integrals 　　2: finding $v(t)$ 　　1: answer (b) 2 points 　　1: solving the limit 　　1: answer

BC Model Examination 1

Section I
Part A (pages 302–305)

1. (A) $10 \sin 10x$

2. (D) $x = e$

3. (A) $2(e^t - e + 1)$

4. (C) 0

5. (E) I, II, and III

6. $f(x)$ is continuous but not differentiable at $x = 1$.

7. (A) $\dfrac{e^2 + 1}{4}$

$u = \ln x \qquad dv = x\, dx$

$du = \frac{1}{x}\, dx \qquad v = \frac{x^2}{2}$

$\displaystyle\int_1^e x \ln x\, dx$

$= \frac{x^2}{2} \ln x - \displaystyle\int_1^e \frac{x}{2}\, dx$

$= \frac{x^2}{2} \ln x - \frac{x^2}{4}\Big|_1^e$

$= \left(\frac{e^2}{2} \ln e - \frac{e^2}{4}\right) - \left(\frac{1}{2} \ln 1 - \frac{1}{4}\right)$

$= \frac{e^2}{4} + \frac{1}{4}$

8. (C) $8 \ln(6) + 6 \ln\left(\dfrac{3}{2}\right)$

$\displaystyle\int_5^{10} \frac{14x + 16}{x^2 + x - 20}\, dx$

$= 2 \displaystyle\int_5^{10} \frac{4}{x - 4} + \frac{3}{x + 5}\, dx$

$= 8 \ln(x - 4) + 6 \ln(x + 5)\Big|_5^{10}$

$= 8 \ln(6) + 6 \ln\left(\frac{3}{2}\right)$

9. (B) $\displaystyle\int_0^\pi \sqrt{1 + \cos^2 x}\, dx$

10. (B) $a = \dfrac{1}{4}, c = -1$

For $f(x)$ to be continuous and differentiable, two conditions must be satisfied: the two functions must have the same f value at 2, and the two functions must have the same derivative at 2.

$f'(x) = 1$ for $x > 0$
$f'(2) = 1$
$f'(x) = 2ax$ for $x \le 2$
$f'(2) = 4a = 1$

$a = \frac{1}{4}$

$f(x) = \frac{1}{4} x^2$ (first condition satisfied)

$$f(2) = \frac{1}{4} \cdot 2^2 = 1$$

$2 + c = 1$ (second condition satisfied)

11. (A) $y = \ln x$

12. (C) $\sqrt{34}$

$$\frac{dx}{dt} = 2t + 1$$

When $t = 1$, $\frac{dx}{dt} = 5$.

$$\frac{dy}{dt} = 3$$

By the Pythagorean Theorem, $5^2 + 3^2 = s^2$.

13. (B) $\dfrac{1}{g(x)} - \dfrac{2}{(g(x))^3}$

$$u = f(x),\ u' = g(x),\ v = (g(x))^2,\ v' = \frac{2g(x)}{f(x)}$$

$$\frac{(g(x))^2 g(x)}{((g(x))^2)^2} - \frac{f(x)\frac{2(g(x))}{f(x)}}{((g(x))^2)^2}$$

$$= \frac{(g(x))^3 g(x)}{(g(x))^4} - \frac{2(g(x))}{(g(x))^4} = \frac{1}{g(x)} - \frac{2}{(g(x))^3}$$

14. (E) I, II, and III

15. (D) 6

16. (D) $4y + 10$

17. (E) $\dfrac{3}{4}$

18. (A) $6x - y = 11$

19. (C) $\dfrac{f(4) - f(0)}{4}$

20. (B) $-\dfrac{1}{3}$

21. (C) 16

$$\int_{-3}^{3} \left(2\,\frac{(\sqrt{9 - x^2})}{3} \right)^2 dx = 16$$

22. (E) 36

23. (E) does not exist

24. (A) $-2 \tan x$

25. (B) $y = -\dfrac{1}{e}x + e$

26. (C) $\dfrac{1}{2e}$

$$\int_{1}^{\infty} xe^{-x^2}\,dx = \lim_{b \to \infty} \int_{1}^{b} xe^{-x^2}\,dx$$

$$= \lim_{b \to \infty} \left(-\frac{1}{2}e^{-x^2} \right)\Big|_{1}^{b}$$

$$= \lim_{b \to \infty} \left(-\frac{1}{2}e^{-b^2} + \frac{1}{2}e^{-1} \right) = \frac{1}{2e}$$

27. (B) 0

28. (C) -2

$$\int_{2}^{5} f(x)\,dx = F(5) - F(2)$$

$9 = 7 - F(2)$, and $F(2) = -2$

Section I
Part B (pages 306–308)

1. (C) 5.278

$$\int_{0}^{8} \left(\sqrt[3]{x} \right)^2 dx = \frac{3x^{5/3}}{5}\Big|_{0}^{8} = \frac{96}{5}$$

$$\frac{3k^{5/3}}{5} = \frac{48}{5}$$

$$k = 4\sqrt[5]{2^2} \approx 5.278$$

2. (C) I and II

3. (A) $\dfrac{1 - \cos 2t}{t}$

4. (C) 1

$$x \ln y + e^x = y$$

$$\frac{dy}{dx} = \frac{x^2 \ln y}{2} + \frac{x}{y} + e^x$$

$$\frac{0^2 \ln 1}{2} + \frac{0}{1} + e^0 = 1$$

5. (D)

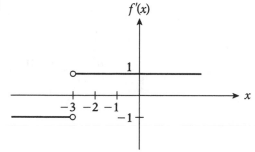

6. (E) does not exist

$$f(x) = f'(x) = \frac{1}{2}(x^2 - x)^{-1/2}(2x - 1)$$

$$= \frac{2x - 1}{2\left(\sqrt{x(x-1)}\right)}$$

7. (C) $\lim_{x \to 2} f(x) = 2$

8. (D) D

9. (E) $e^{\frac{1}{4}x} = \sum_{n=0}^{\infty} \frac{\left(\frac{1}{4}x\right)^n}{n!}$, which simplifies to (E).

10. (B) one relative minimum and one relative maximum

11. (C) 0

$$f''(x) = \frac{2x(x^2 - 3)}{(x^2 + 1)^3}$$

$$x = 0, x = \sqrt{3}, \text{ or } x = -\sqrt{3}$$

$$f'(0) = 0, f'\left(\sqrt{3}\right) = -\frac{1}{8}, \text{ and}$$

$$f'\left(-\sqrt{3}\right) = -\frac{1}{8}$$

12. (E) $-e^{-t} + c$

13. (E) 4π

$$\int_0^{2\pi} \left((2 - \cos\theta) - \cos\theta\right) d\theta$$

14. (A) converges by the Comparison Test

15. (E) 14.697

16. (A) 10.0 mph

17. (D) 5

Section II
Part A (page 309)

1.

(a) $A = \int_{\frac{\pi}{4}}^{\frac{5\pi}{4}} (\sin x - \cos x)dx = 2.828$	(a) 2 points
	    1: definite integral
	    1: answer

(b) $V = \pi \int_{\frac{\pi}{4}}^{\frac{5\pi}{4}} \left[(\sin x + 1)^2 - (\cos x + 1)^2\right] dx = 5.657\pi = 17.771$	(b) 4 points
	    3: definite integral
	       1: integrand must be in the form of $R^2 - r^2$
	       1: limits
	       1: π
	    1: answer

(c) $V = \int_{\frac{\pi}{4}}^{\frac{5\pi}{4}} (\sin x - \cos x)^2 dx = \pi$	(c) 3 points
	    2: definite integral
	       1: limits, no π
	       1: integrand
	    1: answer

2.

(a) $\dfrac{dy}{dt} = 0.03y(100 - y)$
 	
 $\quad 0.03y(100 - y) = 0$
 $\qquad\qquad\quad y = 0 \text{ and } y = 100$
 $y(-1)' = -101.03$, so the interval before $y = 0$ is decreasing.
 $y(1) = 2.97$, so the interval $[0, 100]$ is increasing.
 $y(101) = -303$, so the interval after $y = 100$ is decreasing.
 Thus, the interval where y is increasing is $0 < y < 100$.
	(a) 2 points
	     1: finding $y = 0$ and $y = 100$
	     1: answer

(b) $y'' = 3 - 0.06y$
 $\quad 3 - 0.06y = 0$
 $\qquad\qquad y = \dfrac{3}{0.06} = 50$
 	
 Thus, $y = 50$ is increasing the fastest.
	(b) 2 points
	     1: the second derivative
	     1: answer

(c) $y(t) = 10 + (0.03(y)(100 - y)t)$
 $\quad y(0) = 10$
 $\quad y(0.1) = 10 + (0.03(10)(100 - 10))0.1 = 12.7$
 $\quad y(0.2) = 12.7 + (0.03(12.7)(100 - 12.7))0.1 = 16.026$
 $\quad y(0.3) = 16.026 + (0.03(100 - 16.026))0.1 = 20.063$
	(c) 5 points
	     3: definite integral
	         2: integrand
	         1: finding the value of c
	   2: answer

3.

(a) absolute minimum = $(2, -1.18)$
     absolute maximum = $(1.55, 2.55)$
 	
 To find the absolute maximum, set $\dfrac{dy}{dt} = 0$.
 	
 $\dfrac{dy}{dt} = 2 - \dfrac{1}{2} e^{t/2} = 0$
 	
 $t = \ln 16$
 $x \approx 1.55, y \approx 2.55$
 Since there is only one solution found when we set the derivative equal to zero, the absolute minimum must occur at one of the endpoints. It occurs at $t = 5$.
	(a) 3 points
	     1: derivative
	     1: absolute minimum
	     1: absolute maximum

(b) $\dfrac{dy}{dt} = 2 - \dfrac{1}{2} e^{t/2} = 2 - \dfrac{1}{2} e$ when $t = 2$ and $\dfrac{dx}{dt} = \dfrac{1}{5}$.
 	
 $\dfrac{\frac{dy}{dt}}{\frac{dx}{dt}} = \dfrac{dy}{dx} = 10 - \dfrac{5}{2} e \approx 3.20$
	(b) 3 points
	     2: derivative
	     1: answer

The slope of the tangent line at $t = 2$.

$y = 3.20x - 2.2$

$3.20x - 2.2 = 0$

0.69 is the x-intercept.

(c) **METHOD 1** $\quad t = 2$ corresponds to the point $(1.4, 2.28)$. Use this with the slope to get the x-intercept.

The arc length is $\int_0^5 \sqrt{\left(\frac{1}{5}\right)^2 + \left(2 - \frac{1}{2}e^{\frac{t}{2}}\right)^2}\, dt \approx 6.43$.

METHOD 2

$x = \frac{t}{5} + 1$

$t = 5(x - 1)$

$y = 2(5x - 5) - e^{\frac{5x-5}{2}} + 1$

$y = 10x - e^{\frac{5x-5}{2}} + 9$

$\int_0^5 \sqrt{\left(1 + \left(10 - \frac{5}{2}e^{\frac{5x-5}{2}}\right)\right)^2}\, dx \approx 6.43$

(c) 3 points
   2: definite integral
      1: limit
      1: integrand
   1: answer

Section II
Part B (page 310)

4.

(a) $y' = \dfrac{x^2}{\sqrt[3]{(x^3 - 1)^2}}$

$x^2 = 0$ for the horizontal tangent line.

$\sqrt[3]{(x^3 - 1)^2} = 0$ for the vertical line.

The tangent line is vertical at $(1, 0)$, and horizontal at $(0, -1)$.

(b) $\displaystyle\lim_{x \to \infty} \frac{\sqrt[3]{x^3 - 1}}{x} = 1$ and $\displaystyle\lim_{x \to -\infty} \frac{\sqrt[3]{x^3 - 1}}{x} = 1$

The end behavior of the graph indicates that the function is asymptotic to the line $y = x$

(c) Sketches will vary.

(a) 3 points
   1: solving derivative
   1: the point where the tangent line is vertical
   1: the point where the tangent line is horizontal

(b) 3 points
   2: solving both limits
   1: answer

(c) 3 points
   1: curve looks as if tangent is horizontal at $(0, -1)$ and vertical at $(1, 0)$
   1: slope of tangent is always positive
   1: graph approaches line $y = x$ at ends

5.

(a) $\dfrac{1}{1+2x} = 1 - 2x + 4x^2 - 8x^3 + \cdots = \displaystyle\sum_{n=0}^{\infty} (-1)^n (2x)^n$

The interval of convergence is $|x| < \dfrac{1}{2}$.

(b) $\dfrac{1}{(1+2x)^2} = -\dfrac{1}{2} \dfrac{d}{dx}\left(\dfrac{1}{1+2x}\right)$

$\qquad = -\dfrac{1}{2}(-2 + 8x - 24x^2 + \cdots)$

$\qquad = 1 - 4x + 12x^2 - \cdots$

$\qquad = \displaystyle\sum_{n=1}^{\infty} (-1)^{n+1} n(2x)^{n-1}$

The interval of convergence is $|x| < \dfrac{1}{2}$.

(c) $\ln(1 + 2x) = 2\displaystyle\int \dfrac{1}{1+2x}\,dx$

$\qquad = c + 2x - 2x^2 + \dfrac{8}{3}x^3 - 4x^4 + \cdots$

Let $x = 0$. Then $c = 0$, and

$\ln(1 + 2x) = 2x - 2x^2 + \dfrac{8}{3}x^3 - 4x^4 + \cdots$

$\qquad = \displaystyle\sum_{n=0}^{\infty} (-1)^n \dfrac{(2x)^{n+1}}{n+1}.$

The interval of convergence is $-\dfrac{1}{2} < x \le \dfrac{1}{2}$.

(a) 3 points
  1: first four terms of Maclaurin series
  1: sigma notation
  1: interval of convergence

(b) 3 points
  1: first four terms of Maclaurin series
  1: sigma notation
  1: interval of convergence

(c) 3 points
  1: first four terms of Maclaurin series
  1: sigma notation
  1: interval of convergence

6.

(a) $g(0) = \displaystyle\int_0^0 f(t)\,dt = 0$

$g(2) = \displaystyle\int_0^2 f(t)\,dt = 1 + \dfrac{\pi}{4}$

(b) Set $g'(x) = 0$. Since $g' = f$ by the Fundamental Theorem, solve $f(x) = 0$. $x = \pm\dfrac{3}{2}$.

There is a relative minimum at $x = -\dfrac{3}{2}$, and a relative maximum at $x = \dfrac{3}{2}$.

(a) 2 points
  1: $g(0)$
  1: $g(2)$

(b) 3 points
  1: critical points of g
  1: relative minimum at $x = -\dfrac{3}{2}$, relative maximum at $x = \dfrac{3}{2}$
  1: justification

The First Derivative Test

Since g' changes from $-$ to $+$ at $x = -\frac{3}{2}$, $g\left(-\frac{3}{2}\right)$ is a relative minimum.

Since g' changes from $+$ to $-$ at $x = \frac{3}{2}$, $g\left(\frac{3}{2}\right)$ is a relative maximum.

(c) Solve $g''(x) = 0$ or is undefined. Since $g'' = f'$, find values where $f'(x) = 0$ or f' is undefined.
If $f'(x) = 0$, then $x = 0$. If f' is undefined, then $x = \pm1$.

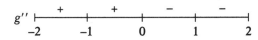

Since g'' changes sign at $x = 0$, it is the only point of inflection.

(d) Graph of $g(x)$.

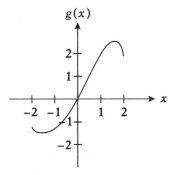

(c) 2 points
   1: points of inflection
   1: justification

(d) 2 points
   1: one relative maximum and one relative minimum
   1: one point of inflection

BC Model Examination 2

Section I
Part A (pages 311–314)

1. (D) $\frac{9}{16}$

2. (A) $3x + y = 7$

3. (D) $\frac{3}{4}$

4. (D) -5

5. (E) divergent
$$\int_0^\infty \frac{\ln(x)}{x}\,dx = \left.\frac{(\ln(x))^2}{2}\right|_0^\infty$$

6. (B) $a = \frac{1}{4}$ $c = -1$

For $f(x)$ to be continuous and differentiable, two conditions must be satisfied: the two functions must have the same f value at 2, and the two functions must have the same derivative at 2.

$f'(x) = 1$ for $x > 0$
$f'(2) = 1$
$f'(x) = 2ax$ for $x \le 2$
$f'(2) = 4a = 1$

$a = \frac{1}{4}$

$f(x) = \frac{1}{4}x^2$ (first condition satisfied)

$f(2) = \frac{1}{4} \cdot 2^2 = 1$

$2 + c = 1$ (second condition satisfied)

7. (B) 0

If you try to substitute directly, you get an indeterminate form; therefore, use L'Hôpital's Rule.

$$\lim_{x \to \infty} \frac{\ln(\ln(x))}{\ln(x)} = \lim_{x \to \infty} \frac{\frac{1}{\ln(x)} \cdot \frac{1}{x}}{\frac{1}{x}}$$

$$= \lim_{x \to \infty} \frac{1}{\ln(x)} = 0$$

8. (C) 0

$$\lim_{x \to \infty} x^5 e^{-x/5} = \lim_{x \to \infty} x^5 \frac{1}{e^{x/5}} = \infty \times 0 = 0$$

9. (E) $-\dfrac{5}{24}$

$$\frac{dx}{5x^2} = dt$$

$$\frac{1}{5x} + c = t$$

$$c = \frac{1}{25}$$

$$\frac{1}{5x} + \frac{1}{25} = 1$$

$$x = -\frac{5}{24}$$

10. (B) $\dfrac{\pi}{2} - 1$

$$\int_2^{\frac{\pi}{2}} t\cos(t)\,dt = t\sin(t) + \cos(t) \Big|_0^{\frac{\pi}{2}} = \frac{\pi}{2} - 1$$

11. (C) $e^{\frac{x^3}{3}+x} - 1$

$$\frac{dy}{dx} = y(x^2 + 1) + (x^2 + 1)$$

$$\frac{dy}{(y+1)} = (x^2 + 1)\,dx$$

$$y = e^{\frac{x^3}{3}+x} - 1$$

12. (A) $\ln|x^2 - 2x| = \ln(x^2 - 2x)$, when $x < 0$ or $x > 2$.

$\ln|x^2 - 2x| = \ln(2x - x^2)$, when $0 < x < 2$.

In either case, the derivative is $\dfrac{2x - 2}{x^2 - 2x}$.

13. (E) $(-\infty, \infty)$

14. (C) $\ln(x - 1)$

15. (A) -25

16. (E) $50.50

Let x be the number of widgets not sold.

Then $R(x) = (1{,}000 - x)(0.10x + 1.00)$

$$= 1{,}000 + 99x - \frac{x^2}{10}.$$

If you set $\dfrac{dR}{dx} = 0$, you get $x = 495$, so the selling price is $(0.10)495 + 1.00$.

17. (A) $\dfrac{2}{7}(x + 1)^{7/2} - \dfrac{4}{5}(x + 1)^{5/2}$
$+ \dfrac{2}{3}(x + 1)^{3/2} + C$

18. (E) 0

19. (E) II and III

20. (A) $\displaystyle\sum_0^{\infty}(-1)^n(5x)^n$

21. (C) 21

If $a(t) = 2t + 2$, then $v(t) = t^2 + 2t + C$.

$v(1) = 4$

$C = 1$

Because the arc length formula requires the derivative of $x(t)$, we do not need to integrate again in order to find that derivative.

$$\int_0^3 \sqrt{1 + (x'(t))^2}\,dt$$

$$= \int_0^3 \sqrt{1 + (t^2 + 2t + 1)^2}\,dt$$

22. (C) $y = \frac{\pi}{4}x + \frac{\pi(\pi - 4)}{16}$

First, find the slope of the tangent line by using the derivative.

$\frac{2\arctan(x)}{x^2 + 1}$ at $x = 1$ is $\frac{\pi}{4}$.

Use the point $\left(1, \frac{\pi^2}{16}\right)$ with the slope to find the equation of the line.

23. (E) $\pi - \frac{3\sqrt{3}}{2}$

24. (B) $\frac{2}{e}$

25. (D) $\frac{2x - 2}{x^2 - 2x}$

26. (B) $\frac{2}{\pi}(\sin^2(3\pi^2))$

$2\left(\frac{1}{\pi}\right)\frac{1 - \cos(2 \times 3\pi^2)}{2} = \frac{2}{\pi}(\sin^2(3\pi^2))$

27. (D) $\frac{19}{3}$

$F(x) = \int(-2x^2 + 4x)dx$

$= \frac{-2}{3}x^3 + 2x^2 + C$

$F(0) = 5$

$C = 5$

28. (C) 1.5

Section I
Part B (pages 315–317)

1. (A) 0.0024

$g(x) = 1, g'(x) = \frac{1}{2}, g''(x) = \frac{1}{4}, g''(x) = \frac{1}{8}$

$1 - \frac{1}{2} + \frac{1}{8} - \frac{1}{48}$

$\frac{1}{\sqrt{e}} - 1 - \frac{1}{2} + \frac{1}{8} - \frac{1}{48} = 0.0024$

2. (E) I, II, and III

3. (A) 0.443

$\int_0^{\frac{1}{2}} (2x)\, dx + \int_{\frac{1}{2}}^1 \left(\frac{1}{x} - 1\right) dx$

4. (D) 4.587

5. (B) f has a point of inflection in $[a, b]$.

Consider two points on a parabola that have the same y value.

6. (E) does not exist

7. (D) $\frac{\pi}{2}$

The integral is $\arcsin(x)$.

8. (A) 2π

$\int_0^\pi (2 + 2\cos\theta)d\theta$

9. (A) (1.333, 5.333)

The intercepts are at $x = 0$ and $x = 2$.

$\frac{dy}{dx} = 4 - 3x^2$

The tangent line at $x = 0$ is $y = 4x$.

The tangent line at $x = 2$ is $y = -8x + 16$.

10. (C) $\frac{1}{3e}$

11. (B) 0.267

12. (B) 1.771

13. (E) 0.73024

$$h'(x) = \frac{f'(x) \cdot \cos(f(x))}{2 \cdot \sqrt{\sin(f(x))}}$$

$$\frac{e \cdot \cos\left(\frac{\pi}{3}\right)}{2 \cdot \sqrt{\sin\left(\frac{\pi}{3}\right)}} \approx 0.73024$$

14. (D) 6,913 gallons

15. (C) 2

16. (A) 1

$$g(x) = \int_0^x (\ln(1 + t))^2 dt$$
$$= (x + 1) \ln(x + 1)^2 - 2(x + 1) \ln(x + 1)$$
$$+ 2x$$
$$g'(x) = \ln(x + 1)^2$$
$$g'(e - 1) = 1$$

17. (A) none

Section II
Part A (page 318)

1.

(a) $f(x) \approx 1 + \frac{1}{2}(x - 1) + \frac{1}{4}(x - 1)^2 + \frac{1}{16}(x - 1)^3$
 	
 $f(1.2) \approx 1.1105$
 	
 (b) $F(x) \approx x - 1 + \frac{1}{4}(x - 1)^2 + \frac{1}{12}(x - 1)^3 + \frac{1}{64}(x - 1)^4$
 	
 The exact value of $F(2)$ cannot be determined.
 	
 (c) $g'(x) \approx 1 + (x - 1) + \frac{3}{4}(x - 1)^2$
 	
 $g'(2) \approx 2.75$
	(a) 2 points
	    2: answer
	 (b) 3 points
	    2: correct expansion
	    1: answer
	 (c) 4 points
	    2: understanding that to have 4 distinct values of x, the polynomial of $f^{(3)}(x)$ must be a fourth-degree polynomial
	    1: derivatives
	    1: answer

2.

(a) $\dfrac{1}{(e + 1) - 2}\displaystyle\int_2^{e+1} \ln(x - 1)dx$
 	
 $\dfrac{1}{e - 1} \approx 0.582$
 	
 (b) The area under the curve from 2 to $e + 1$ is 1. (Integrate with that bound.)
 	
 Area $= \displaystyle\int_2^{e+1} \ln(x - 1)dx = 1$
 	
 $\displaystyle\int_2^{k} \ln(x - 1)dx = \frac{1}{2}, k \approx 3.156$
 	
 (c) Use the integral $2\pi \displaystyle\int_0^1 (1 - y)(e + 1 - (e^y + 1))dy$.
 	
 $\pi(4 - e) \approx 4.03$
	(a) 3 points
	    1: identifying the integral
	    1: solving the integral
	    1: answer
	 (b) 3 points
	    1: identifying the integral
	    1: solving the integral
	    1: answer
	
	 (c) 3 points
	    1: identifying the integral
	    1: solving the integral
	    1: answer

3.

(a) Equation of tangent line at $x = a$: $\quad y - (a^2 + 2) = 2a(x - a)$.	(a) 2 points $\quad$ 1: $f'(x)$ $\quad$ 1: equation of tangent line at $x = a$
(b) Base of triangle $= 4 - \dfrac{a^2 - 2}{4a}$. $\quad$ Area of triangle $= \dfrac{1}{2}\left(4 - \dfrac{a^2 - 2}{2a}\right)(a^2 + 2)$.	(b) 2 points $\quad$ 1: base of triangle $\quad$ 1: area of triangle
(c) $A' = \dfrac{16a^3 - 3a^4 - 4}{4a^2}$ $\quad$ If $A' = 0$, then $x = 0.658$. $$A' \vdash\!\!\!\overset{-}{\underset{0 \quad 0.658}{+}}\!\!\!\overset{+}{\underset{4}{\rule{0pt}{0pt}}}\!\dashv$$ $\quad$ Since A' changes from $-$ to $+$ at $x = 0.658$, $A(0.658)$ is a relative minimum.	(c) 5 points $\quad$ 1: finding A' $\quad$ 1: setting $A' = 0$ $\quad$ 1: solving $A' = 0$ $\quad$ 1: justification that solution is a minimum $\quad$ 1: only one solution shown between 0 and 4

Section II
Part B (page 319)

4.

(a) 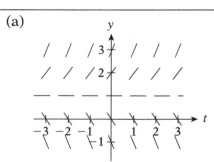	(a) 5 points $\quad$ 5: graph
(b) $y = 1 + 4e^{5t}$	(b) 2 points $\quad$ 2: answer
(c) $y = 1$	(c) 2 points $\quad$ 2: answer

5.

(a) $\dfrac{dV}{dt} = 4\pi r^2 \dfrac{dr}{dt}$	(a) 3 points 3: finding the formula 1: answer
(b) $\dfrac{dr}{dt} = \dfrac{5}{\pi(10^2)} = \dfrac{2}{20\pi} \approx 0.0159154$	(b) 1 point 1: answer
(c) $\dfrac{dV}{dt} = 4\pi r^2 \dfrac{dr}{dt} - e^{-\frac{V}{3}}$	(c) 3 points 2: finding the formula 1: answer
(d) $20 = 4\pi(10^2)\dfrac{dr}{dt} - e^{-\frac{1}{3}\left(\frac{4}{3}\pi(10)^3\right)}$, $\dfrac{dr}{dt} = \dfrac{20 + e^{-\frac{4,000}{9}\pi}}{4\pi(10^2)} \approx 0.0159$ in./sec	(d) 2 points 1: using $v = 0$ 1: answer

6.

(a) If y is odd, then y' is even.	(a) 3 points 1: the derivative 2: answer
(b) $(-\infty, 0) \cup (0, \infty)$	(b) 1 point 1: the answer
(c) The graph has no points of inflection since the part that is concave down (where x is negative) is separated by a vertical asymptote at $x = 0$ from the part that is concave up. Substitute positive and negative values into the second derivative to verify this.	(c) 2 points 2: answer
(d) $(0, \infty)$	(d) 1 point 1: answer
(e) $(-\infty, 0) \cup (0, \infty)$	(e) 2 points 2: answer

Index